A2
B1

CULTURE & COMMUNICATION

Community

ANGLAIS 2DE

Relecture pédagogique

Frédéric Chotard
IA-IPR
Académie de Nantes (44)

Kristell Dazy
Professeure certifiée
Lycée Jacques Feyder (93)

Natacha Godaillier
Professeure agrégée
Lycée Emmanuel Mounier (92)

Scot Esposito
Professeur, formateur et chargé de développement
International House World Organisation

Sophie Wright
Professeure, formatrice et chargée de développement
International House World Organisation

Grammaire et précis grammatical

Stephan Wilhelm
Professeur agrégé et chercheur
Lycée Claude Louis Berthollet (74)
Laboratoire TIL de l'Université
de Bourgogne (21)

EDITIONS
maison des langues

Découvrez vos fichiers MP3

Téléchargez tous les fichiers MP3 élève sur www.community.emdl.fr.

Unit 1 — Fichier

p. 15 Toolbox 1
p. 17 Toolbox 2
p. 18 Pronunciation: *L'accentuation des phrases* 3
p. 18 Toolbox 4
p. 21 Toolbox 5

Unit 2 — Fichier

p. 23 Toolbox 6
p. 25 Toolbox 7
p. 26 Toolbox 8
p. 27 Pronunciation: *L'accentuation des mots en* **-ity** *et* **-ion** 9
p. 29 Toolbox 10
p. 30 Reading: *Divergent* 11
p. 34 Toolbox 12

Unit 3 — Fichier

p. 37 Toolbox 13
p. 38 Pronunciation: *Les différentes prononciations du « **a** »* 14
p. 39 Toolbox 15
p. 39 Pronunciation: *L'accent texan* 16
p. 40 Toolbox 17
p. 43 Toolbox 18
p. 44 Reading: *Travels with Charley: In Search of America* 19
p. 48 Toolbox 20

Unit 4 — Fichier

p. 51 Toolbox 21
p. 52 Pronunciation: *Les différentes prononciations du « **o** »* 22
p. 52 Toolbox 23
p. 55 Toolbox 24
p. 56 Toolbox 25
p. 58 Reading: *Notes from a Small Island* 26
p. 62 Toolbox 27

Unit 5 — Fichier

p. 65 Toolbox 28
p. 67 Pronunciation: *Les groupes de sens* 29
p. 67 Toolbox 30
p. 69 Toolbox 31
p. 70 Toolbox 32
p. 72 Reading: *The Food of the Gods* 33
p. 76 Toolbox 34

Unit 6 — Fichier

p. 79 Toolbox 35
p. 81 Toolbox 36
p. 82 Toolbox 37
p. 83 Pronunciation: *Transmettre l'indignation* 38
p. 84 Toolbox 39
p. 86 Reading: *The Buddha of Suburbia* 40
p. 90 Toolbox 41

Unit 7 — Fichier

p. 93 Toolbox 42
p. 95 Toolbox 43
p. 96 Pronunciation: *La prononciation du « **-ed** »* 44
p. 96 Toolbox 45
p. 99 Toolbox 46
p. 100 Reading: *Sonny's Blues* 47
p. 104 Toolbox 48

Unit 8 — Fichier

p. 107 Toolbox 49
p. 108 Toolbox 50
p. 110 Toolbox 51
p. 111 Pronunciation: *Le « **i** » court et le « **i** » long* 52
p. 112 Toolbox 53
p. 114 Reading: *The Art of Fielding* 54
p. 118 Toolbox 55

Unit 9 — Fichier

p. 121 Toolbox 56
p. 122 Pronunciation: *Forme forte ou forme faible ?* 57
p. 123 Toolbox 58
p. 125 Toolbox 59
p. 126 Toolbox 60
p. 128 Reading: *A Christmas Carol* 61
p. 132 Toolbox 62

Unit 10 — Fichier

p. 135 Toolbox 63
p. 136 Pronunciation: *Les liaisons* 64
p. 137 Toolbox 65
p. 139 Toolbox 66
p. 140 Toolbox 67
p. 142 Reading: *Code Talker: A Novel about the Navajo Marines of World War Two* 68
p. 146 Toolbox 69

Workbook — Fichier

p. 4 *Audio spécial* Workbook 70

Crédits 71

Coordination éditoriale : Florence Pitti • Eduard Sancho
Responsable de projet : Karine Couly
Conception graphique : Guillermo Bejarano • Roser Cerdà • Per Fritsche
Couverture : Guillermo Bejarano • Luis Luján
Mise en page : Evelyne Boyard • Joëlle Parreau
Relecture et correction : Julia Galmiche • Gracie Glowiak
Illustrations : David Revilla
Iconographie et droits : Karine Couly • Gracie Glowiak
Cartographie : AFDEC

ISBN : 978-2-35685-337-0
ISBN spécimen : 978-2-35685-336-3

Bienvenue dans *Community*

Dear students:

Les programmes d'enseignement indiquent que la classe de Seconde se consacre à **« l'art de vivre ensemble »**... C'est un beau et vaste projet ; un sujet complexe aussi quand on tente de comprendre le monde qui nous entoure et les hommes et femmes qui y vivent. Le monde anglophone, en particulier, est d'une immense variété. Nous vous proposons dans ce manuel d'en ouvrir quelques portes et de vous donner envie d'en apprendre davantage.

Le nom de « ***Community*** » renvoie directement vers cet art de vivre ensemble : qu'est-ce qui constitue une communauté humaine, une famille, une nation dans les sociétés anglophones d'aujourd'hui ? La réponse n'est jamais simple ni unique, et notre défi consiste à la fois à vous aider à mieux pratiquer l'anglais et à vous forger une conscience citoyenne individuelle, réfléchie et responsable, loin des réponses toutes faites ou des jugements trop rapides.

Nous avons donc choisi de mettre prioritairement en lumière différents **éléments culturels**, mais toujours dans une **logique d'interrogation et de problématisation**. Au sein de chaque unité du manuel, vous aurez l'occasion de découvrir et d'approfondir un thème, présenté sous plusieurs facettes parfois contradictoires. Vous réaliserez des productions individuelles ou collectives, orales ou écrites, dans une **démarche actionnelle**. Pour vous y préparer, vous serez amenés à lire, écouter, parler et écrire, et à développer ainsi un discours de plus en plus complexe et informé.

Nous nous sommes efforcés de répondre aux besoins de **différenciation pédagogique**, en imaginant des activités qui impliquent la classe entière, mais dans lesquelles chacun(e) peut progresser à son niveau – à condition de s'en donner les moyens ! Nous avons choisi de mettre en avant de nombreuses activités de **compréhension orale**, grâce à des supports audio et vidéo authentiques et de formats variés. Les pages *Reading* et *Art Mag* vous permettront aussi d'aller plus loin dans les domaines littéraire et artistique, et d'enrichir votre **bagage culturel**. Afin d'affiner la qualité de vos productions, vous bénéficierez des apports de la **grammaire énonciative** qui permet de travailler l'anglais en contexte et de bien saisir les mécanismes de cette langue parfois si différente du français.

Dans notre petite « *community* » d'auteurs et d'éditeurs, nous avons pris grand plaisir à réaliser ce manuel et à le rendre aussi intéressant et stimulant que possible. Nous espérons que vous y trouverez matière à réfléchir, apprendre et progresser – mais désormais **tout dépend de vous**... Nous proposons ici une base de travail ; vos professeurs vont vous guider et vous diriger vers les tâches à accomplir ; mais seuls vos efforts et votre implication personnels vous permettront d'améliorer vraiment vos connaissances et vos compétences. « *Learning is not a spectator sport* », donc ne baissez jamais les bras !

L'équipe de *Community*

Votre manuel de page en page

Les pictos : mode d'emploi

Expression orale en continu

Expression orale en interaction

Compréhension de l'oral

Compréhension de l'écrit

Expression écrite

Anticipate
Activité d'anticipation

GO FURTHER...
Lien vers une vidéo complémentaire sur www.community.emdl.fr

Digital ZONE
Activité TICE

CD 3 PISTE 24 MP3 18
Renvoi aux CD classe et aux fichiers MP3 élève sur www.community.emdl.fr

Video Time DVD 3 PISTE 24
Renvoi au DVD classe

WB p. 16
Renvoi au Workbook

community.emdl.fr exercices interactifs
Renvoi aux exercices interactifs sur le site compagnon de la méthode

Zoom sur la structure des unités

L'ouverture

La **problématique**, c'est-à-dire la question qui sous-tend toute l'unité.

La ou les **notions** du programme traitées dans l'unité.

Un peu de **réflexion** pour entrer en douceur dans le thème.

L'annonce de votre **projet final** et des **tâches intermédiaires** qui vous y prépareront dans les leçons.

Des **documents authentiques** et une ou plusieurs **citations** pour découvrir la thématique.

L'introduction du **champ lexical de l'unité**.

Les trois doubles pages de documents

L'annonce de la **tâche intermédiaire** que vous réaliserez à la fin de la double page.

La **problématique propre à chaque double page**, qui s'inscrit dans la problématique globale.

L'**activité langagière** principalement travaillée.

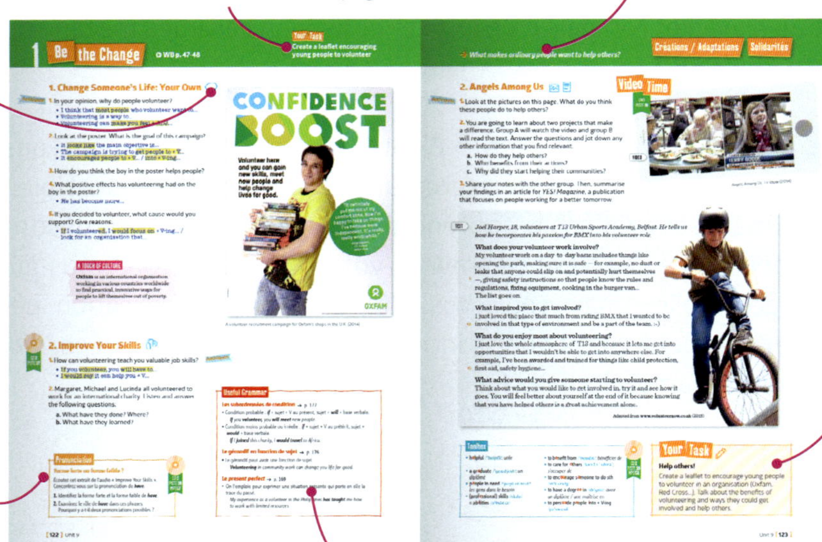

Des **activités de phonologie**, en lien avec un document audio ou vidéo, pour améliorer votre prononciation.

La **tâche intermédiaire** qui conclut le travail sur chaque double page de documents.

L'essentiel à retenir au niveau **grammatical**.

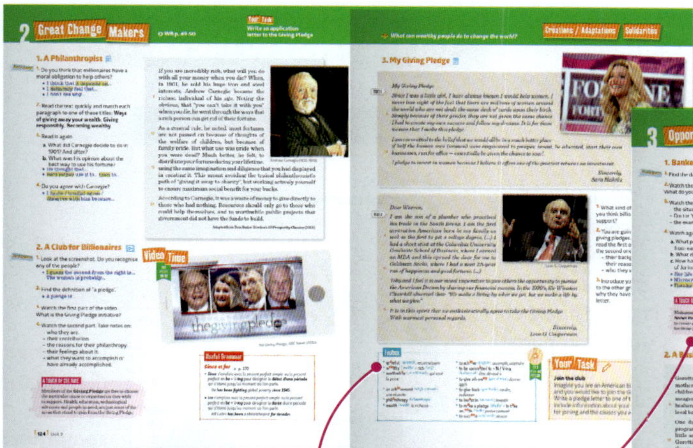

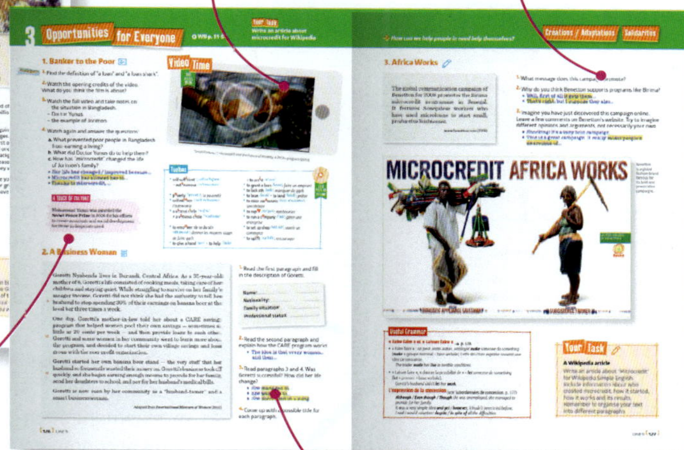

Des **supports variés** et toujours **authentiques**.

Des **activités qui font sens** et **vous préparent** aux tâches intermédiaires et finales.

Des **aides lexicales** pour réaliser les activités de production écrite et orale.

Des **informations culturelles** sur le monde anglophone.

Des **amorces** pour enrichir votre expression et vous donner des idées.

Reading

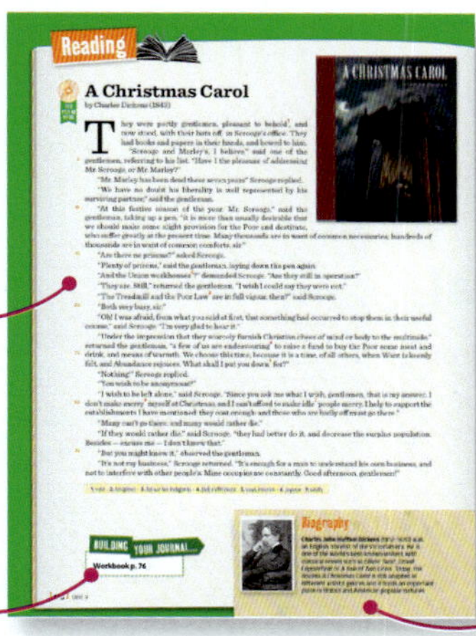

Un **texte long**, d'un écrivain célèbre, pour élargir la thématique et consolider votre bagage littéraire.

Une **fiche à compléter** dans le Workbook pour garder une trace de vos lectures.

Une **courte biographie** pour découvrir l'auteur.

Art Mag

Un coup de projecteur sur un **aspect culturel du monde anglophone**, toujours en lien avec le thème de l'unité.

Une **activité TICE** pour poursuivre l'entraînement à la tâche finale en utilisant les outils numériques.

Une **fiche à remplir** dans le Workbook pour mémoriser l'essentiel.

Let's Practise Grammar

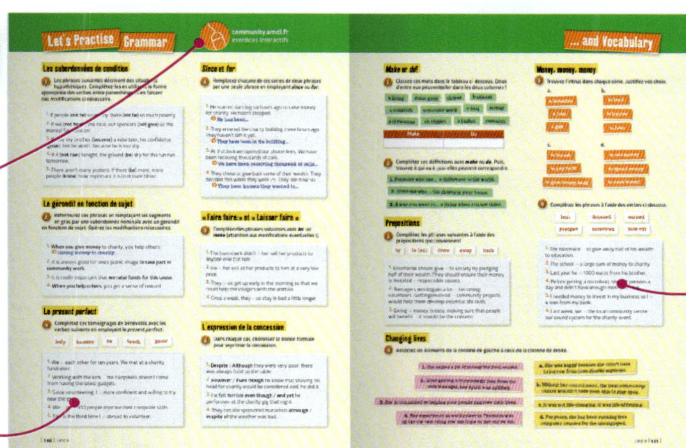

Des **exercices interactifs et autocorrectifs supplémentaires** à réaliser en autonomie sur le site www.community.emdl.fr.

Des **activités d'entraînement**, souvent actionnelles, pour manier les faits de langue dans des situations de communication concrètes.

... and Vocabulary

Des **exercices ludiques** pour mémoriser le lexique de l'unité et enrichir votre expression personnelle.

Votre manuel de page en page

Your Final Task

Une **rubrique lexicale** pour que votre prestation soit aussi authentique que possible.

L'**objectif de la tâche finale** qui clôt l'unité.

Les **étapes à suivre** pour atteindre l'objectif.

Un **exemple**, des **amorces** ou des **idées** pour vous aider et vous inspirer.

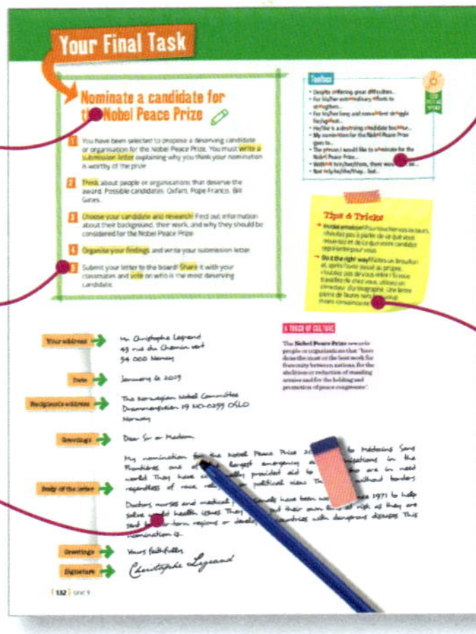

Des **conseils méthodologiques** pour travailler sereinement et en toute autonomie.

On Your Way to the Exam

Une **grille détaillée** pour prendre connaissance des critères d'évaluation de la tâche finale et vous y préparer au mieux.

Une **activité d'évaluation de votre compréhension de l'oral**, à partir d'un audio ou d'une vidéo.

Une **activité d'évaluation de votre compréhension de l'écrit**, conforme à celle du baccalauréat… mais de niveau A2/B1.

Une **activité** de réflexion ou d'imagination pour évaluer votre **expression écrite**.

Et en annexe…

• Un dossier de méthodologie

Huit **fiches pratiques** pour maîtriser les techniques de production et de réception écrites et orales.

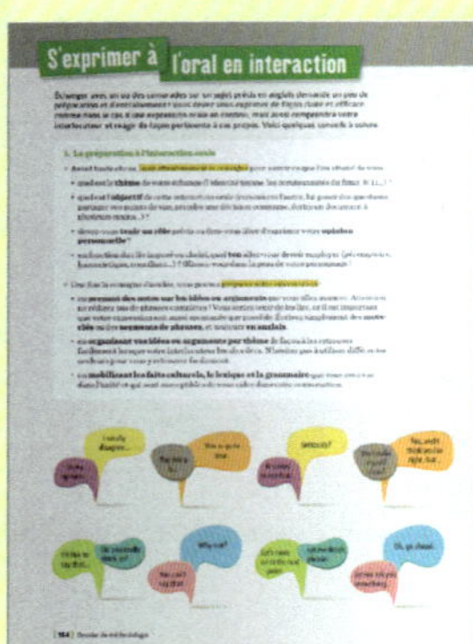

• Un précis grammatical

Un **mémo à consulter régulièrement** pour mieux comprendre le fonctionnement de la langue anglaise grâce à la grammaire énonciative.

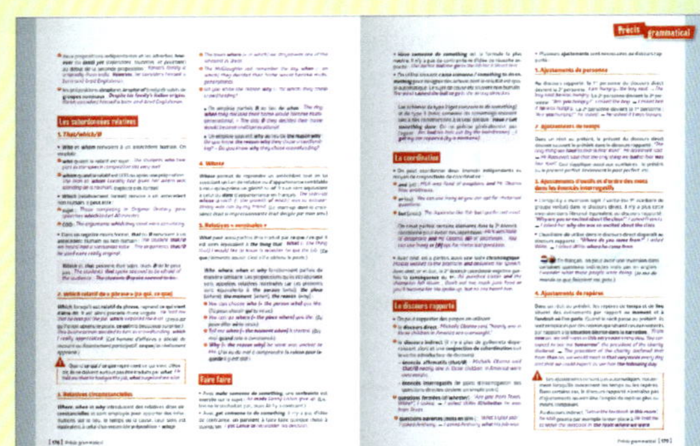

• Une banque d'exercices

Des **exercices d'application**, classés par fait de langue, pour poursuivre l'entraînement proposé dans les unités.

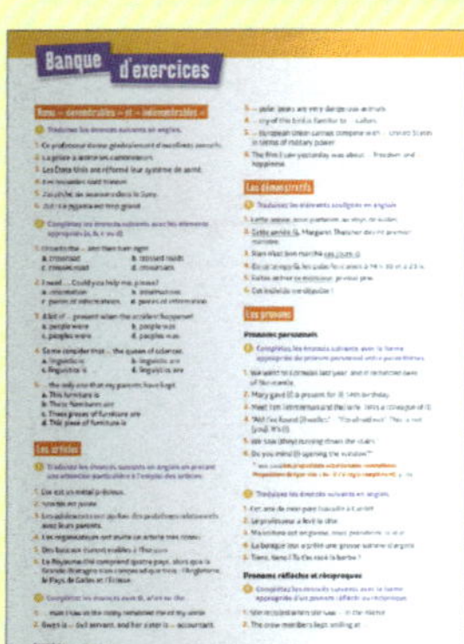

• Les verbes irréguliers

La **liste classique** des verbes irréguliers mais aussi une **liste par champ lexical**, pour les mémoriser plus facilement.

Bookquest: Exploring Community

Grammaire, lexique, méthodologie, verbes irréguliers, prononciation... Votre manuel recèle de précieux outils auxquels vous pourrez vous référer à tout moment de l'année, dès que vous aurez besoin d'un peu d'aide. Apprenez donc à le connaître sur le bout des doigts en répondant aux questions suivantes sur votre cahier !

The cover

1. Look at the cover. What facets of community life are represented?

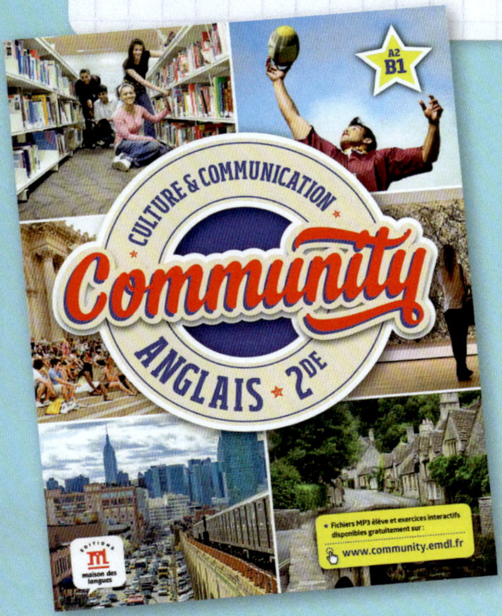

The table of contents

Find the table of contents of your book and answer these questions.

2. How many units are there in your book?

3. What language skills *(compétences)* are you going to develop in each unit?

4. What is the Magazine section about?

5. Look at the pictograms (, , , ,). What skills are they referring to?

Zoom in on the opening pages of a unit

Have a quick look at the opening pages of unit 6 (p. 78-79) and answer these questions.

6. What is the goal of these two pages?

7. Read the title of the unit and the *Issue at stake*. Why are they going to be useful?

8. Can you explain what a final task is?

9. If you need help with vocabulary, where can you turn to?
Take a closer look at this section:

a. What do the **bold** red letters correspond to?

b. What about the symbols between / /?

c. What does this symbol ' indicate?

d. Are all the words translated? Why (not)?

Zoom in on the inside of a unit

Browse through unit 6 (p. 80-91) and answer these questions.

10. What colour is the box that can help you improve your pronunciation?

11. What colour is the box that can help you improve your grammar?

12. Find the pink boxes. What information do they give you?

13. Read the three **Your Task** boxes and explain why they are at the end of each double page.

14. If you want to practise the grammar and vocabulary you have seen in this unit, where do you go?

15. Turn to pages 90-91. Why is it crucial for you to read the chart on the right page before doing the final task?

The appendices

Now turn to the end of your book.

16. What can you find from page 148 to page 157? Why are these pages helpful?

17. In the same section, find the page where the phonetics symbols and their pronunciation are listed.

18. Where can you find help on grammar?

19. Where can you practise grammar?

20. If you don't remember all the irregular verbs (shame on you!), where can you find the list?

1 Speak Your Mind!

How can speaking your mind make you a better person? Sentiment d'appartenance

Final Task Participate in a speech competition p. 21

Join the Club

How do American schools encourage students to speak up? p. 16
Singularités / Solidarités
- Forensics
- The Power of Language

Mini Task Create a radio ad promoting a speech club

2 Better Together

Where is our society heading in terms of lifestyles and social relationships?
Visions d'avenir

Final Task Present and promote a community p. 34

Under One Roof

What changes in communal living are under way? Adaptations p. 24
- Multigenerational Homes
- Come Work with Us!
- Resident Employees

Mini Task Write about your new life as an employee in a startup company

Sharing is Caring

What is the sharing economy? p. 26
Créations
- What's Mine is Yours
- Crowdfunding
- Join the Movement

Mini Task Present an idea for a new sharing economy service

3 T for Texas

Do Texan stereotypes reveal the true identity of Texas? Mémoire

Final Task Create a promotional newsletter of Texas p. 48

Everything is Bigger in Texas

What is so unique about Texas? p. 38
Héritages
- Don't Mess With Texas
- It's Dry and We're Proud!
- How I Became Texan

Mini Task Write an email describing Texas

Remember the Alamo

What are the origins of the strong Texan identity? Héritages / Ruptures p. 40
- Fighting for Independence
- Texas' Most Popular Attraction
- A Folk Hero

Mini Task Record an audio guide of the Alamo

4 A Little "Brit" Different

Why do British people like to be different? Sentiment d'appartenance

Final Task Create a book cover about Great Britain p. 62

The Unique Kingdom

What makes Britain so unique? p. 52
Solidarités
- Another Planet
- The British Thing to Do
- Quintessentially British

Mini Task Write a post for an international travel blog sharing your experiences in Great Britain

Always a Step Ahead

What is so great about Great Britain? p. 54
Singularités
- The Swinging City
- Britain is Great

Mini Task Create a poster promoting a British city

The Gift of the Gab

What can we learn from the best? p. 18
Singularités / Solidarités

- A Few Tips
- Inspirational Speeches

Mini Task Help a friend give a great speech

Language Skills

Grammar

- Le présent simple p. 17
- Les prépositions nominalisées en *to* + V p. 17
- Les énoncés interrogatifs p. 19

Pronunciation

- L'accentuation des phrases p. 18

Back to Basics

Are there any alternatives to a traditional society? Créations p. 28

- Sustainable Communities
- Dancing Rabbit Ecovillage
- Smaller is Better

Mini Task Write a questionnaire for people who want to join an ecovillage

Language Skills

Grammar

- Le présent en *be* + V*-ing* p. 25
- Les pronoms relatifs p. 25
- Le *present perfect simple* p. 26
- Le *present perfect* en *be* + V*-ing* p. 26

Pronunciation

- L'accentuation des mots en *-ity* et *-ion* p. 27

Magazine

Reading

Divergent by Veronica Roth p. 30

Art Mag

Floating Cities: Construction on Water p. 31

The Texas Triangle

How are the four biggest Texan cities different from classic Texas clichés? p. 42
Ruptures

- Visit the "Big D"!
- Let's Go to Houston!
- Keep Austin Weird
- Unforgettable San Antonio

Mini Task Create a radio ad to promote a Texan city

Language Skills

Grammar

- Les comparatifs p. 39
- Les superlatifs p. 39
- Le prétérit simple p. 41
- Les énoncés à l'impératif p. 41

Pronunciation

- Les différentes prononciations du « *a* » p. 38
- L'accent texan p. 39

Magazine

Reading

Travels with Charley: In Search of America by John Steinbeck p. 44

Art Mag

Texas Music p. 45

Eccentrics United

How do the Brits express their eccentricity? Singularités / Solidarités p. 56

- What Does it Mean to Be Eccentric?
- Nutty Aristocrats
- Chap Olympiads

Mini Task Present an eccentric event

Language skills

Grammar

- Le contraste p. 53
- Le gérondif p. 53
- L'article zéro (Ø) p. 54
- L'obligation, la nécessité, l'absence d'obligation et l'interdiction p. 56
- Les superlatifs p. 56

Pronunciation

- Les différentes prononciations du « *o* » p. 52

Magazine

Reading

Notes fom a Small Island by Bill Bryson p. 58

Art Mag

Zaha Hadid: Architectural Eccentricity p. 59

5 Feed Your Future

What are the ingredients of a food revolution? Visions d'avenir

Final Task Present a revolutionary product at the "Food Trends & Innovations" exhibition p. 76

Bad Habits

What food issues do we face? Adaptations p. 66

- Wasted food
- A Nation in Danger
- The Problems with Eating Meat

Mini Task Send a tweet

A New Food Culture

Is change already on the way in the U.S.? Adaptations p. 68

- Jamie Oliver's Crusade
- Eating Local
- Changing Taste

Mini Task Write the rules of a foodie club

6 Double Identity

What is it like having two different cultural identities? Sentiment d'appartenance

Final Task Create a class blog about the pros and cons of having a multicultural circle of friends p. 90

A War Zone, 24/7

What conflicts can arise when cultures collide? Singularités p. 80

- Surviving at School
- A Difficult Integration
- Family Conflicts

Mini Task Choose a well-known figure with mixed origins and present him/her to the class

Identity Crisis

How can teenagers define their own identity? Singularités p. 82

- Between Two Worlds
- Where Do I Belong?
- Mexican-Americans

Mini Task Take part in a poster contest to raise consciousness about biculturalism

7 Say it Loud

What role does music play in the history of the African-America community? Mémoire

Final Task Participate in an exhibition about African-American music and culture p. 104

I've Got the Blues

What made the blues? Héritages p. 94

- The Song of the Slaves
- Discovering the Blues
- The Blues Highway

Mini Task Write a short article about the history of blues music to be published in a children's magazine

The Songs of the Civil Rights Movement

How did music help the Civil Rights Movement? Ruptures p. 96

- Soundtrack for a Revolution
- It's Been a Long Time Coming
- A Song of Protest

Mini Task Pick and present a song representative of the Civil Rights Movement

8 Fair Play?

How can athletes serve as good role models for society? Sentiment d'appartenance

Final Task Participate in a BBC documentary about the greatest sporting moments in history p. 118

Team Spirit

Does sport encourage positive values? Solidarités p. 108

- Sport and Charity
- The Miracle League
- Pro Athletes Giving Back

Mini Task Invite a famous athlete to attend a charity event

The Dark Side of Sport

How much corruption is there in sport? Singularités p. 110

- Sending the Wrong Message
- The Fix Was On
- One Big Liar

Mini Task Broadcast your own sports news report

The Taste of Tomorrow

What is the future of food? p. 70
Créations
- Food Fiction
- Futuristic Food Trends

Mini Task Present a futuristic restaurant

Language Skills

Grammar
- L'expression du conseil p. 67
- Les quantifieurs p. 67
- La référence à l'avenir p. 68
- Les subordonnées de condition p. 71

Pronunciation
- Les groupes de sens p. 67

Magazine

Reading
The Food of Gods by Arthur C. Clarke p. 72

Art Mag
Ralph Goings: Photorealistic Food p. 73

The Best of Both Worlds

How does cultural diversity enrich our lives? Solidarités p. 84
- Culinary Diversity
- A Mixed Couple
- Bilingual, Bicultural and Bi-happy

Mini Task Give a speech to present the Eva Longoria Foundation

Language Skills

Grammar
- Les subordonnées de temps p. 81
- L'expression de l'obligation, du devoir et de l'interdiction p. 82
- L'expression de la capacité p. 83
- Les comparatifs p. 84

Pronunciation
- Transmettre l'indignation p. 83

Magazine

Reading
The Buddha of Suburbia by Hanif Kureishi p. 86

Art Mag
Reggae Britannia p. 87

What is Hip-Hop?

What does hip-hop really stand for? p. 98
Héritages / Ruptures
- Origin
- Hip-Hop Controversy
- Explicit Lyrics

Mini Task Stage a debate about hip-hop music and the influence it has had on the African-American community

Language Skills

Grammar
- Le prétérit simple p. 95
- La voix passive p. 95
- Les subordonnées de but p. 95
- Les subordonnées relatives p. 97

Pronunciation
- La prononciation du « *-ed* » p. 96

Magazine

Reading
Sonny's Blues by James Baldwin p. 100

Art Mag
Wild Styles p. 101

Is Sport Political?

When does sport get political? p. 112
Solidarités
- The "Auld Enemy"
- Political Games
- Black Power

Mini Task Write a tweet in response to a pro athlete's hashtag

Language Skills

Grammar
- Les subordonnées de condition p. 109
- Le gérondif p. 109
- Le prétérit simple, le *past perfect*, le prétérit en ***be*** + V*-ing* p. 111
- Le style indirect dans un récit au prétérit p. 111

Pronunciation
- Le « *i* » court et le « *i* » long p. 111

Magazine

Reading
The Art of Fielding by Chad Harbach p. 114

Art Mag
The Photographer of Boxing p. 115

9 Get Involved

Why and how do people get involved?
Visions d'avenir / Sentiment d'appartenance

Final Task Nominate a candidate for the Nobel Peace Prize p. 132

Be the Change

What makes ordinary people want to help others? Créations / Adaptations / Solidarités p. 122

- Change Someone's Life: Your Own
- Improve Your Skills
- Angels Among Us

Mini Task Create a leaflet encouraging young people to volunteer

Great Change Makers

What can wealthy people do to change the world? Créations / Adaptations / Solidarités p. 124

- A Philanthropist
- A Club for Billionaires
- My Giving Pledge

Mini Task Write an application letter to the Giving Pledge

10 Don't Forget: Celebrate!

How is collective memory passed on from generation to generation? Mémoire

Final Task Participate in a "time capsule" project p. 146

Living History

What can we do to keep the past alive? Héritages p. 136

- A Place to Remember
- Preserving What Has Disappeared
- A Way to Remember

Mini Task Make a report about a significant historical event

Telling History

How do we pass on our history from generation to generation? Héritages p. 138

- Flower of Scotland
- A Master Storyteller
- Based on True Facts

Mini Task Design a poster for a historical film

Et en +

Bookquest

- Bookquest p. 7

Bookquest: Exploring Community

Dossier de méthodologie

- Comprendre un texte p. 148
- Écrire un essai ou un récit p. 149
- Comprendre un document oral p. 150
- Prendre des notes p. 151

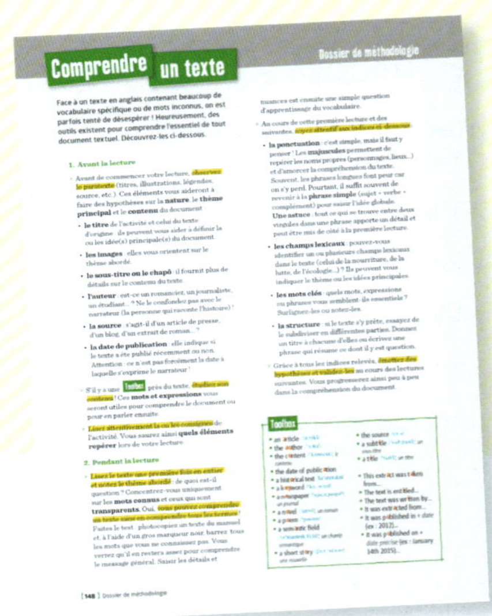
Comprendre un texte

Opportunities for Everyone

How can we help people in need help themselves? Créations / Adaptations / Solidarités — p. 126

- Banker to the Poor
- A Business Woman
- Africa Works

Mini Task Write an article about microcredit for Wikipedia

Language Skills

Grammar

- Les subordonnées de condition — p. 122
- Le gérondif en fonction de sujet — p. 122
- Le *present perfect* — p. 122
- *Since* et *For* — p. 124
- « Faire faire » et « Laisser faire » — p. 127
- L'expression de la concession — p. 127

Pronunciation

- Forme forte ou forme faible ? — p. 122

Magazine

Reading

A Christmas Carol by Charles Dickens — p. 128

Art Mag

A Family of Philanthropists — p. 129

Celebrating History

Do we always know what we are celebrating? Héritages / Ruptures — p. 140

- A Day to Remember
- A Day to Forget
- The Notting Hill Carnival

Mini Task Participate in a debate about Columbus Day

Language Skills

Grammar

- Le prétérit et le *present perfect* — p. 137
- Le *past perfect* — p. 137

Pronunciation

- Les liaisons — p. 136

Magazine

Reading

Code Talker: A Novel About the Navajo Marines of World War Two by Joseph Bruchac — p. 142

Art Mag

The Story Behind the Photo — p. 143

Grammaire

- S'exprimer à l'oral en continu — p. 152
- S'exprimer à l'oral en interaction — p. 154
- Participer à un débat — p. 156
- Relire ses devoirs — p. 157
- Précis grammatical — p. 158
- Banque d'exercices — p. 180
- Verbes irréguliers par forme — p. 188
- Verbes irréguliers par champ lexical — p. 190

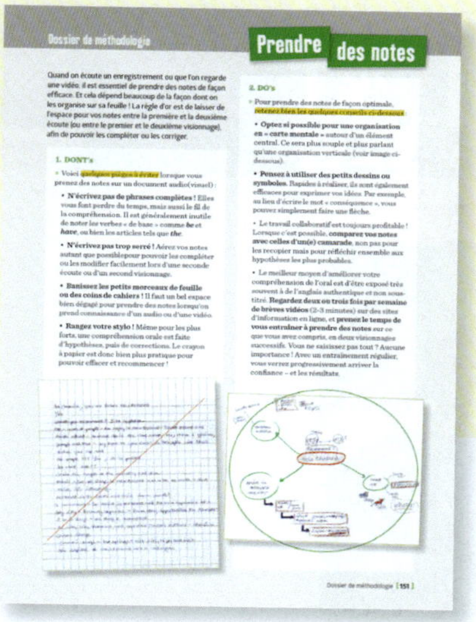

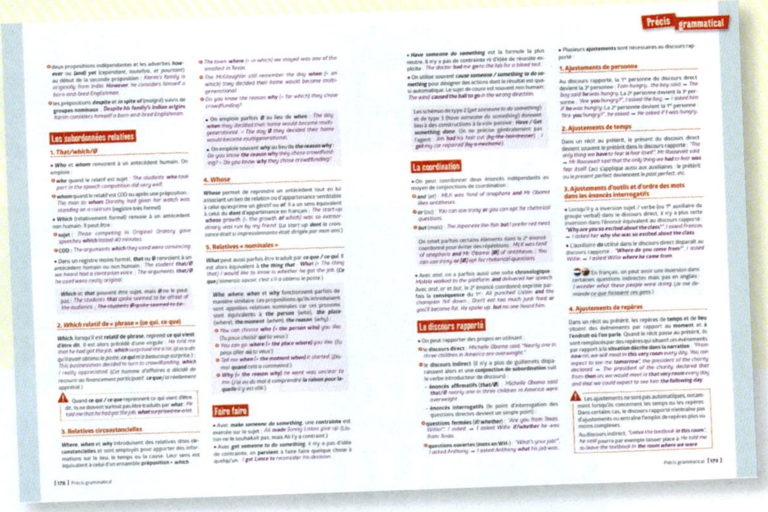

1 Speak Your Mind!

ISSUE AT STAKE

How can speaking your mind make you a better person?

ON YOUR WAY TO THE TASK

1 **Join the Club**

Create a radio ad promoting a speech club

2 **The Gift of the Gab**

Help a friend give a great speech

YOUR FINAL TASK

Participate in a speech competition

2

British actress Kate Winslet

1

Australian football coach Michael Malthouse

Sentiment d'appartenance

4

American media celebrity Oprah Winfrey

3

South African politician Nelson Mandela

> Stand before the people you fear and speak your mind – even if your voice shakes.
>
> Maggie Kuhn, American activist

1. Read the quote by Maggie Kuhn and choose the sentence that best sums it up:
- It is normal to be afraid of speaking in front of people.
- Don't be afraid to let others speak for you.
- You must say what you think, even if you are afraid.

2. Choose one of the pictures and imagine the occasion, goal of the speech, the speaker's feelings, etc.
- I would say that Kate Winslet is...
- She looks + ADJ...
- I think Mandela is talking at a...
- Michael Malthouse is trying to...

3. What was the last occasion when you spoke in front of people (at school, a wedding, etc.)? How did you feel?

Toolbox

CD 1 PISTE 1 MP3 1

- anxious /'æŋkʃəs/
- at ease /æt iːz/: *à l'aise* ≠ ill-at-ease /ɪlə'tiːz/: *mal à l'aise*
- moved /'muːvd/: *ému*
- self-conscious /self'kɒnʃəs/: *gêné, mal à l'aise*
- thrilled /θrɪld/: *ravi*

- to convey (a message / feelings) /kən'veɪ/: *faire passer, transmettre*
- to convince /kən'vɪns/: *convaincre*
- to give / deliver (a speech) /dɪ'lɪvəʳ/: *prononcer (un discours)*
- to go blank /gəʊ blæŋk/: *avoir un trou*
- to motivate /'məʊtɪveɪt/
- to speak up = to speak one's mind: *s'exprimer*
- to stutter /'stʌtəʳ/: *bafouiller, bégayer*
- to voice /vɔɪs/ = to express /ɪk'spres/: *exprimer*

GO FURTHER... www.community.emdl.fr

Watch and learn about something many people fear.
1. What fear does the video portray?
2. How can this fear manifest physically?
3. What advice is suggested to fight against it?

1 Join the Club

WB p. 3

Your Task
Create a radio ad promoting a speech club

A Texas Christian University poster (2014)

A TOUCH OF CULTURE

What do Brad Pitt, Oprah Winfrey, Bill Clinton and Nelson Mandela have all in common? They all belonged to a "Speech and Debate" club. This club (also called Forensics club) is one of the many extracurricular activities offered by American schools and universities.

1. Forensics

CD 1 PISTE 2

1. Look at the poster. What is Forensics? **Anticipate**

- I guess / believe that…
- It seems to me that…
- I would say that…

2. Listen to Hailey and Rachel from Portage Northern High School in Michigan. Make a list of the words you understand to help you identify what Forensics is about.

3. What are the benefits of Forensics according to the students?

- Forensics helps them (to) develop…
- It allows them to…

4. In your opinion, why is it useful to learn how to speak in public?

- Well, it can teach you how to…

2. The Power of Language

1. Read texts 1 and 2. What are the common points between the narrator (text 1) and the journalist (text 2)?

2. What message are the teacher (text 1) and the journalist (text 2) trying to convey?

- They are basically saying that…
- They are both trying to convey the idea that…

TEXT 1

Frances is a Chinese-American student at a Californian school in the 1980s. She has always been very obedient to her mother who wants her to be a straight-A student so that she can go to medical school. In this excerpt, she is discovering an unusual class.

The new teacher turns quickly and writes her name on the chalkboard. Ms. Taylor. Then she faces us. (…)

"Okay. Why speech?" she asks, as if reading my thoughts. Her bright eyes shine with intensity. Everyone is silent. "Why is speech important?" she asks. Again, more silence, not even the sound of breathing. Ms. Taylor walks slowly from one end of the room to the other. (…)

"Language is power," says Ms. Taylor. "We as women have the power to define ourselves and persuade others, to change the ideas of our society and to pass that down for generations to come."

However unconventional this class may be, I'm feeling excited. I'm having a feeling that this will be my favourite class this semester, if not my best class ever.

"You ladies are lucky," Ms. Taylor continues. "You're going to St. Elizabeth's, an elite all-girls school. Here you will be heard. Here you will have the chance to nurture and strengthen your own voice. That's why you've enrolled in this speech course. To develop your own unique, individual voices."

Cara Chow, ***Bitter Melon*** (2010)

TEXT 2

Morgan Levy is a student at Livingston High School in New Jersey. She is President of the Forensics Speech and Debate Team. In this article, she explains why she loves Forensics.

If, walking into high school, somebody had told me that I would willingly join a competitive public speaking team, loving it so much that I would eventually become President, I would reply that the chances of that happening are lower than those of Miley Cyrus becoming President.

At the time, I feared public speaking. Standing in front of an audience made me tremble. This is exactly why I thought it would be a great idea to join the Forensics team. Walking into my first tournament, I was beyond nervous. Yet I walked out wanting more. Forensics gave me a voice, a group of other passionate individuals to speak to and pushed me to conquer my fears.

I compete in a variety of events: Declamation (presenting a memorised speech that was given by somebody else), Extemporaneous Speaking (presenting limited preparation speeches on current affairs) and Original Oratory (presenting an original speech). The most powerful event of all is Original Oratory. Over the course of the last season I have been mesmerised, listening to the diverse range of opinions and speeches. Topics have included tragedy, stereotypes and even lactose intolerance. But what stood out to me was not only the variety of topics, but also the passion each speaker possesses.

More teenagers today need to speak up and give Forensics a chance, conquer that fear of public speaking, and let their voices be heard.

Adapted from Morgan Levy, "Why I Love Forensics", ***The Huffington Post*** (2014)

3. Pick out words and expressions that qualify:
- the power of language in text 1.
- the power of Forensics in text 2.

4. In pairs, compare your findings. Agree on the main benefit of public speaking.
- For us, public speaking is really beneficial as it helps us to...
- It pushes / allows us to...

5. Use the texts to match each word with its synonym:

a. to nurture	**1.** to be hypnotized
b. to strengthen	**2.** to feed
c. to enroll	**3.** to catch one's attention
d. to stand out	**4.** to make stronger
e. to be mesmerized	**5.** to join

6. Would you like to join a speech club? Why (not)?
- I would definitely like to join...
- I'm not really sure about joining...

Useful Grammar

Le présent simple → p. 168
- Forme affirmative : base verbale avec *I / you / we / they*.
  base verbale + **-s** avec *he / she / it*.
  *I **compete** in a variety of events.*
  *She **explains** why she loves Forensics.*
- Forme négative : auxiliaire **do** avec *I / you / we / they* (ou **does** avec *he / she / it*) + **not** + base verbale. Contraction : **don't** / **doesn't**.
  *I **don't like** speaking in public. It **doesn't suit** me.*

Les propositions nominalisées en *to* + V → p. 176

*Joining our club will **help you to develop** the skills you need to become a better public speaker.*
*It **pushed me to conquer** my fears.*
*Forensics **allowed me to have** more confidence.*
*I **advise everybody to join** the Forensics club.*

Toolbox

CD1 PISTE 3 MP3 2

- beneficial /ˌbenɪˈfɪʃəl/: *bénéfique*
- useful /ˈjuːsfʊl/: *utile*
- forensics /fəˈrenzɪks/: *l'art du discours*
- to enable /ɪˈneɪbl/ = to allow: *permettre*
- thanks to: *grâce à*

Your Task

Join our speech club!

Create a 30-second radio ad for your school's speech club to encourage other students to join. Explain the different events and benefits of this club.

2 The Gift of the Gab

WB p. 4

Your Task
Help a friend give a great speech

1. A Few Tips

Anticipate **1.** What qualities are required to speak well in public?

- I think you **need**...
- You definitely **should**...

2. Watch this video about public speaking and jot down everything you understand.

3. Watch again and answer these questions:

a. How do we send signals when we speak?
b. What effect can they have on people?
c. What pieces of advice are given?
d. What does the speaker recommend not to do?

- He **advises** / **recommends us (not) to**...
- He **makes us realise** the importance of...

Video Time

DVD PISTE 1

Tips for becoming a better public speaker, by Ian Patterson (2011)

Pronunciation

CD 1 PISTE 4 MP3 3

L'accentuation des phrases

"We're going to look at simple preparation and presentation ideas that will make you the kind of speaker that people want to hear from."

1. Écoutez cette phrase et repérez les mots sur lesquels le locuteur insiste.
2. En lisant seulement ces mots, pouvez-vous déduire l'idée générale véhiculée ?
3. Qu'en déduisez-vous sur l'accentuation des phrases en anglais ?
4. Entraînez-vous à redire cette phrase plusieurs fois, en imitant l'accentuation du locuteur.

Toolbox

CD 1 PISTE 5 MP3 4

- committed /kə'mɪtɪd/: *engagé*
- convincing /kən'vɪnsɪŋ/: *convaincant*
- energetic /ˌenə'dʒetɪk/: *énergique*
- enthusiastic /ɪnˌθuːzɪ'æstɪk/
- inspirational /ˌɪnspə'reɪʃənl/ = motivational /ˌməʊtɪ'veɪʃənl/
- a figure of speech: *une figure de style*
- public speaking: *l'acte de parler en public*
- to have the gift of the gab: *être à l'aise à l'oral*
- to persuade /pə'sweɪd/ = to convince /kən'vɪns/

2. Inspirational Speeches

1. Read these three speeches and determine:
- who the orator is addressing.
- the main message of the speech.

TEXT 1

Don't tell me words don't matter. "I have a dream" — just words? Words? "We hold these truths to be self-evident that all men are created equal" — just words? "We have nothing to fear but fear itself" — just words? Just speeches?

It's true that speeches don't solve all problems. But what is also true is that if we cannot inspire the country to believe again, then it doesn't matter how many policies and plans we have. And that is why I'm running for president of the United States of America.

Barack Obama's speech in Wisconsin (2008)

TEXT 2

I am William Wallace. And I see a whole army of my countrymen, here in defiance of tyranny! You have come to fight as free men. And free men you are! What will you do without freedom? Will you fight? (...) Fight and you may die. Run and you will live, at least a while. And dying in your beds many years from now, would you be willing to trade all the days, from this day to that, for one chance, just one chance, to come back here and tell our enemies that they may take our lives but they will never take our freedom?!

Mel Gibson's speech in the film ***Braveheart*** (1995)

Barack Obama, the 44th President of the United States

TEXT 3

We realise the importance of light when we see darkness. We realise the importance of our voice when we are silenced. In the same way... we realised the importance of pens and books when we saw the guns. (...) Let us pick up our books and our pens — they are the most powerful weapons. One child, one teacher, one book and one pen can change the world. Education is the only solution.

Malala Yousafzai's speech at the United Nations (2013)

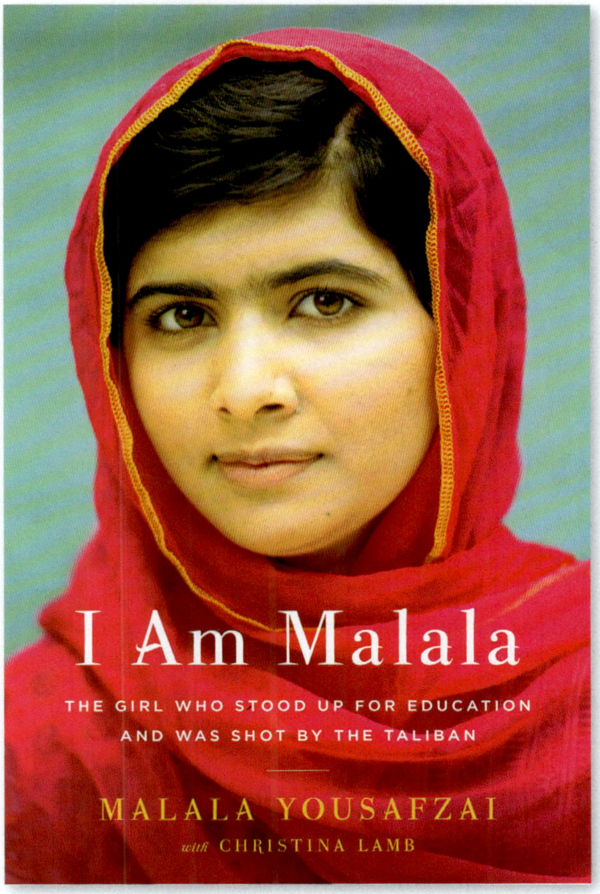

2. Read the definitions of the four figures of speech below. In pairs, find examples in the three extracts. Why have the speakers used them?

→ rhetorical question
Question asked for effect. The speaker does not expect an answer because it is very clear (usually "yes" or "no").

→ antithesis
Contrast between two elements in a sentence.

→ hyperbole
Exaggeration.

→ anaphora
Repetition of a word or phrase at the beginning of a sentence.

Useful Grammar

Les énoncés interrogatifs → p. 173

- Dans les *Yes / No questions* et les questions ouvertes (réponse autre que « oui » ou « non ») qui commencent par un mot interrogatif, il y a **inversion** entre le 1er auxiliaire du groupe verbal et le sujet.
  Do you *have the gift of the gab?*
  Will you *fight?*
  What will we *do without freedom?*
  How can we *fight this problem?*
- **Pas d'inversion** dans les questions ouvertes où ***who*** et ***what*** sont sujets.
  Who gave *that speech about freedom?*
  What led *Malala to fight for girls' education in Pakistan?*

3. Let's focus on Barack Obama's speech (text 1).

a. He mentions three extremely famous quotes. In class or at home, do some research to find more information about them (**when**, **where**, **who**).

CD1 PISTE 6

b. Listen to his speech. Identify the stressed words and the pauses. Why is it so effective in your opinion?

c. Practise giving this speech. Record yourself. Compare your rendition with that of Obama.

Your Task

Music is powerful

Use what you have learned in this lesson to help your friend improve the beginning of a speech entitled "Music is powerful".

"Music is powerful. I really like music. I think it has the power to make you feel better. Music is fantastic. Everybody should listen to music at least once a day."

Le présent simple

1 Traduisez les phrases suivantes.

1. *Elle s'exprime toujours fort et clairement.*

2. *Nous pensons que ce discours transmet un message positif.*

3. *Certaines personnes n'écrivent pas leurs discours seuls, moi si.*

4. *Exprimer mes idées me rend heureux.*

2 Vous avez décidé de faire un discours intitulé *"We teenagers"*. Vous avez prévu de commencer de la façon suivante :

- We teenagers belong to a strange tribe. Adults sometimes don't understand us.

Rédigez quelques phrases supplémentaires de ce discours parlant de vos habitudes « étranges » et de l'incompréhension des adultes.

Les propositions nominalisées en *to* + V

3 Construisez une phrase complète à partir des éléments proposés. Attention aux modifications éventuelles !

1. The teacher wants (**all the students / understand / the power of language**).

2. The journalist is trying to persuade (**they / join a speech club**).

3. This new class will allow (**we / learn / speak in public**).

4. A good speaker gets (**audience / believe / his or her ideas**).

5. My mother forced (**I / work on my speech all weekend**).

6. Laura's parents advised (**she / sign up for / new speech class**).

4 Utilisez les verbes proposés dans les étiquettes (ou d'autres verbes de votre choix) pour former des phrases à partir des éléments suivants.

1. coach / player

2. teacher / student

3. politician / voter

4. employer / employee

5. film director / actor, actress

persuade (sb) to — want (sb) to — push (sb) to — teach (sb) to — get (sb) to — help (sb) to — encourage (sb) to — motivate (sb) to

Les énoncés interrogatifs

5 Transformez les éléments ci-dessous en questions complètes.

1. Why / we / fight each other? (présent en *be -ing*)

2. How / you / feel about this issue? (présent simple)

3. Who / know / the answer? (présent simple)

4. What / you / do to change things? (prétérit simple)

5. When / this nonsense / stop? (avec le modal *will* pour parler de l'avenir)

6 Imaginez deux questions qui invitent au dialogue pour chacun des sujets de discours ci-dessous.

1. Friendship
2. The environment
3. Something you like / hate
4. Your favourite song
5. Aliens
6. Basketball
7. Forensics

- What do people find so fascinating about...?
- Why do so many American students dream of joining...?

Your Final Task

Participate in a speech competition

1. Choose a topic that you are interested in: music, film, a favourite singer/band, a problem that you feel concerned about… the sky is the limit! The goal of the speech is to convince your audience to want to learn more.
2. Brainstorm. Write down everything that comes to mind about the topic. Then, decide on two or three main ideas that you want to share. Find a clear example for each one.
3. Write a catchy introduction and conclusion to grab the audience's attention from the start to the end of your speech. You can use some rhetorical questions to spice it up.
4. Make note of the pronunciation of difficult words. Identify the words and circle them to remind yourself they must be stressed when speaking.
5. Record yourself to practise delivering your speech until you are ready to go.

Toolbox

CD 1 PISTE 7 MP3 5

- Good morning / afternoon, ladies and gentlemen…
- I'm absolutely delighted to be here today…
- I would like to talk to you about…
- I want you to understand that…
- When will we realise the importance of this issue today?
- To sum up…
- Thank you all for listening.

A TOUCH OF CULTURE

Original Oratory (OO) is one of the categories in a Forensics competition. Speakers must deliver an original speech on a topic of their choice.
They are judged on:
- effectiveness (*does the speech make the audience react?*)
- body movement (*does the speaker use body language to convey his/her message?*)
- intonation and enthusiasm (*does the speaker catch the audience's attention?*).

Tips & Tricks

→ **Heads up!** Même si vous devez lire des notes, faites en sorte de regarder vos camarades le plus souvent possible.
→ **Diversify!** Variez les sources pour vos exemples (citations, paroles de chansons, dialogues de films, interviews de personnes de votre entourage…).
→ **Smile!** Ne restez pas statique et souriez !
→ **Spice it up!** Utilisez des extraits de chansons pour votre entrée en scène et des supports visuels (diaporamas, photos…) pendant la présentation.

"I have chosen to discuss my favourite movie in the whole world."

"I have decided to talk about something that I really care about: friendship."

"I know that a lot of us would love to stop going to school. Right? Well, that is wrong! Education is important because…"

2 Better Together

→ **ISSUE AT STAKE**
Where is our society heading in terms of lifestyles and social relationships?

ON YOUR WAY TO THE TASK

1 Under One Roof
Write about your new life as an employee in a startup company

2 Sharing is Caring
Present an idea for a new sharing economy service

3 Back to Basics
Write a questionnaire for people who want to join an ecovillage

YOUR FINAL TASK

Present and promote a community

1

Mother, daughter and grandchildren living together in Brooklyn, New York (U.S.)

> It takes a whole village to raise a child.
>
> Old African proverb

A business team working together

An urban farmers' cooperative in Norwich (U.K.)

Visions d'avenir

> A dream you dream alone is only a dream. A dream you dream together is reality.
>
> Yoko Ono, Japanese artist and peace activist

1. Describe the three pictures. What type of community do you think these people belong to?

- In the first picture, they seem to...
- The people in the second picture all belong to...
- All of them are...

2. Look at the title of the unit and think about the benefits of belonging to a community.

- Working together with other people...
- Being part of a team...

3. Read the three quotes. Choose one that inspires you and explain its meaning to the class.

- I really like the African proverb. I think it means that...

GO FURTHER... www.community.emdl.fr

Watch **"I was here"** by Beyoncé.

1. For what occasion did she sing that song? What do you know about it?
2. What type of actions are shown in the video?
3. What message does Beyoncé want to convey?
4. Can you answer the last question of the video: "What will you do?"

> We must learn to live together as brothers or perish together as fools.
>
> Martin Luther King, American Baptist minister and social activist

3

Toolbox

CD 1 PISTE 8 MP3 6

- collective /kə'lektɪv/ ≠ individual /ˌɪndɪ'vɪdʒʊəl/

- a colleague /'kɒliːg/ = a workmate /'wɜːkmeɪt/
- a mate /meɪt/: *un pote, un copain* (a workmate, a classmate, a roommate: *un collègue, un camarade de classe, un colocataire*)
- mutual support /'mjuːtjʊəl sə'pɔːt/: *un soutien mutuel*
- a neighbour /'neɪbər/: *un voisin*

- to be part of: *faire partie de*
- to belong to sb/sth /bɪ'lɒŋ/: *appartenir à qqn/qqch*
- to collaborate /kə'læbəreɪt/
- to help one another / each other: *s'entraider*
- to share /ʃeə/: *partager*
- to take advantage of /əd'vaːntɪdʒ/ = to benefit from /'benɪfɪt/: *tirer profit de*
- to team up with sb /tiːm ʌp/: *faire équipe avec qqn*

1 Under One Roof

WB p. 5-6

Your Task
Write about your new life as an employee in a startup company

1. Multigenerational Homes

Anticipate **1.** What is a multigenerational home? Look at the cartoon to help you.

- I reckon / think / guess that...
- The cartoonist means to show that...

2. Read the text. Who is living with the McGloughlins?

3. Look for words and expressions that show the advantages and disadvantages of living in a multigenerational home.

Advantages	Disadvantages

4. What does Amy mean when she says "*My kids are getting a better sense of what it is to be a family*" (l. 13-14)?

- I guess she means that her kids are learning to...

AARP (American Association of Retired Persons) Bulletin (2012)

After a tough day at the church where she works as pastor, Amy Yoder McGloughlin comes home and confides in her mother-in-law, Judy, who has lived with her family in a five-bedroom home in Philadelphia for nine years. Amy turns to Judy regularly for advice, support and childcare. She can't imagine how the family would function without her.

"Between my husband and me, we have a mortgage-size student loan debt every month, so Judy's financial contribution really helps," Amy says. "But there's so much more than just financial benefit. We're doing the 'village' thing — my kids are getting a better sense of what it means to be a family."

The McGloughlins are part of a new normal, one in which 17 percent of the population now live in multigenerational households. Of course, no one's saying it's easy to live with your parents or children. Issues of privacy, independence, resource sharing and responsibility must be tackled head-on — ideally in advance of living together. Dividing up and assigning chores is a necessary part of keeping the wheels greased. Strangely, it usually works out. Not everyone likes to cook, and not everyone wants to do laundry.

Robyn Griggs Lawrence, **www.nextavenue.org** (2012)

2. Come Work with Us!

CD 1 PISTES 9-11

1. Look at the website. What does the logo evoke? **Anticipate**

2. Read the full home page. What sort of company is this? How do you know? **Anticipate**

- This company might be specialised in...

3. Listen to the first part of the sound file. Who are Kevin Prentiss and Tony Bacigalupo? What do you learn about the place?

- New Work City offers...
- The amenities include...

4. Listen to the second part. Explain what you understand about this "new trend".

5. Would you rather work at home or in a place like New Work City?

- I'd (much) rather work...

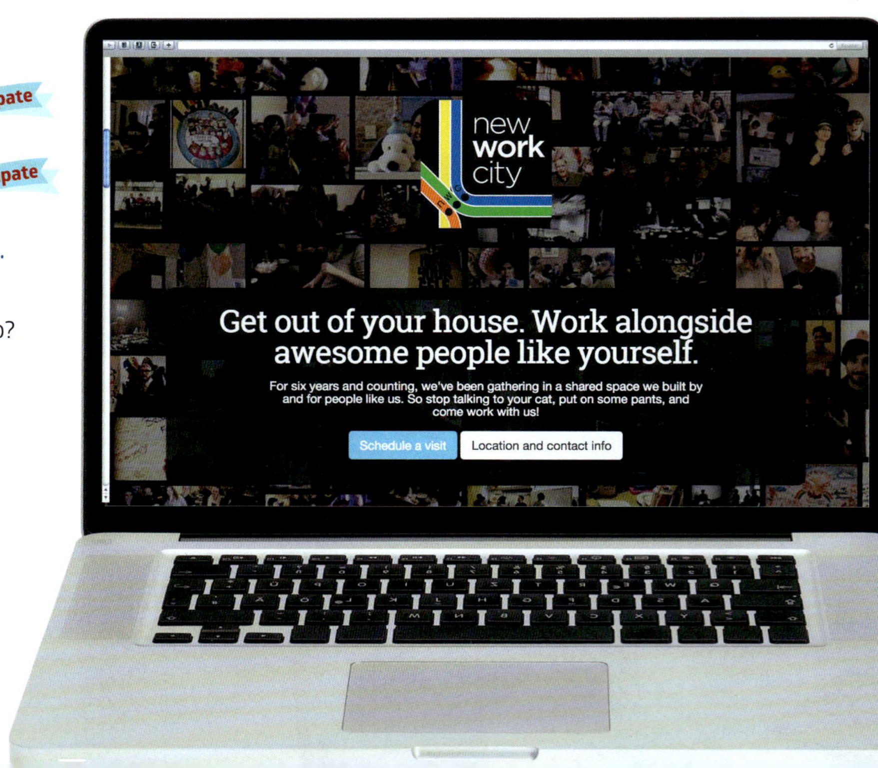

3. Resident Employees

Anticipate **1.** Describe the picture below with as much detail as you can (attitude, atmosphere...).

Anticipate **2.** Focus on the title above and the caption of the photo. What do you think the article is about?

- Given the title, it must be about...

3. Read the text. What company is described? What is unique about it?

- As opposed to other companies, ...
- What is unique about this company is that...

4. In your opinion, who benefits more from this type of organisation?

- I'd say it mostly benefits...

Everyone's heard of startups being "run out of a garage" — from Apple's original home to Facebook's early residence in Palo Alto, working out of a house has been a point of pride for tech entrepreneurs.

Los Angeles-based Enplug, a one-year-old startup that makes interactive displays for bars and restaurants in Southern California, decided to give us an inside look at the home that serves as the main office and residence for the company's team of coders and designers.

By removing the difference between home and office, developers are free to work at any time of day or night. This setup seems equal parts "cultish" (in Enplug CEO and co-founder Nanxi Liu's words) and fun — there's less pressure to work all day when things can be done at night, but it also makes it harder to define when "down time" really is.

Employees I've spoken to have told me that the setup makes working feel like spending time with family. In fact, some of the employees are family: two of the company's developers got married before moving in with Enplug. For their part, they say the free food and rent is worth "the lack of privacy."

Kyle Russell, **www.businessinsider.com** (2013)

One of the employees at Enplug

Toolbox

CD1 PISTE 12 MP3 7

- an amenity /əˈmiːnɪtɪ/ = a facility /fəˈsɪlɪtɪ/: *un équipement, un service*
- a chore /tʃɔː/: *une tâche ménagère*
- a drawback /ˈdrɔːbæk/ = a downside /ˈdaʊnsaɪd/: *un inconvénient*
- privacy /ˈprɪvəsɪ/: *l'intimité*
- workplace: *le lieu de travail*
- to facilitate: *faciliter*
- to offer a service: *offrir un service*
- to provide (sb with sth) /prəˈvaɪd/ = to supply: *fournir (qqch à qqn)*
- to take care of sb/sth: *s'occuper de qqn/qqch*
- to work from home: *travailler de chez soi*

Useful Grammar

Le présent en *be* + V-*ing* → p. 169

- Auxiliaire ***be*** au présent + base verbale + ***-ing***. S'utilise, entre autres, pour décrire une action en cours, se référer à un évènement à venir ou émettre un jugement.
  - *Amy's in the living room with Judy. What* ***is*** *she* ***doing*** *exactly?*
  - *She****'s*** *probably* ***asking*** *for advice.*

Les pronoms relatifs → p. 178

- Antécédent humain seulement : ***who***.
  The guy ***who*** *works at Enplug came to see me yesterday.*
- Antécédent non humain seulement : ***which***.
  The business model ***which*** *the company has developed is really good.*
- Antécédent humain ou non humain : ***that*** ou **Ø** (peu formel). **Ø** ne peut pas être sujet.
  This is a company ***that*** *is worth a visit.*
  That's the woman **Ø** *we want to hire.*
- ***Where***, ***when*** et ***why*** introduisent des relatives circonstancielles de lieu, de temps et de cause. Leur sens est celui de « préposition + ***which*** » : *the place* ***where*** *(= in / at / to which, etc.), the time* ***when*** *(= at / on which), the reason* ***why*** *(= for which)...*
- ***Whose*** : lien d'appartenance (= « dont » en français).
  The company ***whose*** *name I remembered so well was Airbnb.*

Your Task

Living at a startup

Imagine that you have been hired by Enplug. After spending a week there, you are asked to send an email to the CEO, explaining how you are doing so far. Write about your new life. Give details about work, amenities, workmates/flatmates, privacy, leisure...

- Dear Mister Liu,
  So far I'm doing fine. I like it here because... My roommate, who... Work is... What I don't like that much is...

2 Sharing is Caring

WB p. 7-8

Your Task
Present an idea for a new sharing economy service

1. What's Mine is Yours

Anticipate **1.** Look at the picture and react. What is it?

2. Read the text and make a list of all the companies that are cited as examples. What is their business? What do they have in common?

- Airbnb specialises in...
- All these companies...

3. The word "shift" comes up twice in the first paragraph. What does it mean? What "shift" does the article deal with?

- We are increasingly willing to...
- People no longer...

4. What are the benefits of "disownership" according to the text? Find examples.

- Car sharing helps / allows users to...

5. Have you ever used a "sharing economy" service yourself?

- My parents have exchanged...
- I've already shared...

Consumer attitudes and behaviours surrounding renting, borrowing, and leasing items, versus ownership, are shifting. Smart companies are creating innovative business models that offer consumers more flexible choices for accessing the things they want and need. Disownership represents a major cultural shift in consumer behaviour — a shift that benefits our wallets, our planet and our communities.

Airbnb changed the landscape for travel accommodation, giving people the opportunity to stay in other people's homes rather than impersonal and expensive hotels. Ride-sharing companies like Zipcar have made it easier to get around without owning a car, and sites like Rent The Runway and resale marketplaces like Threadflip encourage women to buy, sell, and wear used garments rather than new. Commonly-shared items include vacation houses and rooms, heavy equipment, books, and household tools, cars and trucks, and high-end luxury apparel and accessories.

Even five years ago, the idea of letting a random person on the Internet stay in your home or get in the car with you seemed crazy and potentially dangerous. However, the rise of social networking and crowdsourced information adds in a layer of identity verification and accountability that helps people trust each other.

Rebecca Grant, **www.venturebeat.com** (2013)

Useful Grammar

Le *present perfect simple* → p. 169

- Auxiliaire ***have*** au présent + participe passé. Situation présente qui porte en elle la trace du passé.
  *She **has bought** this gorgeous bag on a website that offers used garments.*

Le *present perfect* en *be* + V-*ing* → p. 170

- Auxiliaire ***have*** au présent + ***been*** + V-***ing***. Situation présente qui porte en elle la trace du passé. On met l'accent sur l'action qui est à l'origine de l'état présent du sujet.
  *Since we**'ve been using** Zipcar, we **have been getting** a better sense of what it means to share.*

Toolbox

CD 1 PISTE 13 MP3 8

- a donation /dəʊ'neɪʃən/
- ownership /'əʊnəʃɪp/: *la propriété*
- a platform /'plætfɔːm/
- a tool /tuːl/: *un outil, un instrument*

- to appeal to sb /ə'piːl/: *plaire à qqn*
- to borrow sth (from sb) /'bɒrəʊ/: *emprunter qqch (à qqn)*
  ≠ to lend (sb sth) /lend/: *prêter (qqch à qqn)*
- to donate /dəʊ'neɪt/: *donner, faire un don*
- to enable /ɪ'neɪbl/: *permettre*
- to exchange /ɪks'tʃeɪndʒ/ = to swap
- to fund /fʌnd/ a project: *financer un projet*
- to own /əʊn/: *posséder*
- to raise funds / money: *collecter des fonds / de l'argent*
- to rent: *louer*

2. Crowdfunding

Crowdfunding is an internet phenomenon in which enterprising artists and business people appeal for micro-donations to fund a project.

The idea first began in 1997 when fans of the British rock band Marillion launched an internet fundraising campaign to bankroll an American tour. More than £35,000 was raised.

Today, crowdfunding is used by filmmakers, charities, technology companies, even football clubs, for projects that would otherwise struggle to get off the ground.

In Britain, it is becoming commonplace for organisations unable to secure state funding to take on this approach.

Sarah Knapton, ***The Telegraph*** (2014)

Graeme Keyes (Irish cartoonist), *Private Eye* magazine (2014)

1. What words do you recognise in "crowdfunding"? What could it mean? **Anticipate**

2. Read the text. How did crowdfunding start? Why is it so popular today?

- A lot of people use these platforms to...
- Crowdfunding is great for + V-ing...

3. Do you know other crowdfunded projects?

- I know a band that has (already) used...

4. Look at the cartoon and describe the story it tells. What message does it convey?

3. Join the Movement

Anticipate **1.** Consider the screenshots and the title of the activity. What might the video be about?

2. Watch the video and list:
- the different types of work that we see
- the things that are shared
- the values and advantages of this new economy

3. Why is this new economy revolutionary? Write a paragraph to present the new economy comparing it with the traditional economy.

4. You are going to create a sharing economy cooperative. List three services that you could offer. Go around to ask your classmates what they can offer. Then, explain the matches you have found.

- I'm offering Marie singing classes, and in return she...

Video Time

DVD PISTE 2

Peers: Growing the sharing economy movement, by www.peers.org (2013)

Pronunciation

CD 1 PISTE 14 MP3 9

L'accentuation des mots en *-ity* et *-ion*

Écoutez ces deux extraits de l'audio « Sustainable communities » en vous concentrant sur la prononciation des mots suivants (dans l'ordre) :
- Extrait 1 : ***transactions***, ***interactions***
- Extrait 2 : ***humanity***, ***community***

1. Repérez la syllabe accentuée dans chaque mot.

2. Qu'en déduisez-vous de l'accentuation des mots en ***-ity*** et ***-ion*** ?

3. Prononcez ces mots en accentuant la syllabe appropriée : ***aspiration***, ***dignity***, ***equality***, ***mission***, ***pronunciation***, ***revolution***, ***sustainability***.

3. Qu'en déduisez-vous sur l'intonation des questions en anglais ?

Your Task

A new service for teenagers

In groups, try to come up with an idea for a sharing economy service that can be useful for teenagers. Every group will present its project to the class. Explain why you have decided to do this, how it works and what the benefits are.

- We've realised that a lot of students... That's why we have come up with...

WB p. 9-10

Your Task
Write a questionnaire for people who want to join an ecovillage

1. Sustainable Communities

Anticipate

1. Look up the definition of "sustainable". Then, discuss what you think a sustainable community might be.

2. Look at the screenshot and focus on the first part of the video just by listening to the soundtrack. What do you think this film is about?

3. Watch the full trailer.

a. What have you learned about this journey?
b. Why did they decide to embark on this adventure?
c. What are the main goals of these communities?

4. If you could create your own community, and if money did not matter at all, what would you do?

- If I could do anything I wanted, I would...
- I'd create a place where...

Video Time

DVD PISTES 3-5

Within Reach: Journey to Find Sustainable Community (2009)

2. Dancing Rabbit Ecovillage

Anticipate

1. Look at the picture and the title above. What kind of things do you think you could find in an ecovillage? What kind of people?

2. Read the first two paragraphs. What is Brian's goal? How has he managed to achieve it in the village?

3. Read the last paragraph. What is the most important thing that Brian has learned?

4. Could you get used to living in an ecovillage?

- I'd find it hard to get used to (not) + V-ing... because...
- It'd be nice to... but at the same time...

5. Imagine a day in the life of Brian. Write a diary entry.

- Today I woke up at...

Brian Ziggy and his partner, April, in front of their hand-built house

In 2006, I found myself visiting an ecovillage in northeast Missouri. My destination was Dancing Rabbit Ecovillage, an intentional community dedicated to ecologically sustainable and socially rewarding lives. I was taken with the place rather quickly and knew that this was the change I wanted in my life, and the following spring, I became a resident.

My goal has been to try to live as mindfully as I can, and as low impact as I am able. The things I have chosen to explore are based on my interests in reducing my carbon footprint. Currently, I live in a hand-built house without electricity (I have access to power and internet usage in a shared Common House, hence my writing this article!). I cook exclusively with wood heat. I grow some portion of my own food with a group of friends, have dabbled in beekeeping and raising chickens, make my own candles for lighting, and practise building with hand tools.

Perhaps the most important lesson I've learned about living environmentally is that it does not happen in isolation. You cannot do it alone. Living ecologically is a collaborative process, and community is the key to creating a sustainable lifestyle.

Brian Ziggy, personal blog from **www.eartheasy.com** (2012)

3. Smaller is Better

CD 1 PISTES 15-18

1. Look at the book cover. What is a "pocket neighbourhood"? **Anticipate**

2. Listen to the first part of the clip. What sort of document is it? Who can you hear?

3. Listen to the second part. What are the differences between small and large communities?

- In pocket neighbourhoods, you find... whereas in large communities...

4. Listen to the third part. What does the speaker say about "privacy"?

5. Prepare a few questions to learn more about your classmates' neighbourhood and community life. Be ready to report your findings.

- Do you live in a city or...?
- How well do you know...?
- Do you ever...?

Useful Grammar

Les énoncés interrogatifs → p. 173

- Dans les *Yes / No questions* et les questions ouvertes (réponse autre que « oui » ou « non ») qui commencent par un mot interrogatif, il y a **inversion** entre le 1er auxiliaire du groupe verbal et le sujet.
  Did you live *in a hand-built house when you were young?*
  Have you been feeling *lonely lately?*
  Who did you see *in the laundry room?*
- **Pas d'inversion** dans les questions ouvertes où ***who*** et ***what*** sont sujets.
  Who wants *to live without electricity?*
  What causes *this feeling of loneliness?*

Pocket Neighborhoods (2011)

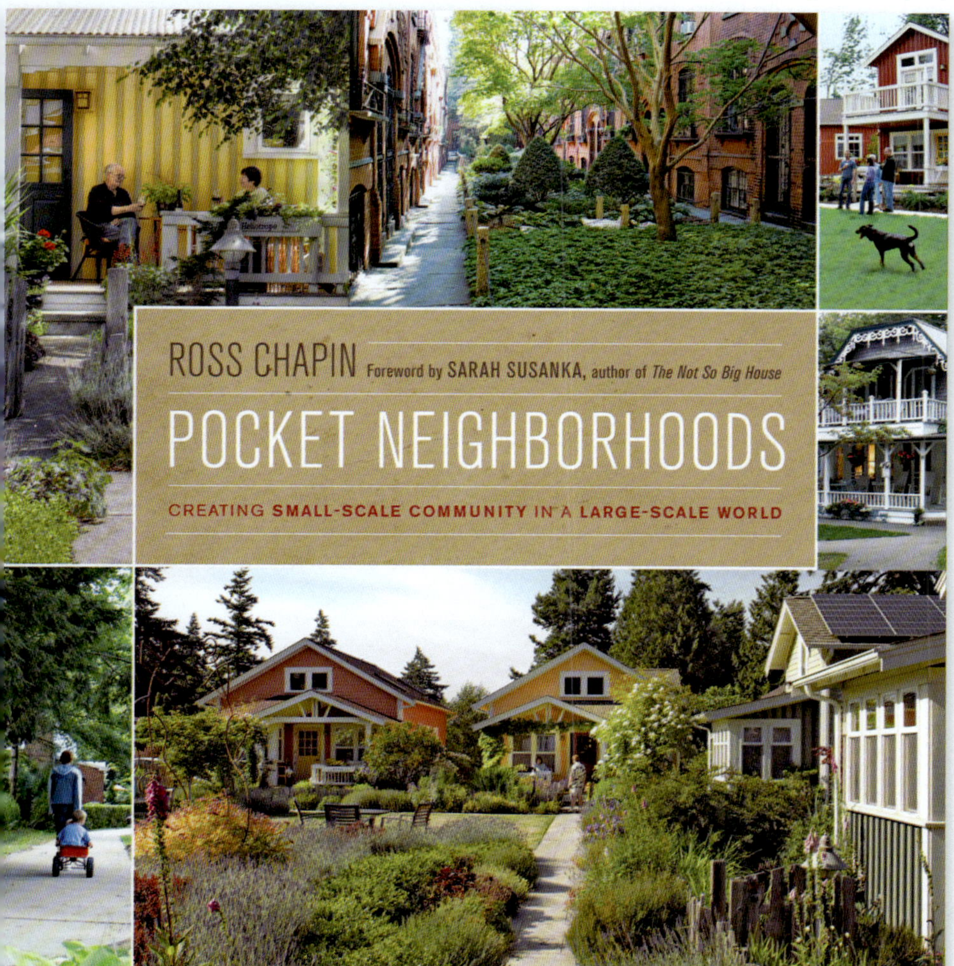

Toolbox

CD 1 PISTE 19 MP3 10

- collaborative /kə'læbərətɪv/
- ecological /ˌiːkə'lɒdʒɪkəl/ = environmental /ɪnˌvaɪərən'mentl/
- hand-built /'hændbɪlt/: *construit à la main*
- mindful /'maɪndfʊl/: *attentif, soucieux*
- rewarding /rɪ'wɔːdɪŋ/: *gratifiant*
- sustainable /səs'teɪnəbl/: *durable*
- upstanding /ʌp'stændɪŋ/: *intègre, droit*

- carbon footprint /'kɑːbən 'fʊtprɪnt/: *l'empreinte carbone*
- a pioneer /ˌpaɪə'nɪə/

Your Task

Who will join us?

Imagine you live in a community like Dancing Rabbit Ecovillage. Write a questionnaire for people who want to join.

- What are your...?
- Have you ever...?

CD 1 PISTE 20 MP3 11

Divergent

by Veronica Roth (2011)

There is one mirror in my house. It is behind a sliding panel in the hallway upstairs. Our faction allows me to stand in front of it on the second day of every third month, the day my mother cuts my hair. I sit on the stool and my mother stands behind me with the scissors, trimming. The strands[1] fall on the floor in a dull, blond ring.

When she finishes, she pulls my hair away from my face and twists it into a knot. I note how calm she looks and how focused she is. She is well-practised in the art of losing herself. I can't say the same of myself.

I sneak a look at my reflection when she isn't paying attention — not for the sake of vanity, but out of curiosity. A lot can happen to a person's appearance in three months.

In my reflection, I see a narrow face, wide, round eyes, and a long, thin nose — I still look like a little girl, though some time in the last few months I turned sixteen. The other factions celebrate birthdays, but we don't. It would be self-indulgent.

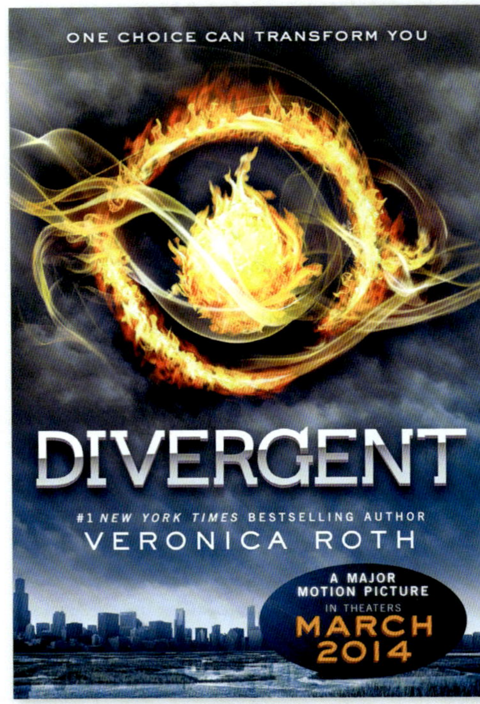

"There," she says when she pins the knot in place. Her eyes catch mine in the mirror. It is too late to look away, but instead of scolding[2] me, she smiles at our reflection. I frown a little. Why doesn't she reprimand me for staring at myself?

"So, today is the day," she says.

"Yes," I reply.

"Are you nervous?" I stare into my own eyes for a moment. Today is the day of the aptitude test that will show me which of the five factions I belong in. And tomorrow, at the Choosing Ceremony, I will decide on a faction; I will decide the rest of my life; I will decide to stay with my family or abandon them.

"No," I say. "The tests don't have to change our choices."

"Right." She smiles. "Let's go eat breakfast."

"Thank you. For cutting my hair."

She kisses my cheek and slides the panel over the mirror. I think my mother could be beautiful, in a different world. Her body is thin beneath the gray robe. She has high cheekbones and long eyelashes, and when she lets her hair down at night, it hangs in waves over her shoulders. But she must hide that beauty in Abnegation. We walk together to the kitchen. On these mornings when my brother makes breakfast, and my father's hand skims[3] my hair as he reads the newspaper, and my mother hums as she clears the table — it is on these mornings that I feel guiltiest for wanting to leave them.

1. les mèches de cheveux - **2.** réprimander - **3.** (ici) caresser

Biography

Veronica Roth (born in 1988 in New York City) is an American novelist and short story writer. She is the author of the young-adult dystopian trilogy *Divergent* (*Divergent*, *Insurgent*, and *Allegiant*). The first book explores themes such as adult authority and the transition from childhood to maturity and has been wildly popular. It was made into a film released in March 2014.

BUILDING YOUR JOURNAL...

Workbook, p. 62

Floating Cities:
Construction on Water

It may look like science fiction, but the time has come for life on the water. Due to climate change, sea levels are rising, floods are prevalent, and cities are put at risk due to overpopulation. Will the solutions be found in the work of 98 year-old Floridian Jacque Fresco? Let's take a look...

Philosophy: A Strong Foundation

Jacque Fresco believes in one thing, communities. This "Modern-Day DaVinci" designs floating cities that incorporate sustainability and revolutionary philosophy in their design. He advocates for a "resource-based economy," which means ensuring all the resources on Earth are shared equally by all people. This visionary is convinced that if society wants to survive, we need dramatic changes in life and through engineering.

Floating structures can accommodate millions of people and relieve the land-based population pressures.

In the Venus Project system, technology would help maximise the quality of life rather than profit.

The Venus Project

To Fresco, it's crucial to re-think architecture and the way we live. This critical view of modern economy has led him to develop the Venus Project, a combination of his ideology and engineering expertise. The Venus Project provides hope that globally, there is a solution to waste, pollution, overcrowding, and even illness. Eco-friendly constructions, including use of alternative power sources and automated self-repairing on both land and water, will relieve congestion in cities and be able to house millions of people.

Digital ZONE

Create your own Art Mag page. Search the internet for a futuristic and sustainable building. Take notes on what you read. Then, in a text document, write two paragraphs about it. Don't forget to include a title, a subtitle or a short introductory paragraph and a couple of photos with captions. You can send your work to anglais@emdl.fr.

BUILDING YOUR JOURNAL...

Workbook, p. 63

Let's Practise Grammar

community.emdl.fr
exercices interactifs

Le présent en *be* + V-*ing*

1 Complétez les phrases avec les verbes suivants au présent en ***be*** + V-***ing*** ou au présent simple.

build | try | make | water | be | feed | do

1. In the morning, we ... the chickens. Then, we ... the garden.

2. A lot of tech companies ... housing communities for their employees these days.

3. Hi. I can't talk to you right now because I ... some candles. Can I call you back later?

4. One of Facebook's goals ... to take care of many aspects of its employees' lives.

5. – What ... you ... on your laptop?
– I ... to find a ride on Zipcar.

Les pronoms relatifs

2 Complétez la conversation suivante entre Lori et Robin en utilisant les relatifs appropriés. Plusieurs solutions sont parfois possibles. Puis, pour mieux mémoriser ces formes, recopiez le texte dans votre cahier en mettant chaque relatif en couleur.

Lori: So, how was your trip to Naples?

Robin: It was great. I especially liked the place **when** / **whose** / **where** we stayed.

Lori: How did you find it?

Robin: We used that website **who** / **which** / **Ø** is called Airbnb. You look on their webpage, decide **who** / **whose** / **where** you need a place to stay and **who** / **whose** / **when** you want to go, and they give you a list of people **when** / **whose** / **where** flats or houses are available.

Lori: And what did you find?

Robin: We found a cute flat **that** / **Ø** / **who** was right in the city centre. It's owned by a very friendly woman **who** / **Ø** / **which** rents her place quite cheaply.

Lori: That sounds perfect! We're going to Athens in April. It's a place **whose** / **when** / **Ø** we've been dreaming of visiting for years, and **whom** / **that** / **where** we'd really like to spend a couple of days.

Les énoncés interrogatifs et le *present perfect*

3 Joyce King s'est installée dans l'écovillage de Generous Iguana en septembre dernier. Reformulez les questions qui lui sont posées par un journaliste à l'aide des éléments entre parenthèses. Choisissez les combinaisons temps/outils appropriées (prétérit simple, *present perfect* simple ou *present perfect* en ***be*** + V-***ing***).

1. – When (**you first hear**) about Generous Iguana, Joyce?
– Well, a couple of years ago.

2. – So when (**you arrive**) in the village, and how long (**you live**) here?
– In June. So, it's been about six months now.

3. – And what (**you learn**) here?
– That it's possible to live sustainably by making a few changes in your life.

4. – What (**you do**) so far today?
– I've been cooking breakfast, picking strawberries and doing other chores.

5. – (**you ever feel**) that you wanted to leave this place?
– Sometimes. I remember once when it was winter and I wanted a hot shower. I thought, "That's it!" But I stayed.

6. – Who (**help**) you adjust to this new life?
– Everyone. This is a collective space.

... and Vocabulary

Verbs, nouns and adjectives

1 Trouvez l'intrus et justifiez votre choix.

1.
- to supply
- to provide
- to own
- to offer

2.
- difficulty
- drawback
- advantage
- downside

3.
- to benefit
- to collaborate
- to team up
- to cooperate

4.
- eco-friendly
- trendy
- ecological
- sustainable

Adverbs

2 Complétez le tableau avec des adverbes formés à partir des adjectifs de la colonne de gauche.

Adjectives	Adverbs
potential	potentially
sustainable	
equal	
ecological	
social	

Maintenant, associez chacun des adverbes trouvés à l'un des mots ci-dessous et complétez les phrases.

shared — dangerous — live — rewarding — sustainable

1. The goal of many people nowadays is to ... in order to protect the environment.

2. The use of fossil fuels is no longer ... . We must find new ways to produce energy.

3. In Dana's house, all of the chores are ... among all of the family members.

4. Environmentalists strongly believe that nuclear energy is a ... way of producing energy.

5. Volunteering is a great way to do something in your free time that is ...

Phrasal verbs

3 Associez chaque *phrasal verb* à sa définition.

1. drop in	a. search for
2. look for	b. make tidy
3. pitch in	c. make an informal visit
4. clean up	d. find a solution
5. work out	e. do your part of a collective effort

Maintenant, utilisez ces *phrasal verbs* pour compléter l'histoire de Daniel.

Daniel felt lonely running his Internet start-up business from home; he wanted to ... more social interaction. A friend told him about a shared office space in the neighbourhood. One day, he decided to ... and see if he liked it. There were a lot of people and a friendly woman explained how it worked. "You get a place to sit and connect your laptop. Everyone has to ... for the expenses, like coffee and toilet paper. You also have to ... your space when you're finished working. If there are any problems, you have to go to a meeting so that everyone can ... the problem together." Daniel decided to become a member immediately.

Prepositions

4 Choisissez la bonne préposition et recopiez la question complète dans votre cahier. Puis, répondez aux questions et partagez vos réponses avec votre partenaire.

1. Who do you confide (**out** / **in** / **off**) more: friends or family?

2. Who can you turn (**out** / **in** / **to**) when you have a serious problem?

3. Do you know the differences (**than** / **of** / **between**) working in an office and working in a collective space?

4. Have you ever heard (**of** / **out** / **in**) a Time Bank where you live?

5. How dedicated are you (**to** / **in** / **up**) helping the community in your neighbourhood?

Your Final Task

Present and promote a community

1 You have been selected to represent one of the following communities at the Open Day. As one of the oldest members, your task is to give a speech to the visitors.

2 Choose one of the communities. Think about your own experience (why you moved there, how long you have been living there), what life is like, the amenities, the lessons that you have learned, etc.

3 Organise your material and write a draft. You can structure the presentation in three parts: introduction, body, conclusion.

4 Rehearse your presentation until you are ready to deliver it to the class. Good luck!

Toolbox

CD 1 PISTE 21 MP3 12

- a community service
- a multicultural community
- a resident
- a tight-knit community
- to be worth a visit

- Shall we start?
- Good morning / afternoon, ladies and gentlemen.
- We are delighted to have you here today...
- I would like to talk to you about...
- What I mean is...
- To sum up...
- So, in conclusion...
- Are there any questions?
- Thank you all for your attention.

Tips & Tricks

→ **Be articulate and enthusiastic!** Souvenez-vous que votre but est d'attirer des visiteurs.

→ **Keep it simple!** Utilisez des phrases simples afin de retenir l'attention du public.

→ **Make it engaging and personal!** Servez-vous d'exemples tirés de votre expérience personnelle et partagez des anecdotes.

→ **Smile!** Votre public réagira positivement si vous êtes souriant et détendu.

→ **Don't rush!** On vous comprendra mieux s'il y a des pauses régulières dans votre prononciation.

An art commune

A nine-bedroom urban home in Dublin (Ireland) for people of all ages interested in art who are looking for a greater sense of community belonging and togetherness.

A skater community

A sustainable community and learning centre for skate lovers willing to help each other and practise their beloved sport in a breathtaking setting on the west coast of Scotland.

Let's prepare your final task

Lorsque vous vous entraînez à faire votre discours, prêtez attention aux critères d'évaluation ci-dessous. Où vous situez-vous dans chaque ligne ?

	Niveau 1	Niveau 2	Niveau 3 (→ B1)	Niveau 4
Réalisation de la tâche	Le thème (*present and promote a community*) est en partie traité mais les idées sont juxtaposées sans vraie organisation. **A1**	La plupart des éléments demandés (*introduction, body, conclusion*...) apparaissent même si la structure du discours reste globalement floue. Des efforts basiques de liaison des idées entre elles (***and*, *but*, *because***...). **A2**	Tous les éléments demandés sont traités. Des efforts pour complexifier le propos (structures relatives, mots de liaison variés...), le rendre vivant et s'approcher d'un discours authentique. **B1**	Le discours produit est remarquable pour la pertinence de son contenu et la qualité formelle de sa réalisation. Le propos est argumenté et convaincant. **B2**
Qualité de la production orale	La prononciation est compréhensible avec des efforts, malgré une lecture serrée des notes. **A1**	La prononciation est suffisamment claire pour être généralement comprise malgré un net accent étranger. **A2** Quelques tentatives pour regarder son auditoire, mais le recours aux notes est encore très fréquent.	Le discours est assez naturel et fluide. La prononciation est toujours intelligible même si on perçoit un accent étranger et malgré quelques erreurs de prononciation. **B1** La lecture des notes est occasionnelle et la gestuelle est souvent adaptée au message transmis.	La prononciation se rapproche de l'authenticité. Un auditeur natif n'aurait pas de mal à comprendre. **B2** Le discours est totalement fluide et le recours aux notes rare. La gestuelle est parfaitement adaptée au message, le contact visuel presque permanent.
Maîtrise de la grammaire et du vocabulaire	Les phrases sont très brèves. Les formes grammaticales sont assez intelligibles mais limitées et répétitives. Emploi d'un répertoire très restreint de mots simples. **A1/A1+**	Les phrases sont simples mais généralement correctes. Des erreurs élémentaires sont possibles. Des efforts pour employer certaines des structures de l'unité (pronoms relatifs, ***present perfect***...). Exploitation d'une partie du lexique étudié, mais le répertoire est encore restreint. **A2/A2+**	Les phrases ne comportent pratiquement pas d'erreurs élémentaires. Les structures vues en cours (pronoms relatifs, *present perfect*, present ***be*** + V-*ing*...) sont fréquemment réutilisées et bien maîtrisées. De nombreux éléments lexicaux du cours sont réexploités. **B1**	Les phrases ne comportent aucune erreur élémentaire. Les structures employées vont au-delà de ce qui a été étudié en cours. Emploi d'un répertoire lexical plus riche que celui qui a été étudié dans l'unité. **B2**
Valeur chiffrée (équivalences)	De 5 à 9/20	De 10 à 15/20	De 16 à 20/20	Au-delà des attentes de 2de : objectifs du cycle terminal en vue.

Let's read two texts

Your teacher will give you two texts. Read them and answer the questions.

Women exchanging clothes, shoes and accessories they no longer need or wear

Let's listen to a short recording

CD-1 / PISTE-22

Listen to the document and answer the questions your teacher will give you.

Living in an intentional community

Let's write

You are a journalist visiting one of the two communities from p. 34. Write an article about this community.

3 T for Texas

> You can take the girl out of Texas, but not Texas out of the girl.
>
> Janine Turner, American actress

→ **ISSUE AT STAKE**

Do Texan stereotypes reveal the true identity of Texas?

ON YOUR WAY TO THE TASK

1 Everything is Bigger in Texas
Write an email describing Texas

2 Remember the Alamo
Record an audio guide of the Alamo

3 The Texas Triangle
Create a radio ad to promote a Texas city

YOUR FINAL TASK

Create a promotional newsletter of Texas

> People either passionately love Texas or passionately hate it.
>
> John Steinbeck, American writer

“I'd rather be a fence post in Texas, than the king of Tennessee.”
Chris Wall, American singer-songwriter

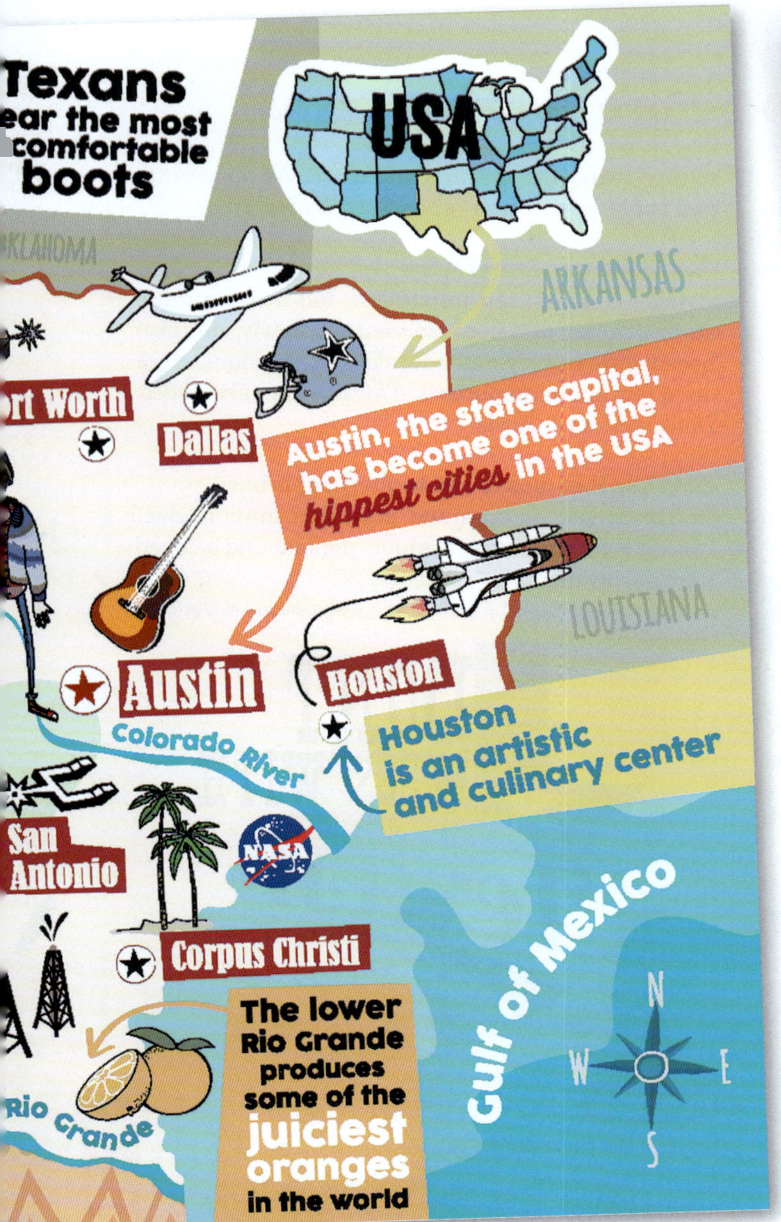

1. Look at the map and list three facts about Texas related to: **food, oil, size**.

2. Do you know anything else about Texas?

- I know that...
- Texas is known for...
- Texas is said to be...

3. Pick one of the items or cities on the map without text and write it yourself.

- Buddy Holly is one of the most influential...
- San Antonio's basketball team...

4. Read the four quotes and think about what they mean. Then, match them to the sentences below:

a. It's better to be unimportant in Texas than very important somewhere else.
b. Texas leaves no one indifferent.
c. If you are from Texas, part of you will always be Texan.
d. Texans love being Texan.

5. What do all of these quotes have in common?

- They all mean that...
  insist on...
  convey the idea that...

GO FURTHER... www.community.emdl.fr

Listen to the song **"Blame it on Texas"** and read the lyrics. Can you summarise the song in one sentence?

Toolbox

CD 1 PISTE 23 MP3 13

- conservative /kən'sɜːvətɪv/
- dynamic /daɪ'næmɪk/
- hip /hɪp/: *branché*
- proud /praʊd/: *fier*

- the capital /'kæpɪtl/
- a cowboy /'kaʊbɔɪ/
- pride /praɪd/: *la fierté*
- a rodeo /'rəʊdɪəʊ/

- to be celebrated for /'selɪbreɪtɪd/: *être réputé pour*

“If a man's from Texas, he'll tell you. If he's not, why embarrass him by asking?”
John Gunther, American journalist and author

 WB p. 11-12

Your Task Write an email describing Texas

1. Don't Mess with Texas

1. Read the text. Look for similarities and differences between Texas and France. Write a list to compare with your classmates.

- In France, there are more... than in Texas.
- French people are (not) as... as Texans.

2. Focus on the fourth paragraph and determine the meaning of one of the two expressions.

3. Would you like to visit Texas? Why or why not?

- I'd absolutely love to visit Texas because...
- I really have no interest in visiting Texas because...
- Texas looks like a fun place because...

4. Write the "Five things to know" for Texan tourists who might visit **your** region.

Five things to know before visiting Texas

1. We are proud

The old adage goes that everything is bigger in Texas. I know a whole bunch of Texans that would argue that everything is also better in the Lone Star State. Yes, we Texans are a very proud bunch, and rightfully so.

2. We don't measure distance in miles, but rather time

Texas includes 7.4% of the nation's total area. El Paso in West Texas is closer to California than it is to Beaumont in East Texas. Texas is larger than France. So, you want to know how far it is from Houston to Austin? It's about three hours.

3. Learning our pronunciation is essential for communication

Texans are not fast talkers. We have a drawl that seems to turn two-syllable words into three. We apparently don't care for the letter "g" on the end of words.

4. We like our expressions

It takes a Texan ten minutes to tell a five-minute story. It's not just because we talk slowly, but also because we're very much into our expressions. Here are a few common phrases: *This ain't my first rodeo. Don't mess with Texas.*

5. When it comes to bar-b-que, beef is boss

In Texas, beef is boss and pork is a minion. Beef brisket is far-and-away the most popular and beloved item on any menu.

Adapted from Leah Walker, **www.LeahTravels.com** (2013)

2. It's Dry and We're Proud!

CD1 PISTE 24

1. Gloria is a Texan girl. Read the title of the activity and try to predict the topics that she will talk about. **Anticipate**

2. Listen to the interview and check your ideas.

3. Listen again and take notes about each topic.

Pronunciation

CD1 PISTE 25 MP3 14

Les différentes prononciations du « a »

Écoutez ces deux extraits audio en vous concentrant sur la prononciation de la lettre « **a** » des mots suivants (dans l'ordre) :
- Extrait 1 : ***Texas, a, than, Japan, many, climates***
- Extrait 2 : ***what, favourite, part***

1. Classez ces mots en fonction de leur prononciation : /æ/, /e/, /ɪ/, /ɑː/, /eɪ/ ou /ə/.
2. Repérez l'accent des mots. Que remarquez-vous sur la prononciation du « **a** » dans les syllabes non accentuées ?
3. ***A***, ***than*** et ***what*** sont prononcés de la même manière. Pourquoi ?

3. How I Became Texan

Anticipate

1. Look at the title above and the photo and brainstorm what the excerpt might be about.

2. Read the text. Who is the narrator and what is she talking about?

3. How did Renee's attitude and feelings towards Texas change as she got older?

- At first she was... but as she grew older / later on she...

4. Imagine you have been living in Texas for two months. Write a post for blogexpat.com to explain what you miss most and least about home, and what you like most and least about Texas.

Dressed as a cowgirl in my early childhood

I grew up in a rural area outside of San Antonio, Texas, USA. Throughout my childhood, and especially as a teenager, I was a country hipster, pushing away the stereotypes that people around me lived out. As soon as I heard the sound of country music, I rolled my eyes.

When I applied for college, I was eager to shed the identity I had had my entire life and get to know as many different people as I could.

Over the next two years, Texas started growing on me so slowly, I didn't notice. But it was only when I came to Costa Rica that I understood more about my Texan identity. Since I've been here, I've written an essay about the Alamo and the Hill Country, I've recounted the Texas Revolution as many times as I had a chance to, I've gotten excited over Texas flag sightings, I've worked the fact that Texas was an independent country into conversations, I've explained "y'all" and "fixin' to" to ticos, I've told all that San Antonio, the hill country, and Big Bend are the most awesome places in the world, and I always tell people I'm from Texas, rather than the United States, when they ask.

I always thought I would settle in another country, or at least another state, but now I think that once the wanderlust leaves me, I'll probably settle in San Antonio, where I can find the best chips and queso and go to the greatest rodeos; where I can see my dearest cousins and aunts and uncles on holidays.

It's not that I think that Texas is a better place than others, it's just that there's a part of me that will never be at home as much as there.

Renee Mazurek, adapted from ***The Quest for Pura Vida*** (2013)

Toolbox

CD 1 PISTE 26 MP3 15

- **aw**esome /'ɔːsəm/: *impressionnant, génial*
- be**lo**ved /bɪ'lʌvɪd/: *bien-aimé, adoré*
- roots /ruːts/: *les racines*
- to be **ho**mesick /'həʊmsɪk/: *avoir le mal du pays*
- to be**long** to /bɪ'lɒŋ/: *appartenir à, faire partie de*
- to care for sth /keəʳ/: *être attaché à qqch*
- to id**ea**lise /aɪ'dɪəlaɪz/: *idéaliser*
- to **rea**lise sth /'rɪəlaɪz/: *se rendre compte de qqch*
- to re**bel** /rɪ'bel/: *se rebeller*
- to re**ject** /rɪ'dʒekt/: *rejeter*

Pronunciation

CD 1 PISTE 27 MP3 16

L'accent texan

Écoutez un Texan parler et essayez d'identifier les particularités de son accent :

He always says that time is on his side.
My mother loves singing traditional songs.
I'm a farmer and I love country music.

Useful Grammar

Le comparatif de supériorité → p. 164

- Adjectif d'une syllabe : dans la plupart des cas, adjectif + ***-er*** (+ ***than***).
  *Texans think they are cool**er than** other Americans.*
- On tend à faire de même avec les adjectifs de 2 syllabes terminés par ***-er*** (*clever* → *clever**er***), ***-ow*** (*narrow* → *narrow**er***) et ***-y*** (*funny* → *funn**ier***).
- Autres adjectifs : ***more*** + adjectif (+ ***than***).
  *Texas is said to be **more** conservative **than** other American states.*

Les comparatifs d'égalité / inégalité (interprétée comme infériorité) → p. 164

- ***(not) as*** + adjectif + ***as***.
  *France is **not as** big **as** Texas.*

Les superlatifs → p. 165

- Adjectif d'une syllabe : dans la plupart des cas, ***the*** + adjectif + ***-est***.
  *Houston is **the** bigg**est** city in Texas.*
- On tend à faire de même avec les adjectifs de deux syllabes terminés par ***-er***, ***-ow*** et ***-y***.
  *Her sister is **the** funn**iest** girl in Texas.*
- Autres adjectifs : ***the*** + ***most*** + adjectif.
  *The Hill Country and Big Bend are **the most** awesome places in the world.*

Your Task

Texas in a nutshell

Imagine you have been living in Texas for a year. A group of foreign students who know nothing about the state are visiting for a few days. Send them an email with the essential information that they should know: geography, customs, must-sees...

2 Remember the Alamo

WB p. 13-14

Your Task
Record an audio guide of the Alamo

1. Fighting for Independence

Anticipate

1. Look at the title above and the screenshot. Which of the events in the timeline is the video about?

- It's probably / definitely (going to be) about...
- It might / must be about...

2. Take notes as you watch the video using the chart.

The historical context	The battle

3. Read these sentences. Watch again and put them in the order they are mentioned in the video.

a. The Mexican army outnumbered the courageous Texans that defended the Alamo.
b. The site of the Battle of the Alamo is in San Antonio.
c. The Spanish educated the indigenous population.
d. Some famous people participated in the battle.
e. The Battle of the Alamo was fought because Texas wanted to become independent from Mexico.
f. The mission was built in the 18th century by the Spanish Empire.
g. The Texans fought hard but were ultimately defeated.

4. In your opinion, what does the Alamo represent today?

Video Time

DVD PISTE 6

The Alamo, Travel Thru History (2014)

Toolbox

CD 1 PISTE 28 MP3 17

- adventurous /əd'ventʃərəs/
- brave /breɪv/ = courageous /kə'reɪdʒəs/
- loyal /'lɔɪəl/
- a hero /'hɪərəu/
- a legend /'ledʒənd/
- a memory /'memərɪ/: *un souvenir*
- a mission /'mɪʃən/
- a symbol /'sɪmbəl/
- to beat /biːt/: *vaincre*
- to claim /kleɪm/: *revendiquer*
- to defeat /dɪ'fiːt/: *battre*
- to demand /dɪ'mɑːnd/: *exiger*
- to settle /'setl/: *s'installer*
- to struggle /'strʌgl/: *lutter*
- to symbolise /'sɪmbəlaɪz/: *symboliser*

2. Texas' Most Popular Attraction

CD 1 PISTE 29

1. Listen to three people describing their visit to the Alamo and take notes about the **good things** and the **not so good things** that they mention.

2. Think about an attraction (the Eiffel Tower, Big Ben, the Colosseum in Rome, Buckingham Palace...) that you have visited and explain your experience to the class.

- Visiting... was an amazing experience because...
- It was (kind of) disappointing to visit... because...

A view of the Alamo with lots of tourists lined up waiting to enter inside (2010)

19th Century
Before 1821
Spain owned a large part of North America, including Texas. **An American, Moses Austin, planned to be the first to establish an English-American settlement in Spanish Texas**, but died before his dream came true.

1821
Mexico won independence from Spain.

1821-1827
Stephen Austin, Moses' son, founded the first American colonies in Texas.

1830
Concerned about Americans having too much influence on Texans, **the Mexican government banned American immigration to Texas**.

1833
The Mexican government rejected the attempt by Texans to create their own **Constitution**.

3. A Folk Hero

nticipate **1.** Look at the title above and the picture. What is "a folk hero"?

- In my opinion, ...
- It seems to me that...
- I would say that...

nticipate **2.** Do you know Davy Crockett? How do you think he is connected to the history of Texas?

3. Read the excerpt and make a timeline with the main events of Davy Crockett's life.

4. Read again and make a list of the words and phrases that are used to describe him.

5. Discover the elements that made Crockett a folk hero. Discuss.

- What made him a folk hero was...

6. Do you know any other folk heroes? What did they do?

- Well, Robin Hood was certainly a folk hero. As the legend goes, ... / Legend has it that...
- Buffalo Bill was also...

A Davy Crockett comic book (1954)

Embodied as the King of the Wild Frontier, Davy Crockett became an icon of a rough, tough, and savvy expanding nation. In his autobiography, he claims to have killed a bear at the age of three, quit school by age nine, traveled all of Tennessee and other states, become a hunter, trapper, and excellent marksman, and returned home before he was fifteen.

While some of his story has gone down as legend or myth, it is known that Davy Crockett was a man who kept his word, worked hard, and became a member of the House of Representatives and a congressman.

In his autobiography, Davy Crockett also says he told his constituents that if he were not re-elected into the House of Representatives again, "... they could all go to hell and I will go to Texas". Davy kept his word and when he wasn't re-elected, he joined the Texas Revolution in 1835, where he would be granted several thousands of acres for his service. When he joined the revolution, he had only 139 men under his command. When the entire group was killed after a surprise attack by Mexican forces, he left and went to fight the Battle of the Alamo. His feat at the Texas Revolution went down in history because the 139 men held off thousands of Mexican soldiers for over eleven days. When Davy Crockett's men were finally killed, over two thousand Mexicans had been slain. Legend, lore, and myth live on about what happened in those days of battle, but Davy Crockett is still considered a martyr for the cause and spirit of the United States.

www.biographyshelf.com (2014)

Useful Grammar

Le prétérit simple → p. 169

- Le prétérit sert à faire part d'évènements révolus.
- Forme affirmative : base verbale + ***-ed*** (sauf verbes dits « irréguliers »).
  *Only 186 people **defended** the Alamo against the Mexican army.*
- Formes interrogative et négative : ***did*** (auxiliaire ***do*** au prétérit) + ***not*** + base verbale.
  *They **did not** / **didn't** defeat the Mexicans.*

Your Task

A field trip

Your English class is going to Texas on a field trip. Your teacher is putting together an audio guide for everyone to listen to while they are sightseeing. You are asked to do the part about the Alamo. You should talk about: the context, the two sides, the battle, the consequences, etc. Record your guide.

1836

The first battle between Texans and Mexicans took place at an old mission that was used as a fort: **the Alamo**. The Texans were defeated.

During the battle of San Jacinto, General **Sam Houston defeated the Mexicans** and made them sign a treaty, thus ending the war and paving the way for the Republic of Texas.

Texas declared itself **The Lone Star Republic**. Sam Houston was elected president.

1845

The United States integrated Texas, the only state in the Union that was a nation on its own before becoming a state.

3 The Texas Triangle

WB p. 15-16

Your Task
Create a radio ad to promote a Texas city

1. Visit the "Big D"!

Anticipate **1.** What do you think the "Big D" is? The map of Texas below can help you.

2. Read the article and make a list of things to do in Dallas.

3. If you went to Dallas, what things would you like to see? What things could you skip?

- If I went to Dallas, I'd like to see...
- I could definitely skip... because...

4. Do you know what U.S. cities these nicknames refer to? *Big Apple, City of Angels, Motor City, Sin City, Windy City, City that Never Sleeps.*

- I'd say that... is the Motor City.
- The Windy City? Maybe it refers to... because...

Dallas is one of the largest, most diverse, most metropolitan cities in the world. Its gleaming glass skyscrapers, colossal sport stadiums, luxury shopping venues, high-rolling nightlife and world-class cuisine are the pride of its residents and the envy of cities across the country.

Eating: When you're exploring Dallas for the first time you'll need to fill your tank with the proper fuel. And by that we mean the national dish of Texas: Tex-Mex. Few places do it better than Pepe's & Mito's. (...)

Activities: An indoor rodeo arena, Texas-sized dance floor and regular visits from country music's biggest stars make Billy Bob's a monument to all things Texas. (...) The one place that is an absolute must-see on your first trip is also the site of one of this city's darkest and most dramatic moments. The exhibits inside the Sixth Floor Museum at Dealey Plaza chronicle the life and death of President John F. Kennedy, who was assassinated as his motorcade passed by this building during a visit to Dallas in November of 1963. Few visitors will leave the museum without feeling its impact.

Nikki and Dusty Green, ***USA Today*** (2014)

The exact spot where JFK was murdered in 1963

A TOUCH OF CULTURE

The Texas Triangle is one of eleven mega-regions in the U.S. It contains the cities of Dallas, Austin, Houston and San Antonio.

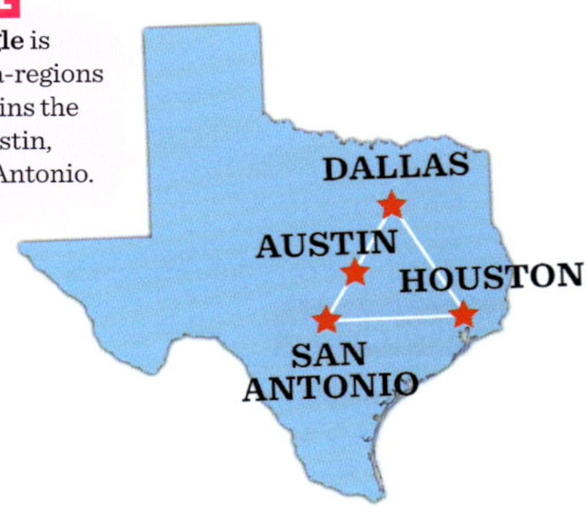

2. Let's Go to Houston!

Anticipate **1.** What do you know about Houston? Does the phrase "Houston, we've got a problem" ring a bell?

2. Watch a promotional video for Houston and take notes about the following topics: **size**, **recreation**, **culture** and **business**.

3. Why do you think Houston has become the fourth largest city in the U.S.?

- Houston has most likely become the fourth largest city because...

Video Time

DVD PISTE 7

Discover Houston, Greater Houston Partnership (2013)

Useful Grammar

Les énoncés à l'impératif → p. 173

- Forme affirmative (2ᵉ personne du singulier/pluriel) : base verbale.
  Visit *Texas; the Lone Star State.*
- Forme négative (2ᵉ personne du singulier/pluriel) : ***don't*** + base verbale.
  Don't *go to Amarillo; go to Dallas.*

3. Keep Austin Weird

While Austin is booming and topping national lists as a number one place to work and play, the city's laid-back vibe remains. After all, it is a city where flip-flops are considered business casual and a decent pair of boots always passes as formal attire. It's a mecca for musicians, software engineers, artists, environmentalists and creative entrepreneurs. Each year, the SXSW music festival reinforces Austin's bragging rights as a world capital of live music.

Austin is not a tourist town. The city lacks a single main attraction that most larger cities offer, and instead offers uniquely appealing surprises in every neighborhood. The "Keep Austin Weird" mantra is a successful campaign to promote local businesses, and demonstrates a commitment to support authenticity. With this ethos comes the freedom to create, the freedom to prosper and the freedom to wear whatever you please. It's a city to truly be yourself and explore in any way you like.

Michael Esposito, ***Texas Report*** (2015)

1. Read the title of the activity and look at the photo. What kind of city does Austin seem to be? **Anticipate**

- It looks like / seems to be a very...
- It must be a...

2. Read the text and check your perceptions.

3. Read the article again and decide if these sentences are **true** or **false**. Explain.

a. Austin is a centre of creativity.
b. Austin is a very stressful city.
c. Austin is the world capital of country dancing.
d. Austin is a tourist town.

4. In groups, try to come up with a slogan for Austin.

4. Unforgettable San Antonio

Anticipate **1.** Think about the title above and look at the screenshot. What do you imagine San Antonio is like?

- It looks like / seems to be a very...
- It seems to have...

2. Watch the video and jot down all the adjectives used to describe the city.

3. Watch again and make a list of the top 3 things that you would like to do if you were in San Antonio.

- My top 3 would be...
- I'd definitely love to...
- I wouldn't miss... for anything.

Video Time

DVD PISTE 8

Unforgettable San Antonio, SA Convention & Visitors Bureau (2014)

Toolbox

CD 1 PISTE 30 MP3 18

- fascinating /'fæsɪneɪtɪŋ/: *fascinant*
- genuine /'dʒenjʊɪn/: *authentique*
- mythical /'mɪθɪkəl/: *mythique*
- touristy /'tʊərɪstɪ/: *trop touristique*
- trendy /'trendɪ/ = hip: *branché*

- a heritage /'herɪtɪdʒ/: *un patrimoine*
- a monument /'mɒnjʊmənt/

- a must-see /mʌst-siː/: *un incontournable*
- the night life /naɪt laɪf/: *la vie nocturne*

- to explore /ɪks'plɔː/
- to go for a walk / drive / ride / sail: *se promener à pied / en voiture / à cheval / en bateau*

Your Task

You're on air!

You're going to record a radio ad to promote one of these Texan cities. Choose the one that appeals to you the most and write a script. Make sure the city is advertised as an interesting place.

CD 1 PISTE 31 MP3 19

Travels with Charley: In Search of America

by John Steinbeck (1962)

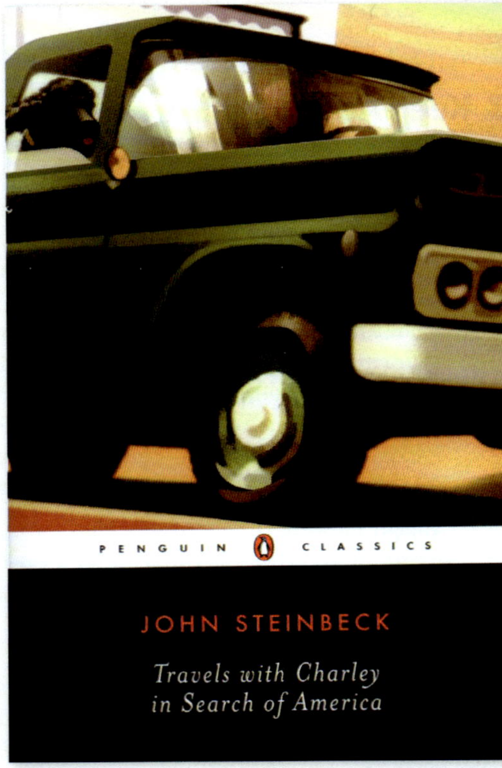

Outside their state, I think Texans are a little frightened and very tender in their feelings, and these qualities cause boasting, arrogance, and noisy complacency — the outlets[1] of shy children. At home Texans are none of these things. The ones I know are gracious, friendly, generous, and quiet. In New York, we hear them so often bring up[2] their treasured uniqueness. Texas is the only state that came into the Union by treaty. It retains the right to secede at will[3]. We have heard them threaten to secede so often that I formed an enthusiastic organization — The American Friends for Texas Secession. This stops the subject cold. They want to be able to secede but they don't want anyone to want them to. (...)

Again — the glorious defense to the death of the Alamo against the hordes of Santa Anna is a fact. The brave bands of Texans did indeed wrestle their liberty from Mexico, and "freedom", "liberty", are holy words. One must go to contemporary observers in Europe for a non-Texan opinion as to the nature of the tyranny that raised need for revolt. Outside observers say the pressure was twofold[4]. The Texans, they say, didn't want to pay taxes and, second, Mexico had abolished slavery in 1829, and Texas, being part of Mexico, was required to free its slaves. Of course there were other causes of revolt, but these two are spectacular to a European, and rarely mentioned here.

I have said that Texas is a state of mind, but I think it is more than that. It is a mystique closely approximating a religion. And this is true to the extent that people either passionately love Texas or passionately hate it and, as in other religions, few people dare to inspect it for fear of losing their bearings[5] in mystery and paradox. Any observations of mine can be quickly canceled by opinion or counter-observation. But I think there will be little quarrel with my feeling that Texas is one thing. For all its enormous range of space, climate, and physical appearance, and for all the internal squabbles[6], contentions, and strivings[7], Texas has a tight cohesiveness perhaps stronger than any other section of America. Rich, poor, Panhandle, Gulf, city, country, Texas is the obsession, the proper study, and the passionate possession of all Texans. (...) To attack one Texan is to draw fire from all Texans. The Texas joke, on the other hand, is a revered institution, beloved and in many cases originating in Texas.

1. (ici) les exutoires - **2.** évoquer - **3.** faire volontairement sécession - **4.** double - **5.** les repères - **6.** les querelles - **7.** les efforts

BUILDING YOUR JOURNAL...

Workbook, p. 64

Biography

John Steinbeck (1902-1968) is one of the finest novelists of the 20th century. Born in California, he achieved success as a writer in 1935 with *Tortilla Flat*. Four years later, his novel *The Grapes of Wrath*, about the migration of a family from Oklahoma to California, won a Pulitzer Prize. In 1962, he published *Travels with Charley: In Search of America* in which he depicted a road trip around the U.S. in the company of his dog, Charley. Also in 1962, he received the Nobel Prize for Literature.

Texas Music

Texas music is truly unique. Covering a wide array of genres, including blues, jazz, Tejano, country, pop, rock and roll, and many others, Texas music perfectly captures the state's rich history and the enormous ethnic and cultural influence that Spanish, French, German, Polish and African immigrants had. But besides this rich and diverse tradition, Texas is also the birthplace of several musicians that have been instrumental in shaping modern American music. Let's find out who they are...

Janis Joplin's jaw-dropping performance at the legendary Monterey Pop Festival in 1967 catapulted her to stardom.

★ Buddy Holly

Born in Lubbock, Texas, Buddy Holly (1936-1959) is often described as the most influential of the early rock 'n' roll musicians. With hits such as "Peggy Sue" and "That'll Be the Day", he was a rising star when he was killed in a tragic plane crash in 1959 at age 22.

Buddy Holly and The Crickets pose for a group shot on the set of the BBC television show "Off The Record" during their U.K. tour.

★ Janis Joplin

One of America's most brilliant and tormented stars, Joplin was born in Port Arthur, Texas, in 1943. She grew up listening to blues musicians, such as Bessie Smith, and singing in the local choir. She left Texas for San Francisco in 1963 and went on to become a prominent figure of the Haight-Ashbury hippy scene. When she died in 1970, an entire generation of Americans mourned her loss.

ZZ Top in Las Vegas (2007)

★ Willie Nelson

Nelson was born in the 1930s in Abbot, Central Texas. He is a singer, animal rights activist, occasional actor, and has written some of the most popular country songs of all time. Often sporting a cowboy hat or a bandana, he has become a Texan icon and an American folk hero.

Nelson on stage in Amsterdam (2002)

★ ZZ Top

ZZ Top are a veteran rock band from Houston, well-known for their long beards. They have toured constantly since the early 1970s, building a national and international following, and selling millions of albums along the way.

Digital ZONE

Make a playlist on YouTube or Spotify of great Texan songs.
Choose at least 5 songs, write a descriptive title and upload the playlist.

BUILDING YOUR JOURNAL...
Workbook, p. 65

Let's Practise Grammar

community.emdl.fr
exercices interactifs

Les comparatifs

1 Complétez le dialogue avec des comparatifs en utilisant les adjectifs suivants.

hot | disappointing | beautiful | good | brave | friendly

Carolyn: **How was your trip to Texas?**

Matthew: Well, I had a wonderful time. In fact, Texas was ... I thought it was going to be. We had a great time.

Carolyn: **What did you do there?**

Matthew: We went to visit the Alamo. It was ... I expected. There were too many people and there wasn't much information. We could have skipped it. The one thing I did learn is that Davy Crockett was ... most other men.

Carolyn: **Did you experience any nature?**

Matthew: Yes, that was really incredible. We went trekking along the Rio Grande River. That was ... anything else I'd ever seen — there were so many colours and birds to see. It was really pretty.

Carolyn: **And how was the Big D?**

Matthew: Oh, Dallas, well, the weather was ... even our summers here, so we had to wear shorts and sandals all the time. I wouldn't recommend the rodeo, though.

Carolyn: **And what about the people?**

Matthew: Well, everyone says they're so kind, but I didn't think that they were ... the people in Chicago.

2 Écrivez une phrase pour comparer les deux éléments de chaque étiquette.

1. Texas / France
2. The Loire River / The Colorado River
3. Notre Dame / The Alamo
4. Austin / Clermont-Ferrand

Les superlatifs

3 Trouvez la ville texane à laquelle se réfère chacune de ces phrases.

1. It's one of the hippest cities in the U.S.
2. The city has the most popular attraction in Texas!
3. It's the fourth largest city in the U.S.
4. It has the richest Hispanic heritage in Texas.
5. It's the most laid-back Texan city.

Le prétérit simple

4 Complétez l'histoire à l'aide des verbes suivants au prétérit simple, soit à la forme affirmative, soit à la forme négative.

visit | begin | like | eat | fly | drive | swim | have

When I was 16, my family travelled to Texas. We ... our trip in San Antonio where we ... the Alamo. We ... authentic Tex-Mex food there, but we ... it because it was too spicy. After that we ... to Austin. We had a great time there. We saw the Colorado River but ... in it. Then we saw a rodeo in Dallas. And finally, two weeks later, we ... home. We ... a great time!

Les énoncés à l'impératif

5 L'Alamo est considéré comme un lieu sacré, ce qui implique de suivre des règles bien précises. Complétez les phrases à l'aide des verbes suivants à la forme affirmative ou négative.

touch | take off | get | put away | eat | wear | turn off

1. ... your telephone.
2. ... your camera. No photography is allowed.
3. ... or drink anything inside.
4. ... your hat.
5. ... the walls or displays.

Additional advice:

6. ... there early to avoid long lines.
7. ... comfortable shoes.

Adjectives

1 Classez ces mots dans l'une des quatre catégories ci-dessous.

great | casual | enjoyable | awesome | trendy | entertaining | laid-back | hip

fantastic	fashionable	fun	relaxed

Types of meat

4 Associez les mots de chaque colonne.

1. beef
2. pork
3. veal
4. lamb
5. venison

a. deer
b. young cow or bull
c. pig
d. young sheep
e. cow or bull

Fighting words

2 Complétez le texte à l'aide des mots suivants.

victory | rebellion | beat | battle | defeat | fight | army | war

There was a terrible ... being fought between a dictator and a group of rebels. The dictator had a larger ... but the rebels wanted ... . There was a huge ... and both men and women had to ... . Many men and women died. However, in the end it was a terrible ... for the dictator. Finally, it was announced in the newspapers that the ... had been successful. They had managed to ... the dictator.

Cool words

5 Associez ces mots aux définitions qui leur correspondent.

vibe | bragging rights | awesome | mecca | wanderlust | hipster

1. A place that attracts a lot of people.
2. The atmosphere of a place.
3. A person who is very trendy.
4. Fantastic.
5. The right to talk highly about yourself, where you are from, your team, etc. Especially used in sport.
6. A strong desire to travel.

Personality adjectives

3 Complétez ces phrases à l'aide des mots suivants.

laid-back | brave | tough | adventurous | proud | passionate

1. Texans are often described as ... people. They love their state, their culture and their achievements.
2. Cowboys are extremely ... men. They often ride a horse for 8 hours a day and sometimes sleep outside.
3. The people at the music festival were really ... . People were relaxing and just listening to the music.
4. Uncle Billy was ... about rodeo. He used to go almost every weekend and spent the whole day there.
5. My cousins are very ... . They trekked all the way across Texas with only their rucksacks.
6. The Texans who fought in the Alamo are remembered for being quite ... . They refused to be afraid of the Mexican Army.

Your Final Task

Create a promotional newsletter of Texas

1 *Texas Tourism* is going to launch a newsletter to promote travel to Texas among 15-25 year olds. To gather ideas, they have organised an international competition.

2 Look back through this unit and find useful information. You can also check the Internet.

3 Use your notes to create your newsletter. You want to attract a lot of travellers to Texas with this campaign, so try to make it as attractive as possible. You can use the structure below.

Toolbox

CD 1 PISTE 32 MP3 20

- to be into + noun
- to fancy + noun / V-*ing*
- to go sightseeing

- Texas is the land of...
- Have you ever wondered what... would be like?
- Have you ever wanted to...?
- Why not escape the stress of life back home and...?
- Pack your bags because / and...
- Discover the wonders / beauty / adventure / thrill of...
- You can start your adventure at / in...
- You can find everything from... to...
- Don't miss...

Tips & Tricks

→ **Shape it!** Structurez votre newsletter pour que le lecteur puisse choisir les informations qui l'intéressent.

→ **Make it catchy!** Le titre principal (**headline**) doit refléter le contenu de votre newsletter, mais aussi être accrocheur, ou on ne vous lira pas !

→ **Make it short!** Préférez les textes courts ; une newsletter doit se lire rapidement.

→ **Keep it engaging!** N'oubliez pas que votre newsletter s'adresse aux 15-25 ans. Trouvez des sujets variés, mais tous susceptibles de les intéresser !

→ **Link it!** N'hésitez pas à insérer un ou des liens internet pour que votre lecteur puisse en savoir plus s'il le souhaite.

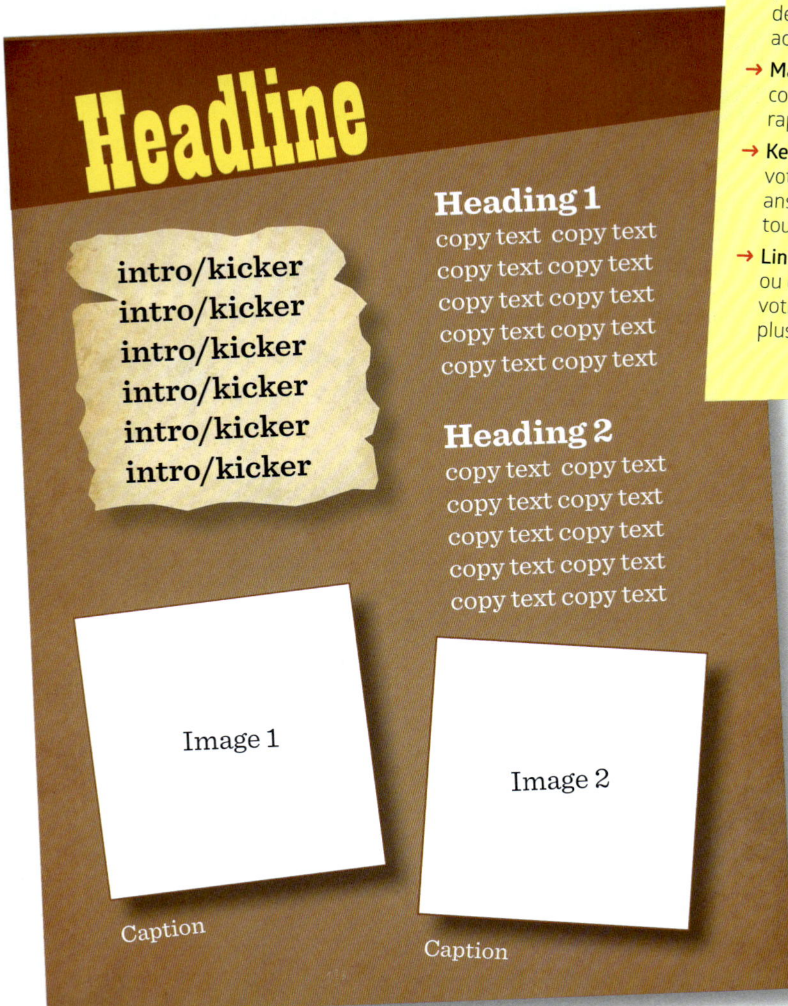

On Your Way to the Exam

Let's prepare your final task

Une fois le brouillon de votre newsletter élaboré, lisez attentivement les critères d'évaluation ci-dessous : où vous situez-vous dans chaque ligne ?

	Niveau 1	Niveau 2	Niveau 3 (→ B1)	Niveau 4
Réalisation de la tâche	Le thème du Texas est traité. Quelques-uns des éléments typiques d'une newsletter sont présents (*headline*, *introduction*, *headings*...).	La newsletter comprend plusieurs idées susceptibles d'intéresser les 15-25 ans. La plupart des éléments typiques de ce support sont présents, même si le texte est bref et élémentaire.	Les idées présentées sont toutes propres à intéresser les 15-25 ans. Tous les éléments demandés sont présents et les textes se rapprochent de ceux d'une newsletter authentique.	Le produit rendu ressemble en tous points à une newsletter authentique. Effort remarquable de mise en page, éventuellement assistée par ordinateur.
Cohérence et organisation		Les idées sont présentées de façon organisée et liées entre elles par des mots de liaison simples (*and*, *but*, *because*...), même si elles sont peu élaborées. **A2**	Des efforts pour enrichir les textes avec des structures complexes (relatives en *who*, *which*, *that*, mots de liaison variés...). **B1**	Tous les éléments de la newsletter sont articulés de façon très cohérente et fluide. **B2**
Maîtrise de la grammaire	Les phrases sont très brèves. Les formes grammaticales sont assez intelligibles mais limitées et répétitives. **A1/A1+**	Les phrases sont simples mais généralement correctes. Des erreurs élémentaires sont possibles (confusion des temps, conjugaisons approximatives...). Des efforts pour utiliser certains des faits de langue de l'unité (impératif, comparatifs...). **A2/A2+**	Usage, avec une correction suffisante, d'un répertoire de tournures et expressions fréquemment utilisées. Comparatifs et/ou superlatifs bien employés. **B1**	Les structures et formes employées montrent une prise de risque pour étoffer le propos et construire un discours plus complexe. Des erreurs sont possibles, mais le texte reste toujours intelligible. **B2**
Maîtrise du vocabulaire	Répertoire très restreint de mots simples. **A1**	Exploitation d'une partie des mots et expressions vus en cours, mais le répertoire est encore restreint. **A2**	Bonne maîtrise du lexique élémentaire. Beaucoup d'éléments du cours sont ré-exploités. **B1**	Le texte va au-delà du lexique étudié pour enrichir le propos. De la variété et une assez grande précision. **B2**
Valeur chiffrée (équivalences)	**De 5 à 9/20**	**De 10 à 15/20**	**De 16 à 20/20**	**Au-delà des attentes de 2de : objectifs du cycle terminal en vue.**

Let's read

Your teacher will give you two excerpts. Read them and answer the questions.

James Griffin's books are traditional Westerns portraying strong heroes with good character and moral values. *A Ranger to Ride With* was published in 2014.

Let's listen to a short recording

CD-1 / PISTE-33

Listen to the document and answer the questions your teacher will give you.

Dallas Cowboys' legendary quarterback Roger Staubach

Let's write

Use what you have learned to answer the following question: Would you like to live in Texas? Why (not)?

4 A Little "Brit" Different

→ **ISSUE AT STAKE**
Why do British people like to be different?

ON YOUR WAY TO THE TASK

1 The Unique Kingdom
Write a post for an international travel blog sharing your experiences in Great Britain

2 Always a Step Ahead
Create a poster promoting a British city

3 Eccentrics United
Present an eccentric event

YOUR FINAL TASK
Create a book cover about Great Britain

"It's celebrated in British culture to be eccentric."
Paloma Faith, British actress

"The British do not want to be happy. They want to be right."
Quentin Crisp, British writer

"When the British are heartbroken, we don't scream in your face with tears. We go home and cry on our own."
Michael Caine, British actor

> We have not journeyed across the centuries, across the oceans, across the mountains, across the prairies, because we are made of sugar candy.
>
> Winston Churchill, British politician

> Amazing what the British do with language; the nuances of politeness. The world's great diplomats, surely.
>
> Anne Rice, American author

1. The title of this unit is a play on words. What does it mean? What do you think the unit will be about?

2. What is the first thing that comes to mind when you hear the word "British" or "Great Britain"?

- I immediately think of...

3. Read the quotes. What do they tell us about British people?

- According to what the quotes say, British people are renowned for...

GO FURTHER... www.community.emdl.fr

Listen to "I'm British" by Professor Elemental. List five or six things that are common among British people according to the song.

Toolbox

CD 1 PISTE 34 MP3 21

- brave /breɪv/: *courageux*
- creative /kriː'eɪtɪv/
- diplomatic /dɪplə'mætɪk/
- polite /pə'laɪt/: *poli*
- pragmatic /præg'mætɪk/
- reserved /rɪ'zɜːvd/: *timide, réservé*
- steady /'stedɪ/: *mesuré, posé*
- stubborn /'stʌbən/: *têtu, obstiné*

- typically /'tɪpɪkəlɪ/ = quintessentially /kwɪntɪ'senʃ(ə)lɪ/: *typiquement*

- the British = (the) British people = the Brits
- a pun /pʌn/ = a play on words

1 The Unique Kingdom

WB p. 17-18

Your Task

Write a post for an international travel blog sharing your experiences in Great Britain

1. Another Planet

1. Look at the pictures. What are they? What do they advertise?
- They are both...

2. Focus on the two characters. Where are they? What do they represent?
- I guess the first one represents... whereas the other one may...

3. Focus on the slogan and the pictures. What is the message of the campaign?
- It aims at + V-ing...
- The goal is to...

4. You have been chosen to create a 15-second radio ad for this campaign. Get ready to have your message heard across the waves!

2. The British Thing To Do

CD 1 PISTE 35

1. Can you explain the title of the cartoon ("Anarchy in the UK")? *Anticipate*

2. Charlie McDonnell is a young British video blogger. Watch the video. Why does he drink tea? Listen and take notes.
- He finds tea + ADJ...
- He drinks tea to + V... / because...

3. What about you? What food or drink is "a part of who you are"?
- I would say that...
- I love... so much that I eat / drink it every day.

Hugleikur Dagsson, *Dj Set* (2013) (www.dagsson.com)

Pronunciation

CD 1 PISTE 36 MP3 22

Les différentes prononciations du « *o* »

Écoutez ces trois extraits de l'audio « *The British Thing To Do* » en vous concentrant sur la prononciation de la lettre « ***o*** » des mots suivants (dans l'ordre) :
- Extrait 1 : ***reason, love, so, born***
- Extrait 2 : ***to, slowly-formed, stroppy***
- Extrait 3 : ***don't, know, to, do***

1. Classez ces mots en fonction de leur prononciation : /ɒ/, /ʌ/, /ɔ:/, /əʊ/, /u:/ ou /ə/.

2. ***Born*** et ***formed*** sont prononcés de la même manière. Pourquoi ?

Toolbox

CD 1 PISTE 37 MP3 23

- characteristic /ˌkærɪktəˈrɪstɪk/ = distinctive /dɪsˈtɪŋktɪv/
- humorous /ˈhju:mərəs/: *plein d'humour*
- quirky /ˈkwɜ:ki/ = bizarre /bɪˈzɑ:r/
- unique /ju:ˈni:k/
- an alien /ˈeɪlɪən/: *un extraterrestre*
- Buckingham Palace /ˈbʌkɪŋəm ˈpælɪs/
- a catchphrase /ˈkætʃfreɪzv
  = a slogan /ˈsləʊgən/
- a trait /treɪt/: *une caractéristique*
- to be obsessed with /əbˈsest/
- can't help + V-ing /kɑ:nt help/: *ne pas pouvoir s'empêcher de*

3. Quintessentially British

Here are five traits and institutions that are quintessentially British:

1. Come rain, shine, wind or snow, we are endlessly talking about the weather.
Almost 70 per cent of British people check the weather forecast at least once a day.

2. "I'm sorry": Britons always apologise, even when it's not their fault.
We are so desperate to avoid confrontation that we are prepared to take the blame for things just to maintain the status quo.

3. Our quirky sense of humour that foreigners just don't get.
Our distinctive sense of humour, often based around sarcasm and self-deprecation, leaves foreigners scratching their heads.

4. Love them or hate them, we are obsessed by the Royal Family.
More than 24 million of us tuned in to watch Prince William and Kate Middleton get married in 2011.

5. Fry ups: how do you like yours?
They may not be the best for our health, but the traditional English breakfast is a national treasure.

James Edgar, "What makes Britain great?", *The Telegraph* (2014)

1. Look at the cartoon. Who is the British child? How do you know?

2. *The Telegraph*'s editor wants you to illustrate this article. Take a few minutes to create your illustration.

3. Swap with a classmate and comment on his/her work. Which one best illustrates the article. Why?

4. What about French people? Think about some traits that define us and make comparisons with the British.

- Unlike the British, the French are obsessed with...
- We are always talking about... whereas...

Karsten Schley (2012)

Three little kids and their first words. Can you find out which one is the British kid?

Useful Grammar

Le contraste (voir Usages divers des prépositions, p. 166 et Subordonnées de contraste, p. 177)

- Pour exprimer le contraste, on peut employer des propositions subordonnées introduites par des conjonctions comme ***whereas*** et ***while***, ou encore des prépositions comme ***unlike*** :
  French people like coffee ***whereas*** *English people like tea.*
  While *English people like tea, French people like coffee.*
  Unlike *French people, English people like tea.*

Le gérondif (voir V-*ing* (le « gérondif »), p. 176 et Usages divers des prépositions, p. 166)
On emploie le gérondif :

- dans les subordonnées nominales dont la fonction est sujet.
  Drinking *tea is one of their favourite pastimes.*
- dans les subordonnées nominales, après un verbe exprimant l'appréciation d'une activité déjà réalisée ou connue.
  They ***love*** *talk**ing** about the weather.*
- dans les subordonnées nominales, après les prépositions et les verbes prépositionnels.
  British people are obsessed ***with*** *queu**ing**.*
- après ***by*** pour indiquer le moyen.
  By *us**ing** this slogan, they present London as a cosmopolitan city.*

Your Task

Living in England

You are living with a British family and writing for travelexperience.com. Today, you are going to write about what has surprised you most about British people so far.

- This is my Xth day in London and
  I have already + V-en...
  English people (really) love...
  I was also surprised to discover
  that, unlike us, they...

2 Always a Step Ahead

WB p. 19-20

Your Task
Create a poster promoting a British city

1. The Swinging City

Anticipate **1.** What do you know about London?

- London is famous for...

It's the summer of 1966... The city glows. It echoes. It pulses. This is how it's always going to be: smashing clothes, brilliant music, easy sex, eternal youth, the eyes of everybody, everyone's first thought, the top of the world, right here, right now: Swinging London.

In *Ready, Steady, Go!* Levy captures the spirit of the sixties in all its exuberance. A portrait of London from roughly 1961 to 1969, it chronicles the explosion of creativity — in art, music and fashion — and the revolutions — sexual, social and political — that reshaped the world. Levy deftly re-creates the fast pace and daring experimentation of the times, from the utter transformation of rock 'n' roll by the Beatles and the Rolling Stones to the new aesthetics introduced by fashion designers like Mary Quant, haircutters like Vidal Sassoon, photographers like David Bailey, actors like Michael Caine and Terence Stamp and filmmakers like Richard Lester and Nicolas Roeg to the wild clothing shops and cutting-edge clubs that made Carnaby Street and King's Road the hippest thoroughfares in the world.

Adapted from the blurb of Shawn Levy's ***Ready, Steady, Go!*** (2002)

Ready, Steady, Go!, a fascinating portrait of London in the sixties (2003)

A TOUCH OF CULTURE

Carnaby Street is located in London's Soho. During the 1960s, it was packed with both hippie and modern fashion boutiques.

2. Read the text and jot down:
- words and phrases that express change and innovation.
- artistic fields that underwent a transformation.

3. Read again. What is the book about?

- The book is about / portrays / chronicles / is an account of...

4. Do you know any of the people and bands mentioned in the text? Research one of them and present it to the class.

- The Rolling Stones are a London-based band. They formed in... and became famous for...

5. Think of another moment in time that caused a big social change. Explain it to the class.

- I think we are currently living...
- In 1989, there was a... It led to...

Useful Grammar

L'article zéro (Ø) → p. 160

On emploie l'article zéro :

- pour désigner des personnes ou des choses en général.
  Ø Music *played a large part in popular London culture in the 1960s.*
- devant les noms de continents, de pays (sauf s'ils sont constitués à partir d'un nom commun : *the United Kingdom*), de rues et de langues.
  Ø Britain *has produced a lot of outstanding musicians.*
- devant les noms précédés d'un titre.
  Ø Queen Elizabeth II *is one of the most famous women in the world.*

Les superlatifs → p. 165

- Adjectif d'une syllabe : dans la plupart des cas, ***the*** + adjectif + ***-est***.
  Soho is one of ***the*** *cool****est*** *neighbourhoods in London.*
- On tend à faire de même avec les adjectifs de 2 syllabes terminés par ***-er*** (*clever* → ***the*** *clever****est***), ***-ow*** (*narrow* → ***the*** *narrow****est***) et ***-y*** (*funny* → ***the*** *funn****iest***).
- Autres adjectifs : ***the*** + ***most*** + adjectif.
  Which city in England is ***the most*** *beautiful?*

2. Britain is Great

ticipate **1.** In your opinion, what is great about Great Britain?

- In my opinion, what makes Britain great is...
- Britain is a place where / which...
- England is one of the most...

2. Group A watches the first video and group B the second one. First, each group picks out nouns and adjectives about Britain and its people. Then, each group watches their video again and answers these questions:

Group A: Do you recognise any of the artists? What can you say about them? What makes Britain musically unique?

Group B: Where does creativity start? Jot down as much information as you can about the different youth movements that are mentioned.

3. Now, each group informs the other about what they have discovered.

- British music is known for...
- British fashion gets a lot of inspiration from...
- If you want to succeed in the U.K., you have to...

National Tourism Agency of Great Britain (2011)

Video Time

DVD PISTE 9

VIDEO 1

Live Music is Great, National Tourism Agency of Great Britain (2011)

Video Time

DVD PISTE 10

VIDEO 2

Fashion is Great, National Tourism Agency of Great Britain (2011)

Toolbox

CD 1 PISTE 38 MP3 24

- buzzing /ˈbʌzɪŋ/: *plein de vie*
- fashionable /ˈfæʃnəbl/: *à la mode*
- groundbreaking /ˈgraʊnd͵breɪkɪŋ/: *révolutionnaire*
- innovative /ˈɪnəʊ͵veɪtɪv/: *novateur, innovant*
- open-minded /ˈəʊpən-maɪndɪd/: *ouvert d'esprit*
- swinging /ˈswɪŋɪŋ/: *animé, qui bouge*

- a metamorphosis /͵metəˈmɔːfəsɪs/
- a must-see /mʌst-siː/: *un incontournable*

- to be a step ahead /əˈhed/: *être précurseur, en avance sur*
- to be at the heart of /hɑːt/: *être au cœur de*

Your Task

The greatest city in the world

You are doing an internship at the City Hall in one of the following cities: Edinburgh, Glasgow, Liverpool or Cardiff. You are working on a campaign promoting the city around the world. Prepare a poster with: a slogan, 1 or 2 photos and a short promotional text.

WB p. 21-22

Your Task
Present an eccentric event

1. What Does It Mean to Be Eccentric?

Anticipate **1.** Think of some famous eccentrics. What makes them unconventional?

- I would say... is rather eccentric because...
- ... is (quite) an eccentric character because...

"If people did not dare to be different, the world would be a much more boring place," says author David McKie. (...)

Britain has produced more than its fair share of eccentric characters throughout history. Some of the greatest have helped shape the very essence of Britishness, contributing to what we now embrace as our national identity. In every field, from politics to physics and fashion to food, true talent is often synonymous with more than a touch of madness. While inventing the telephone, for example, Scotland-born inventor Alexander Graham Bell tried to teach his dog to talk, and renowned genius Sir Isaac Newton is said to have stuck a large darning needle into his eye socket and twiddled it around — just to see what would happen, presumably. (...)

Perhaps the British are particularly prone to and proud of eccentricity because, as an island nation, we like to feel a little cut off from the mainstream. "Like so much else in our traditions and culture, we take special pleasure and pride in diversity," agrees McKie.

Jessica Tooze, "Great British Eccentrics", ***The Official Magazine*** (2013)

2. Read the text and identify who David McKie, Alexander Graham Bell, Isaac Newton and Jessica Tooze are.

3. What are the similarities between Alexander Graham Bell and Isaac Newton?

- They both...

4. Find sentences in the text that prove that eccentricity is appreciated by the British.

5. Why does the author mention the fact that Britain is an "island nation"?

Useful Grammar

L'obligation, la nécessité, l'absence d'obligation et l'interdiction
(voir Les modaux, p. 171 et Modaux et périphrases en *to*, p. 172)

- L'obligation et la nécessité
  - ***must*** : obligation qui provient de celui qui parle.
  - ***have to*** : obligation ou nécessité due à des contraintes extérieures.
  - ***need to*** : exprime le besoin, la nécessité.

  *You **must** take part in the Chap Olympiads with me!*
  *Lord Rokeby's servants often **had to** drag him out of the water.*
  *In my opinion, you **need to** be rich to be eccentric.*
- L'absence d'obligation ou de nécessité : ***don't have to***, ***don't need to***, ***needn't***.
  *You **don't have to / don't need to** be an aristocrat to be a little nutty.*
  *You **needn't** study for the exam. It's been postponed.*
- Interdiction : ***mustn't*** (l'interdiction provient de celui qui parle).
  *You **mustn't** talk in here!*

Toolbox

CD 1 PISTE 39 MP3 25

- eccentric /ɪk'sentrɪk/
- talented /'tæləntɪd/: *talentueux*
- weird /wɪəd/ = odd /ɒd/: *bizarre*
- a chap /tʃæp/: *un type, un gars*
- creativity /kri:eɪ'tɪvɪtɪ/
- an event /ɪ'vent/: *un évènement*
- a rule /ru:l/: *une règle*
- singularity /sɪŋgjʊ'lærɪtɪ/
- a trial /'traɪəl/: *une épreuve*
- to be prone to sth /prəʊn/: *être sujet à qqch*
- to conform to/with sth /kən'fɔ:m/: *se conformer à qqch*
- to dare to do sth /deəʳ/: *oser faire qqch*
- to take part in = to participate to /pɑ:'tɪsɪpeɪt/

2. Nutty Aristocrats

The UK may be a small country, but it seems to have more true eccentrics than many larger countries. The old aristocracy supplied many of the most bizarre ones, because to have a really odd lifestyle, you require a large personal fortune and the arrogance to ignore the reactions of your fellow countrymen.

Lord Rokeby decided that he would like to spend all his life near or in water. He spent hours in the sea off the Kent beaches, and his servants often had to drag him out on to dry land, unconscious.

Francis Henry Egerton, the eighth Earl of Bridgewater, preferred dogs to people. He had no time for women, and he declared that dogs were better behaved than gentlemen. The dogs ate with him every day, (...) each with a clean, white napkin around their necks.

Lord Cornbury, the third Earl of Clarendon, was Queen Anne's cousin. (...) The Queen made him her representative as Governor of New York and Jersey in America. He took it all very seriously and decided that as he represented a woman, he would dress as a woman.

Ben Johnson, "British Eccentrics", **www.historic-uk.com** (2015)

1. Read the text. According to the first paragraph, what are the two requirements to be a true British eccentric?

- To be a true eccentric, you must... / have to...

2. Identify the best nickname for each aristocrat. Justify your answers.

- The Good-Mannered
- The Loyal Royal
- The Sailing Aristocrat
- The Earl of Pets
- The Lady
- The Lord of Clocks

- Lord Cornbury could be called... because...

3. Choose one of the remaining nicknames and imagine what was eccentric about him or her. Be inventive!

- The "Lord of Clocks" was a really peculiar character who... He used to...

3. Chap Olympiads

CD1 PISTE 40

Anticipate

1. Look at the pictures and imagine what type of competition the Chap Olympiads are.

- The Chap Olympiads must be some kind of...

2. Listen and jot down as much information as you can about:
- the goal.
- the reasons why the competition was created.
- the events.

3. Listen again. Are the following sentences right or wrong?

a. Participants are nice, honest people.
b. The event honors British eccentrics.
c. The British are great at sports.
d. A torch is used at the opening ceremony.

Your Task

Only for eccentrics

Look for an existing eccentric event or invent one. Take notes about what it consists in, the rules, the origins, the participants... Present it to the class with the help of pictures.

- Let me tell you about...
  Unlike other events, this one...
  Participants have to... but they mustn't...

Reading

Notes from a Small Island

CD 1 PISTE 41 MP3 26

by Bill Bryson (1995)

So let's talk about John Fallows. One day in 1987, Fallows was standing at a window in a London bank waiting to be served when a would-be robber named Douglas Bath stepped in front of him, brandished a handgun and demanded money from the cashier. Outraged, Fallows told Bath to "bugger off[1] to the back of the line and wait his turn", to the presumed approving nods of others in the queue. Unprepared for this turn of events, Bath meekly[2] departed from the bank empty-handed and was arrested a short distance away.

I bring this up here to make the point that if there is one golden quality that characterises the British, it is an innate sense of good manners and you defy it at your peril. Deference and a quiet consideration for others are such a fundamental part of British life, in fact, that few conversations could even start without them. Almost any encounter with a stranger begins with the words "I'm terribly sorry but", followed by a request of some sort, "could you tell me the way to Brighton?", "help me find a shirt my size", "get your steamer trunk off my foot". And when you've fulfilled their request, they invariably offer a hesitant, apologetic smile and say sorry again, begging forgiveness for taking up your time or carelessly leaving their foot where your steamer trunk[3] clearly needed to go. I just love that.

As if to illustrate my point, when I checked out of the hotel the other day, I arrived to find a woman ahead of me wearing a helpless look and saying to the receptionist: 'I'm terribly sorry but I can't seem to get the television in my room to work.' She had come all the way downstairs, you understand, to apologize to them for their TV not working. My heart swelled[4] with feelings of warmth and fondness for this strange and unfathomable[5] country.

And it is all done so instinctively, that's the other thing. I remember when I was still new to the country arriving at a railway station one day to find that just two of the dozen or so ticket windows were open. (For the benefit of foreign readers, I should explain that, as a rule in Britain, no matter how many windows there are in a bank, post office or rail station, only two of them will be open, except at very busy times, when just one will be open.) Both ticket windows were occupied. Now, in other countries one of two things would have happened. Either there would be a crush[6] of customers at each window, all demanding simultaneous attention, or else there would be two slow moving lines, each full of gloomy people convinced that the other line was moving faster.

Here in Britain, however, the waiting customers had spontaneously come up with a much more sensible and ingenious arrangement. They had formed a single line a few feet back from both windows. When either position became vacant, the customer at the head of the line would step up to it and the rest of the line would shuffle forward a space. It was a wonderfully fair and democratic approach and the remarkable thing was that no one had commanded it or even suggested it. It just happened.

1. décamper - **2.** humblement - **3.** grande malle de voyage - **4.** se remplir - **5.** difficile à comprendre - **6.** une foule

BUILDING YOUR JOURNAL...

Workbook, p. 66

Biography

Bill Bryson was born in 1951 in Des Moines, Iowa, but for most of his adult life has lived in Britain. He has written many humorous travel books, including *Notes from a Small Island*, his book about British culture. In 2003 it was voted the book which best sums up British identity.

Zaha Hadid

Architectural Eccentricity

Zaha Hadid is an Iraqi-born British architect whose buildings challenge people to reconsider what their urban surroundings could look like. Often called the most prominent contemporary female architect, Hadid has the honor of being the first and only woman to have won the Pritzker Architecture Prize.

The Guangzhou Opera House in China is shaped to resemble two rocks on the Pearl River, creating a dialogue between the natural and urban landscape.

Thinking 'Tomorrow'

More than buildings, Hadid builds our future. Complex, intense, current and fluid, her style evokes the chaos of modern life. This visionary architect constantly pushes the boundaries of architecture with futuristic lines. These curves are produced with the most advanced digital technology, and shape the future of some of the biggest cities around the world.

The Aquatics Centre was built for both the 2012 Summer Olympics and the Paralympics in London. The structure mimics the flowing qualities of water in motion.

Worldwide Fame

Sometimes considered difficult to work with and a bit eccentric, Hadid admits that both her work and personality might be challenging. As a woman working in a masculine world, she faces many obstacles. Initially her ideas were opposed and criticised. As a result, she pushed back and put British creativity on the map of the world.

Digital ZONE

Record an introductory speech for Zaha Hadid. Imagine you have been chosen to present the Pritzker Prize to Zaha Hadid. Prepare your speech by briefly summing up her life and talking about her accomplishments. Conclude by thanking her and presenting her the award.

BUILDING YOUR JOURNAL...

Workbook, p. 67

Let's Practise Grammar

community.emdl.fr
exercices interactifs

Le contraste

1 Complétez les phrases en utilisant ***unlike*** ou, au choix, ***whereas/while***.

1. English people like tea, ... French people prefer coffee.
2. She thinks jelly cake is quite yucky, ... Charlie, who likes it.
3. We like to go to the mountains for a holiday, ... our children always want the seaside.

2 Écrivez trois phrases sur les différences entre Britanniques et Français. Utilisez ***whereas***, ***while*** ou ***unlike***.

Le gérondif

3 Complétez les phrases de manière logique en utilisant un gérondif.

1. British people are obsessed with ...
2. My British friends love ...
3. ... is fun.
4. ... is quite a British habit!
5. I hate ...
6. ... about the weather is quite common in England.
7. I passed the exam by ...
8. ... fun of other people is not nice.
9. Nowadays I really enjoy ...

L'article zéro

4 Traduisez les phrases suivantes.

1. *Je suis un grand fan de la mode britannique. Je vais tous les ans à la Fashion Week, à Londres.*
2. *La politesse et la diplomatie sont des qualités typiquement britanniques.*
3. *Il y a de grandes différences culturelles entre la France et le Royaume-Uni.*
4. *Le Prince Charles est le fils aîné de la Reine Elizabeth II.*
5. *Les Anglais adorent le thé.*

Les superlatifs

5 Mettez les adjectifs entre parenthèses au superlatif.

1. Brits are ... (**talented**) and (**creative**) people.
2. He is ... (**quirky**) man I have ever met.
3. Winston Churchill was one of ... (**brave**) British politicians.
4. This is ... (**interesting**) book I have read on Great Britain.
5. The author has really focused on ... (**good**) traits of the Brits in his book.

L'obligation, la nécessité, l'absence d'obligation et l'interdiction

6 Remplacez les éléments en gras par un modal ou une périphrase en ***to***. Plusieurs solutions sont parfois possibles.

1. **It is forbidden to** run in the corridors.
2. **It is necessary to** follow the rules.
3. **It is unnecessary to** be very talented to do this job.
4. We **are obliged to** move to another house because we can't pay the rent.
5. **It is prohibited to** feed the animals.
6. **It is not necessary to** be physically fit to participate in the Chap Olympiads.

Personalities and nuances

1 Trouvez l'adjectif qui qualifie le mieux les personnes ou choses suivantes.

1. He insists on taking the long route, even though he knows it's shorter to go this way.
2. He's my favourite comedian. His observaticns about life never fail to make me laugh.
3. Recently, instead of keeping to his normal routine, he's been acting kind of strange.
4. By the age of 4, she was able to read music and by the age of 8, she could play three instruments.
5. He didn't think twice about saving the baby from the burning building.
6. As the middle child, I was always the one who calmed everyone down and helped my siblings come to a compromise.
7. Her fashion sense has always been slightly strange, but somehow she makes a pink tutu and Dr Martens work.

Traits

2 Formez des noms à partir des adjectifs suivants.

a. polite
b. talented
c. mad
d. innovating
e. creative
f. singular
g. fashionable
h. diplomatic
i. young
j. eccentric
k. buzzing
l. proud

Great Britain

3 Recopiez cette carte mentale et complétez-la avec le plus d'éléments possibles. Vous pouvez ajouter autant de branches que vous le souhaitez.

Compound words

4 Formez des mots en associant un élément de la colonne de gauche à un élément de la colonne de droite.

1. weather
2. open-
3. old-
4. video
5. good-
6. self-
7. must-
8. travel

a. guide
b. mannered
c. minded
d. blogger
e. forecast
f. fashioned
g. deprecation
h. see

Prepositional verbs

5 Complétez les phrases avec la préposition qui convient.

with – to – from – for – of

1. Rowan Atkinson is known ... his leading role in "Mr. Bean".
2. Big Ben, the symbol of London, is made ... red bricks.
3. The British are obsessed ... the Queen.
4. You will have to conform ... the British traditions if you study in Great Britain.
5. I'm too shy, I wouldn't dare ... speak English.
6. The United Kingdom is an island. It is cut off ... the rest of Europe.
7. Beware! You are not allowed ... take pictures in museums.
8. But it's not my fault! I don't want to take the blame ... Laura!

Your Final Task

Create a book cover about Great Britain

1 You are self-publishing a book about Great Britain's uniqueness. Determine the subject and the genre (novel, travel guide, historical, children's book, biography...).

2 Focus on the front cover. Come up with a title and a subtitle that will make the average person think, "I want to know more".

3 Focus on the back cover. Write a blurb and a few reviews by famous people or prominent newspapers. Don't forget about the spine!

4 Design the front cover, spine and back cover. Then, print it and paste it on cardboard to make it look like a real book.

Toolbox

CD 1 PISTE 42 MP3 27

- astonishing /əˈstɒnɪʃɪŋ/: *sidérant, étonnant*
- impressive /ɪmˈpresɪv/: *impressionnant*
- must-have /mʌst-hæv/: *indispensable*
- remarkable /rɪˈmɑːkəbl/
- riveting /ˈrɪvɪtɪŋ/: *captivant*
- splendid /ˈsplendɪd/
- terrific /təˈrɪfɪk/: *formidable*

- a masterpiece /ˈmɑːstəpiːs/: *un chef-d'œuvre*

- A compelling story of...
- A fine portrait of...
- A funny and touching tale about...
- A prodigious work of research...
- One of the finest...

Tips & Tricks

→ **Make it snappy!** La quatrième de couverture doit être descriptive, mais aussi accrocheuse : il faut donner envie aux futurs lecteurs d'acheter ce livre !

→ **Keep it short!** Les avis cités sur la couverture doivent être brefs et enthousiastes : pensez aux superlatifs et évitez les phrases complètes.

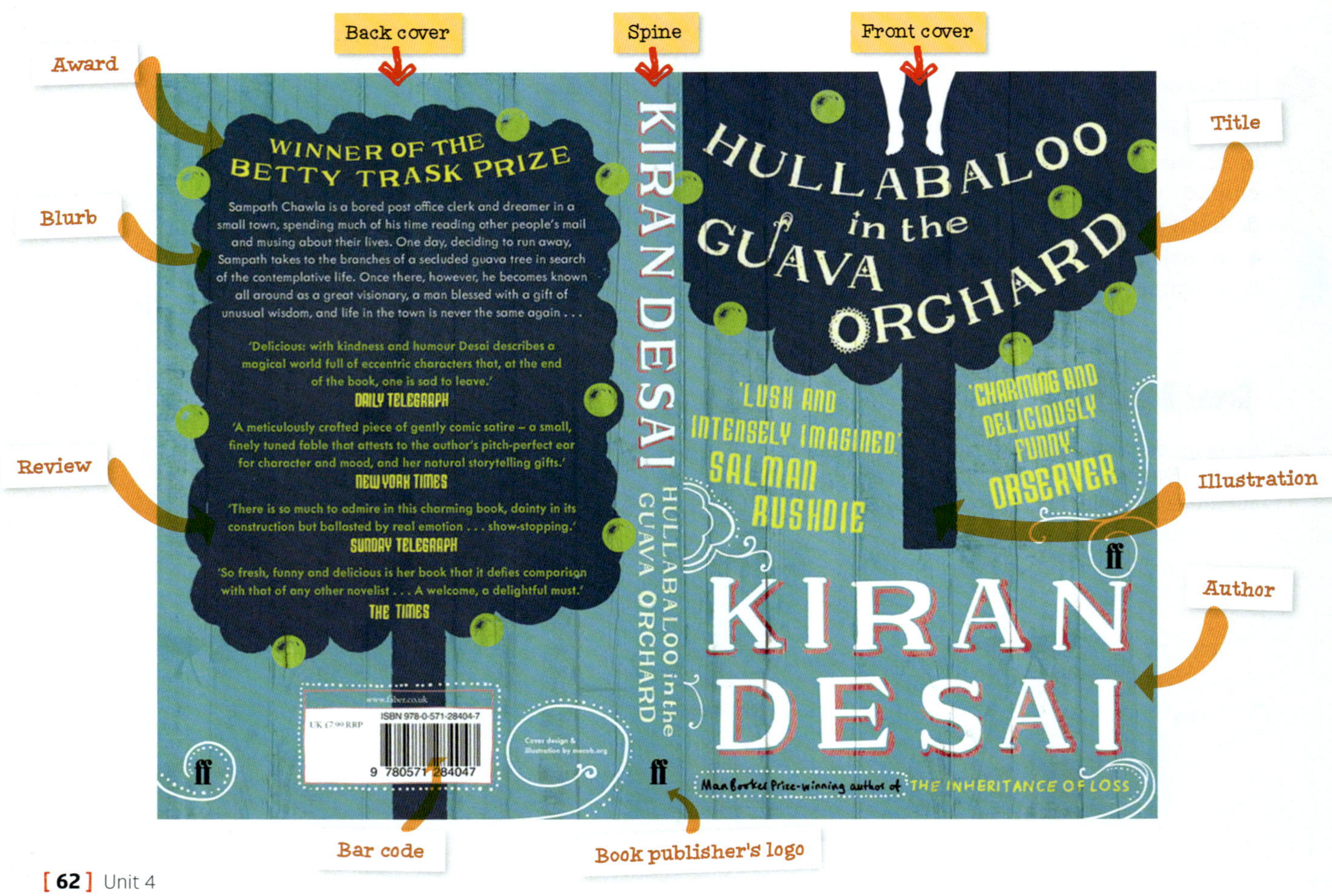

On Your Way to the Exam

Let's prepare your final task

Une fois le brouillon de votre couverture élaboré, lisez attentivement les critères d'évaluation ci-dessous : où vous situez-vous dans chaque ligne ?

	Niveau 1	Niveau 2	Niveau 3 (→ B1)	Niveau 4
Réalisation de la tâche		La plupart des éléments demandés (*front cover*, *spine*, *blurb*…) sont présents, même si la quatrième de couverture est brève et élémentaire et les critiques restent simples.	Tous les éléments demandés sont présents et les textes proposés se rapprochent de ceux que l'on trouve sur une couverture authentique.	Le produit rendu ressemble en tous points à une couverture authentique de livre. Un effort de présentation remarquable.
Cohérence et organisation		Les éléments sont placés de façon logique. Dans le texte de la quatrième de couverture, les idées sont présentées de manière organisée et reliées entre elles par des mots de liaison simples (*and*, *but*, *because*…). **A2**	Des efforts pour enrichir le texte de la quatrième de couverture avec des structures complexes (relatives en *who*, *which*, *that*, mots de liaison variés…). **B1**	Tous les éléments de la quatrième de couverture sont articulés de façon très cohérente et fluide. **B2**
Maîtrise de la grammaire	Les phrases sont très brèves. Les formes grammaticales sont assez intelligibles mais limitées et répétitives. **A1/A1+**	Les phrases restent simples mais généralement correctes. Des erreurs élémentaires sont possibles. **A2** Des efforts pour employer certaines des structures de l'unité (contraste, gérondif, superlatifs…).	Les phrases ne comportent pratiquement pas d'erreurs élémentaires. Les structures étudiées en cours (contraste, gérondif, superlatifs…) sont fréquemment réutilisées et assez bien maîtrisées. **B1**	Les phrases ne comportent aucune erreur élémentaire. Les structures employées vont au-delà de ce qui a été étudié en cours. **B2**
Maîtrise du vocabulaire	Emploi d'un répertoire très restreint de mots simples. **A1**	Exploitation d'une partie des mots et expressions vus en cours, mais le répertoire est encore restreint. **A2**	Beaucoup d'éléments du cours sont réexploités. **B1**	Emploi d'un répertoire très riche et précis qui va au-delà du lexique étudié dans l'unité. **B2**
Valeur chiffrée (équivalences)	De 5 à 9/20	De 10 à 15/20	De 16 à 20/20	Au-delà des attentes de 2de : objectifs du cycle terminal en vue

Let's read a text

Your teacher will give you a text. Read it and answer the questions.

A guide to the quirky gems hidden across Britain and the weird things the British do (2011)

Let's watch a funny clip

DVD / PISTE-11

Watch the video and answer the questions.

Awfully Thorough Guide to Being British, a MeMo Interactive video (2013)

Let's write

You've heard about an eccentric London club that you want to join to be recognised as a true eccentric. Write your cover letter.

5 Feed Your Future

→ ISSUE AT STAKE

What are the ingredients of a food revolution?

ON YOUR WAY TO THE TASK

1 Bad Habits
Send a Tweet

2 A New Food Culture
Write the rules of a foodie club

3 The Taste of Tomorrow
Present a futuristic restaurant

YOUR FINAL TASK

Present a revolutionary product at the "Food Trends & Innovations" exhibition

“One of the delights of life is eating with friends; second to that is talking about eating.”

Laurie Colwin, American actor

1

2

3

> Cooking demands attention, patience, and above all, a respect for the gifts of the earth. It is a way of giving thanks.
>
> Judith Jones, American editor

> If slaughterhouses had glass walls, everyone would be a vegetarian.
>
> Paul McCartney, English singer and composer

4

1. Match the following word(s) to one of the quotes on the page: **pleasure**, **way of life**, **gratitude**, **meat consumption**, **sharing**, **guilt**. Explain your choices.

- To me "gratitude" is the word that best describes... because...

2. Which of the three quotes do you most agree with? Why?

3. These four magazine covers are all related to food. What is the theme of each magazine issue?

- "The Atlantic" addresses the issue of...
  deals with...
  covers...

GO FURTHER... www.community.emdl.fr

Watch the beginning of a BBC documentary entitled **"Future of Food"**. Jot down every food problem that is mentioned.

Toolbox

CD 1 PISTE 43 MP3 28

- (un)healthy /ʌn'helθɪ/: *(mal)sain*

- a dish /dɪʃ/: *un plat*
- greens /griːns/ = green vegetables: *des légumes verts*
- junk food /dʒʌŋk fuːd/: *la malbouffe*
- obesity /əʊ'biːsɪtɪ/
- organic food /ɔː'gænɪk fuːd/: *la nourriture bio*
- pleasure /'pleʒəʳ/: *le plaisir*
- a vegetable /'vedʒɪtəbl/: *un légume*

- to enjoy /ɪn'dʒɔɪ/: *apprécier*
- to grow /grəʊ/ = to farm /fɑːm/ = to cultivate /'kʌltɪveɪt/: *cultiver*

WB p. 23-24

1. Wasted Food

1. Look at the image. What is it? What is the goal of the document?

- It aims at + V-ing...

2. Can you explain the paradox regarding food waste in the U.S.?

3. What do you think people in the U.S. should do to avoid wasting so much food?

- They should / shouldn't buy...

4. You have been chosen to create a 15-second radio ad for this campaign. Get ready to have your message heard across the waves!

Kate Emma (American designer), *Food Waste in America* (2013)

2. A Nation in Danger

Over the past three decades, childhood obesity rates in America have tripled, and today, nearly one in three children in America is overweight or obese. (...)

Thirty years ago, most people led lives that kept them at a healthy weight. Kids walked to and from school every day, ran around at recess, participated in gym class, and played for hours after school before dinner. Meals were home-cooked with reasonable portion sizes and there was always a vegetable on the plate. Eating fast food was rare and snacking between meals was an occasional treat.

Today, children experience a very different lifestyle. Walks to and from school have been replaced by car and bus rides. Gym class and after-school sports have been cut; afternoons are now spent with TV, video games, and the Internet. Parents are busier than ever and families eat fewer home-cooked meals.

Michelle Obama at the ***Let's Move!*** launch (2010)

1. Do you have healthy habits (eating, sleeping...)? Is there anything you should change? **Anticipate**

- I usually... but maybe I should try to...
- I tend to... but it's a problem because...

2. Explain how different is your lifestyle today compared to that of your parents when they were your age. **Anticipate**

- Today, we spend more time + V-ing...
- My parents used to...

3. Read Michelle Obama's speech and try to summarise it in one sentence.

4. What should the government, schools, parents and children do to solve this health problem?

- I think that parents should...

GO FURTHER... www.community.emdl.fr

Watch the trailer of the spoof film "**Snackpocalypse**".
1. What other films does it evoke?
2. Does it look like a real film?
3. Do you know any of the actors?
4. Explain the title of this parody.

3. The Problems with Eating Meat

CD 1 PISTE 44

1. How much meat do you eat? What type of meat is it? **Anticipate**

- I eat a lot / quite a bit / some / not so much...
- I usually eat...

2. Look at the title of this activity. What are the problems with eating meat in your opinion? **Anticipate**

3. Listen to an interview with a food expert and take notes. What problems does he address?

4. Listen again and put the following ideas in the right order:

a. A big part of what animals eat becomes waste.
b. Animal waste pollutes the water and the air.
c. Crops are used for feeding animals and people.
d. Too many crops can cause environmental damage.
e. It takes a lot of land and crops to produce the meat we consume.

5. Your friend Scott has just posted this message on his Facebook wall. React to his post.

- That's great. / Well done. / Congrats.
- You can't be serious. / Are you kidding?
- A lot of people are not aware of...

Pronunciation

Les groupes de sens

CD 1 PISTE 45 MP3 29

"A third of all the crops that people grow all across the world go to feeding animals."

1. Écoutez cette phrase et repérez les moments où l'interlocuteur fait une courte pause. Le bloc de mots compris entre chaque pause se nomme un « groupe de sens ».

2. À votre avis, à quoi servent les groupes de sens ?

3. En vous basant sur l'exemple, expliquez comment on délimite un groupe de sens.

4. Entraînez-vous à répéter cette phrase, en focalisant sur les pauses et les groupes de sens.

Toolbox

CD 1 PISTE 46 MP3 30

- a consumer /kən'sju:məʳ/: *un consommateur*
- exercise /'eksəsaɪz/: *l'exercice physique*
- the leftovers /'leftəʊvəz/: *les restes (de nourriture)*
- overweight /ˌəʊvə'weɪt/: *le surpoids*
- a producer /prə'dju:səʳ/: *un producteur*
- waste /weɪst/: *le gaspillage, les déchets*

- to consume /kən'sju:m/: *consommer*
- to cut down on /kʌt daʊn ɒn/ = to reduce /rɪ'dju:s/: *réduire*
- to exercise /'eksəsaɪz/: *exercer, faire travailler*
- to pollute /pə'lu:t/: *polluer*
- to produce /prə'dju:s/: *produire*
- to raise awareness on /reɪz ə'weənɪs/
- to throw away /θrəʊ ə'weɪ/: *jeter*
- to waste /weɪst/: *gaspiller*
- to watch /wɒtʃ/: *faire attention à*

Useful Grammar

L'expression du conseil (voir **Les modaux**, p. 171)

- Si celui qui donne le conseil se présente comme directement à l'origine de celui-ci : ***should* / *shouldn't***.
  *You **shouldn't** eat so much.*
- Si celui qui donne le conseil ne se présente pas comme directement à l'origine de celui-ci : ***ought to***.
  *You **ought to** eat fruits and vegetables every day.*

Les quantifieurs → p. 162

*Americans eat **a lot of** meat.*
***Lots of** people eat junk food.*
*Are there **many** children that will face health problems?*
*There's not **much** food left.*
*There's **some** tea left.*
*There isn't **any** ice-cream in the freezer.*
*American families eat **few** home-cooked meals.*

Your Task

Let's improve our habits!

Your Biology and English teachers have created the hashtag **#betterhabits** to raise awareness of students' lifestyles and eating habits. Use everything that you have learned to send a couple of tweets about your own recommendations, personal resolutions, reactions, information, etc.

2 A New Food Culture

WB p. 25-26

Your Task
Write the rules of a foodie club

1. Jamie Oliver's Crusade

Anticipate **1.** Consider the screenshot and the title of this activity. Jamie Oliver is a British chef. What do you think the video is about?

- It might be about...

2. Watch the video and take notes. Work with a partner and write a short paragraph to summarise what you have understood.

3. Watch the video a second time and answer these questions:

a. What does Jamie Oliver's crusade consist in?
b. What obstacles does he face?
c. What specific actions does he take to carry out his revolution?

4. Do you think he will be successful or not? Give reasons.

- I'm sure he will...
- It will be easy / hard for him to...
- I don't think that he's going to... because...

Video Time
DVD PISTE 12

Jaime Oliver's Food Revolution, TV show that aired on ABC (2010)

Useful grammar

La référence à l'avenir → p. 173

- ***Will*** + base verbale : simple prévision/prédiction ou expression d'une volonté.
  *In 2050, everyone **will eat** liver and kidneys.*
  *I'm sorry, but I **won't eat** this hamburger.*
- ***Be going to*** + base verbale : on s'appuie sur des éléments présents pour dire ce qui va se passer.
  *I'm concerned that I'**m going to be** overweight.*

N.B. : La nuance est souvent fine entre ***will*** et ***be going to***, et dans certains cas les deux formules sont interchangeables.

2. Eating Local

CD 1 PISTE 47

1. Read the comic strip:

a. Define "locavore".
b. Is the penguin really a locavore?
c. Why do you think a lot of people are becoming locavores nowadays?

2. Take notes as you listen to the interview with Barbara Kingsolver, using the following chart:

Barbara	Decision	Reason(s)	New relationship with food

3. Let's debate about locavores. What do you think about her decision? Would you become a locavore? Do you have any objections to this way of life?

- I'd love to...
- Being a locavore seems impossible to me because...

Alex Hallatt (English cartoonist), *articcirclecartoons.com* (2008)

3. Changing Taste

How will historians look back on our times food-wise? Anthony Bourdain, the bad boy chef and author weighs in on the Americans' late arrival to the delights of food culture.

It won't be surprising if cultural historians look back on the first two decades of this century as The Era of Crazed Oral Gratification. I'm speaking of the fascination for food, for cooking and eating, for watching other people cooking and eating.

"We are changing societally, and our values are changing, so that we are becoming more like Italians and Chinese and Thais and Spaniards, where we actually think about what we're eating, what we ate last night, and what we're considering eating tomorrow. When I grew up in the '60s, we'd go to see a movie, then we would go to a restaurant. And we would talk about the movie we just saw. Now, you go right to dinner and you talk about the dinner you had last week and the dinner you're going to have next week, while you're taking pictures of the dinner you're having now."

Along with that, he says, is the evolution of the American palate. "The moment Americans decided that raw fish was desirable. Huge! Nothing could be more repulsive to the traditional American table than raw fish. And yet suddenly, very quickly, we all wanted it. People are learning to like liver and kidneys. They're learning to enjoy textures that would have been profoundly repulsive to them earlier in their lives. It is powerful."

Adapted from Ron Rosenbaum, ***Smithsonian Magazine*** (2014)

Taking pictures of food has become so widespread that it has gained its own catchphrase: "Camera eats first".

ticipate **1.** Has your taste changed over the years? Give specific examples.

- When I was a kid, I hated... but now...
- When I was younger, I used to... but now...

ticipate **2.** What's your relationship with food?

- I love eating, but I hate cooking...
- I'm always taking photos of...
- I dislike / couldn't care less about...

3. Read the article. In two columns, write about America's relationship with food in the past and what it is like today.

4. What does the future of food look like to you? In groups, imagine what the situation will be like in 30 or 40 years' time.

- I think we'll no longer eat... because...
- Maybe people won't... due to...

Toolbox

CD 1 PISTE 48 MP3 31

- attractive /ə'træktɪv/: *alléchant*
- cooked /kʊkt/: *cuit*
- delicious /dɪ'lɪʃəs/: *délicieux*
- raw /rɔː/: *cru*
- repulsive /rɪ'pʌlsɪv/: *répugnant*
- a fascination /ˌfæsɪ'neɪʃn/: *une fascination*
- food-wise /fuːdwaɪz/: *côté nourriture*
- to be conscious of /'kɒnʃəs/ = to be aware of /ə'weəʳ/: *être conscient de*
- to be fascinated with /'fæsɪneɪtɪd/: *être fasciné par*
- to eat out /i:t aʊt/: *manger dehors*

Your Task

A foodie club

Imagine you belong to a foodie club at a British school. For the next meeting, you have to come up with 10 rules or good eating practises that you will follow. Discuss and be ready to read them aloud.

- From now on, all of us will...
- What we'll do is...
- We're not going to... any more.
- We've decided to (no longer) + V...

3 The Taste of Tomorrow

WB p. 27-28

Your Task
Present a futuristic restaurant

1. Food Fiction

Anticipate

1. When you eat out with friends or family, where do you go? What do you order? What do you drink?
- I usually / sometimes / never...
- Most of the time, I...

2. Read the text and try to guess in which time period it takes place.

3. Read again and jot down every type of food that is mentioned. What is surprising about the menu?
- Moby's offers a wide variety of...
- What's suprising / odd / shocking is...

4. In your opinion, why is there such a huge price difference between the two types of meat?
- I'd say that real meat has become...

5. Make a list of the pros and cons of this futuristic eating experience.

6. Imagine that you could time-travel to the year 2035, and go to Moby's. What would you order? Give reasons.
- If I went to Moby's in 2035, I would...

Toolbox

CD 1 PISTE 49 MP3 32

- affordable /ə'fɔ:dəbl/: *abordable*
- disgusting /dɪs'gʌstɪŋ/: *dégoûtant*
- (in)edible /(ɪn)'edɪbl/: *(im)mangeable*
- efficient /ɪ'fɪʃənt/: *efficace*
- exotic /ɪg'zɒtɪk/
- money-saving /'mʌnɪ 'seɪvɪŋ/: *économique*
- practical /'præktɪkəl/: *pratique*
- rare /reə/: *saignant*
- spicy /'spaɪsɪ/: *épicé*
- tasteless /'teɪstləs/: *fade*
- tasty /'teɪstɪ/: *savoureux*
- time-consuming /'taɪmkən,sju:mɪŋ/: *chronophage, qui prend du temps*
- (un)usual /(ʌn)'ju:ʒʊəl/: *(in)habituel, (peu) commun*
- weird /wɪəd/: *bizarre*

- a bug /bʌg/ = an insect /'ɪnsekt/
- hunger /'hʌŋgə/: *la faim*
- a luxury item /'lʌkʃərɪ 'aɪtəm/: *un objet de luxe*

Imagine that you are extremely hungry. You choose to go to Moby's, a pub on Tejon Street. You sit down in a booth. You check out the menu on your 10G iPhone.

Moby's has a "Real Beef Burger" special tonight — a quarter pound of grass-fed, free-range, antibiotic-free Hereford, topped with Balinese long pepper, served with homemade papaya ketchup, a side of cassava fries and choice of soup or salad. Sounds fine. It's sixty dollars — it's by far the most expensive thing on the menu.

The waitress, detecting your price point discomfort notes that "it's real meat". She suggests another burger — that's almost as good— and is only ten dollars. "We have cow meat, bison, chicken, and pork — all fresh out of the bioreactor. We have an excellent meat-grower."

You order a soup — it's unbearably spicy. Inedible. You gasp. You then ask for the "Zanzibari pizza" — it tastes nothing like pizza. It has Indian spices, and thin slices of rabbit meat, in a bed of naan. It's amazingly good.

"Mystery Box Burger", *Fat & Furious Burger* (2014)

Moby's provides copious information on all of its food — ingredients, health issues, production methods, chemicals used and not used, place of origin. The 60-dollar beef burger? 17% fat, 602 calories, slaughtered two days ago at the Gunnison Ranch, sixty-five miles away.

Josh Schonwald, ***The Taste of Tomorrow: Dispatches from the Future of Food*** (2012)

2. Futuristic Food Trends

1. Have you ever eaten anything that you thought was unusual?

- I haven't tried anything weird, but my sister once tried... and said that...
- I remember tasting...

2. Look at the pictures. What does each of them show?

- The blonde girl looks like she's about to...

3. Insects contain a lot of protein and vitamins and they emit very few greenhouse gases. A lot of people say they are the food of the future. Do you agree with this prediction? Explain why or why not.

- I (don't) think we'll be eating...
- Even if...

4. Choose one of the other two trends — 3D-printed food or Soylent — and think about the pros and cons.

- If we all had..., we'd...
- If every family owned..., we'd no longer...

1

2

A food-creating 3D printer in action

3

Soylent: the drink that claims to be able to replace all your meals (one package = 1 day's worth of food)

Useful Grammar

Les subordonnées de condition → p. 177

- Condition probable : ***if*** + présent, + ***will*** + base verbale.
  If *you* ***like*** *meat, you* ***will like*** *this new restaurant.*
- Condition moins probable ou irréelle : ***if*** + prétérit, + ***would*** + base verbale.
  If *we* ***had*** *more Soylent, we* ***could*** *help people in developing countries.*
- Irréel du passé : ***if*** + *past perfect*, + ***would*** + ***have*** + infinitif parfait.
  (Voir aussi Modaux avec V + ***have -en***, p. 172)
  If *you* ***had tried*** *insects, you* ***would have realised*** *that they are tasty.*

Your Task

The best restaurant ever

You have just opened a futuristic restaurant in your hometown. Think about the name of the place, the slogan, the dishes that you offer, what the guest experience is like, what makes your restaurant special, the reasons why people should go there, etc. Then, present it to the class.

CD 1 PISTE 50 MP3 33

The Food of the Gods

by Arthur C. Clarke (included in *The Wind from the Sun*, 1990)

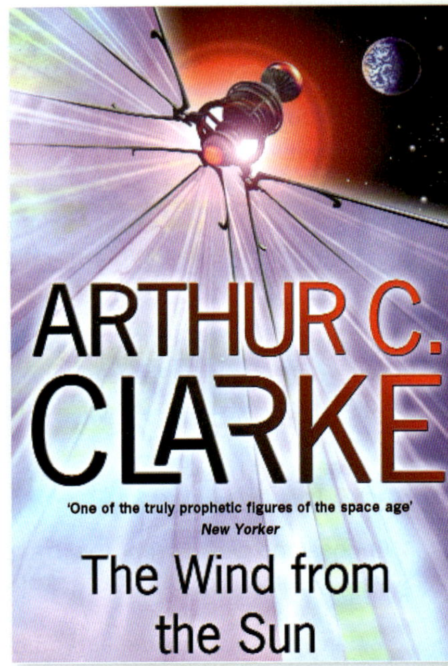

It's only fair to warn you, Mr. Chairman, that much of my evidence will be highly nauseating (...). But I am afraid that they have to be faced; there are times when the veil of hypocrisy has to be ripped away, and this is one of them.

You and I, gentlemen, have descended from a long line of carnivores. I see from your expressions that most of you don't recognise the term. Well, that's not surprising – it comes from a language that has been obsolete for two thousand years. Perhaps I had better avoid euphemisms and be brutally frank, even if I have to use words that are never heard in polite society. I apologise in advance to anyone I may offend. Until a few centuries ago, the favourite food of almost all men was meat – the flesh[1] of once living animals. I'm not trying to turn your stomachs; this is a simple statement of fact, which you can check in any history book. (...)

Well, if I may continue. Until modern times, all food fell into two categories. Most of it was produced from plants – cereals, fruits, plankton, algae and other forms of vegetation. It's hard for us to realise that the vast majority of our ancestors were farmers, winning food from the land or sea by primitive and often back-breaking techniques; but that is the truth. The second type of food, if I may return to this unpleasant subject, was meat, produced from a relatively small number of animals.

Luckily for all of us, the biochemists solved the problem; as you may know, the answer was one of the countless by-products[2] of space research. All food – animal or vegetable – is built up from a very few common elements. Carbon, hydrogen, oxygen, nitrogen, traces of sulphur and phosphorus – the half-dozen elements, and a few others, combine in an almost infinite variety of ways to make up every food that man has ever eaten or will ever eat. Faced with the problem of colonising the moon and planets, the biochemists of the twenty-first century discovered how to synthesise any desired food from the basic raw materials of water, air and rock. It was the greatest, and perhaps the most important, achievement[3] in the history of science. (...)

New foods, gentlemen, are invented every week. It is hard to keep track of them. They come and go like women's fashions, and only one in a thousand becomes a permanent addition to the menu. It is extremely rare for one to hit the public fancy overnight[4], and I freely admit that the Ambrosia Plus line of dishes has been the greatest success in the entire history of food manufacture. (...)

I really must congratulate my competitor. He has at last made available unlimited quantities of what is, from the nature of things, the ideal food for mankind. (...) Yes, Triplanetary's chemists have done a superb technical job. Now you have to resolve the moral and philosophical issues. When I began my evidence, I used the archaic word "carnivore." Now I must introduce you to another: I'll spell it out for the first time: C-A-N-N-I-B-A-L...

1. la chair - **2.** d'innombrables produits dérivés - **3.** la réussite - **4.** du jour au lendemain

BUILDING YOUR JOURNAL...

Workbook, p. 68

Biography

Arthur C. Clarke (1917–2008) was a British science fiction writer who was most famous for co-writing the screenplay for *2001: A Space Odyssey*, which is considered one of the most influential films of all time. In addition, Clarke was the author of more than 100 books, most of them exploring humanity's position in the near and distant future of the universe.

Ralph Goings

Photorealistic food

Ralph Goings (born in 1928) is one of the leading figures of Photorealism, a painting style that uses near-microscopic detail to achieve an appearance similar to a photo. In his works, Goings documents ordinary aspects of America in the 50s, 60s and 70s. One of his favourite topics is diners.

Condiment containers and napkin holders showing Going's fascination with light

The extraordinary ordinary

Making ordinary food such as hamburgers and ketchup interesting was Ralph Goings' specialty when he painted traditional American diners. While his subjects are quite like those of the Pop Art movement – such as Andy Warhol's Campbell's soup can – Goings devoted more attention to detail and became a pioneer in the photorealist movement.

Donut (1995), oil on canvas / Collection of Ann & Donovan Moore, Brooklyn, N.Y.

What's on the menu?

Goings' paintings are about much more than just food. They reveal familiar aspects of the American culture and lifestyle, an interesting mix between optimism and nostalgia of old values.

BUILDING YOUR JOURNAL...
Workbook, p. 69

Digital ZONE

You are going to create a photography exhibition about culinary tradition in your region.
Choose a photo that matches the theme of your exhibition; for instance, a traditional dish, a traditional restaurant, etc. Scan, title and (if you can) edit the photo. Then, put it in a text document and accompany it with a short description: what it portrays, why you selected it, etc. The whole class will hang their art in the classroom.

Let's Practise Grammar

community.emdl.fr
exercices interactifs

L'expression du conseil

1 Réécrivez chacune de ces opinions en utilisant le mot ou l'expression entre parenthèses.

1. "I think it's a good idea that you see a doctor." (**should**)
2. "I feel the best thing to do is to prohibit genetically modified foods." (**shouldn't**)
3. "They need to lose some weight". (**ought to**)
4. "It's better not to eat much meat." (**shouldn't**)

Les quantifieurs

2 Choisissez l'option correcte dans chacune de ces phrases.

1. We can't cook this soup! There are too (**few** / **many** / **much**) ingredients to buy.
2. Eating out is expensive here. There aren't (**much** / **few** / **any**) cheap restaurants.
3. My mom doesn't like fondue because she says there's too (**few** / **many** / **much**) cheese in it.
4. If you go to that café, you will see (**a few** / **a lot of** / **any**) unusual desserts. There are more than twenty.
5. Is there (**any** / **a few** / **many**) lemonade?
6. I was so thirsty that I drank (**any** / **a lot of** / **a few**) water.

3 Complétez ces phrases avec *some, any, many, much, little* ou *a little*. Attention : il y a parfois plusieurs possibilités !

1. They have **...** time to make dinner on Tuesdays so they usually just have pizza.
2. Bill often goes to the cafeteria because he doesn't have **...** time to cook.
3. If Martin has **...** spare time this weekend, he will bake a chocolate cake.
4. There must be **...** restaurants around here where we can get a good steak.
5. Her parents don't eat **...** red meat because they're concerned about the environment.
6. Not **...** people I know could be true vegetarians; most of my friends love meat.

4 Complétez les phrases ci-dessous avec des informations personnelles.

1. I don't really eat much... because...
2. I tend to eat too much...
3. I eat way too many...
4. When I go to the supermarket I buy a lot of...
5. I ate very little... when...
6. In my fridge, there are a few...

La référence à l'avenir

5 Complétez les phrases suivantes en donnant votre avis.

1. In the future, people will eat more... because...
2. In the future, people won't eat... anymore because...
3. Tonight for dinner, I'm going to have...
4. Tomorrow for breakfast, I'm going to have...

Les subordonnées de condition

6 Complétez ces phrases en fonction de votre expérience ou de votre avis personnel.

1. If I'm hungry in school, I usually...
2. I would eat insects if...
3. If you ate at McDonald's every day, you would...
4. If he had exercised more in the summer, he...

Talking about food

1 Trouvez le mot correspondant à chaque définition.

1. A food that might burn your tongue, like a chili pepper, is...
S _ _ _ _

2. A food that you cannot eat is...
I _ _ _ _ _ _ _

3. A food that isn't cooked is...
R _ _

4. A food with no flavor is...
T _ _ _ _ _ _ _ _

5. Some people think that food from Asia or Africa is...
E _ _ _ _ C

6. A food you find extremely disgusting is...
R _ _ _ _ _ _ _ _

Odd word out

2 Trouvez l'intrus dans chacune des trois listes de mots ci-dessous. Justifiez vos choix.

1.	2.	3.
beef	cook	palate
lamb	order	crops
spices	grow	farm
liver	meal	land

Phrasal verbs

3 Associez chaque *phrasal verb* au verbe ou à l'expression qui lui correspond.

1. Eating too much sugar can **turn into** a big problem for your health.
2. I'm going to **get rid of** this milk because it expired last week.
3. Many students **look back on** their education as lacking creativity.
4. Some children **grow up** thinking sweets and fizzy drinks are healthy.
5. The class is going to **carry out** a survey on our favourite restaurants.
6. Even though the recipe looks complicated, I think I'll be able to **pull it off**.
7. Have you **checked out** that new vegan restaurant?

a. dispose of
b. think of something of the past
c. do or complete something successfully
d. complete something despite it being difficult
e. try something to see if it's good or bad
f. become
g. change from a child to an adult

Compound words

4 Reliez les mots de chaque colonne pour former un mot composé ou une expression.

1. fast	a. free
2. antibiotic-	b. saving
3. grass-	c. cooked
4. money-	d. food
5. home-	e. waste
6. organic	f. fed
7. climate	g. change
8. animal	h. food

5 Classez les mots trouvés dans l'exercice 4 dans ces trois catégories selon qu'ils ont, d'après vous, un effet positif, négatif ou neutre sur l'environnement ou la santé.

Positive effect	Negative effect	Neutral effect

Portions and packages

6 Reliez les éléments de chaque colonne.

1. a slice of	a. crisps, biscuits, pasta
2. a portion of	b. pizza, bread, cheese
3. a packet of	c. tuna, peas, soup
4. a tin of	d. meat, vegetables, rice

Your Final Task

Present a revolutionary product at the "Food Trends & Innovations" exhibition

1 Think about a specific way to solve some of the problems with food we have seen in the unit. It could be a new product, a new service, a new plant, a new technology... Use your imagination!

2 In pairs, brainstorm and discuss your ideas. What is the name of the product? The target group? The benefits? The cost?

3 Present your product at the exhibition.

4 After watching the presentations of all the groups, the class will give three awards: an award to the most original, the most eco-friendly, and the healthiest invention.

Toolbox

CD 1 PISTE 51 MP3 34

- Good morning / afternoon, everybody...
- I'm absolutely delighted to present...
- We'll be talking about...
- I'd like to introduce my colleague...
- Please feel free to interrupt if you have questions...
- We'd now like to move on to...
- To sum up...
- Thank you all for listening.
- We'd be glad to answer any questions you might have.

Tips & Tricks

→ **The sky is the limit!** Votre produit n'a pas besoin d'être absolument réaliste. Laissez parler votre imagination !

→ **Use visuals!** Si possible, réalisez un prototype ou dessinez une maquette de votre produit.

→ **Be a pro!** Pour convaincre, vous devez paraître sûr de vous et avoir l'air de connaître votre produit sur le bout des doigts !

"We have created a hybrid plant that grows tomatoes at the top and pears at the bottom...
This new type of plant, which we call "pearato", will allow us to..."

"We have created a fork that tells you when you have eaten enough..."

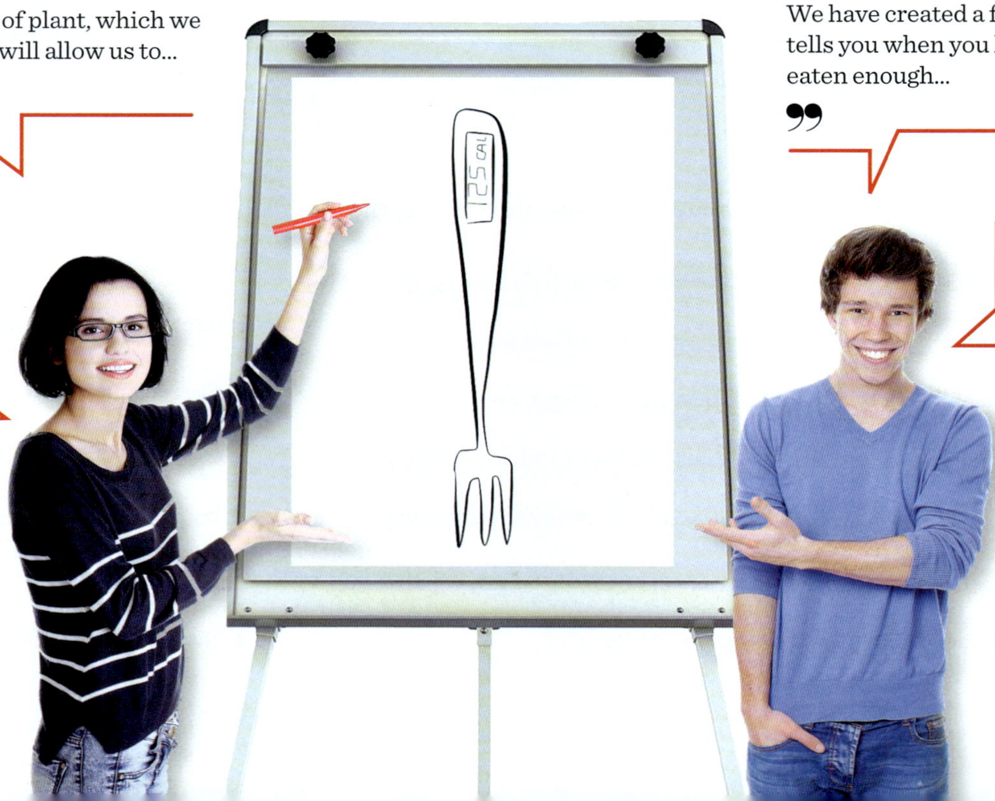

"If every garden had this plant, we could...
If you don't have much space at your disposal, "pearato"..."

"It will be a bit expensive, but... I think it will please a lot of people because..
It will be on the market starting next year..."

On Your Way to the Exam

Let's prepare your final task

Lorsque vous préparez votre présentation orale, lisez attentivement les critères d'évaluation ci-dessous.

	Niveau 1	Niveau 2	Niveau 3 (→ B1)	Niveau 4
Réalisation de la tâche		La plupart des critères imposés (nom du produit, cible, bienfaits, coût...) sont respectés, mais présentés de manière peu élaborée. Des efforts basiques de liaison des idées entre elles (*and*, *but*, *because*...).	Tous les critères imposés sont respectés. La présentation du produit est organisée et se base sur un support visuel. Des efforts pour complexifier le propos (emploi de relatives en *who*, *which*, *that*, de l'expression du contraste...).	La présentation du produit est très aboutie et originale. Le propos est argumenté et convaincant. Un support visuel de qualité est utilisé.
Qualité de la production orale	La prononciation est compréhensible avec des efforts, malgré une lecture serrée des notes. A1	La prononciation est suffisamment claire pour être généralement comprise, malgré un net accent étranger. A2 Quelques tentatives pour regarder son auditoire, mais le recours aux notes est encore très fréquent.	Le discours est assez naturel et fluide. La prononciation est toujours intelligible malgré un accent étranger et quelques erreurs de prononciation. B1 La lecture des notes est occasionnelle et la gestuelle souvent adaptée au message transmis.	La prononciation se rapproche de l'authenticité. Un auditeur natif n'aurait pas de mal à comprendre. B2 Le discours est fluide et le recours aux notes rare. La gestuelle est adaptée au message, le contact visuel presque permanent.
Maîtrise du vocabulaire	Emploi d'un répertoire très restreint de mots simples. A1/A1+	Exploitation d'une partie des mots et expressions vus en cours, mais le répertoire est encore restreint. A2/A2+	Beaucoup d'éléments du cours sont ré-exploités. B1	Emploi d'un répertoire très riche et précis qui va au-delà du lexique étudié dans l'unité. B2
Maîtrise de la grammaire	Les phrases sont très brèves. Les formes grammaticales sont assez intelligibles mais limitées et répétitives. A1/A1+	Les phrases restent simples mais généralement correctes. Des erreurs élémentaires sont possibles. Des efforts pour employer certains des faits de langue de l'unité (if, quantifieurs, conseil...). A2/A2+	Les phrases ne comportent pratiquement pas d'erreurs élémentaires. Les structures étudiées en cours (*if*, quantifieurs, conseil...) sont fréquemment réutilisées et bien maîtrisées. B1	Les phrases ne comportent aucune erreur élémentaire. Les structures employées vont au-delà de ce qui a été étudié en cours. B2
Valeur chiffrée (équivalences)	**De 5 à 9/20**	**De 10 à 15/20**	**De 16 à 20/20**	**Au-delà des attentes de 2de : objectifs du cycle terminal en vue.**

Let's listen to a short recording

CD-1 / PISTE-52

Listen to the recording and answer the questions.

Making Cronuts, a croissant-donut hybrid, in New York (2014)

Let's read a text

Your teacher will give you a text. Read it and answer the questions.

Let's write

Use what you have learned to answer the following question: Why do you think cooking shows and cooking classes are becoming more and more popular?

6 Double Identity

ISSUE AT STAKE
What is it like having two different cultural identities?

ON YOUR WAY TO THE TASK

1 **A War Zone, 24/7**
Choose a well-known figure with mixed origins and present him/her to the class

2 **Identity Crisis**
Take part in a poster contest to raise awareness about biculturalism

3 **The Best of Both Worlds**
Give a speech to present the Eva Longoria Foundation

YOUR FINAL TASK

Create a class blog about the pros and cons of having a multicultural circle of friends

1

2

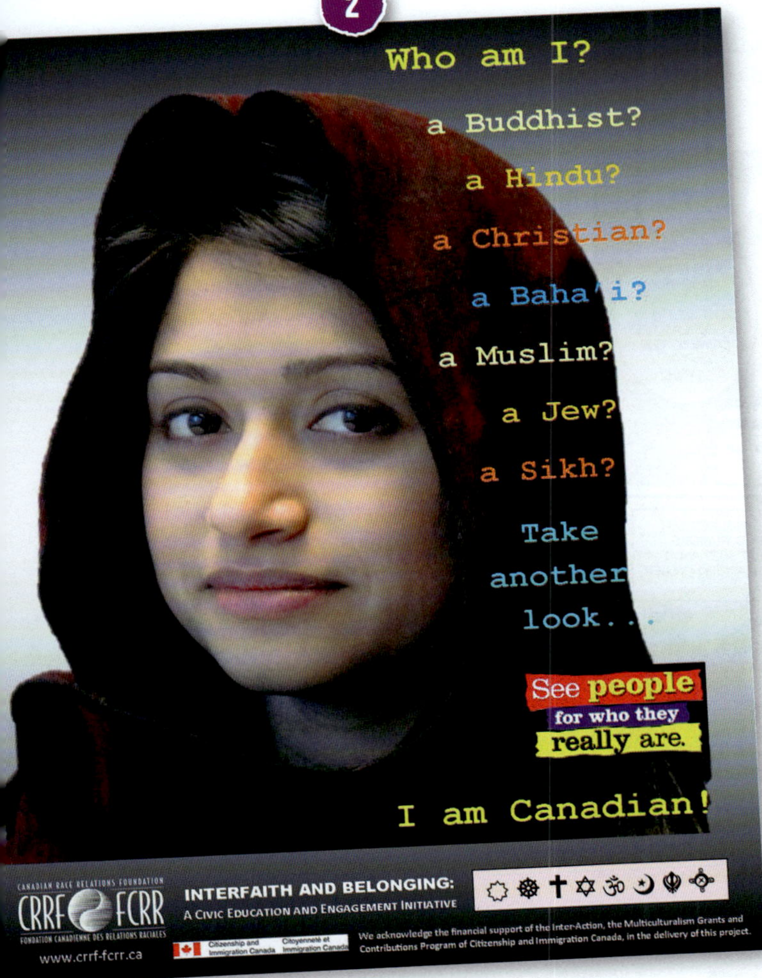

3

> Diversity is not about how we differ. Diversity is about embracing one another's uniqueness.
>
> Ola Joseph, Nigerian-born author and speaker

1. Consider the posters and the title of this unit. Why do you think it is called "Double Identity"?

- Well, these are all pictures of people who...

2. Where are the people in the posters from? What makes you think that?

- The girl in picture 1 might be... because...
- The boy wearing the headphones looks like he's from...

3. What stereotypes are they challenging?

- The boy is saying that just because he's black doesn't mean that...
- Picture 2 means / wants to show that...

4. Do you agree with Ola Joseph's quote on diversity? Create your own definition of diversity.

- What diversity means to me is...
- For me, diversity means...

Toolbox

CD 2 PISTE 1 MP3 35

- deceptive /dɪ'septɪv/: *trompeur*

- biculturalism /baɪ'kʌltʃərəlɪzəm/
- culture /'kʌltʃə/
- mixed origins /mɪkst 'ɒrɪdʒɪns/: *des origines mixtes, métisses*
- multiculturalism /ˌmʌltɪ'kʌltʃərəlɪzəm/
- prejudice /'predʒʊdɪs/: *les préjugés*
- skin colour /skɪn 'kʌləʳ/: *la couleur de peau*
- uniqueness /jʊ'ni:knəs/: *l'unicité, la spécificité*

- to be prejudiced against someone /bi: 'predʒʊdɪst ə'genst/: *avoir des préjugés contre qqn*
- to break a stereotype /breɪk ə 'sterɪətaɪp/ = to debunk a stereotype /di:'bʌŋk/: *démonter un stéréotype*
- to challenge a view /'tʃælɪndʒ ə vju:/: *critiquer une idée, contester un argument*
- to embrace (an idea) /ɪm'breɪs ən aɪ'dɪə/: *adopter, épouser (une idée)*

WB p. 29-30

Your Task
Choose a well-known figure with mixed origins and present him/her to the class

1. Surviving at School

Jin Wang has just moved from San Francisco's Chinatown to a mostly white suburb. It's his first day of school and his teacher introduces him to his new classmates.

Gene Luen Yang, ***American Born Chinese*** (2006)

Anticipate

1. Imagine it's your first day of school in a different country. Discuss what difficulties you might face.

- I think it would be difficult / tough... because...

2. Read the comic strip. Then, close your book and try to tell the story.

3. What is Timmy's reaction to Jin joining the class? What about the teacher's?

4. Why does the narrator mention Suzy?

- I guess it is to show / insist on...

5. Make a list of clichés about French people. Are they real? Can you find arguments to debunk them?

- French people are known for...
- It's a common thought that...
- People tend to think that...

2. A Difficult Integration

Anticipate

1. Read A TOUCH OF CULTURE and look at the image. What do you think the video is about?

- I suppose / reckon it's about...
- It is probably a documentary about...
- It definitely deals with...

2. Watch the first part of the video. Take notes on what you see and hear. Then, report to the class.

- In the past, England used to + V..., but today...

3. Watch the second part and take notes on the different conversations. How do their opinions differ?

- For the shopkeeper...
- According to the young girl, ...
- Nowadays, attitudes have changed...

4. In your opinion, how important is it for immigrants to learn the language of their new country? Why or why not?

- It's essential to...
- On the one hand, ... On the other hand, ...

Video Time
DVD PISTES 13-15

How has immigration changed Britain?, BBC News (2013)

A TOUCH OF CULTURE

India and **Pakistan** became independent from Britain in 1947. Since then, people have been immigrating from these countries to Britain in order to find work and build a new life. Often the only jobs available to them are poorly paid. Nowadays, 1.4 million Indians live in Britain making them the largest ethnic minority group there.

CD 2 PISTE 2

3. Family Conflicts

1. Look at the picture below. What can you tell about Jhumpa Lahiri? *Anticipate*

- From the way she dresses, I think she could be...

2. Group A will listen to Jhumpa's experience with biculturalism. Group B will read about it. Jot down things she tells us about: **problems**, **feelings**, **reactions**.

3. Share your findings with the other group.

4. Use all the information that you have to write a paragraph about Jhumpa's mother's experiences and feelings.

- When she first came to America, ...
- As soon as she realised...
- She probably tried (really) hard to...
- I'm sure she did her best to...

Useful Grammar

Les subordonnées de temps → p. 177

- ***When*** : quand.
  *I argued with my parents **when** I was a teenager.*
- ***As soon as*** : dès que.
  *He started learning English **as soon as** he set foot in England.*
- ***While*** : pendant que.
  ***While** my friends were wearing modern clothes and going to discos, I had to stay at home with my family.*

Jhumpa Lahiri is a writer, winner of the Pulitzer Prize for fiction.

I began to pity my mother; the older I got, the more I saw what a desolate life she led. She had never worked, and during the day she watched soap operas to pass the time. Her only job, every day, was to clean and cook for my father and me. We rarely went to restaurants, my father always pointing out, even in cheap ones, how expensive they were compared with eating at home. When my mother complained to him about how much she hated life in the suburbs and how lonely she felt, he said nothing to placate her. "If you are so unhappy, go back to Calcutta," he would offer, making it clear that their separation would not affect him one way or the other. I began to take my cues from my father in dealing with her, isolating her doubly. When she screamed at me for talking too long on the telephone, or for staying too long in my room, I learned to scream back, telling her that she was pathetic, that she knew nothing about me. (...)

In the end, (...) my mother and I had made peace; she had accepted the fact that I was not only her daughter but a child of America as well. Slowly, she accepted that I dated one American man, and then another, and then yet another, that I slept with them, and even that I lived with one though we were not married. (...) After years of being idle, she decided, when she turned fifty, to get a degree in library science at a nearby university.

Jhumpa Lahiri, "Hell-Heaven", ***Unaccustomed Earth*** (2008)

Toolbox

CD 2 PISTE 3 MP3 36

- heritage /'herɪtɪdʒ/
- lack of /læk əv/: *manque de*
- loneliness /'ləʊnlɪnəs/: *la solitude*
- a misconception /mɪskən'sepʃən/: *une idée fausse*
- narrow-mindedness /ˌnærəʊ 'maɪndɪdnəs/: *l'étroitesse d'esprit*
- a sense of belonging /sens əv bɪ'lɒŋgɪng/: *un sentiment d'appartenance*
- a source of conflict /sɔːs əv 'kɒnflɪkt/
- to be an advocate for /biː ən 'ædvəkɪt fɔːʳ/: *se poser en défenseur de*
- to endure /ɪn'djʊəʳ/: *endurer, supporter*
- to make fun of /meik fʌn əv/: *se moquer de*
- to mix in /mɪks ɪn/: *se mélanger*
- to realise /'rɪəlaɪz/: *se rendre compte*

Your Task

Guess who?

Choose a celebrity from the English-speaking world who could represent biculturalism. Present his/her life story but do not say his/her name: your classmates must guess. Describe his/her cultural origins and what effect being bicultural has had on his/her life.

- My celebrity was born in Hawaii. His father was Kenian and his mother... While he was...

 WB p. 31-32

Your Task
Take part in a poster contest to raise awareness about biculturalism

1. Between Two Worlds

CD 2 PISTE 4

1. Look at the badge. What does it tell you about the person who might wear it? **Anticipate**

- He or she **might be from**... **whereas** / **while**...
- His or her first language **must be**...

Anticipate **2.** You will listen to an interview with Liona Mesta, an American girl with a Mexican father and an American mother. She talks about **family**, **food** and **language**. What do you think she will say about each topic?

3. Listen and check your hypotheses.

4. Do you think parents of bicultural families should expose their children to their culture?

- In my opinion, parents **should** / **shouldn't**...
- When parents are from a different country, they **should** / **shouldn't**...

Toolbox

CD 2 PISTE 5 MP3 37

- ashamed /ə'ʃeɪmd/: *honteux*
- bilingual /baɪ'lɪŋgwəl/: *bilingue*
- frustrated /frʌs'treɪtɪd/
- proud /praʊd/: *fier*
- superior /sʊ'pɪərɪə/ ≠ inferior /ɪn'fɪərɪə/
- tough /tʌf/: *difficile*
- the background /'bækgraʊnd/: *le milieu, l'éducation*
- a burden /'bɜːdən/: *un fardeau*
- lifestyle /'laɪfstaɪl/: *le style de vie*
- roots /ruːts/: *les racines*
- upbringing /'ʌp,brɪŋɪŋ/: *l'éducation*
- to adapt to a situation /ə'dæpt/
- to complain about /kəm'pleɪn əbaʊt/: *se plaindre de*
- to feel torn between /fiːl tɔːn bɪ'twiːn/: *se sentir tiraillé entre*
- to struggle to do sth /'strʌgl/: *avoir des difficultés à faire qqch*

2. Where Do I Belong?

1. Take a minute to read the poster. Then, close the book. In pairs, write a paragraph to describe the poster and its message.

2. You are going to read about two different people. Group A about Claudine, and Group B about Delfín. Answer these questions:

a. What are their origins?
b. What languages can they speak?
c. What difficulties do they face?
d. How do they feel about being bicultural?

An example of a photo campaign launched by the Asian American Alliance aiming to address stereotypes and misconceptions on Asian-American people (2013)

TEXT 1

Claudine Chiawei O'Hearn was born in Hong Kong to an Irish-American father and a Chinese mother. Raised as an American in Singapore, she moved to the United States to attend college.

To be Chinese, to be half Chinese, is work. I often find myself cataloguing my emotions, manners, and philosophies into Chinese and American. How can I be Chinese if I prefer David Bowie to Chinese pop, if I can more easily pass as an American, if I choose to live in New York and not return to Asia where my family still lives, if English is my first language and Chinese remains a distant second? How can I be Chinese when I struggle to communicate with my grandparents? I am unable to tell them about my life and who I have become, and the result is they don't really know me.

For those of us who fall between the cracks, being "black," being "white," being "Chinese," being "Latino," is complicated. Cultural and racial amalgams create a third, wholly indistinguishable category where origin and home are indeterminate.

Adapted from Claudine O'Hearn,
Writers on Growing Up Biracial and Bicultural (1998)

3. Now, present your results and take notes about the other group's character.

4. Write a paragraph comparing Claudine and Delfín.

- Delfín can..., but Claudine can't...
- Both of them feel... yet Claudine...
  Claudine is..., whereas / while Delfín is...

5. In your opinion, what are the positive and negative things about being bicultural?

- I believe that being bicultural can be... but it can also...

Useful Grammar

L'expression de l'obligation, du devoir et de l'interdiction → p. 171-172

- On peut exprimer l'obligation ou le devoir avec le modal ***must*** (celui qui parle se présente comme directement à l'origine de l'obligation) ou avec ***have to*** (celui qui parle ne se présente pas comme directement à l'origine de l'obligation). ***Must*** exprime l'interdiction.

  *We **must** be on alert at all times.*
  *The successful candidate will **have to** speak English perfectly.*

L'expression de la capacité → p. 171

- On peut exprimer la capacité avec le modal ***can*** (***could*** au passé) ou avec ***be able to***.

  *I **could** easily pass for an American.*

TEXT 2

Delfín Carbonell is a renowned lexicographer. He was born in Spain, but was educated in the United States.

Those of us who are bilingual and bicultural, which is the same, if we are worth our salt, have split personalities and a certain sense of being eternal outsiders, and always misunderstood. We must be on the alert at all times because in our daily intercourse we know there are subjects, names, facts, that we cannot mention in one culture because we will not be understood. We must change tones of voice, manners, references, gestures, and avoid certain taboo subjects that in our other culture are fine. Certain jokes will make us laugh in one culture, while in another will make us angry.

It is indeed a rewarding experience to water at different and diverse cultural rivers, of course. (...) But today I just wanted to point out how lonely the bicultural road is, not always paved with wine and roses. Today, especially today, I feel torn between two languages and two cultures, lonely and sad, a stranger.

Delfín Carbonell, ***Fox News Latino*** (2013)
@CarbonellDelfin

3. Mexican-Americans

CD 2 PISTE 6

Anticipate

1. You are going to listen to a film excerpt in which one of the characters says "*Mexican Americans have to be twice as perfect as anybody else.*" Who are Mexican-Americans? Why do you think he makes this claim?

- I suppose he means that they have to...
- He might think that...

2. Listen a couple of times and pick out the topics that he mentions: **language**, **jobs**, **sport**, **Americans**, **celebrities**, **school**, **food**. Take notes about what he says about each.

3. Sum up his opinion about being Mexican-American.

A TOUCH OF CULTURE

Latin American immigration began at the end of the Mexican-American war (1846-1848). The war settled the border dispute and Mexico lost a third of its territory. Since then, Mexicans have been immigrating to the U.S. and today Latinos are the largest immigrant group in the country.

Pronunciation

CD 2 PISTE 7 MP3 38

Transmettre l'indignation

Écoutez deux extraits de l'audio « Mexican-Americans ». Concentrez-vous sur l'intonation de l'homme.

1. Comment transmet-il son indignation ? Repérez plusieurs manières.
2. Qu'en déduisez-vous sur le rôle de l'intonation et de l'accentuation en anglais ?
3. Comparez avec le français.

Your Task

Design biculturalism

A Latino organisation based in the U.S. has launched a poster contest to raise consciousness about the difficulties that Latinos face in the U.S. Design a poster for the contest including:

- an image.
- text (min. 25 words).
- an original slogan.

3 The Best of Both Worlds

WB p. 33-34

Your Task
Give a speech to present the Eva Longoria Foundation

1. Culinary Diversity

Brick Lane, a street in the heart of the London Bangladeshi community, also known as "Banglatown"

A man melting cheese at the vibrant and multicultural Camden Food Market in London

For any culture, its food offering is a massive part of its identity. The London dining scene is probably more diverse and international than that of any city in the world.

Most would agree that the ethnic diversity of London's dining scene is a very good thing, but it's not just about filling your face with something different. On the one hand, this international food is a way for us to experience a foreign culture first-hand. On the other hand, London's multicultural dining scene is an important thing for immigrant communities and their offspring. It's a way for London-based and often British-born families to maintain a connection with their heritage.

Adapted from Ben Norum, ***Pea Soup Magazine*** (2012)
@BenNorum

Anticipate

1. Do you like trying foreign dishes? Why or why not? What different types of food have you tried? Did you enjoy it?
- I love discovering...
- I'm not (too) keen on...
- Eating dishes from other countries is...

2. Read the text and decide what is remarkable about London's food culture.

3. What are the advantages of a multicultural dining scene?

4. What about you? What kind of food evokes memories?
- Onion soup always reminds me of...
- The smell of my grandmother's Hachis Parmentier makes me think of...

Toolbox

CD 2 PISTE 8 MP3 39

- adventurous /əd'ventʃərəs/: *aventureux, audacieux*
- enriching /ɪn'rɪtʃɪŋ/: *enrichissant*
- life-changing /ˌlaɪf'tʃeɪndʒɪŋ/: *qui change la vie*
- open-minded /ˌəʊpən 'maɪndɪd/: *ouvert d'esprit*
- tolerant /'tɒlərənt/

- a cultural background /'kʌltʃərəl 'bækgraʊnd/
- heritage /'herɪtɪdʒ/
- the offspring /'ɔfsprɪŋ/: *la descendance*
- parental disapproval /pə'rentəl dɪsə'pruːvəl/: *la désapprobation des parents*
- the pressure from society /'preʃəʳ frɒm sə'saɪəti/
- to bring back memories /brɪŋ bæk 'memərɪz/: *raviver des souvenirs*
- to experience a culture /ɪk'spɪərɪəns ə 'kʌltʃəʳ/
- to face a challenge /feɪs ə 'tʃælɪndʒ/: *relever un défi*
- to live in poverty / wealth /'pɒvətɪ/ /welθ/: *vivre dans la pauvreté / la richesse*
- to make the most of something /meɪk ðə məʊst əv 'sʌmθɪŋ/: *tirer le meilleur parti de qqch*
- to miss out on something /mɪs aʊt ɒn 'sʌmθɪŋ/: *rater qqch*

Useful Grammar

Les comparatifs de supériorité → p. 164
- Adjectifs d'une syllabe : adjectif + ***-er*** (+ ***than***).
  Chinese food is ***sweeter than*** *Japanese food.*
- Adjectifs de 2 syllabes se terminant par ***-er***, ***-ow*** et ***-y*** : adjectif + ***-er*** (+ ***than***) (***y*** → ***i*** devant ***-er***).
  *Mixed couples are often happ****ier than*** *other couples.*
- Autres adjectifs : ***more*** + adjectif (+ ***than***).
  London's dining scene is now ***more*** *diverse* ***than*** *ever.*

Le comparatif d'égalité et (souvent) d'infériorité → p. 164
- Égalité (infériorité) : ***(not) as*** + adjectif + ***as***.
  A lot of people are ***not as*** *open-minded* ***as*** *you.*

2. A Mixed Couple

Anticipate **1.** Look at the book cover and describe the couple. Imagine the cultural differences they might face.

- He probably isn't as ... as she is.
- She looks (way) more ... than...
- They might find it difficult to...

2. Read the text. Where is she from? What about him?

3. What effects did their marriage have on them?

4. Focus on lines 18 and 19. Discuss what he means by "losing out" and say if you agree.

- Well, I think he means that...
- I suppose he's suggesting that...

Margaret did not know much about German history or WW2 before she met me. She is now interested in these subjects almost as much as I am.

I have also gleaned much from Margaret that I appreciate. Before knowing her, I couldn't pick Nigeria out from a global map of the world. Nowadays, I am at ease prostrating myself in front of elders and can happily discuss the price of yam or sweet potato. (...)

Both of us also feel enlightened by having our minds and souls enriched by our union. It is only as time has gone on that we have begun to realise a lot of people we have bumped into over the years are not as tolerant as we are. Too many are quick to dismiss others as "white trash", "fanta" (a derogatory Yoruba word used against Nigerian women who date white men), "Jamaican yardies", "Muslim terrorist" or "Nigerian fraudsters". This is lazy and will only change if people mix more. (...)

The saddest thing is that the people who stay in their own homogeneous boxes are the ones losing out. You, dear reader, will have to trust our judgement over this issue, as we are writing with plenty of hands-on experience.

Bobby Smith & Margaret Oshindele-Smith, ***One Love Two Colours*** (2007)

3. Bilingual, Bicultural, Bi-happy

CD 2 PISTES 9-11

1. Look at the picture of Eva Longoria. In groups, brainstorm 4 or 5 things you know about her. Anticipate

2. Discuss the mission of her foundation. Anticipate

- The mission of her foundation might be to...

3. Watch the first part of the video and check your hypotheses.

4. Watch the first part again and write down:
- the challenges Latinas face in the U.S.
- the factors that contribute to their success.

5. According to the interviewees, what are the effects of biculturalism and bilingualism on the Latino population?

6. How might speaking another language help you in the future?

- Speaking both French and English would help me to...
- Speaking another language could...

Eva Longoria at a charity event for children with cancer

Your Task

Speed fundraising!

You have volunteereed for a branch of the Eva Longoria Foundation in Miami, FL, and you are about to meet potential sponsors. You will be given a maximum of three minutes to give an oral presentation to raise funds for the foundation. Present the foundation's goals, and explain why you need the money.

Reading

The Buddha of Suburbia

CD 2 PISTE 12 MP3 40

by Hanif Kureishi (1990)

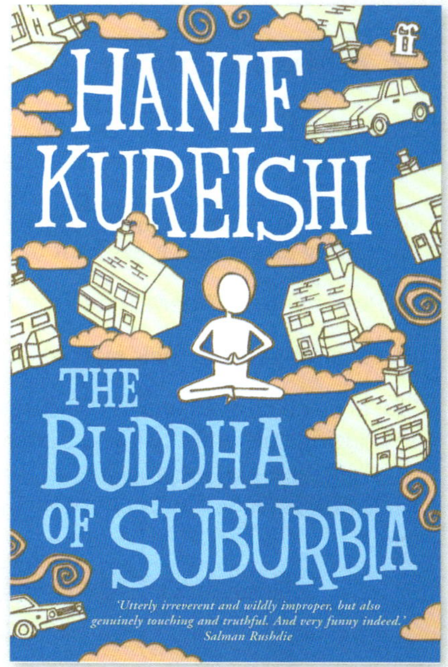

My name is Karim Amir, and I am an Englishman born and bred, almost. I am often considered to be a funny kind of Englishman, a new breed[1] as it were, having emerged from two old histories. But I don't care – Englishman I am (though not proud of it), from the South London suburbs and going somewhere. Perhaps it is the odd mixture of continents and blood, of here and there, of belonging and not, that makes me restless and easily bored. Or perhaps it was being brought up in the suburbs that did it. Anyway, why search the inner room when it's enough to say that I was looking for trouble, any kind of movement, action and sexual interest I could find, because things were so gloomy[2], so slow and heavy, in our family, I don't know why. Quite frankly, it was all getting me down and I was ready for anything.

Then one day everything changed. In the morning things were one way and at bed time another. I was seventeen.

On this day, my father hurried home from work not in a gloomy mood. His mood was high, for him: I could smell the train on him as he put his briefcase away behind the front door and took off his raincoat, chucking it over the bottom of the banisters. He grabbed my fleeing little brother, Allie, and kissed my mother and me with enthusiasm, as if we'd recently been rescued from an earthquake. More normally, he handed Mum his supper: a packet of kebabs and chapatis so greasy their paper wrapper had disintegrated. Next, instead of flopping[3] into a chair to watch the television news and wait for Mum to put the warmed-up food on the table, he went into the bedroom, which was downstairs next to the living room. He quickly stripped to his vest and underpants.

'Fetch the pink towel,' he said to me.

I did so. Dad spread it on the bedroom floor and fell on his knees. I wondered if he'd suddenly taken up religion. But no, he placed his arms beside his head and kicked himself into the air.

'I must practise,' he said in a stifled voice.

'Practise for what?' I said reasonably, watching him with interest and suspicion.

'They've called me for the damn yoga Olympics,' he said. He easily became sarcastic, Dad.

He was standing on his head now, balanced perfectly. His stomach sagged down[4]. (...) The considerable muscles in his arms swelled up and breathed energetically. Like many Indians, he was small, but Dad was also elegant and handsome, with delicate hands and manners; beside him most Englishmen looked like clumsy giraffes. (...)

'By the way, Margaret, coming to Mrs. Kay's tonight?' Mum shook her head. 'Come on, sweetie. Let's go out together and enjoy ourselves, eh?'

'But it isn't me that Eva wants to see,' Mum said. 'She ignores me. Can't you see that? She treats me like dog's muck, Haroon. I'm not Indian enough for her. I'm only English.'

'I know you're only English, but you could wear a sari.' He laughed. He loved to tease, but Mum wasn't a satisfactory teasing victim, not realising you were supposed to laugh when mocked.

1. une race, une espèce - **2.** lugubre, déprimant - **3.** se vautrer - **4.** s'affaisser

BUILDING YOUR JOURNAL...

Workbook, p. 70

Biography

Hanif Kureishi (1954) is a playwright, screenwriter, filmmaker and novelist. Born to a Pakistani father and an English mother in London, he discovered early the casual racism that surrounded his family. His first novel was the semi-autobiographical *Buddha of Suburbia*. It describes a young, bicultural boy's struggle for social and sexual identity, and offers a satirical portrait of race relations in Britain during the 1970s.

Art Mag

REGGAE BRITANNIA

Reggae Britannia… how come? How did Jamaican reggae merge with Britain, the cradle of pop music? Let's find out…

A REBELLIOUS MUSIC

While in America West Indian immigrants were absorbed into existing African-American communities, in Britain Caribbean people found themselves isolated. When reggae music became popular in the 1970s, artists like Linton Kwesi Johnson, Aswad or Steel Pulse voiced the fear and anguish of growing up in a predominantly white society.

This sense of rebellion connected with a part of the working-class British youth, particularly the punks. Reggae and punk listeners were both protesting against the violence, poverty and social injustices of the time and ended up joining forces to change British music forever. In 1977, The Clash – one of the most politicised British punk bands – famously recorded a cover of Junior Murvin's "Police and Thieves" for their debut album.

The Specials in 1980. The band wore mod-style suits and hats. Watch them perform "Too Much Too Young" in 1979 on **www.community.emdl.fr**.

WHITE REGGAE

In the late 1970s, British music transformed and absorbed reggae into the mainstream. The Police's pop-reggae song "Roxanne" became their signature tune and was a tremendous commercial success. Then came The Specials, a multiracial group from Coventry that played a fusion of punk and Jamaican ska. Their song "Too Much Too Young" reached number one in the U.K. In the 1980s, bands like UB40 and Madness continued to take reggae sounds into the charts, but now with a softer approach. By that time, reggae had become a defining element of British multiracial identity. And it still is today!

BUILDING YOUR JOURNAL…

Workbook, p. 71

Digital ZONE

Prepare an audio documentary about a band representative of Reggae Britannia for a TV program.
Pick one of the bands mentioned in the article and look for information about it: the origins, style, members, legacy… Take notes in a text document, select a few short extracts from 2 or 3 of their songs and record the piece.

Let's Practise Grammar

community.emdl.fr
exercices interactifs

Les subordonnées de temps

1 Choisissez l'option la plus adéquate et expliquez à votre partenaire la différence entre les deux mots. Lorsque les deux solutions sont possibles, expliquez la différence de sens entre les deux phrases.

1. **As soon as** / **While** Jin started school, people started to make assumptions about him based on his family origin.

2. **While** / **When** Jhumpa's mother complained, her father would get angry.

3. His father integrated into British culture **when** / **while** he arrived in Britain.

4. **While** / **As soon as** her friends were out having fun, she had to stay at home with her mother.

L'expression de l'obligation, du devoir, de l'interdiction et de la capacité

2 Décidez laquelle des deux options (**a** ou **b**) est la plus proche de la phrase proposée.

1. We must fight stereotypes and misconceptions if we want to change the world.
a. It is our duty to fight stereotypes.
b. It is a good idea to fight stereotypes.

2. Governments have to take more responsibility for integrating immigrants into society.
a. I think it's a good idea for governments to take more responsibility for integrating immigrants into society.
b. It is the government's duty to integrate immigrants into society.

3. You mustn't talk in here. It's a sacred place.
a. It is fordbidden to talk in this place.
b. I disapprove of you talking in this place.

4. Most immigrants can speak the language of the country they are living in.
a. Most immigrants are able to speak the language of the country they are living in.
b. It is possible that most immigrants speak the language of the country they are living in.

3 Imaginez que votre cousin anglais vienne vivre en France. Il est très nerveux. Que diriez-vous pour l'aider à se sentir mieux ? Réfléchissez aux cinq thématiques données ci-dessous. Écrivez au moins cinq phrases. Utilisez ***must***, ***have to***, ***can***, ***be able to*** ou leur forme négative.

keep in touch with friends | the country | the school | make new friends | the food | the language

Les comparatifs

4 Classez les différents types de cuisine ci-dessous par ordre de préférence et donnez les raisons de votre choix en utilisant des comparatifs.

Thai | Greek | French | Indian | Japanese | Spanish | Caribbean | Mexican | Italian | American

- I don't like English food. It isn't as...
- I like hot food, and Thai food is... than...

Compound adjectives

1 Associez chacun des adjectifs composés ci-dessous à la définition qui lui correspond.

life-changing | hard-working | open-minded | British-born | old-fashioned | narrow-minded | mouth-watering | well-known

1. Someone who shows no interest in cultures other than his or her own is...

2. An event that affects you so much that it changes everything is...

3. Someone who was born in Wales is...

4. Food that looks or smells very good is...

5. A person who puts a lot of effort into his or her work is...

6. Someone who is happy to consider ideas and attitudes other than his or her own is...

7. A belief or attitude which is out-of-date or no longer modern is...

8. A person, a place or a fact that many people are aware of is...

2 Associez les mots de chaque colonne pour créer des adjectifs composés. Puis, utilisez ces adjectifs composés dans une phrase. Vous pouvez même créer de petits haïkus, ces très courts poèmes japonais.

London	-lasting
thought	-suffering
sweet	-qualified
well	-based
long (x2)	-tasting
strong	-provoking
	-willed

- A long-lasting friend arrives and he smiles and I feel my heart pound.

Phrasal verbs

3 Associez chaque *phrasal verb* à sa définition.

a. to spend time with
b. to belong to and be accepted by a group
c. to learn or discover more about something
d. to manage to communicate with someone
e. to finally solve or understand something

1. I want to **find out** more about my heritage because I don't know enough and I'm interested in it.

2. I have **figured out** where I get my love of art from — I saw a picture of my great-grandfather and he was painting a picture.

3. When I started at my new school, I was worried that I wouldn't **fit in** and my classmates wouldn't like me.

4. My Chinese grandparents don't understand why I want to **hang out with** my American friends at the mall.

5. Although I tried and tried, I couldn't **get through to** my mother and make her understand how I was feeling.

Personality adjectives

4 Lisez l'opinion que les personnes ci-dessous ont au sujet de leurs camarades de classe. Quel adjectif utiliseriez-vous pour décrire ces personnes ?

tough | ashamed | defiant | weak | reserved | proud

1. I can never tell what he's thinking, or whether he's happy or sad.

2. She told her parents that she wasn't going to have an arranged marriage, even though it is expected of her.

3. He never stands up for himself; he's always doing what other people tell him to do.

4. She's always talking about her heritage and wants to find out more about it.

5. He never wants to be seen out in public with his family.

6. She never gives up, even when it gets difficult! She's really strong.

Your Final Task

Create a class blog about the pros and cons of having a multicultural circle of friends

1. Create a class blog about multiculturalism. Every student or group of students will write a post giving their opinion about the pros and/or cons of having a multicultural circle of friends.
2. Decide if you are going to speak for yourself or if you are going to play a fictitious role.
3. Start your post by introducing yourself and your circle of friends.
4. Give your opinion (positive and/or negative) and illustrate with personal examples to be more persuasive.
5. Read the other posts and leave comments.

Toolbox

CD 2 PISTE 13 MP3 41

- I strongly believe that…
- The biggest pro is…
- What I mean is…
- Let me give an example…
- We also have to take into account that…
- Overall, …
- On the one hand… On the other hand…
- The advantages outweigh the disadvantages…
- There are more pros than cons…

Tips & Tricks

→ **Be respectful!** Respectez les opinions des autres blogueurs.

→ **Be constructive!** Il est plus intéressant de développer vos arguments que de démolir ceux des autres.

→ **Be visual!** N'hésitez pas à ajouter une photo pour illustrer votre propos.

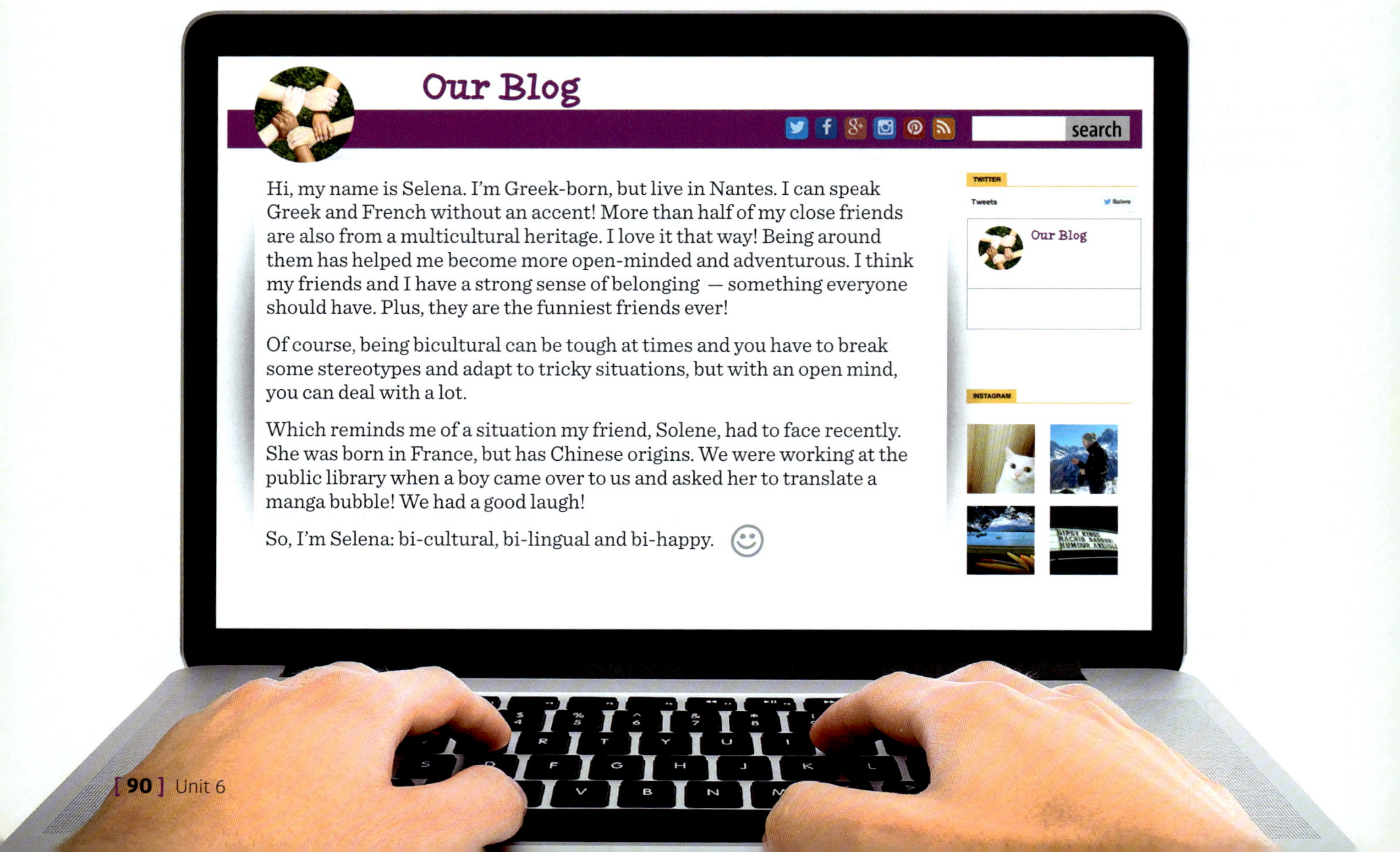

Let's prepare your final task

Avant de mettre votre texte de blog au propre, lisez attentivement les critères d'évaluation ci-dessous : où vous situez-vous dans chaque ligne du tableau ?

	Niveau 1	Niveau 2	Niveau 3 (→ B1)	Niveau 4
Réalisation de la tâche		Le message répond généralement aux critères demandés (présentation, opinion, exemples…), mais reste relativement simple.	Tous les critères demandés sont pris en compte et l'opinion est assez bien argumentée. Des exemples concrets et variés.	Le message est très complet et illustré. Les arguments sont riches et développés.
Cohérence et organisation	Les idées sont simplement juxtaposées. **A1**	Les idées sont présentées de manière organisée et reliées entre elles par des mots de liaison simples (***and***, ***but***, ***because***…). **A2**	Des efforts pour articuler les idées entre elles de manière assez complexe (emploi de structures relatives en ***who***, ***which***, ***that***, mots de liaison variés…). **B1**	Les idées sont articulées entre elles de façon très fluide. Expression précise des contrastes ou des similitudes. **B2**
Maîtrise de la grammaire	Les phrases sont très brèves. Les formes grammaticales sont assez intelligibles mais limitées et répétitives. **A1/A1+**	Les phrases restent simples mais généralement correctes. Des erreurs élémentaires sont possibles (confusion des temps, conjugaisons approximatives…). Des efforts pour employer certaines des structures de l'unité (comparatifs, obligation, capacité…). **A2/A2+**	Les phrases ne comportent pratiquement pas d'erreurs élémentaires. Les structures étudiées en cours (comparatifs, obligation, capacité…) sont fréquemment réutilisées et bien maîtrisées. **B1**	Les phrases ne comportent aucune erreur élémentaire. Les structures employées vont au-delà de ce qui a été étudié en cours. **B2**
Maîtrise du vocabulaire	Emploi d'un répertoire très restreint de mots simples. **A1/A1+**	Exploitation d'une partie des mots et expressions vus en cours, mais le répertoire est encore restreint. **A2**	Beaucoup d'éléments du cours sont réemployés. **B1**	Emploi d'un répertoire très riche et précis qui va au-delà du lexique étudié dans l'unité. **B2**
Valeur chiffrée (équivalences)	**De 5 à 9/20**	**De 10 à 15/20**	**De 16 à 20/20**	**Au-delà des attentes de 2de : objectifs du cycle terminal en vue.**

Let's read a text

Your teacher will give you a text. Read it and answer the questions.

Brick Lane, a book by Bangladeshi-born British writer, Monica Ali

Let's listen to a short recording

CD-2 / PISTE-14

Listen to the audio and answer the questions.

Cheryl Quintana Leader: one-eighth Aztec Indian

Let's write

During an evening at a friend's, you meet Shinan, who arrived from India a couple of weeks ago. You wonder what she thinks and how she feels about her adaptation to France. Write your conversation.

7 Say it Loud

Faith

Single black parent from Compton
raising children of four
That's four innocent bastards
cause papa they don't know
Her day consists of working back
and forth with babysitters
Can't find no one to watch her kids
so she pay her sister

by Kendrick Lamar (2012)

→ **ISSUE AT STAKE**

What role does music play in the history of the African-American community?

ON YOUR WAY TO THE TASK

1 I've Got the Blues

Write a short article about the history of blues music to be published in a children's magazine

2 Songs of the Civil Rights Movement

Pick and present a song representative of the Civil Rights Movement

3 What is Hip-Hop?

Stage a debate about hip-hop music and the influence it has had on the African-American community

YOUR FINAL TASK

Participate in an exhibition about African-American music and culture

Mémoire

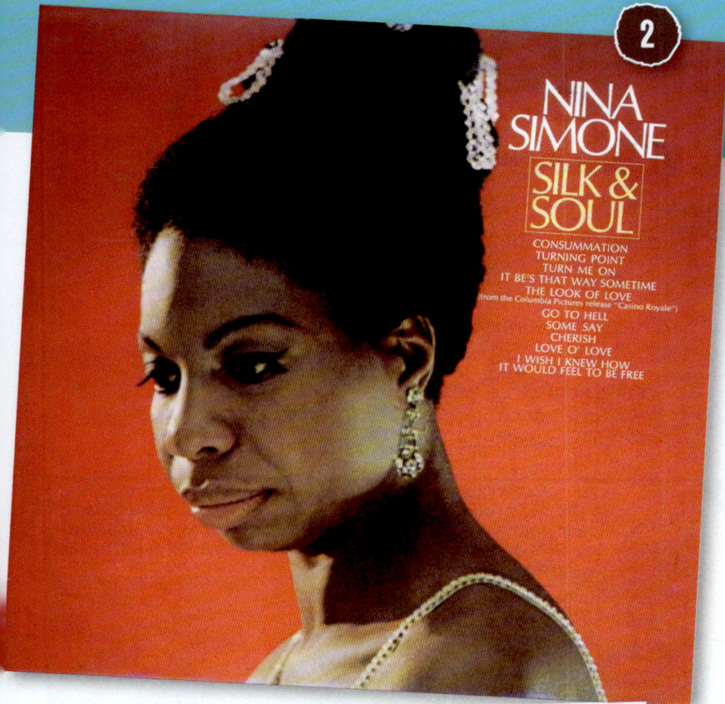

To Be Young, Gifted and Black

Young, gifted and black
We must begin to tell our young
there's a world waiting for you
This is a quest that's just begun

by Nina Simone (1972)

Stones in My Passway

I got stones in my passway
and my roads seem dark as night (x2)
I have pains in my heart
they have taken my appetite

by Robert Johnson (1937)

> Words mean more than what is set down on paper. It takes the human voice to infuse them with meaning.
>
> Maya Angelou, author, actress, singer and Civil Rights activist

1. Read the quotation by Maya Angelou. Can you rephrase it?

2. Read the three song lyric verses. Associate each lyric with one or more of these concepts: **pride**, **struggle**, **black culture**, **hope**, **love**, **poverty**. Explain your choices.

- I feel that "struggle" is the concept that best describes... because...

3. Read Nina Simone's lyrics. What "quest" is she referring to?

- In my opinion, she's referring to... / talking about...

4. Try to determine the three music genres represented.

5. What do these three songs have in common? How are they different?

GO FURTHER... www.community.emdl.fr

Listen to "Say it Loud, I'm Black and I'm Proud" by James Brown. Then, read the lyrics. What is the theme of the song?

Toolbox

CD 2 PISTE 15 MP3 42

- helpless /'helpləs/: *désespéré*
- hopeful /'həʊpfʊl/: *plein d'espoir*
- idealistic /aɪdɪə'lɪstɪk/: *idéaliste*
- proud /praʊd/: *fier*

- lyrics /lɪrɪks/: *paroles*
- pride /praɪd/: *fierté*

- to denounce /dɪ'naʊns/
- to describe /dɪ'skraɪb/
- to inspire /ɪn'spaɪə/
- to protest against /prə'test ə'genst/
- to reflect /rɪ'flekt/
- to struggle with /'strʌgl wɪð/: *lutter contre, avoir des difficultés avec*
- to support /sə'pɔːt/: *défendre, soutenir*

1 I've Got the Blues

WB p. 35-36

Your Task
Write a short article about the history of blues music to be published in a children's magazine

1. The Song of the Slaves

Anticipate **1.** Before you read the text, focus on the title above and imagine what the text might be about.

- In my opinion, ...
- It seems to me that...
- I would say that...

2. Read the text and make a list of words that express either suffering or joy.

3. "*Slaves are the most contented and happy laborers in the world*" (l. 1-3). Is this message conveyed in the text?

The remark is frequently made, that slaves are the most contented and happy laborers in the world. They dance and sing, and make all manner of joyful noises; but it is a great mistake to suppose them happy because they sing. The songs of the slave represent the sorrows, rather than the joys, of his heart; and he is relieved by them, only as an aching heart is relieved by its tears. When the slaves on board of the "Pearl" were overtaken, arrested, and carried to prison — their hopes for freedom blasted — as they marched in chains they sang, and found a melancholy relief in singing. Sorrow and desolation have their songs, as well as joy and peace. Slaves sing more to make themselves happy, than to express their happiness.

Adapted from Frederick Douglass, *My Bondage and My Freedom* (1855)

A TOUCH OF CULTURE
Born a slave, **Frederick Douglass** (1818-95) escaped at age 20 and went on to become a leader of the abolitionist movement. His three autobiographies, among them *My Bondage and My Freedom*, discuss his transition from bondage to liberty.

2. Discovering the Blues

Anticipate **1.** Brainstorm on the meaning of the title of this lesson: "I've Got the Blues".

- I guess / reckon / believe that...

2. Read the comic strip. Explain: Who sang the blues? Why? Where?

- The blues was sung by...
- And they sang (so as) to... / (in order) to...
- The slaves sang because...

Josh Cohen, *The Blues Comic Book* (2011)

17th Century
1649
A Dutch ship brought **20 African** servants to the English colony of Jamestown, Virginia.

19th Century
1848
77 slaves were captured after trying to escape Washington D.C. on a ship called "The Pearl".

1861
The **Civil War began**. Fought over the issue of slavery, it lasted four years. The Union's victory meant the end of slavery in the U.S.

1863
President **Abraham Lincoln's Emancipation Proclamation** freed all slaves in the Confederacy.

1881
Tennessee passed the first of the **"Jim Crow" segregation laws**, segregating state railroad-cars. Other Southern states passed similar laws.

3. The Blues Highway

Anticipate

1. Look at the book cover and discuss what the Blues Highway might be.

- I'd say that it is a...

2. Read the text. Where did many Southern black people go to during the first part of the 20th century? Why?

- They moved... because...
- They migrated (so as) to... / (in order) to... because...

3. How did the blues evolve after the Great Migration?

4. What is the birthplace of rock 'n' roll? How did it originate?

5. Where was the blues amplified and why?

At the end of the bitter Civil War, Southern slaves were freed. But unfair legislation tied blacks to plantations for many years to come. During the first part of the 20th century, the lure of jobs and rights in America's northern cities, most notably Chicago, drew Southern workers North. (...) The growing mechanization of the cotton industry prompted yet more to travel as jobs in the South were lost.

As these itinerant families traveled, so they took music with them. Bluesmen roamed North along the Blues Highway, developing a taste for music in every town and city along the way. Memphis, St. Louis and, finally, Chicago all began to hear the intoxicating rhythms of jazz and blues. That music met other influences and continued to develop. In Memphis, Delta blues, country music from nearby Nashville and Southern gospel fused to create rock 'n' roll. In Chicago, blues developed into a more refined and urban sound and was amplified for the first time to make itself be heard in noisy South Side clubs.

Richard Knight, ***The Blues Highway*** (2003)

Useful Grammar

Le prétérit simple → p. 169
- Le prétérit sert à faire part d'évènements révolus.
- Forme affirmative : base verbale + ***-ed*** (sauf verbes irréguliers).
  *The blues **documented** the experience of Southern blacks.*
- Formes interrogative et négative : ***did*** (auxiliaire ***do*** au prétérit) (+ ***not***) + base verbale.
  *Slaves **did not** / **didn't have** freedom of speech.*

La voix passive → p. 174
- Voix passive : ***be*** conjugué + participe passé. On l'emploie pour parler de ce qui est affecté par un évènement/une démarche plutôt que de l'auteur de celle-ci.
  *In the 1800s, Africans **were kidnapped** from their houses.*

Les subordonnées de but → p. 177
- Pour exprimer le but dans une subordonnée, on utilise ***to***, ***in order to*** ou ***so as to***.
  *Slaves sang **to** make themselves happier.*

Toolbox

- equality /ɪ'kwɒlətɪ/
- freedom /'fri:dəm/: *la liberté*
- integration /ɪntɪ'greɪʃn/
- a job opportunity /dʒɒb ɒpə'tju:nətɪ/: *une perspective d'emploi*
- slavery /'sleɪvərɪ/
- to cope with /kəʊp wɪð/: *faire face à*
- to express /ɪk'spres/
- to let off steam /let ɒf sti:m/: *se défouler*
- to let out sth /let aʊt/: *lâcher, laisser sortir*

CD 2 PISTE 16 MP3 43

Your Task

Be a journalist!

Write a short article about the history of blues to be published in a children's magazine. Talk about the origins, the meaning, and how it evolved.

20th Century

1920s

The **Mississippi Delta** — an area in the south of the U.S. famous both for fertile soil and poverty — is considered the birthplace of the blues. In the 1920s, **Delta Blues** artists like Charlie Patton and Robert Johnson made their first recordings.

1923

Blues diva **Bessie Smith** recorded "Down Hearted Blues", which became a phenomenal success.

1943

Bluesman Muddy Waters left Mississipi and moved to Chicago. This was symbolically known as **the year that the electric Chicago Blues sound was born**. By this time, the Great Migration from the South to the North was at its peak.

2 Songs of the Civil Rights Movement

WB p. 37-38

Your Task
Pick and present a song representative of the Civil Rights Movement

1. Soundtrack for a Revolution

Anticipate **1.** Before watching an extract of a documentary, look at the poster, the screenshot and the timeline and try to imagine what it is about.

- It might / must be about...

Anticipate **2.** Can you define what the Civil Rights Movement was?

3. Watch the video and count the number of people interviewed. Who are they? What are their ideas?

4. Discuss the meaning of the quote, "*You can cage the singer but not the song.*"

5. Do you think music and songs were powerful weapons during the movement?

6. How important is music in **your** life? Explain the power of music for you.

- For me, music is a way to...
- Music calms me down when...

Pronunciation

CD 2 PISTE 17 MP3 44

La prononciation du « -ed »

Écoutez ces trois extraits de « Soundtrack for a Revolution ». Concentrez-vous sur la prononciation du ***-ed*** des verbes ***arrested***, ***liberated***, ***crossed***, ***created***, ***jailed***, ***called***, ***colored***.

1. Classez-les en fonction de leur prononciation : /ɪd/, /t/ ou /d/.

2. Ajoutez ces verbes à votre liste : ***claimed***, ***defended***, ***handcuffed***, ***hummed***, ***influenced***, ***pushed***, ***stopped***, ***walked***, ***waved***.

3. Qu'en déduisez-vous sur la prononciation du ***-ed*** ?

Toolbox

CD 2 PISTE 18 MP3 45

- to claim /kleɪm/ = to demand /dɪˈmaːnd/: *revendiquer, exiger*
- to encourage /ɪnˈkʌrɪdʒ/
- to stand up for sth/sb /stænd ʌp/: *défendre qqch/qqn*
- to struggle for /ˈstrʌɡl fɔː/: *lutter pour*

Video Time

DVD PISTE 16

Bill Guttentag and Dan Sturman's *Soundtrack for a Revolution* (2009)

20th Century

1955
In Montgomery, Alabama, **Rosa Parks** refused to give up her seat to a white person and move to the back of the bus, the space reserved for African-Americans. Her arrest sparked the **Montgomery Bus Boycott**.

1959
Motown Records was founded in Detroit. The label helped transform **soul music** — a new genre of music combining gospel and blues — into a major force. Soul music was an essential part of the Civil Rights Movement.

1960
Four African-American college students **held a sit-in aimed at integrating a Woolworth's lunch counter** in Greensboro, N.C., launching a wave of similar protests across the South.

2. It's Been a Long Time Coming

:icipate

1. Listen to "A Change is Gonna Come" in **www.community.emdl.fr** and think about the style and mood of the song. How does it make you feel?

- It's a song that...
- It makes me feel (like)...
- It gives me a feeling of...

2. Why are some lyrics repeated? What is the "change" that is coming?

3. Is the song positive or negative? What is the main feeling?

- In my opinion, this is a song that...

4. Why does someone tell the narrator "*Don't hang around*" (l. 11)? Who might this be?

3. A Song of Protest

CD 2
PISTE 19

1. Listen to a music expert talk about "A Change is Gonna Come". Jot down the main ideas that you understand.

2. Listen again. What were the three sources of inspiration for this song?

- The singer was inspired by...

3. Why was Sam Cooke ashamed?

4. Look for information on Bob Dylan's song and share it with your classmates.

- I've found that...
- According to Wikipedia, ...

Useful Grammar

Les subordonnées relatives → p. 178

- Antécédent humain seulement : ***who***.
  *The man **who** was singing was white.*
- Antécédent non humain seulement : ***which***.
  *The guitar **which** he played was slightly out of tune.*
- Antécédent humain ou non humain : ***that*** ou **Ø** (peu formel). (**Ø** ne peut pas être sujet.)
  *The song **that** / **Ø** he heard made him feel ashamed.*
  *This is the song **that** made him famous.*

A Change is Gonna Come

I was born by the river in a little tent
Oh and just like the river
I've been running ever since
It's been a long, a long time coming
But I know a change is gonna come, oh yes it will

It's been too hard living but I'm afraid to die
'Cause I don't know what's up there beyond the sky
It's been a long, a long time coming
But I know a change is gonna come, oh yes it will

I go to the movie and I go downtown
Somebody keep telling me, "Don't hang around"
It's been a long, a long time coming
But I know a change is gonna come, oh yes it will

Then I go to my brother
And I say, "Brother, help me please"
But he winds up knockin' me
Back down on my knees

Oh there's been times that I thought
I couldn't last for long
But now I think I'm able to carry on
It's been a long, a long time coming
But I know a change is gonna come, oh yes it will

Sam Cooke, ***"A Change is Gonna Come"***

Your Task

A song that made a difference

Pick and present a song representative of the Civil Rights Movement. Talk about the artist, the lyrics, the mood and the feelings expressed, when it was released, why it is relevant, etc. You can choose one of the following songs: **"Say It Loud - I'm Black And I'm Proud"** by James Brown, **"To Be Young, Gifted and Black"** by Nina Simone, or **"People Get Ready"** by The Impressions.

1963
Iore than **200,000 people marched on Washington, D.C.**, in the largest Civil Rights emonstration ever; Martin Luther King Jr. ave his **"I Have a Dream" speech**.

1964
President Lyndon Johnson signed the **Civil Rights Act** outlawing discrimination based on race, colour, religion, sex, or national origin.

Martin Luther King Jr. was awarded the Nobel Peace Prize.

1967
Aretha Franklin recorded a series of hit singles, including her best-known song, "Respect". She came to be known as the "Queen of Soul".

1968
Martin Luther King Jr. was assassinated in Memphis, Tennessee.

3 What is Hip-Hop?

WB p. 39-40

Your Task

Stage a debate about hip-hop music and the influence it has had on the African-American community

1. Origin

CD 2 PISTE 20

1. Do you like hip-hop? Why (not)? What stereotypes are associated with it? *Anticipate*

- What I like most about hip-hop is...
- I'm not really into hip-hop fashion, because...

Anticipate **2.** Look at the album cover and read the caption. What elements of the photo would you associate with hip-hop?

Anticipate **3.** You are going to listen to a radio program called "Afrika Bambaataa Creates Culture". Imagine what this program might be about.

4. Listen and jot down information on the following categories: **who**, **what**, **where**.

5. What values did Bambaataa hope to pass on?

A TOUCH OF CULTURE

The music genre and culture known as **hip-hop** began in the Bronx, New York City, in the early 1970s.

American hip-hop group Grandmaster Flash & The Furious Five played a significant role in the early development of hip-hop.

2. Hip-Hop Controversy

1. Group A reads the first text and Group B reads the second one. Each group discusses the message and tries to summarise it.

- The author is basically saying that... isn't he?
- His main point is that... isn't it?

2. Each group finds counter-arguments to the main message of their text.

- I think Kool Herc is only partially right because...
- Hip-hop can be..., but it can also be...

3. Now, each group presents the main ideas of their text to the other group, who will respond with counter-arguments.

TEXT 1

To me, hip-hop says, "Come as you are." We are a family. (...). It's about you and me, connecting one to one. That's why it has universal appeal. It has given young people a way to understand their world, whether they are from the suburbs or the city or whatever.

Hip-hop also created a lot of jobs that otherwise wouldn't exist. But even more important, I think, hip-hop has bridged the culture gap. It brings white kids together with black kids, brown kids with yellow kids. They all have something in common that they love. It gets past the stereotypes and people hating each other because of those stereotypes.

Introduction by Kool Herc to ***Can't Stop Won't Stop*** (2005)

TEXT 2

The late 1990s saw the rise in popularity of the "bling bling" lifestyle in rap music, focusing on symbols of wealth and status like money, jewelry, cars, and clothing.

The widespread success of hip-hop, specifically gangsta rap, has also had a significant social impact on the demeanor of modern youth. The sometimes egotistic attitudes often portrayed in the lyrics and videos of certain hip-hop artists have repeatedly shown negative effects on some of their idolizing fans. Because hip-hop music almost always puts an emphasis on hyper-masculinity, its lyrics have been said to reflect a homophobic mindset. Many hip-hop recordings are broadcast in censored form, with offending language blanked out of the soundtrack.

Adapted from **www.urbandictionary.com** (2006)

20th Century

1973
Kool Herc DJed his first party in the South Bronx, an impoverished neighbourhood riddled with gang violence.

1974
Afrika Bambaataa formed the **Universal Zulu Nation**, a socially conscious collective of DJs, graffiti artists and break dancers.

1979
"Rapper's Delight" by the **Sugar Hill Gang** helped bring rap to national prominence.

1988
Two very different records were released: **Public Enemy's** socially conscious "It Takes a Nation of Millions to Hold Us Back" and **N.W.A.'s** "Straight Outta Compton", which made **gangsta rap** popular.

3. Explicit Lyrics

RHYME 1 So while you're imitating Al Capone,
I'll be Nina Simone
From: "Ready or Not" by The Fugees (1996)

RHYME 2 You shouldn't throw stones if you live in a glass house
and if you got a glass jaw, you should watch your mouth
'cause I'll break your face
From: "Patiently Waiting" by 50 Cent (2003)

RHYME 3 Now I'm in the limelight 'cause I rhyme tight
Time to get paid, blow up like the World Trade
From: "Juicy" by The Notorious B.I.G. (1994)

RHYME 4 I learned from my teachers
but became through my music
From: "Ten Thousand Hours" by Macklemore (2012)

RHYME 5 That ghetto life sure is drastic
All the furniture's covered in plastic
From: "In the Ghetto" by Busta Rhymes (2006)

RHYME 6 I'm fighting for the girls that never thought they could win
'Cause before they could begin, you told them it was the end
But I am here to reverse the curse that they live in
From: "I'm the best" by Nicky Minaj (2010)

Nicki Minaj mixes a spunky style and an unpredictable fusion of hip-hop, pop, and electronic music. She has become one of the most powerful figures in the music business.

1. Match each rhyme with one of the following concepts and defend your choices: **peace and love**, **violence**, **city life**, **girl power**, **greed**, **poverty** and **American icons**.

- I guess / reckon / believe that 50 Cent's rhyme is about...

2. Find verses that express the following ideas:

a. "Now is the time to make money and be famous."
b. "I represent girls who feel they have no chance."
c. "Be careful with what you say if you're a weak person."
d. "Life in a poor neighbourhood is tough."
e. "My music helps women overcome men's dominance."
f. "While you use violence, I'll fight peacefully for my people."
g. "School taught me skills but didn't make me who I am."

3. What are the similarities among the musical styles in this unit?

Toolbox

CD 2 PISTE 21 MP3 46

- materialistic /mətɪərɪə'lɪstɪk/
- sectarian /sek'teərɪən/

- a ghetto blaster /'getəʊ 'blɑːstə/ = a boom box /buːm bɒks/: *un gros lecteur de son*
- homophobia /ˌhəʊməʊ'fəʊbɪə/
- misogyny /mɪ'sɒdʒənɪ/
- sneakers (U.S.) /'sniːkə(r)z/ = trainers (U.K.) /'treɪnə(r)z/: *des baskets*

Your Task

A debate about hip-hop

GROUP A: You will argue that hip-hop is a positive force.
GROUP B: You will argue that hip-hop is a bad influence on youth.
GROUP C: You are journalists. Listen to the debate and take notes to write a brief report for a newspaper.

1991
A video recording of four white Los Angeles police officers beating a black man named **Rodney King** was nationally broadcast.

1993
Toni Morrison became the first black American to win the Nobel Prize for Literature.

21st Century
2008
Barack Obama became **the first black president in U.S. history**. One year later, he was awarded the Nobel Peace Prize.

2015
Los Angeles rapper Kendrick Lamar released the follow-up album to the highly-acclaimed "Good Kid, M.A.A.D. City" (2012), which chronicled Lamar's experiences in L.A.'s Compton neighbourhood.

Sonny's Blues

by James Baldwin (included in *Going to Meet the Man*, 1975)

CD 2 PISTE 22 MP3 47

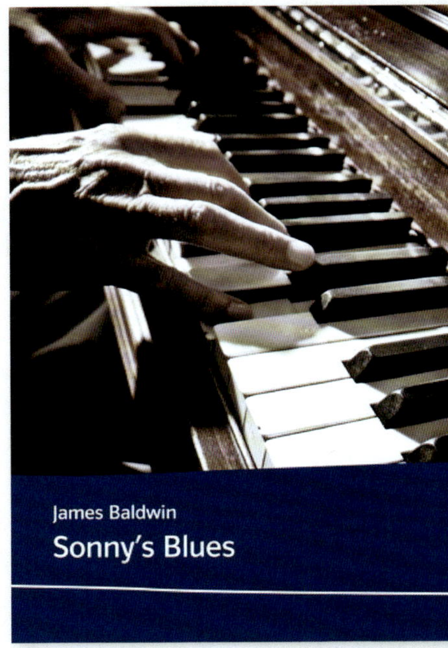

I had never before thought of how awful the relationship must be between the musician and his instrument. He has to fill it, this instrument, with the breath of life, his own. He has to make it do what he wants it to do. And a piano is just a piano. It's made out of so much wood and wires and little hammers and big ones, and ivory. While there's only so much you can do with it, the only way to find this out is to try; to try and make it do everything.

And Sonny hadn't been near a piano for over a year. And he wasn't on much better terms with his life, not the life that stretched before him now. He and the piano stammered[1], started one way, got scared, stopped; started another way, panicked, marked time, started again; then seemed to have found a direction, panicked again, got stuck. And the face I saw on Sonny I'd never seen before. Everything had been burned out of it, and, at the same time, things usually hidden were being burned in, by the fire and fury of the battle which was occurring in him up there.

Yet, watching Creole's face as they neared the end of the first set, I had the feeling that something had happened, something I hadn't heard. Then they finished, there was scattered applause, and then, without an instant's warning, Creole started into something else, it was almost sardonic, it was "Am I Blue". And, as though he commanded, Sonny began to play. Something began to happen. And Creole let out the reins. The dry, low, black man said something awful on the drums, Creole answered, and the drums talked back. Then the horn insisted, sweet and high, slightly detached perhaps, and Creole listened, commenting now and then, dry, and driving, beautiful and calm and old. Then they all came together again, and Sonny was part of the family again. I could tell this from his face. He seemed to have found, right there beneath his fingers, a damn brand-new piano. It seemed that he couldn't get over it. Then, for a while, just being happy with Sonny, they seemed to be agreeing with him that brand-new pianos certainly were a gas.

Then Creole stepped forward to remind them that what they were playing was the blues. He hit something in all of them, he hit something in me, myself, and the music tightened and deepened, apprehension began to beat the air. Creole began to tell us what the blues were all about. They were not about anything very new. He and his boys up there were keeping it new, at the risk of ruin, destruction, madness, and death, in order to find new ways to make us listen. For, while the tale of how we suffer, and how we are delighted, and how we may triumph, is never new, it always must be heard. There isn't any other tale to tell, it's the only light we've got in all this darkness.

1. balbutier, bégayer

BUILDING YOUR JOURNAL...
Workbook, p. 72

Biography

James Arthur Baldwin (1924–1987) was an American writer and social critic. His essay collection, *Notes of a Native Son* (1955), explores the felt, yet unspoken, difficulties of racial, sexual, and class distinctions. His work focuses on America's tensions during the mid-20th century. *Going to Meet the Man* (1965) is his only short story collection.

WILD STYLES

Hip-hop is a form of musical expression and artistic culture that originated in African-American communities during the 1970s in New York City. The four pillars of hip-hop culture are MCing —the act of rapping on a microphone—, DJing, break dancing, and graffiti. Let's take a look at two of them...

GRAFFITI

Graffiti emerged as a form of expression for political activists and gang members, but it soon turned into an art form; the visual expression of hip-hop culture. Children from the Bronx, one of the poorest and most dangerous New York City neighbourhoods in the 1970s, adopted graffiti as a way to express themselves creatively. They mainly practised on subway stations and trains. This was not an easy task, as they had to deal with police patrolling the trains and the yards where they worked. NYC subway graffiti eventually became world famous and their styles and sensibilities were transplanted to other parts of the country and the world, mixing with local traditions and styles in exciting new ways.

From the Platform: Subway Graffiti, 1983-1989 is a great book on the origins of graffiti.

The Rock Steady Crew remains the world's most famous b-boy troupe in the world. Watch them dance on **www.community.emdl.fr**.

BREAKING

Breaking, or break dancing, is a style of street dance that originated in NYC along with the emergence of hip-hop culture in the early 1970s. Kids started spinning on their heads and doing all kinds of acrobatic flips to the beats played by early DJs like Kool Herc. What had begun as a competition of skills at house parties and street jams soon became a pop culture phenomenon.

BUILDING YOUR JOURNAL...

Workbook, p. 73

Digital ZONE

Create an ebook about graffiti art. Look for a photo of an important piece of graffiti. Learn about the piece: Who is the artist? What is his or her technique? What is the meaning of the work? Paste the photo into a text document and explain it in two short paragraphs; one about the artist, the other about the piece. Title your work creatively and make a cover page. Combine your pages with the rest of the class to make a PDF ebook.

Le prétérit simple et la voix passive

1 Formez des phrases à la voix passive à partir des énoncés suivants.

1. In 1807, Congress banned the importation of slaves into the U.S.

➔ In 1807, the importation of slaves...

2. Tears can relieve *(soulager)* an aching *(souffrant)* heart.

3. In the 20s and 30s, people considered Son House, Charlie Patton and Robert Johnson the best Delta blues singers.

4. They amplified the acoustic sound of the Delta blues in Chicago.

5. Chicago eclipsed the Mississippi Delta as the centre of blues music.

6. The song "Respect" perfectly captured the confidence and pride of African-Americans.

2 Présentez à la classe un(e) chanteur(euse) ou un groupe afro-américain que vous aimez en utilisant le prétérit simple et la voix passive chaque fois que possible. Divulguez trois informations à son sujet mais ne donnez pas son nom ! Vos camarades devront trouver l'identité de ces artistes mystères.

- He was an American singer.
  He was called the King of Pop.
  He popularised a dance technique called the moonwalk.

Beyoncé

Pharell Williams

3 Écrivez un bulletin d'information radio au passé. Utilisez tous les mots ci-dessous et faites au moins quatre phrases à la voix passive. Utilisez votre imagination ! Présentez ensuite votre production à la classe.

worldwide | guests | huge crowds | record stores | new album | concert

- A **new album** by Nicki Minaj was launched yesterday at...

Les subordonnées de but

4 Faites des phrases complètes en associant les débuts et les fins de phrases ci-dessous et en ajoutant un marqueur de but.

1. Slaves sang...

2. Kids in the Bronx started to graffiti...

3. Civil Rights activists sang songs...

4. Chicago musicians electrified the blues...

a. express hope and determination.
b. cope with grief.
c. gain fame and recognition.
d. make it sound more appealing to the new urban masses.

Les subordonnées relatives

5 Choisissez la forme correcte.

1. Nina Simone was a singer, pianist and songwriter **Ø** / **who** / **which** used her talent to create a remarkable body of work.

2. Simone was denied admission at the Curtis Institute of Music in Philadelphia for reasons **who** / **whom** /**that** remain unclear.

3. She wrote a song entitled "Mississippi Goddam" in reaction to the assassination of Medgar Evers and to a church bombing **who** / **which** /**Ø** killed four black girls in Birmingham, Alabama.

4. In the late 1980s an event occurred **whom** / **Ø** / **that** literally resurrected her career; her song "My Baby Just Cares For Me" was used in an advert for a famous perfume.

5. She eventually wrote an autobiography **who** / **which** / **Ø** was published in 1992 under the title *I Put a Spell on You*.

Actions, Feelings and Concepts

1 Trouvez l'intrus et justifiez votre choix.

1.
- joyful
- happy
- satisfied
- painful

2.
- sorrow
- melancholy
- desolation
- happiness

3.
- inspire
- mobilise
- neutralise
- add hope

4.
- slavery
- equality
- freedom
- integration

Phrasal Verbs

2 Associez les *phrasal verbs* aux verbes correspondants.

1. Don't **hang around** here. It's too dangerous.
2. I'm sick of hip-hop's misogyny. I **give up**!
3. **Coping with** grief was not easy for the slaves.
4. What does hip-hop really **stand for** these days?
5. The song is about forgetting the past and **moving on**.
6. What she said is not true. She **made it up**.

a. deal with, handle
b. mean, represent
c. continue
d. stay, wait
e. invent
f. stop, abandon

Music Genres

3 Associez chacun des concepts au(x) genre(s) correspondant(s). Justifiez vos choix.

traditional sound · urban sound · gospel-influenced · dance music · universal appeal · work songs · rural music · an artistic culture · explicit lyrics · political songs · passionate interpretations

Musical Instruments

4 Associez le nom de chaque instrument à sa photo. Puis, indiquez quel(s) instrument(s) correspond(ent) aux genres musicaux suivants: **jazz**, **folk**, **blues**, **hip-hop**, **pop**.

a. turntable **b.** fiddle **c.** harmonica
d. accoustic guitar **e.** banjo **f.** drums
g. electric guitar **h.** saxophone **i.** sampler

Your Final Task

Participate in an exhibition about African-American music and culture

1. Look for information in this unit and on the Internet. Decide on a theme for your part of the exhibition.
2. Choose a title and a subtitle. Decide the type of text and the accompanying music that you will include.
3. Create at least two panels including photographs and text.
4. Hang them on the wall next to the panels of your classmates.
5. Take your time to visit the exhibition and choose the part you like the most.
6. You are being interviewed at the end of the visit. Comment on the experience of visiting the exhibition; what you have learned, which part you have enjoyed the most (think about the content and intentions of that particular part).

Toolbox

CD 2 PISTE 23 MP3 48

- It was really/truly educational...
- It was very entertaining/informative...
- It was a bit disappointing because...
- I thought it was impressive...
- I learned a whole lot of things...

Tips & Tricks

→ **Structure it!** Organisez l'information en paragraphes et donnez un titre accrocheur à chacun.

→ **Make it clear!** Utilisez un corps assez gros (16 minimum), consacrez au moins 1/3 de l'affiche aux illustrations et conservez des espaces blancs.

→ **Make it nice!** N'utilisez pas plus de trois couleurs et deux polices par affiche.

“
I was shocked to see...
I really liked the fact that...
The part I liked the most was...
The goal of thid part was to...
It was as much about music as it was about...
”

On Your Way to the Exam

Let's prepare your final task

Une fois vos affiches réalisées au brouillon, lisez attentivement les critères d'évaluation ci-dessous : où vous situez-vous dans chaque ligne ?

	Niveau 1	Niveau 2	Niveau 3 (→ B1)	Niveau 4
Réalisation de la tâche		La plupart des critères imposés (au moins deux affiches, présence de photos...) sont respectés. Les affiches sont proprement présentées. Les textes sont rédigés par l'élève et non pas recopiés sur Internet.	Tous les critères imposés sont respectés et les affiches proposées se rapprochent de celles d'une véritable exposition.	Les affiches réalisées ressemblent en tous points à celles d'une exposition authentique. Les textes sont denses.
Cohérence et organisation		La thématique choisie est assez bien traitée dans les différentes affiches. Les informations culturelles fournies sont peu élaborées mais pertinentes. La plupart des titres et illustrations sont bien choisis. **A2**	La thématique choisie est bien traitée dans les différentes affiches. Les informations culturelles fournies sont élaborées. Les titres et légendes des images sont rédigés avec recherche. **B1**	Les textes des différentes affiches s'articulent de façon très cohérente et fluide. La structure générale et la pertinence du contenu sont remarquables. **B2**
Maîtrise de la grammaire	Les phrases sont très brèves. Les formes grammaticales sont assez intelligibles mais limitées et répétitives. **A1/A1+**	Les phrases sont simples mais généralement correctes même si des erreurs élémentaires sont possibles. Des efforts pour utiliser certains des faits de langue de l'unité (prétérit simple, voix passive, subordonnées relatives...). **A2/A2+**	Les phrases ne comportent presque pas d'erreurs élémentaires. Les structures étudiées en cours (prétérit simple, voix passive, subordonnées relatives...) sont souvent réutilisées et bien maîtrisées. **B1**	Les phrases ne comportent aucune erreur élémentaire. Les structures employées vont au-delà de ce qui a été étudié en cours. **B2**
Maîtrise du vocabulaire	Répertoire très restreint de mots simples. **A1**	Exploitation d'une partie des mots et expressions vus en cours, mais le répertoire est encore restreint. **A2**	Vocabulaire approprié et varié. De nombreux éléments du cours sont réexploités. **B1**	Emploi d'un répertoire très riche et précis qui va au-delà du lexique étudié dans l'unité. **B2**
Valeur chiffrée (équivalences)	De 5 à 9/20	De 10 à 15/20	De 16 à 20/20	Au-delà des attentes de 2de : objectifs du cycle terminal en vue.

Let's read a text

Your teacher will give you a text. Read it and answer the questions.

Maya Angelou was one of the world's most important writers and activists. She first thrilled the world with *I Know Why the Caged Bird Sings* (1969).

Let's listen to a short recording

CD-2 / PISTE-24

Listen to the recording and answer the questions.

Aretha Franklin performs at Radio City Music Hall in New York (2008).

Let's write

Use what you have learned to write a report on the subject, "The Power of Music".

8 Fair Play?

→ **ISSUE AT STAKE**
How can athletes serve as good role models for society?

ON YOUR WAY TO THE TASK

1 Team Spirit
Invite a famous athlete to attend a charity event

2 The Dark Side of Sport
Broadcast your own sports news report

3 Is Sport Political?
Write a tweet in response to a pro athlete's hashtag

YOUR FINAL TASK

Participate in a BBC documentary about the greatest sporting moments in history

1

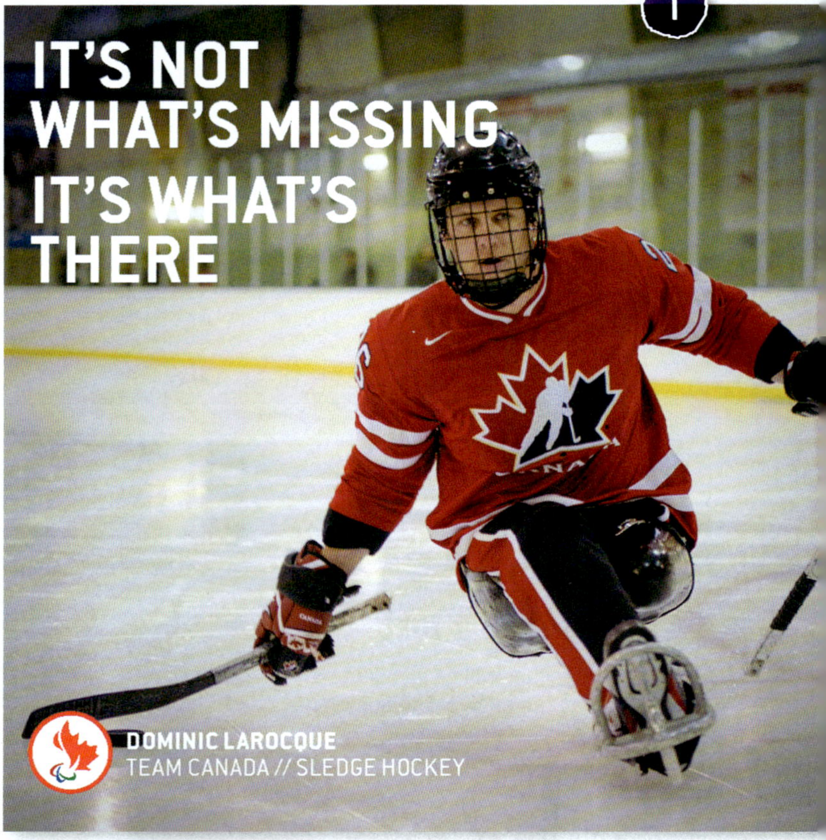

> "Serious sport has nothing to do with fair play. It is bound up with hatred, jealousy, boastfulness, disregard of all rules and sadistic pleasure in witnessing violence."
>
> George Orwell, British author

Sentiment d'appartenance

> I've failed over and over and over in my life and that is why I succeed.
>
> Michael Jordan, American basketball player

1. What sport do you play? How often?

- I play in a football / basketball team.
- I do gymnastics / karate three times a week.
- I go swimming / running every week.

2. Look at the posters. What sport do these athletes play?

3. Choose the word(s) that best describe(s) each poster: **discipline**, **cheating**, **discrimination**, **strength**, **fear**, **pride**, **determination**, **will power**. Explain your choices.

- I feel that... is the word that best describes... because...

4. Complete the sentences and associate each of them with one of the posters:

a. More needs to be done about...
b. Focus on..., not on...
c. Motivation to win comes from..., not from...

5. Read the quotes. What values does Michael Jordan associate with playing sport? What about George Orwell?

- Michael Jordan is actually saying that...
- According to George Orwell, ...

Toolbox

CD 2 PISTE 25 MP3 49

- anti-doping /'æntɪ 'dəʊpɪŋ/
- a disability /dɪsə'bɪlɪtɪ/: *un handicap*
- a disabled person /dɪs'eɪbld 'pɜːsn/: *une personne handicapée*
- a failure /'feɪljə/: *un échec*
- fair-play /feə-pleɪ/
- fear /fɪəʳ/ *la peur*
- pride /praɪd/: *l'orgueil*
- strength /streŋθ/: *la force*
- unfairness /ʌn'feənəs/: *l'injustice*
- to cheat /tʃiːt/: *tricher*
- to fail /feɪl/: *échouer*
  ≠ to succeed /sək'siːd/: *réussir*
- to promote positive values /prə'məʊt 'pɒzətɪv 'væljuːz/: *promouvoir des valeurs positives*

WB p. 41-43

Your Task
Invite a famous athlete to attend a charity event

1. Sport and Charity

1. Read the text. What is a student athlete? What is the overall message of the text?

- A student athlete is someone who…
- One thing they try to do is…

2. List words and phrases that describe the pros of being a student athlete.

3. How would you help your community if you were a student athlete?

- If I were a student athlete, I would + V…

Toolbox

CD 2 PISTE 26 MP3 50

- popular /'pɒpjʊləʳ/
- athletics /æθ'letɪks/: *l'athlétisme*
- a charity /'tʃærɪtɪ/: *une œuvre de bienfaisance*
- a commitment /kə'mɪtmənt/: *un engagement*
- a playing field /'pleɪɪŋ fi:ld/: *un terrain de sport*
- a role model /rəʊl 'mɒdl/: *un modèle*
- selflessness /'selflɪsnəs/: *l'altruisme*
- to encourage /ɪn'kʌrɪdʒ/
- to inspire /ɪn'spaɪəʳ/
- to integrate /'ɪntɪgreɪt/: *intégrer*
- to pass on /pɑ:s ɒn/: *transmettre*
- to volunteer /vɒlən'tɪəʳ/: *faire du bénévolat*

I have had the privilege of being a student athlete. This potential leadership role can open up many opportunities for you to make a difference on the court, in the classroom and also in the lives of others around you. (...) For example, if you go to help clean up a park, this allows for children to have a safer environment to play and makes the landscape look cleaner. This could create a domino effect. If others see that people are caring for their surroundings, this could inspire them to help with another neighborhood project. (...)

You can help your community by serving it with work; however, just as importantly, you can also make a difference by having a good attitude and loving the people around you. Athletics provides a unique opportunity that could be a model of self-lessness instead of being used for self-promotion.

Hannah Woodworth, ***MIAA Student Sportsmanship Essay*** (2011)

2. The Miracle League

CD 2 PISTES 27-29

1. Look at the poster. What could "a league of their own" refer to? **Anticipate**

- This must be a league that…

2. Listen to the first part of the recording. Were you correct? Complete your answer.

3. Finish the recording and answer these questions:

a. Who are the "buddies"?
b. What three roles do they have in the league?
c. What is unique about the playing field?

4. How has the Miracle League had a positive effect on the children?

- The Miracle League has allowed kids to…
- Thanks to the Miracle League…
- By playing in this league…

3. Pro Athletes Giving Back

nticipate

1. Look at the photos of two professional athletes. What do you think they are doing?

2. Group A reads the first text, and group B the second one. Answer the questions. Then, each group will explain what they have read.

a. Who are the excerpts about?
b. How have they helped others?
c. Why do you think they perform these acts of kindness?

3. Brainstorm other ways athletes can help their communities.

- There are a lot of things they can do.
- For instance, they can start / give...

4. How do these actions benefit people, their communities and themselves? Write a few lines about it.

- Visiting hospitals can really make a difference for...
- It probably gives the athletes a sense of...

LeBron James unveiled a legacy project, including a refurbished gymnasium, at the Boys and Girls Club of Southeast Louisiana-Westbank Unit in Gretna, Louisiana (2014).

TEXT 1

On Wednesday, January 9, 2013, LeBron James received a request from a fan on his Facebook page. In the post, James was asked if he would be able to meet Joey Anderson who was battling brain cancer and was going to be in attendance for the Heat's game in Portland. (...) Well, LeBron saw the post and made Joey's dream a reality. He took some time after the Heat's loss in Portland to meet him. (...) Acts like that remind us that professional athletes are regular people just like the rest of us.

Adapted from Christian Marin, **www.prosgiveback.com** (2013)

TEXT 2

American sprinter and 2008 Olympic gold medalist Mary Wineberg is a hero for reasons far beyond her gold medal and many successes on the track. (...) She has been a constant supporter and familiar face with Girls on the Run where she teaches, motivates and encourages young girls to stay active and follow their dreams. (...) She also makes continual visits to children's hospitals and runs after school programs once a month.

"I could never complain about anything because if I were in their shoes what would I do? I would want someone to do the same for me", explained Mary.

Michael Cecchin, **www.prosgiveback.com** (2014)

Mary Wineberg running with a group of young girls (2014).

Useful Grammar

Les subordonnées de condition → p. 177

- Condition relativement peu probable ou irréelle : ***if*** + prétérit modal, ***would*** + base verbale.

  If *we* ***hosted*** *a charity sports event, we* ***would raise*** *money.*

Le gérondif → p. 176

- Peut être utilisé comme sujet dans les subordonnées nominales dont la fonction est sujet.

  Helping *the community should be any pro athlete's goal.*

- Peut être utilisé dans les subordonnées nominales après les prépositions, notamment après ***by***, pour indiquer le moyen.

  You can make a difference ***by having*** *a good attitude.*

Your Task

Looking for a guest

Your community is holding a charity event to raise funds for the local sports centre. Write an email to a famous athlete persuading him/her to attend.

2 The Dark Side of Sport

WB p. 44

Your Task
Broadcast your own sports news report

1. Sending the Wrong Message

1. Read the two tweets. Who do you think Vincent Kompany is?

2. Why did Milan players "leave the pitch"?

3. Racism is not the only problem affecting sport today. Brainstorm 3-4 other issues.

4. What should be done about these problems?

- It's the responsibility of... to eradicate... They should...

2. The Fix Was On

Anticipate **1.** The phrases "*to fix a match*" and "*to make lots of money*" both appear in the text below. What do you think the text will be about?

2. Read the text and write down any information you find about: **people**, **places**, **dates**.

3. Close your book and sum up what you have understood. In pairs, check your work.

4. Put these sentences in chronological order.

a. He was pretending not to pay attention.
b. They were having a meeting.
c. He was told that a game had been fixed before.
d. He was informed that an agreement had been made.

5. What are some of the possible consequences of match-fixing? Think about the players, the fans and the effect on the sport itself.

- It takes away...
- It makes people...

Vincent Kompany
@VincentKompany
proud captain of @MCFC and the @BelRedDevils - @BXBrussels believer and international SOS Children's Villages ambassador
Manchester, UK
facebook.com/vincentkompany

303 Photos

TWEET 1
Vincent Kompany @VincentKompany
I can only salute Milan's decision to leave the pitch. Also noted that the majority of the fans were completely supportive of the players.

TWEET 2
Vincent Kompany @VincentKompany
Acts of racism against Boateng during Milan's game. How about becoming extremely intolerant towards racist idiots? They need to be told.

Toolbox

- a banned substance /bænd 'sʌbstəns/: *une substance interdite*
- a performance-enhancing drug /pə'fɔːmənsɪn'hɑːnsɪŋ drʌg/: *un produit dopant*
- sportsmanship /'spɔːtsmənʃɪp/: *l'esprit sportif*
- to address a problem /ə'dres ə 'prɒbləm/ = to tackle a problem /'tækl/: *s'attaquer à un problème*
- to ban /bæn/: *bannir, exclure, prohiber*
- to be banned /bɪ bænd/: *être exclu*
- to be under pressure /'preʃə/: *être sous pression*
- to benefit from /'benɪfɪt frɒm/: *profiter de*
- to eradicate /ɪ'rædɪkeɪt/
- to fine /faɪn/: *condamner à une amende*
- to fix /fɪks/: *truquer*
- to throw a match /θrəʊ ə mætʃ/: *perdre délibérément un match*

CD 2 PISTE 30 MP3 51

The four men were discussing how to fix a World Cup match in the 2006 finals. It was a little bizarre. In an anonymous, suburban shopping mall in northern Bangkok, the four men were planning to make lots of money and at the same time destroy the dreams of millions of people around the world. (...)

All the time, I was trying to listen as closely as possible, without looking as if I was listening, while trying to maintain my appearance as an overstressed businessman. (...)

At 1:59, I got a phone call. It was Chin. He sounded exultant. The problems were being solved. The fix was on.

Throughout the winter and spring of 2006, Chin and I kept in contact. He had talked about organizing the fix for the World Cup and one country had been mentioned repeatedly: Ghana. According to Chin, back in 2004 at the Olympics in Athens, some of his group were able to get close to some of the Ghana team and get them to throw their last game against Japan. I had no idea how good Ghana could or would be as a soccer team. Chin laughed at my ignorance.

"Do you think Japan could ever beat Ghana? You have to be kidding. Ghana has a good team. There is a player. I paid him $15,000."

Declan Hill, ***The Fix: Soccer and Organised Crime*** (2008)

3. One Big Liar

CD 2 PISTE 31

1. Brainstorm facts about Lance Armstrong. **Anticipate**

2. Find out more about Lance Armstrong. Group A reads the quotes, and group B listens to the recording.

Group A: explain how he defended himself.

- In 2001, he said that...
- He also claimed that...

Group B: sum up Armstrong's confessions to Oprah.

- When he was asked if / whether..., he said / replied / admitted / confessed...

3. Each group presents the main ideas of their document to the other group, who takes notes.

4. Imagine you are a journalist. Write a summary detailing the lies and Lance Armstrong's eventual confession for your newspaper.

5. What are your personal views on Lance Armstrong?

6. Why do you think people cheat in sport?

- I think that most of the time they do it because...
- They must / might do it so as to + V...
- They might be afraid of + V-ing...

DENIAL 1 "Everybody wants to know: what am I on. What am I on? I'm on my bike, busting my ass six hours a day." (Commercial for Nike, 2001)

DENIAL 2 **"Luke's name is Armstrong and people know that name; and when he goes to school I don't want them to say, 'Oh yeah, your dad's the big fake, the doper.' That would just kill me."** (Extract from the book *Every Second Counts*, 2003)

DENIAL 3 "How many times do I have to say it? Well, it can't be any clearer than 'I've never taken drugs'." (Videotaped testimony in lawsuit, 2005)

DENIAL 4 **"I came out of a life-threatening disease. You think I'm going to come back into a sport and say, 'OK, OK doctor, give me everything you've got, I just want to go fast?' No way! I would never do that."** (Public forum, Aspen, 2007)

DENIAL 5 "At the end of the day, I have nothing to hide." (AP interview, 2009)

Pronunciation

CD 2 PISTE 32 MP3 52

Le « *i* » court et le « *i* » long

"Lance Armstrong came clean, almost as if he'd just decided to flip a switch from somewhere deep inside."

1. Écoutez cette phrase et classez les mots avec des voyelles en rouge en fonction de leur prononciation : /ɪ/ ou /iː/.
2. Regardez l'orthographe des mots. Qu'en déduisez-vous sur la prononciation du « *i* » ?
3. Comment sont prononcés ***decided*** et ***inside*** ? Pourquoi la prononciation du « *i* » est-elle différente ?
4. Entraînez-vous à prononcer cette phrase en marquant bien la différence entre les deux « *i* ».

Useful Grammar

Le prétérit simple, le *past perfect*, le prétérit en *be* + V-*ing* → p. 169-170

- Pour faire part d'évènements révolus : prétérit simple.
  *We **kept** in contact throughout the winter.*
- Pour désigner un évènement antérieur à un évènement passé : *past perfect*.
  *In 2005, he insisted that he **had** never **taken** performance-enhancing drugs.*
- Pour décrire une situation, une scène, un cadre pour les évènements du récit : *prétérit en* **be** + V-**ing**.
  *They **were discussing** how to fix a football match.*

Le style indirect dans un récit au prétérit → p. 179

- Le passage au discours indirect passé implique des ajustements au niveau :
  - des adjectifs et des pronoms (***I*** → ***he***/***she*** ; ***me*** → ***him***/***her*** ; ***my*** → ***his***/***her***).
  - des temps (présent → prétérit ; prétérit → *past perfect, present perfect* → *past perfect*).
  - des outils et de l'ordre des mots pour les énoncés interrogatifs.
    ***Did you** feel bad?* → *She **asked him** if **he had felt** bad.*
  - des repères de temps et de lieu (***now*** → ***then*** ; ***here*** → ***there***).

Your Task

Breaking news

Record a 30-second radio segment about an incident of cheating in sport. Use clear, concise sentences to keep the audience's attention. Three, two, one... You're on air!

Is Sport Political?

WB p. 45-46

Your Task
Write a tweet in response to a pro athlete's hashtag

1. The "Auld Enemy"

Anticipate **1.** Look at the cartoon below. What was the cartoonist trying to say about sport?

- Well, it shows how sometimes sport...
- I guess the author wants to show that...

2. Read the text and jot down all the words that refer to some kind of rivalry or opposition.

3. List the different nationalities in the text and explain who opposes who.

4. Explain the meaning of the quote "*This is politics of a different sort*" (l. 3-4).

- Sometimes, sport can serve as...

5. Do you know of any other sport rivalries? Do they have any political connotations?

- I know that in rugby, there's a huge rivalry between...

6. Group A will look for the positive aspects of a sport rivalry, and group B will look for the negative aspects. Then, both groups will participate in a class debate.

- Having a rival can help you to... / can be positive when...
- When / If you have a tough rival..., you...
- That's a good point, but...
- But it can also lead to...
- I agree / disagree...

When the Welsh, Scots and Irish, along with the representatives of some of the former dominions, take on the English, this is politics of a different sort, a response to old wounds and long-distant but never-to-be-forgotten antagonisms (...). When the Welsh win at rugby, the Scots at football, or the Australians at anything at all, victory is all the sweeter because the English have been vanquished. When the Scots take the field against the English at football or rugby, their anthem tells of victory against the "auld enemy" on the battlefield, and their supporters are exhorting the players to repeat the feat on the field of play. They sing of their ancestors "Who fought and died for / Their wee bit hill and glen / And stood against them / Proud Edward's army / And sent them homeward / Tae think again".

Nigel Townson, ***The British at Play. A Social History of British Sport from 1600 to the Present*** (1997)

Mark Knight, Australian cartoonist, *Herald Sun* (2013)

Toolbox

CD 2 PISTE 33 MP3 53

- a political stage /pəˈlɪtɪkəl steɪdʒ/: *une scène politique*
- a rivalry /ˈraɪvəlrɪ/: *une rivalité*
- a showdown /ˈʃəʊdaʊn/: *une confrontation*
- to fight for sth /faɪt fəʳ/ ≠ to fight against sth /faɪt əˈgenst/: *se battre pour / contre qqch*
- to make a statement /meɪk ə ˈsteɪtmənt/: *affirmer un point de vue*
- to protest for / against /prəʊˈtest/
- to show solidarity with /ʃəʊ sɒlɪˈdærɪtɪ/: *faire preuve de solidarité envers*
- to stand up for sth /stænd ʌp fəʳ/: *se battre pour qqch*
- to support /səˈpɔːt/: *soutenir*

20th Century

1936
Berlin. The Nazis used the games to promote the ideology of racial superiority. But the effort backfired when Jesse Owens, a black American track star, won four gold medals.

1960
Rome. South Africa was excluded because of its racist regime. Ethiopian marathon runner Abebe Bikila, running barefoot, became the first black African Olympic champion.

1968
Mexico City. Black American track stars Tommie Smith and John Carlos gave the Black Power salute during the award ceremony.

2. Political Games

1. Match the photos from the Olympics to the stories in the timeline.

- In my opinion, picture 1 was taken at the...
- I reckon that picture 2 was taken...
- Picture 3 goes with... because...

2. You are doing an internship at a photography agency and you have to caption these three photos (description of the scene, context and date) in no more than 50 words. Specify four keywords to archive them.

3. Black Power

nticipate

1. Look at the screenshot. Which of the stories in the timeline relate to the video?

2. Watch the video and try to explain the reasons for their protest.

3. The athletes protested in four different ways. What were they?

4. What point did they want to make? Match the four forms of protest to the points below:

a. to represent workers
b. to protest against the lynching of black people
c. to support the Civil Rights Movement
d. to denounce poverty in the U.S.

5. What happened to the athletes afterwards? Do you think it was right or wrong?

- They should / shouldn't have been allowed to...

Video Time

DVD PISTE 17

Your Task

Tweet!

A pro athlete that you follow on Twitter has created the hashtag #no_politics_in_sports. Tweet your opinion about this hashtag. You can also react to your classmates' tweets.

1980

Moscow. In protest of the invasion of Afghanistan, more than 60 western nations boycotted the Moscow games. In response, the Soviet Union led a boycott of the Los Angeles games four years later.

21th Century

2008

Beijing. The games sparked protests by human rights groups who claimed that allowing China to host the games legitimized its environmental and human rights violations.

2014

Sochi. Equal rights activists around the world gathered in protest in the run-up to the Sochi games, a response to Russia's so-called "gay propaganda" ban.

The Art of Fielding

by Chad Harbach (2011)

CD 2 PISTE 34 MP3 54

After his freshperson year[1] ended, Henry stayed at Westish to train with Schwartz. They met at five thirty every morning. When Henry could run up and down all the stairs in the football stadium without stopping, Schwartz bought him a weighted vest. When he could run five seven-minute miles, Schwartz made him do it on the sand. When he could do it on the sand, Schwartz made him do it with lake water lapping at his knees. Medicine balls, blocking sleds, yoga, bicycles, ropes, tree branches, steel trash cans, plyometrics — no implements or ideas were too mundane[2] or exotic. At seven thirty, the sun still low over the lake, Henry showered and headed to the dining hall to wash breakfast dishes for the summer-school kids. After his shift, he walked to Westish Field, where Schwartz set up the pitching machine and the video camera. Henry hit ball after ball until he could hardly lift his arms. Then they went to the VAC to lift weights. In the evenings, they played on a summer team in Appleton.

Henry had never felt so happy. Freshperson year had been one thing, an adventure, an exhilaration, all in all a success, but it had also been exhausting, a constant struggle and adjustment and tumult. Now he was locked in. Every day that summer had the same framework, the alarm at the same time, meals and workouts and shifts and SuperBoost at the same times, over and over, and it was that sameness, that repetition, that gave life meaning. He savored the tiny variations, the incremental improvements — tuna fish on his salad instead of turkey; two extra reps on the bench press[3]. Every move he made had purpose. While they worked out, Schwartz would recite lines from his favorite philosophers, Marcus Aurelius and Epictetus (...), and Henry felt he understood. *Every day is a war.* Yes, yes it was. *The key is to keep company only with people who uplift you, whose presence calls forth your best.* Done: there was only one of those. He was becoming a baseball player.

By the time his sophomore[4] season began, Henry had gained twelve pounds. He was still one of the smaller guys on the team, but the bat felt different in his hands, lighter and more lively. He batted .348 and was named the first-team Upper Midwestern Small Colleges Athletic Conference shortstop[5]. In thirty-one games he didn't make a single error. He was still shy in class and around campus — he never went to the bars and rarely to parties; there was too much work to do — but among his teammates he flourished[6]. He loved those guys and felt good in their midst, and now that he was undisputedly the best player on the team, he became something of a leader. He wasn't loud like Schwartz, but everyone listened when he spoke. The Harpooners finished .500 for the first time in a decade.

1. première année d'université ou de lycée - **2.** banal - **3.** appareil de musculation - **4.** deuxième année - **5.** arrêt-court (au baseball) - **6.** s'épanouir

BUILDING YOUR JOURNAL...

Workbook, p. 74

Biography

Chad Harbach (born in 1975) grew up in Wisconsin and was educated at Harvard and the University of Virginia. His debut novel, *The Art of Fielding*, follows the baseball team at a small liberal arts college in Wisconsin. The book specifically centers on Henry Skrimshander, the star of the team, and his best friend, Mike Schwartz. Amazon named *The Art of Fielding* the best book of 2011.

The photographer of BOXING

Neil Leifer is probably the world's most iconic sports photographer. His body of work stretches across virtually every sport and well beyond the field of play. Of all the sports that he has covered, "Boxing", says Leifer "is the one I still love shooting." In a recent cover story by the *London Observer* titled "The World's 50 Greatest Sports Photographs", Leifer's Ali vs. Williams photograph was chosen as the number one. The Ali vs. Liston picture was chosen number two. Let's take a good look at both of them.

ALI VS. WILLIAMS

Leifer's favourite photograph was taken from the rafters of the Houston Astrodome looking down on the ring during a fight between the great boxer, Muhammad Ali, and Cleveland Williams in 1966. In this amazing aerial picture, Ali strikes a victory pose as Williams lies unconscious on the white canvas surrounded by spectators and press, the referee counting him out. It's his favourite shot because, "It can never be taken again. Today the ring is a series of ads. You'd never get the clean canvas."

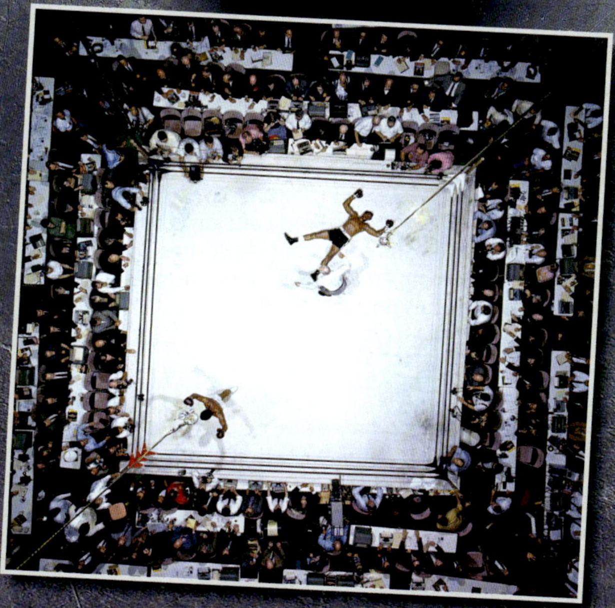

Aerial of Muhammad Ali victorious after knocking out Cleveland Williams.

ALI VS. LISTON

A year earlier, Leifer shot one of the most memorable sport photos of all time. It was taken at the Heavyweight Championship match between Muhammad Ali and Sonny Liston. The picture shows Ali's reaction after knocking out Liston in the first round. Instead of retreating to a neutral corner of the ring, Ali stood over Liston yelling, "Get up and fight, sucker!"

Ali and Leifer hold a print of the photographer's iconic Ali vs. Liston knockout photo.

Digital ZONE

Make a sport photography exhibition. Look for a sport photograph that you like. Paste the photo in a document, write a description, and print it. All the projects will be placed on a classroom wall to make an exhibition.

BUILDING YOUR JOURNAL...

Workbook, p. 75

Let's Practise Grammar

community.emdl.fr
exercices interactifs

Les subordonnées de condition

1 Complétez les dialogues suivants en mettant les verbes entre parenthèses au mode et au temps qui conviennent.

1. SAM: Which trainers (**you / buy**) if you (**be**) me?
BERNIE: Mmm, both are nice. If I (**be**) you, I think I (**get**) the red ones. They're much cooler.

2. NED: Can I borrow your tennis racket?
JOSH: If I (**have**) it, I (**lend**) it to you, but it's being repaired.

3. SHAUN: If you (**can**) meet any famous athlete, dead or alive, who (**it / be**)?
RACHEL: It (**have**) to be Muhammed Ali. He's a legend!

Le prétérit simple, le *past perfect*, le prétérit en *be* + V-*ing*

2 Complétez l'histoire de Fred Lorz, un coureur de fond américain, en conjugant les verbes entre parenthèses aux temps qui conviennent. Plusieurs réponses sont parfois possibles.

It was a hot summer's day and Fred Lorz ... (**get**) ready to compete in the 1904 St. Louis Olympic marathon. He ... (**qualify**) early that month and most people ... (**expect**) him to do well, but nobody thought that he was going to win.

But that is exactly what he did. He ... (**cross**) the finish line with a time of 3 hours and 13 minutes and won the race. Alice Roosevelt, the President's daughter, and Lorz ... (**have**) their picture taken at the award ceremony when suddenly the crowd started to shout, 'Cheat'.

Some spectators ... (**say**) that they ... (**see**) Lorz get into his manager's car at the 14 km mark. Others ... (**claim**) that they ... (**witness**) Lorz getting out of a car at the 18 km mark.

Eventually, Lorz ... (**admit**) that it ... (**all be**) one big practical joke.

Le gérondif

3 Formulez des phrases complètes à partir des éléments suivants, en mettant les verbes en majuscules au gérondif ou à la forme ***by*** + gérondif.

1. WIN the match / Serena Williams / become number one
2. ERADICATE violence in sport / be a priority
3. professional athletes / help communities / ATTEND local charity events
4. COMPETE in the Olympic Games / be an experience like no other in the world
5. FIGHT racism / athletes / send out a positive message to the world
6. TAKE PART in sporting activities / students / learn core values

Le style indirect dans un récit au prétérit

4 Les phrases suivantes ont été transformées au discours indirect. Choisissez la bonne formulation dans chaque cas.

1. "I've run two marathons," Jennifer told us.
a. Jennifer told us that she has run two marathons.
b. Jennifer told us that she had run two marathons.
c. Jennifer told us that she would run two marathons.

2. "I'll meet you here tomorrow," said Sue to Matt.
a. Sue said to Matt that she would meet him there the following day.
b. Sue said to Matt that she would meet him here tomorrow.
c. Sue said to Matt that she will meet him here the following day.

3. "Was it a good match yesterday?" my mother asked.
a. My mother asked if it had been a good match yesterday.
b. My mother asked if had it been a good match the day before.
c. My mother asked if it had been a good match the day before.

4. "How often do you go running?" the doctor asked.
a. The doctor asked how often did I go running.
b. The doctor asked how often I did go running.
c. The doctor asked how often I went running.

... and Vocabulary

Compound nouns

1 Créez des noms composés en utilisant les mots ci-dessous. Puis, utilisez-les pour compléter les phrases proposées.

charity · playing · model · student · stage · field · fair · play · political · athletes · role · event

1. Messi is a good ... for many young boys because he does a lot of charity work.
2. Some athletes have used the Olympics as a ... to get their messages across to the world.
3. Holding a ..., such as a concert, helps to raise money for people in need.
4. The match was called off because the ... was in such poor condition.
5. ... should help younger children in their community to improve their lives.
6. The referee's job is to ensure ..., but today he let the other team cheat.

Good sportsmanship?

2 Classez ces mots selon qu'ils renvoient, d'après vous, à des valeurs ou à des problèmes existant dans le monde du sport. Expliquez chacun de vos choix en une phrase.

teamwork · ambition · resilience · match-fixing · rivalry · doping · respect · pressure · jealousy · discipline · fair play

Sport actions

3 Avec quel verbe associe-t-on ces sports ? Placez chacun d'eux dans la colonne du tableau qui lui correspond.

tennis • sailing • skiing • karate • football
chess • gymnastics • skating • yoga

play	do	go

4 Dans quels sports pouvez-vous effectuer les actions suivantes ?

1. to win a set
2. to score a touchdown
3. to checkmate
4. to shoot a 3-pointer
5. to score a homerun
6. to take a penalty

5 Quel verbe ne peut pas s'employer avec le mot en gras ? Trouvez l'intrus dans chaque liste.

a. beat / win / lose / draw **a match**
b. beat / defeat / lose to / win **an opponent**
c. score / miss / make / let in **a goal**
d. hold / do / break / set **a record**
e. cheat / fix / throw / cheat at **a game**
f. get / take / do / give **a penalty**

Talking about principles

6 Utilisez les éléments ci-dessous pour reformuler les phrases proposées. Attention aux modifications éventuelles !

give up · stand up for something · believe in something/someone · pass something on · show solidarity with something

1. Even though he lost the year before, it didn't stop him trying to win the next year.
   → He never...
2. Although they knew that they might lose their medals, the girls defended gay rights.
   → The girls ... gay rights.
3. He hoped that by teaching his daughter to play chess, he would teach her the value of patience.
   → He hoped to ... by teaching her to play chess.
4. His father always knew his son would succeed in life.
   → His father never stopped ... his son.
5. They demonstrated their support by joining the black community on the march.
   → They ... the black community by joining them on the march.

Your Final Task

Participate in a BBC documentary about the greatest sporting moments in history

1 The BBC has asked teenagers worldwide to film a short video clip explaining a memorable sporting moment or event. Clips should be 30 seconds to 2 minutes long.

2 Brainstorm and look on the Internet. Here are some ideas: France winning the soccer World Cup in 1998; Michael Phelps winning 8 gold medals in the 2008 Olympics; Usain Bolt winning the 100 metre dash; Maradona and the hand of God, the London 2012 Olympics, etc.

3 Jot down details of the event: place, date, players/teams, what happened, why it is a great moment in sporting history, your memories of the event (if you have any)...

4 Action! Record your clip.

Toolbox

CD 2 PISTE 35 MP3 55

- One moment that will always stick in my mind...
- ... is by far one of the most memorable moments...
- The crowd was behind him/her/them.
- It was a demonstration of sheer determination / power.
- It was an unbelievable / jaw-dropping performance.
- People will talk about it for years to come.
- It/He/She will go down in history as being...

Tips & Tricks

→ **Rehearse, rehearse, rehearse!** Entraînez-vous devant un miroir ou enregistrez-vous jusqu'à ce que votre discours soit fluide et vos gestes naturels.

→ **Look the part!** Pour être diffusée par la BBC, votre vidéo doit être de qualité ! Choisissez bien le lieu du tournage, faites attention au son et à l'image, et soignez votre apparence.

→ **Spruce it up!** Pour capter l'attention des auditeurs et illustrer votre propos, n'hésitez pas à montrer des photos à l'écran ou à faire écouter un témoignage.

“After the game, Nadal said that it was impossible to explain what he felt when he won the last point.”

“I'm not a big fan of Nadal, but that day, he showed the world his strength of character by fighting for every point and never giving up.”

“In my opinion, the 2008 Wimbledon final is the greatest match ever played. It was an epic final.”

On Your Way to the Exam

Let's prepare your final task

Lorsque *vous vous entraînez à témoigner pour le documentaire de la BBC, prêtez attention aux critères d'évaluation ci-dessous : où vous situez-vous dans chaque ligne ?*

	Niveau 1	Niveau 2	Niveau 3 (→ B1)	Niveau 4
Réalisation de la tâche	Présentation d'une vidéo d'environ 30 secondes. Le thème (*a memorable sporting moment*) est traité. Les idées sont simplement juxtaposées.	La plupart des éléments demandés (lieu, date, sportif(s) impliqués, etc.) sont traités, mais présentés de manière peu élaborée. La vidéo dure près d'une minute, mais se limite à un plan fixe.	Tous les éléments demandés sont traités. Des efforts pour complexifier le propos et le rendre vivant. La vidéo dure près de deux minutes et offre quelques idées de mise en scène.	Le témoignage produit est remarquable pour l'intérêt de son contenu et la qualité formelle de sa réalisation (son et image). Le propos est argumenté et convaincant.
Qualité de la production orale	La prononciation est compréhensible avec des efforts, malgré une lecture serrée des notes. A1	La prononciation est suffisamment claire pour être généralement comprise, malgré un net accent étranger. A2 Quelques tentatives pour regarder son auditoire, mais le recours aux notes est encore très fréquent.	Le discours est assez fluide. La prononciation est toujours intelligible, malgré un accent étranger et quelques erreurs de prononciation. B1 La lecture des notes est occasionnelle et la gestuelle est souvent adaptée au message transmis.	La prononciation se rapproche de l'authenticité. Un auditeur natif n'aurait pas de mal à comprendre. B2 Le discours est fluide et le recours aux notes rare. La gestuelle est adaptée au message, le contact visuel presque permanent.
Maîtrise de la grammaire et du vocabulaire	Les phrases sont très brèves. Les formes grammaticales sont assez intelligibles mais limitées et répétitives. Emploi d'un répertoire très restreint de mots simples. A1/A1+	Les phrases restent simples mais généralement correctes. Des erreurs élémentaires sont possibles. Des efforts pour employer certains des faits de langue de l'unité (style indirect, prétérit...). Exploitation d'une partie des mots et expressions vus en cours, mais le répertoire est encore restreint. A2/A2+	Les phrases ne comportent pratiquement pas d'erreurs élémentaires. Les structures étudiées dans l'unité sont fréquemment réutilisées et bien maîtrisées. De nombreux éléments lexicaux du cours sont réemployés. B1	Les phrases ne comportent aucune erreur élémentaire. Les structures employées vont au-delà de ce qui a été étudié en cours. Emploi d'un répertoire lexical riche et précis. B2
Valeur chiffrée (équivalences)	**De 5 à 9/20**	**De 10 à 15/20**	**De 16 à 20/20**	**Au-delà des attentes de 2de : objectifs du cycle terminal en vue.**

Let's read a text

Your teacher will give you a text. Read it and answer the questions.

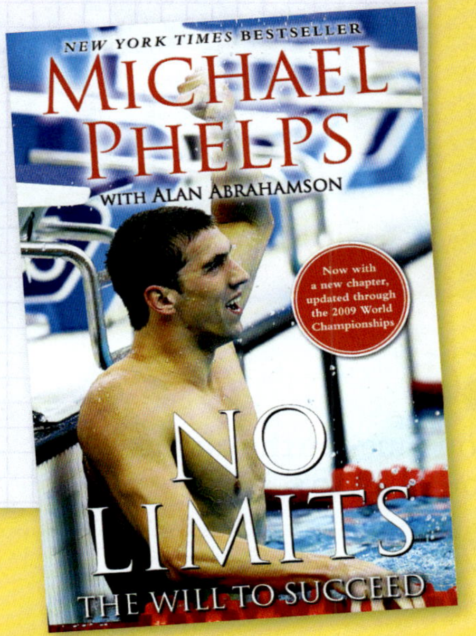

Michael Phelps is one of the greatest competitors the world has ever seen. In *No Limits* (2008) he explores the hard work, commitment, and sacrifice that go into reaching any goal.

Let's watch a video

DVD / PISTE-18

Watch the video and answer the questions your teacher will give you.

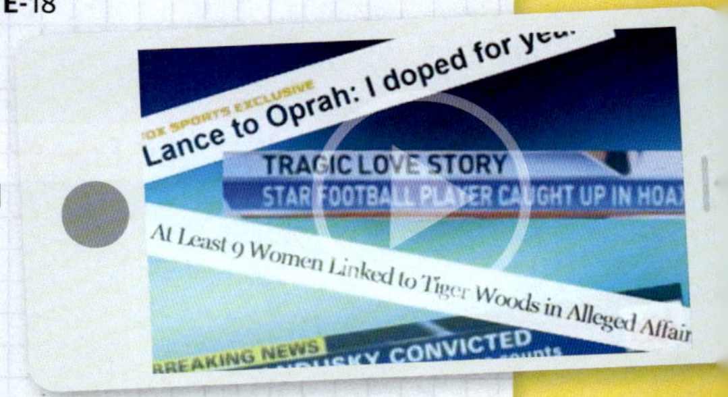

Inside the Numbers: Athletes as Role Models, a program aired on SportsKnight (2013)

Let's write

Use what you have learned to answer the following question: Are athletes role models to you? Why or Why not?

9 Get Involved

> We make a living by what we get, but we make a life by what we give.
>
> Winston Churchill, British politician

→ **ISSUE AT STAKE**

Why and how do people get involved?

ON YOUR WAY TO THE TASK

1 **Be the Change**

Create a leaflet to encourage young people to volunteer

2 **Great Change Makers**

Write an application letter to the Giving Pledge

3 **Opportunities for Everyone**

Write an article about microcredit for Wikipedia

YOUR FINAL TASK

Nominate a candidate for the Nobel Peace Prize

1

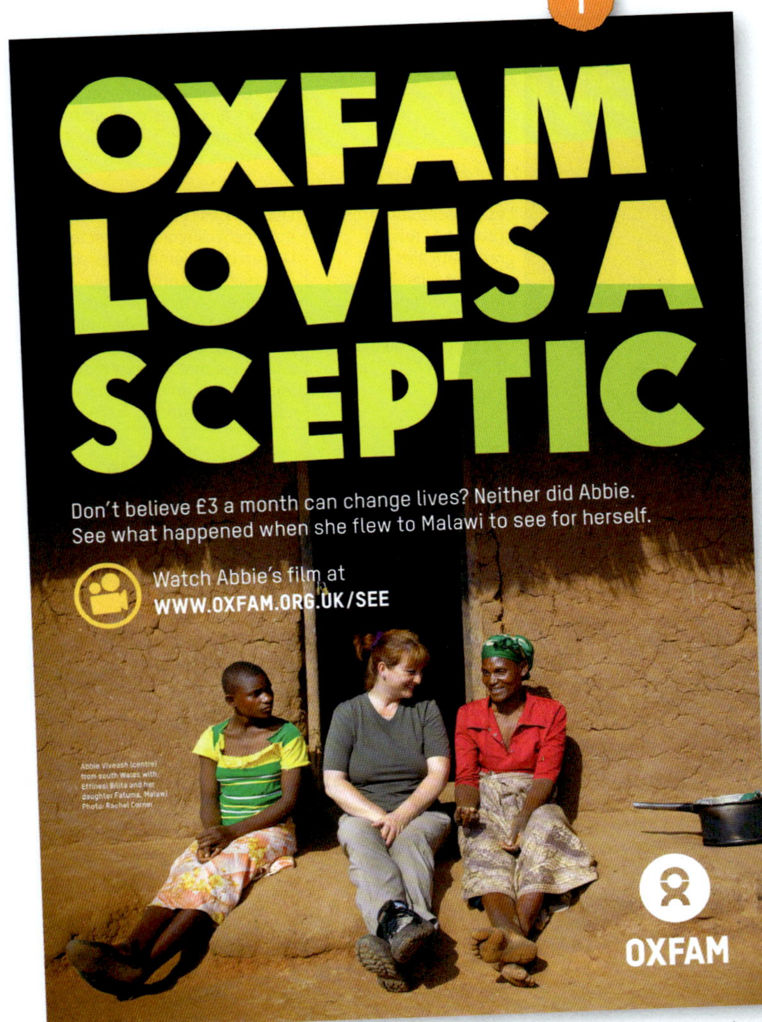

Oxfam fundraising campaign (2012)

> You must be the change you want to see in the world.
>
> Mahatma Gandhi, leader of India's independence movement

A Singapore Red Cross campaign (2010)

2

3

British Heart Foundation raises money by running at the London Marathon (2013)

> The man who dies rich, dies disgraced.
>
> Andrew Carnegie, Scottish-American industrialist and philanthropist

> The best way to cheer yourself up is to cheer somebody else up.
>
> Mark Twain, American author

1. Associate each poster with one or more of these concepts: **donating**, **raising money**, **making a difference**, **volunteering overseas**, **saving lives**. Give your reasons.

- I would say that the Oxfam campaign is about…
- Quite obviously, number 3 is about…

2. Read the quotes. Use your own words to explain what you think each person meant.

- Gandhi is basically saying that…
- This one is about the importance of + N / V-ing…
- Mark Twain argues that if you help others…

3. Which quote(s) ring(s) true to you?

- Twain's quote rings true to me because…
- I like Churchill's quote best because…

GO FURTHER… www.community.emdl.fr

Watch a Starbucks campaign promoting local volunteerism that uses **"Grassroots Movement"**, a song by MC Yogi.

1. List all the rhymes that you understand.

2. What is the message of the song?

Toolbox

CD 2 PISTE 36 MP3 56

- disgraced /dɪs'greɪst/: *déshonoré*
- generous /'dʒenərəs/
- selfless /'selflɪs/ ≠ selfish /'selfɪʃ/: *altruiste ≠ égoïste*

- a charity /'tʃærɪtɪ/: *une association caritative*
- a contribution /ˌkɒntrɪ'bjuːʃən/
- a donor /'dəʊnər/: *un donateur*

- to cheer sb up /tʃɪər 'sʌmbədɪ ʌp/: *réconforter qqn*
- to contribute to /kən'trɪbjuːt/: *contribuer à*
- to donate /dəʊ'neɪt/ = to give /gɪv/
- to earn a salary /ɜːn ə 'sælərɪ/ / to earn a living /ɜːn ə 'lɪvɪŋ/: *gagner un salaire / sa vie*
- to get involved /get ɪn'vɒlvd/: *s'impliquer*
- to promote /prə'məʊt/: *promouvoir*
- to raise funds /reɪz fʌndz/: *collecter des fonds*
- to support /sə'pɔːt/ = to advocate /'ædvəkeɪt/

 WB p. 47-48

Your Task
Create a leaflet encouraging young people to volunteer

1. Change Someone's Life: Your Own

Anticipate

1. In your opinion, why do people volunteer?
   - I think that most people who volunteer want to...
   - Volunteering is a way to...
   - Volunteering can make you feel + ADJ...

2. Look at the poster. What is the goal of this campaign?
   - It looks like the main objective is...
   - The campaign is trying to get people to + V...
   - It encourages people to + V... / into + V-ing...

3. How do you think the boy in the poster helps people?

4. What positive effects has volunteering had on the boy in the poster?
   - He has become more...

5. If you decided to volunteer, what cause would you support? Give reasons.
   - If I volunteered, I would focus on + V-ing... / look for an organisation that...

A TOUCH OF CULTURE

Oxfam is an international organisation working in various countries worldwide to find practical, innovative ways for people to lift themselves out of poverty.

A volunteer recruitment campaign for Oxfam's shops in the U.K. (2014)

2. Improve Your Skills

CD 2 PISTE 37

1. How can volunteering teach you valuable job skills? Anticipate
   - If you volunteer, you will have to...
   - I would say it can help you + V...

2. Margaret, Michael and Lucinda all volunteered to work for an international charity. Listen and answer the following questions:
   - a. What have they done? Where?
   - b. What have they learned?

Pronunciation

CD 2 PISTE 38 MP3 57

Forme forte ou forme faible ?

Écoutez cet extrait de l'audio « Improve Your Skills ». Concentrez-vous sur la prononciation de ***have***.

1. Identifiez la forme forte et la forme faible de ***have***.
2. Examinez le rôle de ***have*** dans ces phrases. Pourquoi y a-t-il deux prononciations possibles ?

Useful Grammar

Les subordonnées de condition → p. 177
- Condition probable : ***if*** + sujet + V au présent, sujet + ***will*** + base verbale.
  *If you **volunteer**, you **will meet** new people.*
- Condition moins probable ou irréelle : ***if*** + sujet + V au prétérit, sujet + ***would*** + base verbale.
  *If I **joined** this charity, I **would travel** to Africa.*

Le gérondif en fonction de sujet → p. 176
- Le gérondif peut avoir une fonction de sujet.
  ***Volunteering** in community work can change you life for good.*

Le *present perfect* → p. 169
- On l'emploie pour exprimer une situation présente qui porte en elle la trace du passé.
  *My experience as a volunteer in the Philippines **has taught** me how to work with limited resources.*

2. Angels Among Us

icipate

1. Look at the pictures on this page. What do you think these people do to help others?

2. You are going to learn about two projects that make a difference. Group A will watch the video and group B will read the text. Answer the questions and jot down any other information that you find relevant:

- **a.** How do they help others?
- **b.** Who benefits from their actions?
- **c.** Why did they start helping their communities?

3. Share your notes with the other group. Then, summarise your findings in an article for *YES! Magazine*, a publication that focuses on people working for a better tomorrow.

Video Time

DVD PISTE 19

VIDEO

Angels Among Us, TV show (2014)

TEXT

Joel Harper, 18, volunteers at T13 Urban Sports Academy, Belfast. He tells us how he incorporates his passion for BMX into his volunteer role.

What does your volunteer work involve?
My volunteer work on a day-to-day basis includes things like opening the park, making sure it is safe — for example, no dust or leaks that anyone could slip on and potentially hurt themselves —, giving safety instructions so that people know the rules and regulations, fixing equipment, cooking in the burger van... The list goes on.

What inspired you to get involved?
I just loved the place that much from riding BMX that I wanted to be involved in that type of environment and be a part of the team. :-)

What do you enjoy most about volunteering?
I just love the whole atmosphere of T13 and because it lets me get into opportunities that I wouldn't be able to get into anywhere else. For example, I've been awarded and trained for things like child protection, first aid, safety hygiene...

What advice would you give someone starting to volunteer?
Think about what you would like to get involved in, try it and see how it goes. You will feel better about yourself at the end of it because knowing that you have helped others is a great achievement alone.

Adapted from **www.volunteernow.co.uk** (2015)

Toolbox

CD 2 PISTE 39 MP3 58

- helpful /ˈhelpfl/: *utile*
- a graduate /ˈgrædjuɪt/: *un diplômé*
- people in need /ˈpiːpl ɪn niːd/: *les gens dans le besoin*
- (professional) skills /skɪlz/ = abilities /əˈbɪlɪtɪz/
- to benefit from /ˈbenɪfɪt/: *bénéficier de*
- to care for others /keə fə ˈʌðəˈz/: *s'occuper de*
- to encourage someone to do sth /ɪnˈkʌrɪdʒ/
- to have a degree in /dɪˈgriː/: *avoir un diplôme / une maîtrise en*
- to persuade people into + V-ing /pəˈsweɪd/

Your Task

Help others!
Create a leaflet to encourage young people to volunteer in an organisation (Oxfam, Red Cross...). Talk about the benefits of volunteering and ways they could get involved and help others.

WB p. 49-50

Your Task
Write an application letter to the Giving Pledge

1. A Philanthropist

Anticipate

1. Do you think that millionaires have a moral obligation to help others?
- I think that it depends on...
- I definitely feel that...
- I don't see why...

2. Read the text quickly and match each paragraph to one of these titles: **Ways of giving away your wealth**, **Giving responsibly**, **Becoming wealthy**.

3. Read it again.

a. What did Carnegie decide to do in 1901? And after?

b. What was his opinion about the best way to use his fortune?
- He thought that...
- He'd rather use it to... than to...

4. Do you agree with Carnegie?
- I (quite / totally) agree / disagree with him because...

Andrew Carnegie (1835-1919)

If you are incredibly rich, what will you do with all your money when you die? When, in 1901, he sold his huge iron and steel interests, Andrew Carnegie became the richest individual of his age. Noting the obvious, that "you can't take it with you" when you die, he went through the ways that a rich person can get rid of their fortune.

As a general rule, he noted, most fortunes are not passed on because of thoughts of the welfare of children, but because of family pride. But what use was pride when you were dead? Much better, he felt, to distribute your fortune during your lifetime, using the same imagination and diligence that you had displayed in creating it. This meant avoiding the typical philanthropist's path of "giving it away to charity", but working actively yourself to ensure maximum social benefit for your bucks.

According to Carnegie, it was a waste of money to give directly to those who had nothing. Resources should only go to those who could help themselves, and to worthwhile public projects that government did not have the funds to build.

Adapted from Tom Butler-Bowdon's ***50 Prosperity Classics*** (2008)

2. A Club for Billionaires

Anticipate

1. Look at the screenshot. Do you recognise any of the people?
- I guess the second from the right is...
  The woman is probably...

2. Find the definition of "a pledge".
- A pledge is...

3. Watch the first part of the video. What is the Giving Pledge initiative?

4. Watch the second part. Take notes on:
- who they are.
- their contribution.
- the reasons for their philanthropy.
- their feelings about it.
- what they want to accomplish or have already accomplished.

Video Time

DVD PISTES 20-22

The Giving Pledge, ABC News (2010)

A TOUCH OF CULTURE

Members of the **Giving Pledge** are free to choose the particular cause or organization they wish to support. Health, education, technological advances and people in need, are just some of the areas that stand to gain from the Giving Pledge.

Useful Grammar

Since* et *for → p. 170

- ***Since*** s'emploie avec le *present perfect simple* ou le *present perfect* en ***be*** + V-***ing*** pour désigner le **début d'une période** qui s'étend jusqu'au moment où l'on parle.
  *He **has been fighting** global poverty **since 1945**.*
- ***For*** s'emploie avec le *present perfect simple* ou le *present perfect* en ***be*** + V-***ing*** pour désigner la **durée** d'une période qui s'étend jusqu'au moment où l'on parle.
  *Bill Gates **has been** a philanthropist **for decades**.*

3. My Giving Pledge

Sara Blakely (2013)

TEXT 1

My Giving Pledge

Since I was a little girl, I have always known I would help women. I never lose sight of the fact that there are millions of women around the world who are not dealt the same deck of cards upon their birth. Simply because of their gender, they are not given the same chance I had to create my own success and follow my dreams. It is for those women that I make this pledge.

I am committed to the belief that we would all be in a much better place if half the human race (women) were empowered to prosper, invent, be educated, start their own businesses, run for office — essentially be given the chance to soar!

I pledge to invest in women because I believe it offers one of the greatest returns on investment.

Sincerely,
Sara Blakely

Leon G. Cocperman

TEXT 2

Dear Warren,

I am the son of a plumber who practised his trade in the South Bronx. I am the first generation American born in my family as well as the first to get a college degree. (...) I had a short stint at the Columbia University Graduate School of Business, where I earned an MBA and this opened the door for me to Goldman Sachs, where I had a near 25-year run of happiness and good fortune. (...)

Toby and I feel it is our moral imperative to give others the opportunity to pursue the American Dream by sharing our financial success. In the 1930's, Sir Winston Churchill observed that: "We make a living by what we get, but we make a life by what we give."

It is in this spirit that we enthusiastically agree to take the Giving Pledge.
With warmest personal regards,

Sincerely,
Leon G. Cooperman

Anticipate

1. What kind of causes do you think billionaires will support?

2. You are going to read two giving pledges. Group A will read the first one, and group B the second one. Take notes on:
- their background.
- their reasons for pledging.
- who they want to help.

3. Introduce your billionaire(s) to the other group and explain why they have written the letter.

Toolbox

CD 2 PISTE 40 MP3 59

- grateful /'greɪtfl/: *reconnaissant*
- wealthy /'welθɪ/ = rich /rɪtʃ/
- worthwhile /ˌwɜːθ'waɪl/: *qui vaut la peine*
- an achievement /ə'tʃiːvmənt/: *une réussite*
- philanthropy /fɪ'lænθrəpɪ/
- wealth /welθ/: *la richesse*
- to achieve /ə'tʃiːv/: *accomplir, atteindre*
- to be committed to + N / V-ing /kə'mɪtɪd/: *être dévoué à*
- to give sth away /gɪv ə'weɪ/: *donner qqch*
- to give back /gɪv bæk/: *rendre, redonner*
- to invest in /ɪn'vest/: *investir*
- to make a pledge /pledʒ/ = to take an oath /'əʊθ/: *prêter serment*
- to succeed /sək'siːd/: *réussir*

Your Task

Join the club

Imag ne you are an American billionaire and you would like to join the Giving Pledge. Write a pledge letter to one of the founders. Include information about your life, reasons for jo ning and the causes you wish to support.

3 Opportunities for Everyone

WB p. 51-54

Your Task
Write an article about microcredit for Wikipedia

1. Banker to the Poor

Anticipate

1. Find the definition of "a loan" and "a loan shark".

2. Watch the opening credits of the video. What do you think the film is about?

3. Watch the full video and take notes on:
   - the situation in Bangladesh.
   - Doctor Yunus.
   - the example of Jorimon.

4. Watch again and answer the questions:
   a. What prevented poor people in Bangladesh from earning a living?
   b. What did Doctor Yunus do to help them?
   c. How has "microcredit" changed the life of Jorimon's family?

- Her life has changed / improved because...
- Microcredit has allowed her to...
- Thanks to microcredit, ...

Video Time

DVD PISTES 23-25

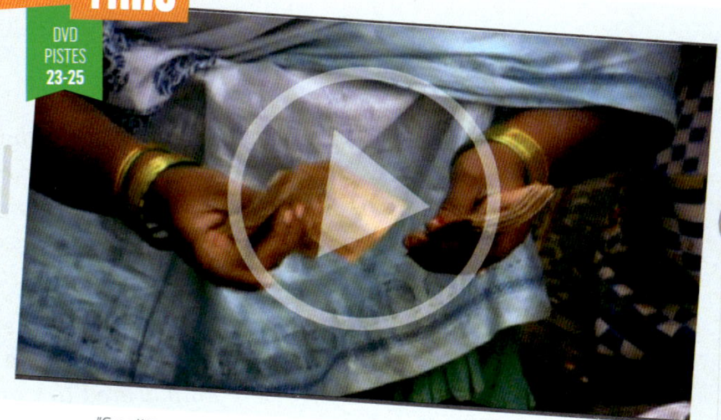

"Small Fortunes", *Microcredit and the Future of Poverty*, a BYUtv program (2010)

A TOUCH OF CULTURE

Muhammad Yunus was awarded the **Nobel Peace Prize** in 2006 for his efforts to create economic and social development for those in desperate need.

Toolbox

CD 2 PISTE 41 MP3 60

- self-sufficient /ˌselfsəˈfɪʃənt/ = autonomous /ɔːˈtɒnəməs/
- poverty /ˈpɒvətɪ/: *la pauvreté*
- self-reliance /ˌself-rɪˈlaɪəns/: *l'autonomie*
- a vicious circle /ˈvɪʃəs/ ≠ a virtuous circle /ˈvɜːtjʊəs/
- to empower sb to do sth /ɪmˈpaʊəʳ/: *donner les moyens à qqn de faire qqch*
- to give a hand /gɪv/ = to help /help/ = to assist /əˈsɪst/
- to grant a loan /ləʊn/: *faire un emprunt*
- to lack sth /læk/: *manquer de qqch*
- to loan /ləʊn/ = to lend /lend/: *prêter*
- to raise awareness /reɪz əˈweənɪs/: *sensibiliser*
- to repay /riːˈpeɪ/: *rembourser*
- to run a company /rʌn/: *gérer une entreprise*
- to set up shop /set ʌp/: *ouvrir un commerce*
- to uplift /ʌpˈlɪft/: *encourager*

2. A Business Woman

Goretti Nyabenda lives in Burundi, Central Africa. As a 35-year-old mother of 6, Goretti's life consisted of cooking meals, taking care of her children and staying quiet. While struggling to survive on her family's meager income, Goretti did not think she had the authority to tell her husband to stop spending 30% of their earnings on banana beer at the local bar three times a week.

One day, Goretti's mother-in-law told her about a CARE savings program that helped women pool their own savings — sometimes as little as 20 cents per week — and then provide loans to each other. Goretti and some women in her community went to learn more about the program, and decided to start their own village savings and loan group with the non-profit organization.

Goretti started her own banana beer stand — the very stuff that her husband so frequently wasted their money on. Goretti's business took off quickly, and she began earning enough income to provide for her family, send her daughters to school, and pay for her husband's medical bills.

Goretti is now seen by her community as a "husband-tamer" and a smart businesswoman.

Adapted from *International Museum of Women* (2010)

1. Read the first paragraph and fill in the description of Goretti.

Name: ....
Nationality: ....
Family situation: ....
Professional status: ....

2. Read the second paragraph and explain how the CARE program works.
   - The idea is that every woman... and then...

3. Read paragraphs 3 and 4. Was Goretti successful? How did her life change?
   - She managed to...
   - She was able to...
   - She succeeded in + V-ing...

4. Come up with a possible title for each paragraph.

3. Africa Works

The global communication campaign of Benetton for 2008 promotes the Birima microcredit programme in Senegal. It features Senegalese workers who have used microloans to start small, productive businesses.

www.benetton.com (2008)

1. What message does this campaign promote?

2. Why do you think Benetton supports programs like Birima?

- Well, first of all it gets them...
- That's right, but I suppose they also...

3. Imagine you have just discovered this campaign online. Leave a few comments on Benetton's website. Try to imagine different opinions and arguments, not necessarily your own.

- Shocking! It's a very bold campaign...
- This is a great campaign. It really raises people's awareness of...

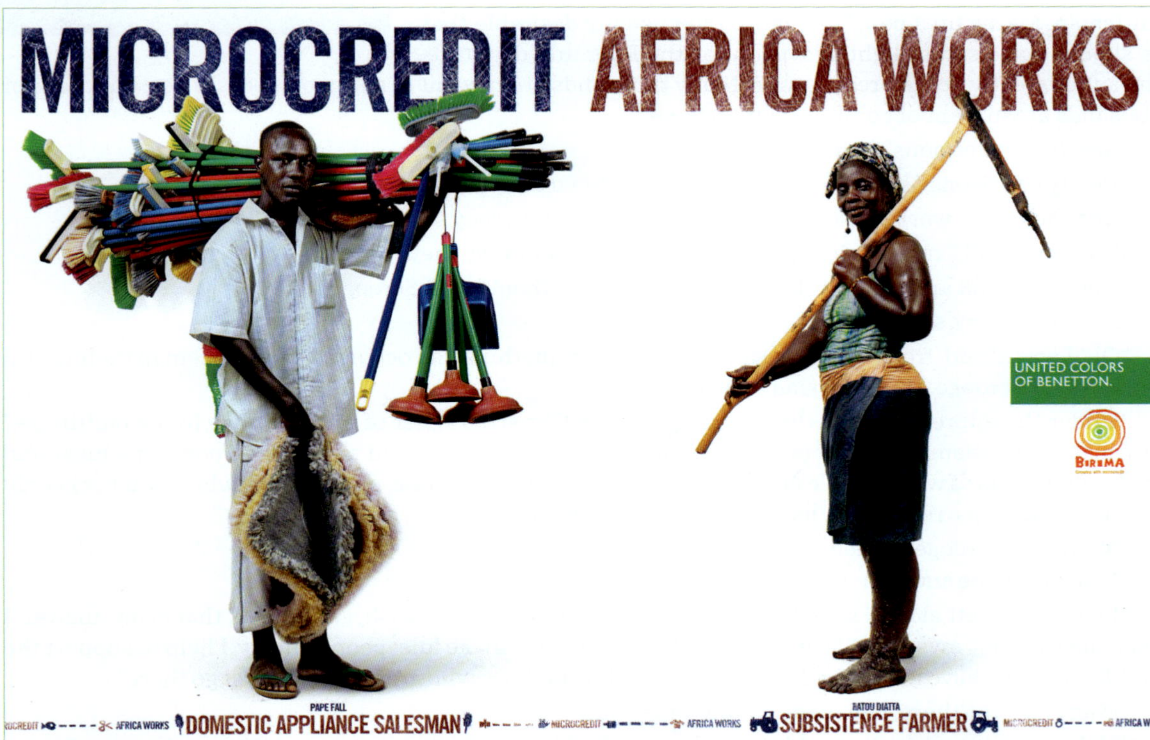

Benetton is a global fashion brand, famous for its bold and provocative campaigns.

Useful Grammar

« Faire faire » et « Laisser faire » → p. 178

- « Faire faire » : on peut, entre autres, employer ***make*** *someone do something* (***make*** + groupe nominal + base verbale). Cette structure exprime souvent une idée de contrainte.
  *The trader **made** her **live** in terrible conditions.*
- « Laisser faire », « donner la possibilité de » = ***let*** *someone do something* (***let*** + pronom + base verbale).
  *Goretti's husband didn't **let** her **work**.*

L'expression de la concession (voir Subordonnées de concession, p. 177)

__Although__ / __Even though__ / __Though__ she was unemployed, she managed to provide for her family.
It was a very simple idea __and yet__ / __however__, it hadn't been tried before.
I said I would volunteer __despite__ / __in spite of__ all the difficulties.

Your Task

A Wikipedia article

Write an article about "Microcredit" for Wikipedia Simple English. Include information about who created microcredit, how it started, how it works and its results. Remember to organise your text into different paragraphs.

Reading

A Christmas Carol

CD 2 PISTE 42 MP3 61

by Charles Dickens (1843)

They were portly gentlemen, pleasant to behold[1], and now stood, with their hats off, in Scrooge's office. They had books and papers in their hands, and bowed to him.

"Scrooge and Marley's, I believe," said one of the gentlemen, referring to his list. "Have I the pleasure of addressing Mr. Scrooge, or Mr. Marley?"

"Mr. Marley has been dead these seven years" Scrooge replied.

"We have no doubt his liberality is well represented by his surviving partner," said the gentleman.

"At this festive season of the year, Mr. Scrooge," said the gentleman, taking up a pen, "it is more than usually desirable that we should make some slight provision for the Poor and destitute, who suffer greatly at the present time. Many thousands are in want of common necessaries; hundreds of thousands are in want of common comforts, sir."

"Are there no prisons?" asked Scrooge.

"Plenty of prisons," said the gentleman, laying down the pen again.

"And the Union workhouses[2]?" demanded Scrooge. "Are they still in operation?"

"They are. Still," returned the gentleman, "I wish I could say they were not."

"The Treadmill and the Poor Law[3] are in full vigour, then?" said Scrooge.

"Both very busy, sir."

"Oh! I was afraid, from what you said at first, that something had occurred to stop them in their useful course," said Scrooge. "I'm very glad to hear it."

"Under the impression that they scarcely furnish Christian cheer of mind or body to the multitude," returned the gentleman, "a few of us are endeavouring[4] to raise a fund to buy the Poor some meat and drink, and means of warmth. We choose this time, because it is a time, of all others, when Want is keenly felt, and Abundance rejoices. What shall I put you down[5] for?"

"Nothing!" Scrooge replied.

"You wish to be anonymous?"

"I wish to be left alone," said Scrooge. "Since you ask me what I wish, gentlemen, that is my answer. I don't make merry[6] myself at Christmas, and I can't afford to make idle[7] people merry. I help to support the establishments I have mentioned: they cost enough: and those who are badly off must go there."

"Many can't go there; and many would rather die."

"If they would rather die," said Scrooge, "they had better do it, and decrease the surplus population. Besides — excuse me — I don't know that."

"But you might know it," observed the gentleman.

"It's not my business," Scrooge returned. "It's enough for a man to understand his own business, and not to interfere with other people's. Mine occupies me constantly. Good afternoon, gentlemen!"

1. voir - **2.** hospices - **3.** loi sur les indigents - **4.** (ici) s'efforcent - **5.** vous inscrire - **6.** joyeux - **7.** oisifs

BUILDING YOUR JOURNAL...

Workbook p. 76

Biography

Charles John Huffam Dickens (1812-1870) was an English novelist of the Victorian era. He is one of the world's best-known writers with classical novels such as *Oliver Twist*, *David Copperfield* or *A Tale of Two Cities*. Today, the novella *A Christmas Carol* is still adapted in different artistic genres and it holds an important place in British and American popular cultures.

A FAMILY OF PHILANTHROPISTS

Guggenheim... The name may seem familiar as it is one of the most famous museums in the world. But did you know the Guggenheims were a family who made their great fortune in mining and smelting? They dedicated their lives (and money) to art by building museums and commissioning artists. Let's learn more about one of them, Peggy, who played a key role in the world of art.

The Guggenheim Museum in New York, commissioned by Solomon Guggenheim (Peggy's uncle) and designed by famous architect Frank Lloyd Wright in 1939.

The Guggenheim Bilbao constructed in 1997 by Canadian-American architect Frank Gehry along the Nervion River.

PAINTINGS FOR THE PUBLIC

New York, Venice, Bilbao, Berlin, Las Vegas... All cities where the Guggenheim family has built museums for artists to publicly show their work. The famous American expressionist, Jackson Pollock, displayed his first solo-exhibition in Peggy Guggenheim's gallery in New York, in 1943. This made him the first abstract expressionist to earn a living from his work.

> *"Having plenty of time and all the museum's funds at my disposal, I put myself on a regime to buy one picture a day."*

ARTIST APPRECIATION

Peggy Guggenheim helped other artists, giving Wassily Kandinsky his first-ever showing in London, and bringing lesser-known American artists to Europe. Without her help, the American Expressionist movement would not be what it is today. After her death in 1979, Peggy's home was converted into an eclectic collection, revealing her life commitment to the ideal that art is to be loved and remembered. Today, the Foundation maintains the family's vision and expands further by opening museums in Helsinki and Abu Dhabi.

Peggy Guggenheim "The Mistress of Modernity" and one of her 14 beloved Lhasa Apso dogs at the entrance of the Peggy Guggenheim Collection in Venice, Italy.

Digital ZONE

Create the first track of the New York Guggenheim audioguide.
Look for general information about the museum (location, the building, selected works in the collection...), take notes and record the track, which should last between 1' and 1'30''.

BUILDING YOUR JOURNAL...

Workbook p. 77

Let's Practise Grammar

community.emdl.fr
exercices interactifs

Les subordonnées de condition

1 Les phrases suivantes décrivent des situations hypothétiques. Complétez-les en utilisant la forme appropriée des verbes entre parenthèses et en faisant des modifications si nécessaire.

1. If people (**not be**) so greedy, there (**not be**) so much poverty.
2. If we (**not finish**) the race, our sponsors (**not give**) us the money! So come on!
3. If only my brother (**become**) a volunteer, his confidence (**grow**), but he won't, because he is too shy.
4. If it (**not rain**) tonight, the ground (**be**) dry for the fun run tomorrow.
5. There aren't many posters. If there (**be**) more, more people (**know**) how important it is to donate blood.

Le gérondif en fonction de sujet

2 Reformulez ces phrases en remplaçant les segments en gras par une subordonnée nominale avec un gérondif en fonction de sujet. Opérez les modifications nécessaires.

1. **When you give money** to charity, you help others.
   ➔ Giving money to charity...
2. It is always good for one's public image **to take part in community work**.
3. It is really important that **we raise funds for this cause**.
4. **When you help others**, you get a sense of reward.

Le *present perfect*

3 Complétez ces témoignages de bénévoles avec les verbes suivants en employant le *present perfect*.

help | become | be | teach | know

1. We ... each other for ten years. We met at a charity fundraiser.
2. Working with the kids ... me happiness doesn't come from having the latest gadgets.
3. Since volunteering, I ... more confident and willing to try new things.
4. We ... over 100 people improve their computer skills.
5. This is the third time I ... abroad to volunteer.

Since et *for*

4 Remplacez chacune de ces séries de deux phrases par une seule phrase en employant ***since*** ou ***for***.

1. He started dancing six hours ago to raise money for charity. He hasn't stopped.
   ➔ He has been...
2. They entered the charity building three hours ago. They haven't left it yet.
   ➔ They have been in the building...
3. At 9 o'clock we opened our phone lines. We have been receiving thousands of calls.
   ➔ We have been receiving thousand of calls...
4. They chose to give back some of their wealth. They decided this when they were 25. They are now 50.
   ➔ They have known they wanted to...

« Faire faire » et « Laisser faire »

5 Complétez les phrases suivantes avec ***let*** ou ***make*** (attention aux modifications éventuelles !).

1. The loan shark didn't ... her sell her products to anyone else but him.
2. He ... her sell all her products to him at a very low price.
3. They ... us get up early in the morning so that we could help the villagers with the animals.
4. Once a week, they ... us stay in bed a little longer.

L'expression de la concession

6 Dans chaque cas, choisissez la bonne formule pour exprimer la concession.

1. **Despite** / **Although** they were very poor, there was always food on the table.
2. **However** / **Even though** he knew that shaving his head for charity would be considered odd, he did it.
3. He felt terrible **even though** / **and yet** he performed at the charity gig that night.
4. They ran the sponsored marathon **although** / **in spite of** the weather was bad.

Make or do?

1 Classez ces mots dans le tableau ci-dessous. Deux d'entre eux peuvent aller dans les deux colonnes !

a living · some good · chores · business · a donation · volunteer work · a deal · money · a difference · an impact · a basket · research

Make	Do

2 Complétez ces définitions avec ***make*** ou ***do***. Puis, trouvez à qui ou à quoi elles peuvent correspondre.

1. Someone who has ... a difference to the world.
2. Someone who ... the chores in your house.
3. A way you want to ... a living when you are older.

Prepositions

3 Complétez les phrases suivantes à l'aide des prépositions qui conviennent.

by · in (x2) · from · away · back

1. Billionaires should give ... to society by pledging half of their wealth. They should ensure their money is invested ... responsible causes.
2. Teenagers would gain a lot ... becoming volunteers. Getting involved ... community projects would help them develop essential life skills.
3. Giving ... money is easy, making sure that people will benefit ... it should be the concern.

Changing lives

4 Associez les éléments de la colonne de gauche à ceux de la colonne de droite.

1. She raises a lot of money for local causes.
2. After getting a microcredit loan from the bank manager, her spirit was uplifted.
3. She is committed to helping poor people improve their lives.
4. Her experience as a volunteer in Tanzania was by far the best thing she has done in her entire life.

a. She was happy because she didn't have to borrow from loan sharks anymore.
b. Without her commitment, the local community centre wouldn't have been able to stay open.
c. It was not life-changing, it was life-affirming.
d. For years, she has been running free computer courses for the unemployed.

Money, money, money

5 Trouvez l'intrus dans chaque série. Justifiez vos choix.

a. a donation · a loan · a gift

b. to lend · to borrow · to loan

c. to invest · to pay back · to give money back

d. to use money · to spend money · to save money

6 Complétez les phrases à l'aide des verbes ci-dessous.

lent · donated · earned · pledged · borrowed · took out

1. The billionaire ... to give away half of his wealth to education.
2. The school ... a large sum of money to charity.
3. Last year he ... 1000 euros from his brother.
4. Before getting a microloan, she ... 2 pennies a day and didn't have enough money to save.
5. I needed money to invest in my business so I ... a loan from my bank.
6. Last week, we ... the local community centre our sound system for the charity event.

Your Final Task

Nominate a candidate for the Nobel Peace Prize

1 You have been selected to propose a deserving candidate or organisation for the Nobel Peace Prize. You must write a submission letter explaining why you think your nomination is worthy of the prize.

2 Think about people or organisations that deserve the award. Possible candidates: Oxfam, Pope Francis, Bill Gates...

3 Choose your candidate and research! Find out information about their background, their work, and why they should be considered for the Nobel Peace Prize.

4 Organise your findings and write your submission letter.

5 Submit your letter to the board! Share it with your classmates and vote on who is the most deserving candidate.

Toolbox

CD 2 PISTE 43 MP3 62

- Despite suffering great difficulties...
- For his/her extraordinary efforts to strengthen...
- For his/her long and non-violent struggle for/against...
- He/She is a deserving candidate because...
- My nomination for the Nobel Peace Prize goes to...
- The person I would like to nominate for the Nobel Peace Prize...
- Without him/her/them, there would not be...
- Not only he/she/they... but...

Tips & Tricks

→ **Invoke emotion!** Pour toucher vos lecteurs, n'hésitez pas à parler de ce que vous ressentez et de ce que votre candidat représente pour vous.

→ **Do it the right way!** Faites un brouillon et, après l'avoir passé au propre, n'oubliez pas de vous relire ! Si vous travaillez de chez vous, utilisez un correcteur d'orthographe. Une lettre pleine de fautes sera beaucoup moins convaincante.

A TOUCH OF CULTURE

The **Nobel Peace Prize** rewards people or organisations that "have done the most or the best work for fraternity between nations, for the abolition or reduction of standing armies and for the holding and promotion of peace congresses".

Your address → Mr. Christophe Legrand
43 rue du Chemin vert
54 000 Nancy

Date → January 6, 2015

Recipient's address → The Norwegian Nobel Committee
Drammensveien 19 NO-0255 OSLO
Norway

Greetings → Dear Sir or Madam,

Body of the letter → My nomination for the Nobel Peace Prize 20... to Médecins Sans Frontières, one of the largest emergency a... nisations in the world. They have co... ally provided aid to ... who are in need regardless of race, reli... or political view. Th... without borders.

Doctors, nurses and medical p... sionals have been wo... nce 1971 to help solve world health issues. They ... put their own lives at risk as they are sent to war-torn regions or develo... countries with dangerous diseases. This nomination is...

Greetings → Yours faithfully,

Signature → Christophe Legrand

Let's prepare your final task

Une fois votre lettre rédigée au brouillon, lisez attentivement les critères d'évaluation ci-dessous : où vous situez-vous dans chaque ligne ?

	Niveau 1	Niveau 2	Niveau 3 (→ B1)	Niveau 4
Réalisation de la tâche		L'objectif de la lettre (*propose a candidate for the Nobel Peace Prize*) est clairement indiqué. La plupart des éléments attendus sont présents même si la lettre reste brève et son contenu élémentaire. La présentation respecte globalement la forme attendue.	Tous les éléments demandés sont présents et le texte proposé se rapproche d'une lettre de recommandation authentique.	Le texte rendu ressemble en tous points à une lettre de recommandation officielle.
Cohérence et organisation		Des efforts visibles d'organisation des éléments sur la page (paragraphes...). Des arguments sont avancés mais peu élaborés. Des efforts basiques de liaison des idées entre elles (***and***, ***but***, ***because***...). A2	La lettre est assez développée et détaillée. L'argumentation est visible et souvent convaincante. Des efforts pour employer des structures complexes (relatives, mots de liaison variés, cause / conséquence...). B1	Les différentes parties de la lettre s'enchaînent de façon très cohérente et fluide. B2
Recevabilité linguistique	Les phrases sont très brèves. Les formes grammaticales sont assez intelligibles mais limitées et répétitives. A1/A1+	Les phrases sont simples mais généralement correctes. Des erreurs élémentaires sont possibles. Des efforts pour utiliser certains des faits de langue de l'unité (***since***, ***for***, *present perfect*...). Exploitation d'une partie des mots et expressions vus en cours, mais le répertoire est encore restreint. A2/A2+	Les phrases ne comportent presque pas d'erreurs élémentaires. Les structures étudiées en cours (***since***, ***for***...) sont souvent réutilisées, et de façon correcte. Bonne maîtrise du lexique élémentaire, notamment celui vu en cours. Peu ou pas de fautes d'orthographe. B1	Les phrases ne comportent aucune erreur élémentaire. Une volonté visible d'enrichissement et de prise de risque. Des erreurs sont possibles sur des points plus complexes, mais le texte reste toujours intelligible. Emploi d'un lexique varié et précis. B2
Valeur chiffrée (équivalences)	**De 5 à 9/20**	**De 10 à 15/20**	**De 16 à 20/20**	**Au-delà des attentes de 2de : objectifs du cycle terminal en vue.**

Let's read a text

Your teacher will give you a text. Read it and answer the questions.

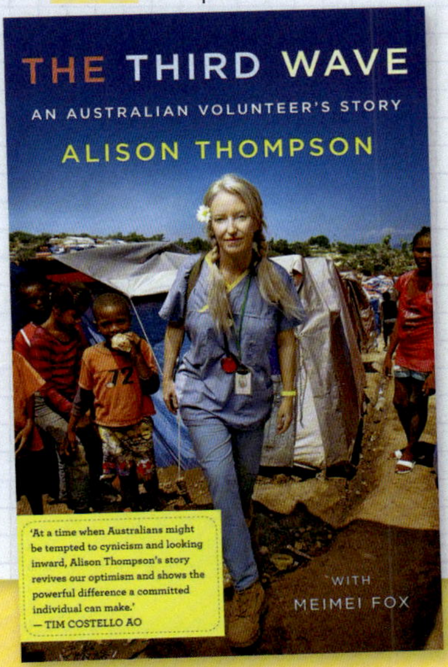

In *The Third Wave* (2011), Alison Thompson provides an inside glimpse into what really happens on the ground after a disaster — and a road map for what anyone can do to help.

Let's listen to a short recording

CD-2 / PISTE-44

Listen to the audio and answer the questions.

Scott Harrison, on a trip to Ethiopia

Let's write

Write about a time you decided to help someone without expecting anything in return: focus on why you wanted to do it and how you felt.

10 Don't Forget: Celebrate!

ISSUE AT STAKE

How is collective memory passed on from generation to generation?

Re-enactors gather in Manassas, Virginia, U.S. (2012)

ON YOUR WAY TO THE TASK

1 **Living History**
Make a report about a significant historical event

2 **Telling History**
Design a poster for a historical film

3 **Celebrating History**
Participate in a debate about Columbus Day

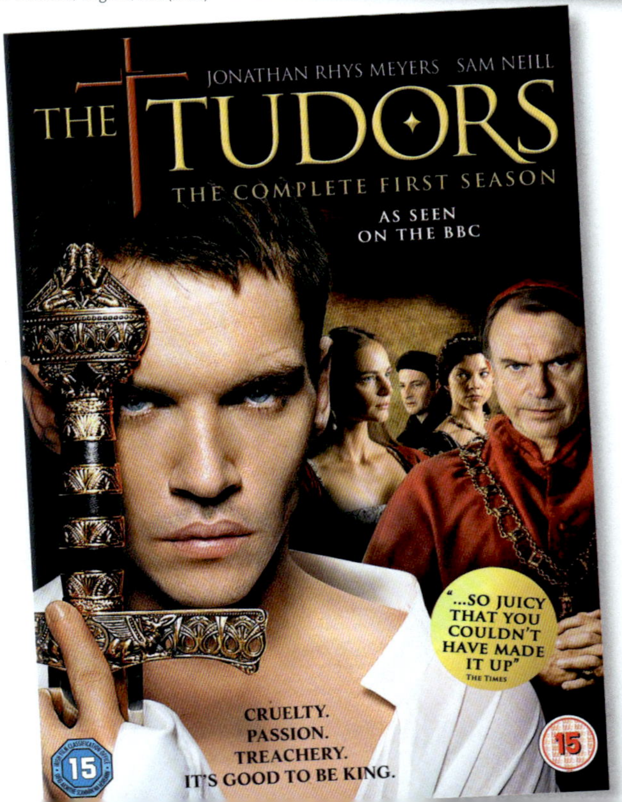

The Tudors, a historical fiction television series created by Michael Hirst (2010)

YOUR FINAL TASK

Participate in a "time capsule" project

3

Freedom from Want, an oil painting by American artist Norman Rockwell (1942)

> The more you know about the past, the better prepared you are for the future.
>
> Theodore Roosevelt, 26th American president

4

People looking at a wall of pictures in the Ellis Island Museum, New York, U.S. (2010)

> If you don't know history, then you don't know anything. You are a leaf that doesn't know it is part of a tree.
>
> Michael Crichton, American novelist

1. Look at the pictures and find the common point(s).

- All of these pictures...
- They all...

2. Match each picture with the appropriate historical reference: **Thanksgiving, King Henry VIII of England, the Civil War, immigration to the U.S.**

3. Picture 2 shows a way of teaching history through television. Look at the other three pictures and identify the other ways.

4. In your opinion, what is the best way of learning history?

- I'd rather learn about history by... than by...
- The most appealing way these days is...

5. Both quotes talk about the importance of history. Is it important in your opinion to know about the past? Why?

GO FURTHER... www.community.emdl.fr

Watch the first twenty seconds of the song "All Together Now" and explain the context (**who**, **what**, **when**). Then, watch the rest and answer the following questions:

1. What is the song's message? What does it want to celebrate?
2. Do you know any other songs that commemorate a past event?

Toolbox

CD 2 PISTE 45 MP3 63

- historic /hɪˈstɒrɪk/: *mémorable, historique*
- historical /hɪˈstɒrɪk(ə)l/: *qui appartient à l'Histoire, historique*
- an event /ɪˈvent/: *un évènement*
- to capture a moment /ˈkæptʃə/
- to commemorate /kəˈmeməreɪt/
- to learn from one's mistakes /lɜːn frɒm/
- to make memories live on /ˈmeɪk meməriz ˈlɪv ɒn/: *faire perdurer les souvenirs*
- to matter /ˈmætə/: *être important*
- to re-enact /riːɪˈnækt/: *reconstituer (un évènement)*

1 Living History

WB p. 55-56

Your Task
Make a report about a significant historical event

1. A Place to Remember

Anticipate **1.** You are going to watch a report on the 9/11 Museum. Do you know what happened on that day in 2001?

Anticipate **2.** Look at the picture. Explain why this quote was chosen to be displayed on a wall of the museum.

3. Watch the video and take notes about the people featured in the report.

4. Watch it again. Make a list of words describing the feelings people might experience when visiting the museum.

5. Is it important that such museums exist? Why?
- In my opinion, they are important because...
- They help visitors remember that...
- Museums like this one are a reminder of/that...

A quote from Virgil fills a wall of the 9/11 Museum in New York City (2014)

Video Time
DVD PISTE 26

"9/11 Memorial Museum", *The National*, CBC News (2014)

Pronunciation
CD 2 PISTE 46 MP3 64

Les liaisons

"There are even voices of the dead for all to hear."
"Barack Obama was among those today marking the official opening of this place."

1. Écoutez ces deux phrases et repérez les liaisons (quand deux mots ou plus sont prononcés comme un seul).

2. Regardez l'orthographe des mots concernés. Quand est-il possible de faire une liaison ?

3. À quoi servent les liaisons en anglais ? Et en français ?

2. Preserving What Has Disappeared

Anticipate **1.** What is a ghost town?

2. Watch the video and take notes about **the place**, **the people**, and **the problems**.

3. Watch again and try to understand why Kolmanskop, Namibia, became a ghost town.

4. What do you notice about the Namibian guide's accent? How can you explain it?
- Well, it's a bit weird...
- It sounds (a bit) like...

5. You have been asked to create a leaflet to attract tourists to Kolmanskop. Watch the film again and decide which aspects of the ghost town you will include.

Video Time
DVD PISTE 27

"Kolmanskop ghost town in Namibia", *Top Billing*, a TV show by SBC3 (2013)

3. A Way to Remember

nticipate

1. Look at the leaflet and read the caption. What is a "re-enactment"?

2. Read the text below and separate it into three different parts. Give a title to each.

3. Read again from line 16 ("*I hadn't realised...*") to the end and explain it in your own words.

- The writer means that...

4. If you had to take part in a re-enactment, which historical event would you choose? Why?

- I think I'd choose... because...
- I'd love to re-enact...

5. Look for information about the Battle of Hastings to find out why it is such an important historical event.

A leaflet promoting the re-enactment of the Battle of Hastings in Sussex, England (2014)

The history teacher had been given the cursed Friday afternoon lesson which normally consisted of pupils talking among each other and discussing what they were going to do at the weekend while the teacher valiantly tried to get through the material of the lesson in vain. However, the teacher said that we were to have a different lesson that day. He took us all to the drama theatre and passed out a plastic sword and shield and we lined up on the stage. The teacher explained that we were going to re-enact the Battle of Hastings. Throughout the lesson we re-enacted the battle, half the class as Normans, and the other half as Saxons, with the teacher giving step by step analysis of the battle while we acted out what he said. By the end of the lesson we had finished the battle and had even seen a death scene from a student! (...) I hadn't realised that history could be so interesting. I know that the lesson was etched onto my brain because when I took an exam I remembered the lesson vividly.

Michael Reichert & Richard Hawley, ***Reaching Boys, Teaching Boys: Strategies that Work and Why*** (2010)

Useful Grammar

Le prétérit et le *present perfect* → p. 169

- On emploie le **prétérit simple** pour faire part d'évènements révolus.
  *On 9/11, a group of terrorists **attacked** the World Trade Center.*
- On emploie le ***present perfect*** pour montrer qu'une **situation présente** porte en elle la **trace du passé**.
  *The inhabitants of Kolmanskop **have left** but their houses still remain.*

Le *past perfect* → p. 170

- Le ***past perfect*** permet de souligner le fait qu'un évènement est antérieur à un évènement passé.
  *Before that famous lesson, he **had** never **thought** that history could be so interesting.*

Toolbox

CD 2 PISTE 47 MP3 65

- abandoned /ə'bænd(ə)nd/
- memorable /'memərəbl/
- moving /'muːvɪŋ/: *émouvant, touchant*
- profound /prə'faʊnd/
- realistic /riːə'lɪstɪk/
- unforgettable /ʌnfə'getəbl/: *inoubliable*
- vivid /'vɪvɪd/: *vif, vivant*
- a period costume /'pɪərɪəd 'kɒstjuːm/: *un costume d'époque*
- a re-enactment /ˌriːɪ'næktm(ə)nt/: *une reconstitution*
- a reminder /rɪ'maɪndə/: *un rappel*

- to bring to life /brɪŋ/
- to dress up /dres ʌp/: *se déguiser*
- to go back in time /gəʊ bæk/: *remonter dans le temps*
- to relive /riː'lɪv/: *se remémorer*

Your Task

Celebrating French history

Choose a place or event that commemorates a significant part of French history. Gather information about it and prepare an audio or video report that you will present to your English penpal's class when you visit him/her.

2 Telling History

WB p. 57-58

Your Task
Design a poster for a historical film

1. Flower of Scotland

CD 2 PISTE 48

Anticipate

1. Before listening to an audio report about "Flower of Scotland", take a look at the picture and imagine what the audio will be about.

2. Listen and answer these questions:
- **a.** Who wrote the song?
- **b.** What is it about?
- **c.** What made it successful?
- **d.** What is it used for nowadays?

3. Read the lyrics. Find all the pronouns in the text. Who or what do they refer to?

4. Pick out vocabulary that refers to: **war**, **success** and **defeat**. Use it to explain the story of the song.

5. Think about your own national anthem. How do you feel towards it? What historical event does it refer to?

6. Research an anthem from an English-speaking country and be ready to explain its story.

AUDIO

Scottish players stand in line singing "Flower of Scotland" before a rugby match (2010)

TEXT

O Flower of Scotland,
When will we see
Your like again,
That fought and died for,
Your wee bit Hill and Glen,
And stood against him,
Proud Edward's Army,
And sent him homeward,
To think again.

Those days are past now,
And in the past
They must remain,
But we can still rise now,
And be the nation again,
That stood against him,
Proud Edward's Army,
And sent him homeward,
To think again.

Roy Williamson, ***Flower of Scotland*** (1967)

2. A Master Storyteller

Whether it's through music, dancing or his art, Nigerian Jimi Solanke is a master of telling local folk stories. The 70-year-old, who is fondly referred to as "Uncle Jimi", is one of the West African country's most accomplished performing artists, most famous for his storytelling on children's television shows.

Armed with an expressive face and a baritone voice, Solanke is renowned for his uncanny ability to tell stories, moving brilliantly and convincingly between characters and settings. The prolific artist, poet and singer rose to fame in Nigeria with his two children's television shows, *Storyland* and *African Stories*. The successful TV programs were broadcast across the country, entertaining and educating different generations of Nigerian children.

Solanke has also been taking his acting into the rural villages to train local aspiring artists and to help keep his Yoruba culture alive. He says traditions play a big part in his work. "If you lose the depths of your cultural perspectives, you have nothing to sell," says Solanke. "People like us, we will keep the flag of our ancestors flying, no matter what. At least at my age, I've lived it and seen it, I've taught it, I've discussed it, so I believe it can never be totally pushed into extinction," he adds.

Adapted from Teo Kermeliotis, ***CNN*** (2012)

Anticipa

1. Who tells the most stories in your family? Is he/she good at it? What are they about?
- My grandmother always talks about...

2. Read about an inspiring man. Take notes about him and recap them in a short identity card.

3. What kind of themes do you think Solanke talks about in his stories?

4. Find a quote that expresses what Solanke thinks about traditions. Do you agree with him?

5. Imagine you are 50 years older. What stories will you be telling future generations?
- I'll probably be telling them about...
- I'd say that I will often talk about where I was when...

6. Choose one of the stories you have brainstormed and imagine how you would tell it to your grandchildren.
- Let me tell you about...

3. Based on True Facts

1

Mandela, by Justin Chadwick (2013)

2

World Trade Center, by Oliver Stone (2006)

3

The Young Victoria, by Jean-Marc Vallée (2009)

Participate **1.** Do you like historical films? Which one do you remember most? What was it about?

- I really liked *The Book Thief*. It tells the story of...
- I have recently watched *American Sniper*. I have learned about...

2. Look at the posters of these three films. What do you know about the stories that they tell?

- I haven't seen *World Trade Center*, but it must be about...
- This film focuses on..., who / which was...

3. Choose one of the posters and comment on its design: what do the choice of colours, the tagline and the framing reveal about the story?

- *Mandela's* poster conveys an impression of..., thanks to...
- The... suggests that...
- From this poster, we can guess that the story will be...

Toolbox

CD 2 PISTE 49 MP3 66

- eye-catching /aɪ'kætʃɪŋ/: *accrocheur*
- patriotic /peɪtrɪ'ɒtɪk/
- striking /'straɪkɪŋ/: *saisissant, frappant*
- an anthem /'ænθəm/: *un hymne*
- the background /'bækgraʊnd/: *le fond, l'arrière-plan*
- a dying tradition /'daɪɪŋ trə'dɪʃn/: *une tradition en train de disparaître*
- the foreground /'fɔːgraʊnd/: *le premier plan*
- the framing of the shot /'freɪmɪŋ əv ðə ʃɒt/: *le cadrage*
- a tagline /'tæglaɪn/: *un slogan, une phrase d'accroche*
- to become obsolete /bɪ'kʌm 'ɒbsəliːt/: *tomber en désuétude*
- to pass on /pɑːs ɒn/: *transmettre*
- to pay tribute to /peɪ'trɪbjuːt/: *rendre hommage à*

Your Task

A film poster → Ex. 3, p. 145

The European History Council is holding a film poster competition. Design one for a historical event that you think should be filmed. Present your poster to the Council.

WB p. 59-60

Your Task
Participate in a debate about Columbus Day

1. A Day to Remember

1. Look at the two pictures. What celebrations do they refer to? Brainstorm what you know about them and/or make hypotheses.

- ... is celebrated in the U.S. and...
- I don't know much about..., but it looks like...

2. What words come to mind when you look at these images (feelings, activities, goals...)?

3. Think of a "day to remember" in your life. Describe it to the class in detail and explain why it was so memorable.

- I'll always remember Christmas when I was a kid. We used to go to...

1

An advertising poster by Stateside (2013)

2

Thanksgiving, by Jon Darren (2013)

Toolbox

- controversial /kɒntrəˈvɜːʃ(ə)l/
- grateful /ˈgreɪtf(ʊ)l/: *reconnaissant*
- offensive /əˈfensɪv/: *offensant, choquant*

- a family meal /ˈfæmɪlɪ miːl/: *un repas de famille*
- a gathering /ˈgæðərɪŋ/: *un rassemblement*
- gratitude /ˈgrætɪtjuːd/
- a legacy /ˈlegəsɪ/ = a heritage /ˈherɪtɪdʒ/
- minorities /maɪˈnɒrətɪz/
- a national holiday /ˈnæʃ(ə)n(ə)l ˈhɒlɪdeɪ/: *une fête nationale*
- togetherness /təˈgeðənɪs/: *un sentiment d'unité*

- to be worth + V -ing /wɜːθ/: *valoir la peine de + V*
- to celebrate /ˈseləbreɪt/
- to gather /ˈgæðə/: *rassembler, réunir*

CD 2 PISTE 50 MP3 67

2. A Day to Forget

1. Group A reads the song lyrics about the events that are commemorated on Australia Day (text 1), and Group B reads the article about the origin of Thanksgiving (text 2 on the following page).

2. Both groups fill in this chart:

Oppressor	Oppressed	Acts of the oppressor

3. Each group presents the event referred to.

4. All together, find the common point(s) between the two texts.

5. Both groups read text 2 and explain the last paragraph in their own words.

TEXT 1

In 1788 down Sydney Cove,
the first boat-people land.
Said "Sorry boys, our gain's your loss,
we're gonna steal your land.
And if you break our new British laws,
for sure you're gonna hang.
Or work your life like convicts
with chains on your neck and hands. (...)
We're gonna civilise your black barbaric lives
and teach you how to kneel."
But your history couldn't hide the genocide,
the hypocrisy to us was real.

Kev Carmody, "**Thou Shalt Not Steal**" (1989)

TEXT 2

Thanksgiving has never been a celebratory holiday in my family. Whenever my family did cook we always gave thanks that all the Native Americans weren't wiped out when Columbus "discovered" America. I never understood why we were so against Thanksgiving. In school we drew turkeys with our hands and it was a happy time. When I was older though, I was told the truth by my family.

My great, great, great, great grandfather was a part of a band of Black Indians in Florida, hence my unique and Native American-sounding last name.

I learned that in 1637 the body of a white man was discovered dead in a boat. Armed settlers — which we tell our children were God-fearing, gentle, sharing, kind Pilgrims — invaded a Pequot village. They also set the village, which included many children, on fire. Those who were lucky enough to escape the fire were systematically sought, hunted down and killed. While many, including historians, still debate what exactly happened this day, it directly led to the creation of "Thanksgiving Day."

When I finally found out the origins of Thanksgiving, it made me nauseous. Never again will I celebrate a holiday I know nothing about until I investigate its origins. I am very thankful, pun intended, that I learned about the origins of this holiday. It is a reminder that history can be rewritten and if told enough times eventually becomes the truth!

Nicole Breedlove, ***The Huffington Post*** (2013)

3. The Notting Hill Carnival

CD 2 PISTE 51

1. Look at the photos of the Notting Hill Carnival. Make a list of things you would expect to see there. *Anticipate*

- I'd expect to see people dancing...
- For sure, there would be...

2. Listen to the recording once and find out how the carnival started. Jot down information about these categories: **when**, **who**, **why**.

3. Listen again and answer the following questions:
a. Why was the carnival not all "fun and laughs"?
b. How is the carnival different today?

- It has changed a lot...
- The focus is more on... than...

4. Use everything you have understood to write a 50-word summary of the history of the carnival.

- It started because...

5. Would you like to go to the Notting Hill Carnival today? Why/Why not? Have you been to a similar event?

The Notting Hill Carnival parade (2014)

Performers take part in the Notting Hill Carnival (2011)

Your Task

Let's debate!

You are spending a semester in an American high school. You are invited to participate in an event set up by the Debate Club. The topic is "Should we celebrate Columbus Day?" Prepare your intervention.

Reading

CD 2
PISTE 52
MP3 68

Code Talker: A Novel about the Navajo Marines of World War Two

by Joseph Bruchac (2006)

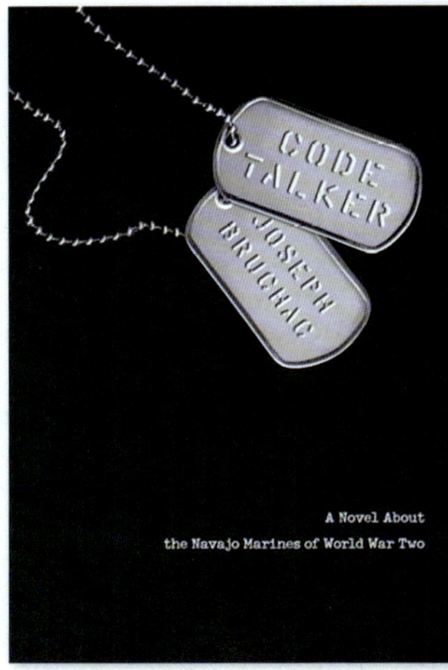

Grandchildren, you asked me about this medal of mine. There is much to be said about it. This small piece of metal holds a story that I was not allowed to speak for many winters. It is the true story of how Navajo Marines helped America win a great war. There is much that I must remember to speak for this medal, to tell its story as it should be told. I must remember not only the great secret with which I was trusted, but also all that happened to me and those like me. That is a lot. But I think that I can do it well enough. After all, I was expected to remember as were the other men trained with me. The lives of many men depended entirely on our memories.

Look here. The man you see riding a horse on the back of this medal was an Indian. He is also one of those raising that flag there behind him. I knew him when we were both young men. His name was Ira Hayes. He was a fine person, even though he was not one of our people, but Akimel O'odam, a Pima Indian. We both fought on a distant island far off in the Pacific Ocean. (...)

I was not one of those who fought to the top of Mount Suribachi, but I had my own special part to play. I helped send the message about our success, about the brave deeds so many Marines did that day for *Nihimà*.

Nihimà, "Our Mother." That is the Navajo word we chose to mean our country, this United States. It was a good name to use. When we Indians fought on those far-off islands, we always kept the thought in our minds that we were defending Our Mother, the sacred land that sustains us.

Nihimà is only one of the Navajo words we chose for places with bilagáanaa names. South America became *Sha-de-ah-Nihimà*, "Our Mother to the South." Because we knew that Britain is an island, we gave it the name of *Tó tah*, "Surrounded by Water." When we did not know much about a place, we described something about the people there. So we named Germany *Béésh bich'ahii*, "Iron Hat," and Japan was *Bináá'ádaálts'ozi*, "Slant-eyed." (...)

But I am getting ahead of myself. I have not even explained to you yet why we made up such names. I have not told you why being able to speak our Navajo language, the same Navajo language they tried to beat out of me when I was a child, was so important during World War Two. It was because I was a Navajo code talker.

What was a code talker and what did we code talkers do? Why was the secret we shared so great that we could not tell even our families about it until long after the war ended?

You cannot weave a rug before you set up the loom[1]. So I will go back to the beginning, pound the posts in the ground, and build the frame. I will start where my own story of words and warriors begins.

1. (ici) Il ne faut pas mettre la charrue avant les bœufs (littéralement : on ne peut pas tisser un tapis avant d'avoir installé le métier à tisser)

BUILDING YOUR JOURNAL...

Workbook, p. 78

Biography

Joseph Bruchac (1942) is an American writer and educator. He comes from English, Slovak and Native American ancestry and is best known for his work as a Native American writer. He is also a performing storyteller and musician.

THE STORY BEHIND THE PHOTO

Photographs can be a valuable way of passing on history to future generations but the truth is not always so easy to see. Do you know the real story behind these two famous pictures?

LUNCH ATOP A SKYSCRAPER

"Lunch atop a Skyscraper" shows 11 construction workers sitting on a girder of the Rockefeller Center during break time, 840 feet above the streets of New York City. Controversy still surrounds this picture. Indeed, some people believe that it was a publicity stunt paid for by the Rockefeller Center to promote their new building. Others, however, are convinced that the American photographer wanted to denounce the extremely dangerous working conditions of these workers, who, as you can see, were not wearing safety harnesses. As a matter of fact, the photograph was taken during the Great Depression and, at the time, a lot of people were ready to accept any type of job — even a dangerous one — to try to make ends meet.

Lunch atop a Skyscraper, attributed to Charles C. Ebbets (1932)

Raising the Flag on Iwo Jima, by Joe Rosenthal (1945)

RAISING THE FLAG ON IWO JIMA

You have also probably seen this picture of U.S. soldiers commemorating the patriotism and heroism of American troops during World War II. For a long time, there was a debate about whether the photo was staged or not. Indeed, when photographer Joe Rosenthal got to the top of Mount Suribachi (on the island of Iwo Jima) on 23 February 1945, the U.S. flag had already been planted. However, it was too small to be seen from a long distance and the soldiers received orders to replace it with a bigger flag. It is this second flag that Rosenthal captured in his photo. What is more, even if this picture has become a symbol of American victory against the Japanese army in the Pacific, it was taken at the beginning of the conflict, which lasted for many more weeks and cost thousands of lives on both sides. This story is told in Clint Eastwood's 2006 film *Flags of our Fathers*.

Digital ZONE

Go online to learn about the history behind some other famous photos.
Choose the one you prefer and be ready to explain it to your schoolmates.

BUILDING YOUR JOURNAL...

Workbook, p. 79

Let's Practise Grammar

community.emdl.fr
exercices interactifs

Le prétérit et le *present perfect*

1 Complétez l'histoire de la création d'Internet en conjugant les verbes entre parenthèses au prétérit ou au *present perfect*.

In 1989, a man called Tim Berners-Lee ... (**create**) the World Wide Web. Since then, life ... (**be never**) the same. The Internet ... (**change**) the way we do business and conduct our personal relationships. Before the Internet, libraries and books ... (**be**) our main sources of information. Nowadays, it is just one easy click away. Business used to be done face-to-face. Nowadays, we deal with people we ... (**never meet**). There was a time when we ... (**write**) long letters to our loved ones to tell them how we were feeling. Now, emoticons and instant texting ... (**take over**) and we know what everybody is feeling all the time. Life will never be the same again.

2 Complétez les phrases ci-dessous avec l'une des deux propositions (**a** ou **b**).

1. I've been to the 9/11 Museum twice...
a. while I was in New York.
b. in the last two years.

2. I went to Luderitz...
a. while I was in Namibia.
b. in the last two years.

3. How long have you taught history...
a. before you became a mother?
b. at this school?

4. They forgot the words to the anthem...
a. but it doesn't matter because the crowd is so loud.
b. but it didn't matter because the crowd was so loud.

5. They have forgotten the words to the anthem...
a. but it doesn't matter because the crowd is so loud.
b. but it didn't matter because the crowd was so loud.

Le prétérit et le *past perfect*

3 Complétez les phrases suivantes en conjugant les verbes entre parenthèses au prétérit ou au *past perfect*.

1. That was fantastic! He ... (**enjoy not**) a history lesson so much for years.

2. There ... (**never be**) a carnival in Notting Hill before the first Caribbean immigrants ... (**arrive**) in London to help with the labour shortage.

3. The guests ... (**have**) to have an x-ray taken before leaving to see if they ... (**try**) to steal a diamond.

4. By 1990, Nelson Mandela ... (**spend**) over 27 years of his life in prison.

5. I thought I ... (**see**) all the exhibits, but then I was told there was another floor.

Le *past perfect*

4 Complétez les phrases ci-dessous à votre guise en utilisant le *past perfect*.

1. Martha didn't want to see *Mandela* because...

2. Before we finally arrived at the museum, ...

3. I understood the book because...

4. My friend Damon knew New Delhi so well because...

5. There was nobody at the theater because...

6. The streets in Notting Hill were wet because...

Opinion adjectives

1 Reformulez les phrases en italique en complétant les amorces proposées avec les adjectifs suivants.

profound | vivid | thought-provoking | unforgettable | moving | controversial

1. *After visiting the war museum, I felt quite emotional. Although I already knew a bit about it, I had a much deeper and clearer understanding of what our ancestors had to go through to protect our country.*

➔ Visiting the war museum was a ... and ... experience which made me appreciate my ancestors more.

2. *I had no idea that celebrating Thanksgiving was such a cause for discussion. When I found out about its history, I have to say that it made me think twice about my own country's celebrations.*

➔ Finding out about Thanksgiving's ... history has been really ... and has made me realise I have no idea why we celebrate our national holidays.

3. *My history lessons were really memorable thanks to my history teacher. He used to give such intense and graphic descriptions of historical events, it was almost like we were there.*

➔ My history lessons were ... because of the ... descriptions my teacher used to give.

Talking about history

2 Complétez ces phrases à l'aide des verbes ci-dessous. Attention aux modifications éventuelles !

look | stick | learn | mark | bring | serve

1. History is an opportunity for us to ... from our ancestors' mistakes and make more informed choices.

2. The statue will ... as a reminder of all those who gave their lives for their country.

3. The Battle of Hastings re-enactment we took part in will always ... in my mind.

4. They ... the anniversary of the end of World War II with a two-minute silence.

5. When we ... back on what the world has achieved, it is really incredible.

6. The film really ... to life what it would have been like to live during medieval times.

Parts of a poster

3 Reliez chaque partie du poster aux éléments ci-dessous.

the release date | the actors and actresses | the background | the foreground | a quote | the director | the title | the tagline

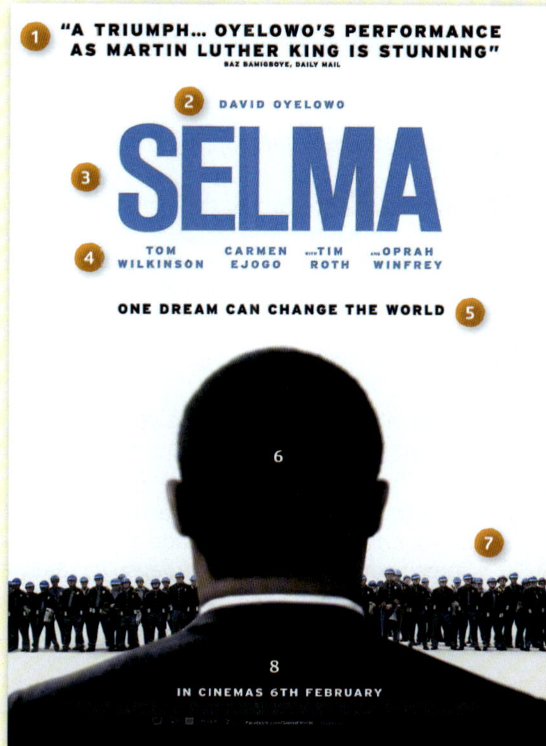

Keeping the collective memory alive

4 Reliez chacun des mots suivants à la définition qui lui correspond.

a memorial | a storyteller | a tradition | a documentary | a national holiday

1. A statue, a building, a place etc. that reminds people of a past event or person.

2. A day when almost everyone in the country does not have to go to school or work.

3. A person who passes on traditions and our ancestor's stories.

4. A film that we watch to find out the true facts about a historical event.

5. A belief and/or way of acting or doing something that has been part of the culture of a group of people for a long time.

Your Final Task

Participate in a "time capsule" project

1 Your school is participating in a time capsule project. Every student has to create a 45-second sound file about a contemporary event they wish to pass on to future generations.

2 Choose an event that happened after you were born.

3 Do some research about the event and take notes of the main information: who, what, where, when, why, how. Think about the consequences (how people reacted, what happened afterwards...) and give your personal opinion.

4 Write your script.

5 Find a picture that symbolises your event to send along with your sound file. Five, four, three, two, one and record!

6 Want to go further? Why not actually create a time capsule on your own? You could include objects, images, texts, etc. Some people keep their time capsules safely at home, but others bury them in a box!

Toolbox

CD 2 PISTE 53 MP3 69

- One of the most significant events in French contemporary history is...
- It took place on / in...
- Never have we seen / experienced anything like it...
- The impact it had on... was huge / massive / harmful.
- Before this, France used to be / didn't use to be...

Tips & Tricks

→ **Use the Six W's!** Pour relater l'évènement choisi, pensez à répondre aux questions **who**, **what**, **where**, **when**, **why** et **how**. N'oubliez pas de parler de l'impact que l'événement a eu sur le pays !

→ **Sign it!** Pensez à indiquer votre nom, votre nationalité et la date d'enregistrement au début de l'audio pour que les générations futures sachent qui s'adresse à eux !

→ **Rehearse, rehearse, rehearse!** Demandez à un camarade de lire votre script pendant que vous vous entraînez à le dire tout haut et de noter les problèmes de prononciation.

"The magazine had published caricatures of the Muslim Prophet Muhammad, something which is forbidden according to some interpetations of Islam."

"Following the terrorist attack, there were huge demonstrations in Paris. The sentence *Je suis Charlie* became a slogan of support in the rallies and in the social media."

"On January the 11th 2015 there was a horrible shooting at the offices of satirical French magazine *Charlie Hebdo*."

"In my opinion, we should never forget..."

On Your Way to the Exam

Let's prepare your final task

Lorsque vous répétez votre témoignage oral, lisez attentivement les critères d'évaluation ci-dessous : où vous situez-vous dans chaque ligne ?

	Niveau 1	Niveau 2	Niveau 3 (→ B1)	Niveau 4
Qualité de la production orale		La prononciation est suffisamment claire pour être généralement comprise malgré une lecture / récitation assez heurtée. Des efforts d'accentuation sont perceptibles. **A2**	La prononciation est toujours intelligible même si un accent étranger est perceptible et quelques erreurs de prononciation persistent. La lecture / récitation est visiblement travaillée (très net effort d'accentuation) et donne un effet de fluidité. **B1**	Le discours est totalement fluide. Le rythme de phrase se rapproche de l'authenticité. Un auditeur natif n'aurait aucun mal à comprendre. **B2**
Réalisation de la tâche	Fichier son de 45 secondes environ. Le sujet (*a contemporary event you wish to pass on...*) est traité, mais les idées sont juxtaposées sans vraie organisation. **A1**	La plupart des éléments demandés (*the Six W's*) sont traités mais présentés de manière peu élaborée. Des efforts basiques de liaison des idées entre elles (***and***, ***but***, ***because***...) même si la structure du discours reste floue. **A2**	Tous les éléments demandés sont traités. Des efforts pour complexifier le propos (structures relatives, mots de liaison variés...), le rendre vivant et s'approcher d'un témoignage authentique. **B1**	Le témoignage produit est remarquable pour l'intérêt de son contenu et la qualité formelle de sa réalisation. Des efforts d'habillage sonore. **B2**
Maîtrise de la grammaire et du vocabulaire	Les phrases sont très brèves. Les formes grammaticales sont assez intelligibles mais limitées et répétitives. Emploi d'un répertoire très restreint de mots simples. **A1/A1+**	Les phrases restent simples mais généralement correctes. Des erreurs élémentaires sont possibles. Des efforts pour employer certains des faits de langue de l'unité (les temps du passé, ***would*** + V...). Réemploi d'une partie du lexique vu en cours. **A2/A2+**	Les phrases ne comportent pratiquement pas d'erreurs élémentaires. Les structures étudiées en cours (les temps du passé, ***would*** – V, ***used to*** + V...) sont fréquemment réutilisées et bien maîtrisées. De nombreux éléments lexicaux du cours sont réemployés. **B1**	Les phrases ne comportent aucune erreur élémentaire. Les structures employées vont au-delà de ce qui a été étudié en cours. Emploi d'un répertoire lexical plus riche que celui qui a été étudié dans l'unité. **B2**
Valeur chiffrée (équivalences)	**De 5 à 9/20**	**De 10 à 15/20**	**De 16 à 20/20**	**Au-delà des attentes de 2de : objectifs du cycle terminal en vue.**

Let's read a text

Your teacher will give you a text and a quote. Read them and answer the questions.

Let's listen to a short recording

CD-2 / PISTE-54

Listen to the document and answer the questions.

The statue of John McDouall Stuart in Alice Springs being turned around (2015)

Let's write

Choose the quote that you like best and use what you have learned to give your opinion about it.

a. "People are hungry for stories. It's part of our very being. Storytelling is a form of history, of immortality too. It goes from one generation to another."

Studs Terkel, American author

b. "History is the torch that is meant to illuminate the past, to guard us against the repetition of our mistakes of other days."

Claude G. Bowers, American historian and politician

Comprendre un texte

Face à un texte en anglais contenant beaucoup de vocabulaire spécifique ou de mots inconnus, on est parfois tenté de désespérer ! Heureusement, des outils existent pour comprendre l'essentiel de tout document textuel. Découvrez-les ci-dessous.

1. Avant la lecture

» Avant de commencer votre lecture, observez le paratexte (titres, illustrations, légendes, source, etc.). Ces éléments vous aideront à faire des hypothèses sur la **nature**, le **thème principal** et le **contenu** du document :

- **le titre** de l'activité et celui du texte d'origine : ils peuvent vous aider à définir la ou les idée(s) principale(s) du document.
- **les images** : elles vous orientent sur le thème abordé.
- **le sous-titre ou le chapô** : il fournit plus de détails sur le contenu du texte.
- **l'auteur** : est-ce un romancier, un journaliste, un étudiant... ? Ne le confondez pas avec le narrateur (la personne qui raconte l'histoire) !
- **la source** : s'agit-il d'un article de presse, d'un blog, d'un extrait de roman... ?
- **la date de publication** : elle indique si le texte a éte publié récemment ou non. Attention : ce n'est pas forcément la date à laquelle s'exprime le narrateur !

» S'il y a une Toolbox près du texte, étudiez son contenu ! Ces **mots et expressions** vous seront utiles pour comprendre le document ou pour en parler ensuite.

» Lisez attentivement la ou les consignes de l'activité. Vous saurez ainsi **quels éléments repérer** lors de votre lecture.

2. Pendant la lecture

» Lisez le texte une première fois en entier et notez le thème abordé : de quoi est-il question ? Concentrez-vous uniquement sur les **mots connus** et ceux qui sont **transparents**. Oui, vous pouvez comprendre un texte sans en comprendre tous les termes ! Faites le test : photocopiez un texte du manuel et, à l'aide d'un gros marqueur noir, barrez tous les mots que vous ne connaissez pas. Vous verrez qu'il en restera assez pour comprendre le message général. Saisir les détails et nuances est ensuite une simple question d'apprentissage du vocabulaire.

» Au cours de cette première lecture et des suivantes, soyez attentif aux indices ci-dessous :

- **la ponctuation** : c'est simple, mais il faut y penser ! Les **majuscules** permettent de repérer les noms propres (personnages, lieux...) et d'amorcer la compréhension du texte. Souvent, les phrases longues font peur car on s'y perd. Pourtant, il suffit souvent de revenir à la **phrase simple** (sujet + verbe + complément) pour saisir l'idée globale. **Une astuce** : tout ce qui se trouve entre deux virgules dans une phrase apporte un détail et peut être mis de côté à la première lecture.
- **les champs lexicaux** : pouvez-vous identifier un ou plusieurs champs lexicaux dans le texte (celui de la nourriture, de la lutte, de l'écologie...) ? Ils peuvent vous indiquer le thème ou les idées principales.
- **les mots clés** : quels mots, expressions ou phrases vous semblent-ils essentiels ? Surlignez-les ou notez-les.
- **la structure** : si le texte s'y prête, essayez de le subdiviser en différentes parties. Donnez un titre à chacune d'elles ou écrivez une phrase qui résume ce dont il y est question.

» Grâce à tous les indices relevés, émettez des hypothèses et validez-les au cours des lectures suivantes. Vous progresserez ainsi peu à peu dans la compréhension du document.

Toolbox

- an article /'ɑ:tɪkl/
- the author /'ɔ:θəʳ/
- the content /'kɒntent/: *le contenu*
- the date of publication
- a historical text /hɪ'stɒrɪkəl/
- a keyword /'ki:.wɜ:d/
- a newspaper /'nju:z,peɪpəʳ/: *un journal*
- a novel /'nɒvl/: *un roman*
- a poem /'pəʊɪm/
- a semantic field /sɪ'mæntɪk fi:ld/: *un champ sémantique*
- a short story /ʃɔ:t 'stɔ:rɪ/: *une nouvelle*
- the source /sɔ:s/
- a subtitle /'sʌb,taɪtl/: *un sous-titre*
- a title /'taɪtl/: *un titre*

- This extract was taken from...
- The text is entitled...
- The text was written by...
- It was extracted from...
- It was published in + *date* (ex: 2012)...
- It was published on + *date précise* (ex: January 14th 2015)...

Écrire un essai ou un récit

De la Seconde à la Terminale, vous serez amené à rédiger nombre d'essais et de récits, sur les thèmes les plus divers. Pour éviter le syndrôme de la page blanche, suivez les conseils suivants.

1. Avant la rédaction

» Avant toute chose, lisez attentivement la consigne pour savoir ce que l'on attend de vous :

- quel est le **sujet** de votre texte (un séjour en Angleterre, les émissions culinaires...) ?
- quel **objectif** votre texte doit-il viser (raconter, commenter, donner votre opinion...) ?
- en fonction de cet objectif, quel **ton** adopterez-vous (nostalgique, virulent...) ?

» Une fois la consigne élucidée vous pouvez préparer la rédaction de votre texte :

- en cherchant dans l'unité **les éléments lexicaux, culturels et grammaticaux** que vous pouvez mobiliser et les **textes de nature similaire** dont vous pouvez vous inspirer.
- en jetant sur le **brouillon**, dans le **désordre** et **en anglais**, toutes les autres idées qui vous viennent à l'esprit.
- en **organisant ensuite ces idées de façon cohérente**. Dans un récit, vous pouvez adopter une structure chronologique. Dans un essai, c'est plutôt la structure logique (introduction, petits paragraphes, conclusion) qui est de mise.
- en réfléchissant aux **formules de transition** et aux **mots de liaison** qui articuleront les différentes parties de votre texte. La **Toolbox** ci-contre peut vous donner des idées !

2. Pendant la rédaction

» Pendant la rédaction, gardez à l'esprit que :

- votre **plan** doit être visible dans votre **mise en page**. N'exprimez qu'une idée par paragraphe, allez à la ligne quand vous changez de partie et commencez à chaque fois un peu en retrait.
- l'**introduction** est essentielle car elle présente le thème de votre texte. Soignez-la !
- vous serez entre autres jugé sur la **richesse du vocabulaire et des structures employés**. Veillez donc à enrichir votre expression avec des propositions subordonnées, des adverbes et des adjectifs.
- les **exemples** et les **anecdotes** donnent de la saveur à votre texte. Réfléchissez : vous avez forcément entendu, vu ou lu quelque chose qui pourra illustrer vos propos de manière vivante. Puisez dans votre propre expérience ou dans celle de vos proches et, au besoin, inventez des exemples (crédibles, bien sûr !)
- la **conclusion** est la dernière impression laissée au lecteur. Ne la bâclez-pas ! Dans un récit, trouvez une fin marquante (étonnante, drôle, tragique...). Dans un essai, résumez vos idées et tentez d'apporter une lumière nouvelle sur le sujet. Finir par une expression idiomatique, des paroles de chansons ou une structure riche (ex : *The more... the more...*) peut vous donner ce petit plus qui fera pencher la balance en votre faveur.

3. Après la rédaction

» Surtout, n'oubliez pas de vous relire plusieurs fois pour vérifier la cohérence de votre texte, mais aussi la qualité de votre expression, de votre orthographe et de votre ponctuation ! La fiche de la p. 157 pourra sans doute vous aider.

Toolbox

Introducing
- From my point of view...
- I (do) believe that...
- There is no doubt that...

Comparing
- although /ɔːl'ðəʊ/ = even though /iːvən ðəʊ/: *bien que*
- in spite of /spaɪt/: *malgré*
- likewise /'laɪkwaɪz/: *de même*
- on the contrary /'kəntrərɪ/
- rather than /'rɑːðəʳ/: *plutôt que*

Expressing cause & consequence
- as a result of /rɪ'zʌlt/: *en conséquence*
- because of /bɪ'kɒz/: *à cause de*
- consequently /'kɒnsɪkwəntlɪ/ = therefore /'ðeərfɔːʳ/: *par conséquent*
- due to /djuː/: *en raison de*
- for this reason /'riːzn/ = that is why /waɪ/: *c'est pourquoi*
- nevertheless /ˌnevəðə'les/: *toutefois*
- since /'sɪns/: *puisque*

Giving details
- for instance /'ɪnstəns/ / for example /ɪg'zɑːmpl/: *par exemple*
- in fact /fækt/: *en fait, en réalité*

Ordering your ideas
- besides /bɪ'saɪds/ = in addition /ə'dɪʃən/ = moreover /mɔː'rəʊvəʳ/: *de plus*
- finally /'faɪnəlɪ/: *enfin*
- first / second / third...
- next: *ensuite, puis*

Concluding
- for the reasons above: *pour les raisons précitées*
- in conclusion
- in short /ʃɔːt/: *en un mot*
- obviously /'ɒbvɪəslɪ/: *de toute évidence, manifestement*
- to sum up /sʌm ʌp/: *en résumé*

Comprendre un document oral

Écouter un enregistrement ou regarder une vidéo en anglais peut être un peu déstabilisant car on ne sait pas toujours bien à quoi se raccrocher. Pourtant, la compréhension d'un document oral mobilise autant l'anglais que la logique ! En suivant ces quelques conseils, vous devriez pouvoir aborder n'importe quel enregistrement ou vidéo avec sérénité.

1. Avant l'écoute / le visionnage

» Dans *Community*, les documents audio et vidéo sont toujours précédés d'un **titre** et souvent accompagnés d'une **image** (photo, dessin, photogramme...), **légendée** ou non. Commencez toujours par lire ce titre et par observer cette image et sa légende. Vous pourrez ainsi émettre des hypothèses sur le thème principal et le contenu du document.

» S'il y a une **Toolbox** sur la double page où figure le document, étudiez son contenu ! Ces mots et expressions seront utiles pour comprendre l'audio ou la vidéo, ou pour en parler ensuite.

» Lisez attentivement les consignes de l'activité. Vous saurez ainsi **quels éléments repérer** lors de l'écoute ou du visionnage.

2. Pendant l'écoute / le visionnage

» Commencez par écouter/regarder le document en entier pour vous faire une idée plus précise du **thème principal**. Ne vous inquiétez pas si vous ne comprenez pas tout !

» Au cours de cette première découverte et des suivantes, soyez attentif aux indices sonores et/ou visuels ci-dessous :

- **les bruits** : ils peuvent indiquer la nature du document (publicité radiophonique, bulletin d'information, interview...) ainsi que l'endroit où se passe l'action (dans une boutique, dans un parc, lors d'une fête...).
- **les voix** : prêtez-y attention pour définir le nombre de locuteurs, leur sexe et leur âge.
- **l'intonation** : elle révèle l'état d'esprit des personnages (joie, colère...) et l'objectif de leur discours (convaincre, expliquer...).
- **l'image** : dans le cas d'une vidéo, vous pouvez bien sûr vous appuyer sur les images. Observez les expressions des personnes filmées, leurs attitudes, leurs regards. Le cadre, les décors et l'ambiance qu'ils contribuent à créer peuvent aussi vous aider à comprendre le document.
- **le lexique** : entendez-vous des mots qui se répètent ? Pouvez-vous identifier un champ lexical dominant ? Ces informations sont essentielles pour déduire le thème principal.
- **les indicateurs temporels** : ils vous permettent de situer l'action dans le temps (*yesterday, last Friday, in 2014...*).
- **les mots de liaison** : repérer les mots de liaison est un bon moyen de faire le lien entre les idées énoncées dans le document (*because, yet, but, whereas...*).

» Grâce aux indices relevés, faites des hypothèses et validez-les lors des écoutes suivantes. Si, par exemple, vous avez compris qu'un problème était soulevé, écoutez attentivement par la suite pour savoir si des solutions sont proposées.

» Prenez des notes au fil des écoutes (voir fiche p. 151). Souvenez-vous : **seuls les mots les plus importants sont accentués** dans une phrase. Repérez-les, notez-les et voyez-les comme les pièces d'un puzzle à assembler. Tout comme vous n'avez pas besoin de toutes les pièces pour comprendre de quelle image il s'agit, vous n'avez pas besoin de tous les mots pour comprendre le sens global du document.

» Souvent, les consignes du manuel vous inciteront dans un second temps à trier et classer vos indices et conclusions pour accéder à une compréhension plus fine du document.

» Acceptez que des zones d'ombre subsistent, ne vous découragez pas et, surtout, entraînez-vous en regardant des séries ou des films en VO et en écoutant des chansons en anglais !

Toolbox

- a debate /dɪ'beɪt/
- a dialogue /'daɪəlɒg/
- an interview /'ɪntəvju:/
- a movie extract /'mu:vɪ ɪk'strækt/: *un extrait de film*
- a news bulletin /nju:z 'bʊlətɪn/: *un bulletin d'informations*
- a radio / TV programme /'reɪdɪəʊ ˌti: 'vi: 'prəʊgræm/
- I suppose /sə'pəʊz/ / reckon /'rekn/ it is about...
- It is probably a documentary about... /ˌdɒkjʊ'mentərɪ/
- The document might be dealing with...

Prendre des notes

Quand on écoute un enregistrement ou que l'on regarde une vidéo, il est essentiel de prendre des notes de façon efficace. Et cela dépend beaucoup de la façon dont on les organise sur sa feuille ! La règle d'or est de laisser de l'espace pour vos notes entre la première et la deuxième écoute (ou entre le premier et le deuxième visionnage), afin de pouvoir les compléter ou les corriger.

1. DONT's

» Voici quelques pièges à éviter lorsque vous prenez des notes sur un document audio(visuel) :

- **N'écrivez pas de phrases complètes !** Elles vous font perdre du temps, mais aussi le fil de la compréhension. Il est généralement inutile de noter les verbes « de base » comme ***be*** et ***have***, ou bien les articles tels que ***the***.
- **N'écrivez pas trop serré !** Aérez vos notes autant que possiblepour pouvoir les compléter ou les modifier facilement lors d'une seconde écoute ou d'un second visionnage.
- **Banissez les petits morceaux de feuille ou des coins de cahiers !** Il faut un bel espace bien dégagé pour prendre des notes lorsqu'on prend connaissance d'un audio ou d'une vidéo.
- **Rangez votre stylo !** Même pour les plus forts, une compréhension orale est faite d'hypothèses, puis de corrections. Le crayon à papier est donc bien plus pratique pour pouvoir effacer et recommencer !

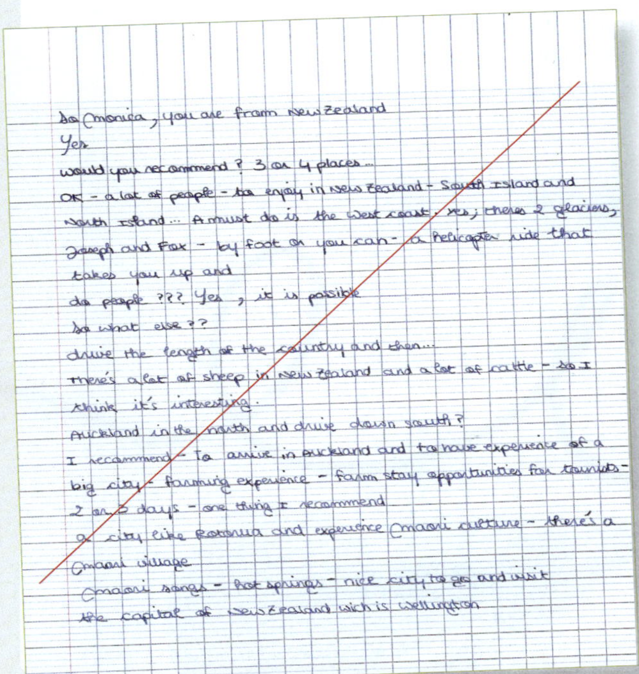

2. DO's

» Pour prendre des notes de façon optimale, retenez bien les quelques conseils ci-dessous :

- **Optez si possible pour une organisation en « carte mentale »** autour d'un élément central. Ce sera plus souple et plus parlant qu'une organisation verticale (voir image ci-dessous).
- **Pensez à utiliser des petits dessins ou symboles**. Rapides à réaliser, ils sont également efficaces pour exprimer vos idées. Par exemple, au lieu d'écrire le mot « conséquence », vous pouvez simplement faire une flèche.
- Le travail collaboratif est toujours profitable ! Lorsque c'est possible, **comparez vos notes avec celles d'un(e) camarade**, non pas pour les recopier mais pour réfléchir ensemble aux hypothèses les plus probables.
- Le meilleur moyen d'améliorer votre compréhension de l'oral est d'être exposé très souvent à de l'anglais authentique et non sous-titré. **Regardez deux ou trois fois par semaine de brèves vidéos** (2-3 minutes) sur des sites d'information en ligne, et **prenez le temps de vous entraîner à prendre des notes** sur ce que vous avez compris, en deux visionnages successifs. Vous ne saisissez pas tout ? Aucune importance ! Avec un entraînement régulier, vous verrez progressivement arriver la confiance – et les résultats.

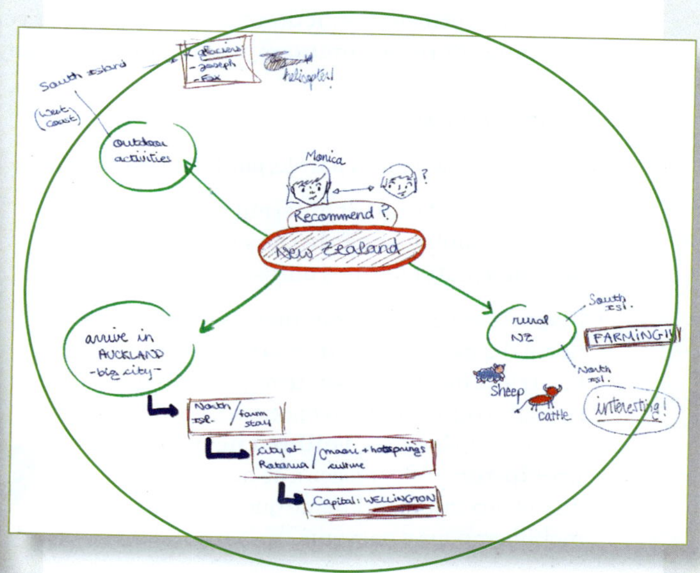

S'exprimer à l'oral en continu

Tout au long de l'année, vous serez régulièrement amené à prendre la parole en continu, devant la classe, pendant quelques secondes ou quelques minutes. Qu'il s'agisse pour vous de défendre une idée, de présenter un objet ou un projet ou encore de convaincre un auditoire, les conseils ci-dessous pourront vous aider à réussir votre prestation.

1. La préparation à la prise de parole

» Avant toute chose, lisez attentivement la consigne pour savoir ce que l'on attend de vous :

- quel est l'**objectif** de votre intervention (expliquer un concept, défendre une cause...) ?
- dans quel **contexte** allez-vous vous exprimer (à la radio du lycée, lors d'une journée portes ouvertes, à l'occasion d'une exposition...) ?
- votre production doit-elle revêtir une **forme** particulière (discours, spot publicitaire, bulletin radiophonique...) ?
- en fonction du contexte et de la forme imposés, quel **ton** allez-vous employer (enthousiaste, professionnel, familier...) ?
- vous est-il demandé de vous appuyer sur un **support** précis (diaporama, photo...) ?
- avez-vous une contrainte de **durée** ?

» Une fois la consigne élucidée, vous pouvez préparer votre intervention :

- en **organisant vos idées** de façon logique et claire (introduction, développement, conclusion) et en **pensant aux mots de liaison** qui pourront les articuler.
- en **prenant des notes en anglais** sur chaque partie de votre discours. Surtout, ne rédigez pas de phrases complètes ! Vous seriez tenté de les lire, or votre expression doit être aussi spontanée que possible. Écrivez seulement des **mots-clés** ou des **segments de phrases** et n'hésitez pas à utiliser des **couleurs** pour vous y retrouver facilement.
- en **pensant aux éléments culturels, lexicaux et grammaticaux** que vous avez étudiés dans l'unité et que vous allez pouvoir réemployer dans votre production.
- en **vous enregistrant** si vous le pouvez pour prendre conscience de la **qualité de votre expression orale** (prononciation, accentuation, rythme et intonation). Si vous êtes chez vous, utilisez les dictionnaires en ligne pour vérifier la prononciation des mots inconnus. Et **recommencez** jusqu'à ce que vous soyez satisfait du résultat !

2. La prise de parole

» Lorsque vous prenez la parole, gardez à l'esprit que :

- le registre de l'oral est différent de celui de l'écrit : il vaut mieux **faire des phrases simples** plutôt que des phrases complexes.
- l'expression orale est rarement parfaite. Il est normal d'hésiter, de faire des pauses, de revenir en arrière quand on s'est trompé ou quand on souhaite reformuler un énoncé. Sans faire de pauses trop longues, **veillez à ne pas vous précipiter** ; réfléchissez à ce que vous voulez dire et aux outils de langue que vous allez mobiliser pour y parvenir.

- lorsque vous hésitez, utilisez des **gap-fillers pour gérer vos silences et formuler votre pensée**. Par exemple : *Er..., Well..., So..., What I mean is..., Let me think..., You know..., You see..., The thing is..., The point is..., I'd say that..., I mean..., I suppose..., I guess..., What I'm trying to say is that..., In other words...*
- vous pouvez vous référer à vos notes, mais **sans les lire** car le **contact visuel** avec votre auditoire est fondamental. Plus vous connaîtrez vos notes, plus vous pourrez vous en passer et regarder votre public. La préparation est la clé de la réussite !
- votre **gestuelle** et vos **mimiques** peuvent grandement faciliter la compréhension de vos propos. N'hésitez pas à utiliser vos bras, vos mains, l'expression de votre visage et le ton de votre voix pour faire passer votre message. Et d'une façon générale, tenez-vous droit, ne mettez pas vos mains dans vos poches et montrez-vous enjoué et sûr de vous !
- votre discours aura plus d'impact s'il est accompagné d'un **support visuel ou auditif**. Même si ce n'est pas spécifié dans la consigne, voyez si vous ne pouvez pas afficher, projeter ou distribuer un document, ou encore utiliser du son pour accompagner votre introduction ou votre conclusion.

Toolbox

Introducing
- First I will deal with... Then... And finally... /'faɪnəlɪ/
- First of all, I'd like to... /fɜ:st/
- I'd like to start by saying...
- I'm going to talk about...
- I will especially focus on... /ɪ'speʃəlɪ 'fəʊkəs/
- I would like to tell you about... /ə'baʊt/
- To begin with... /bɪ'gɪn/ / To start with... /stɑ:t/

Continuing
- I'll now move on to... /mu:v/

Giving your opinion
- I would say...
- In my opinion... /ə'pɪnjən/
- It seems to me that... /si:ms/
- Personally I believe... /bɪ'li:v/
- To my mind... /maɪnd/

Talking to the audience
- As you can see from this text... /si:/
- Do you have any questions? /'kwestʃəns/
- Have a look at this picture... /'pɪktʃəʳ/
- Is that clear? /klɪəʳ/

Clarifying
- In other words... /'ʌðəʳ wɜ:ds/
- What I mean is... /mi:n/

Concluding
- Thank you for your attention. /ə'tenʃən/
- To conclude... /kən'klu:d/ / As a conclusion... /kən'klu:ʒən/
- To sum up... /sʌm ʌp/

English Sounds

Vowels
- /i:/ tree
- /ɪ/ fish
- /e/ pen
- /æ/ bag
- /ɑ:/ car
- /ɒ/ dog
- /ɔ:/ door
- /ʊ/ book
- /u:/ shoe
- /ʌ/ bus
- /ɜ:/ girl
- /ə/ banana

Diphthongs
- /eɪ/ cake
- /əʊ/ boat
- /aɪ/ eye
- /aʊ/ cow
- /ɔɪ/ boy
- /ɪə/ beard
- /eə/ chair
- /ʊə/ tourist

Triphthongs
- /aʊə/ flower
- /aɪə/ fire
- /eɪə/ layer
- /ɔɪə/ employer
- /əʊə/ grower

Consonants
- /ʃ/ shopping
- /tʃ/ beach
- /dʒ/ bridge
- /ŋ/ sing
- /θ/ think
- /ð/ brother

S'exprimer à l'oral en interaction

Échanger avec un ou des camarades sur un sujet précis en anglais demande un peu de préparation et d'entraînement ! Vous devez vous exprimer de façon claire et efficace, comme dans le cas d'une expression orale en continu, mais aussi comprendre votre interlocuteur et réagir de façon pertinente à ses propos. Voici quelques conseils à suivre.

1. La préparation à l'interaction orale

» Avant toute chose, lisez attentivement la consigne pour savoir ce que l'on attend de vous :

- quel est le **thème** de votre échange (l'identité texane, les communautés du futur, 9/11...) ?
- quel est l'**objectif** de cette interaction orale (convaincre l'autre, lui poser des questions, partager vos points de vue, prendre une décision commune, écrire un document à plusieurs mains...) ?
- devez-vous **tenir un rôle** précis ou êtes-vous libre d'exprimer votre **opinion personnelle** ?
- en fonction du rôle imposé ou choisi, quel **ton** allez-vous devoir employer (péremptoire, humoristique, conciliant...) ? Glissez-vous dans la peau de votre personnage !

» Une fois la consigne élucidée, vous pouvez préparer votre intervention :

- en **prenant des notes sur les idées ou arguments** que vous allez avancer. Attention, ne rédigez pas de phrases complètes ! Vous seriez tenté de les lire, or il est important que votre expression soit aussi spontanée que possible. Écrivez simplement des **mots-clés** ou des **segments de phrases**, et toujours **en anglais**.
- en **organisant vos idées ou arguments par thème** de façon à les retrouver facilement lorsque votre interlocuteur les abordera. N'hésitez pas à utiliser différentes couleurs pour vous y retrouver facilement.
- en **mobilisant les faits culturels, le lexique et la grammaire** que vous avez vus dans l'unité et qui sont susceptibles de vous aider dans votre conversation.

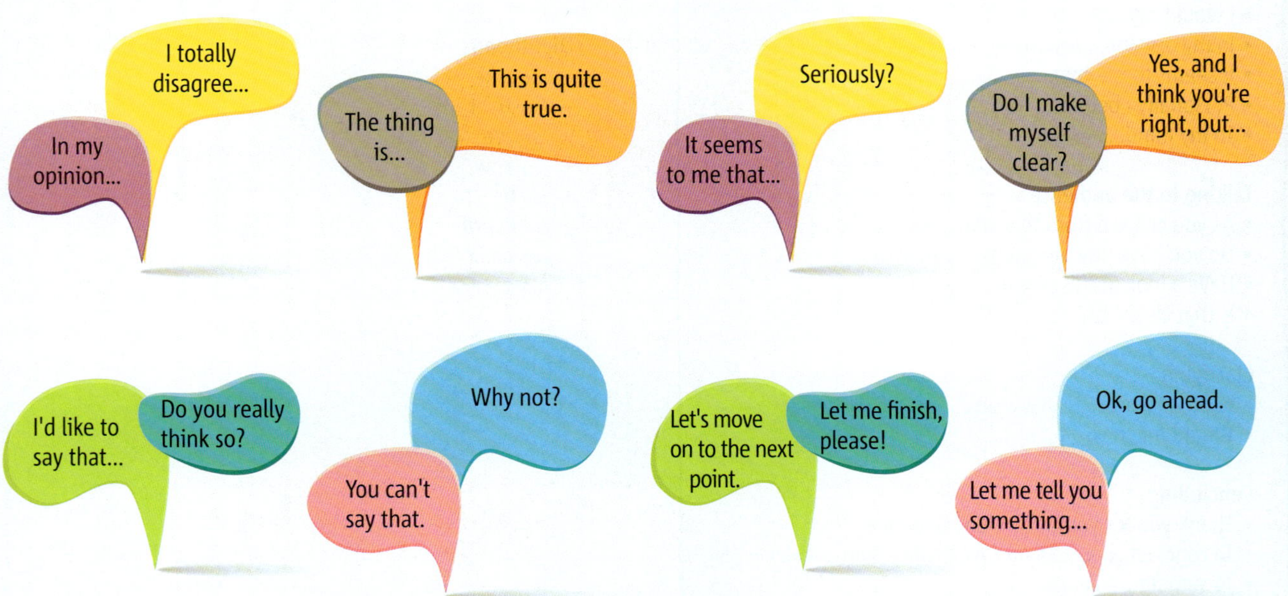

2. L'interaction orale

» Lorsque vous participez à une interaction orale, gardez à l'esprit que :

- vous devez parler **à tour de rôle**. Laissez vos interlocuteurs s'exprimer et respectez leurs points de vue.
- vous devez vous assurer d'avoir **compris vos camarades** avant de réagir à leurs propos. Si ce n'est pas le cas, n'hésitez pas à leur demander de reformuler : *I'm sorry, I didn't get what you said. Can you repeat please?* ; *Would you mind repeating?* ; *Could you speak louder please?* ; *Could you repeat?*
- le registre de l'oral est différent de celui de l'écrit : il vaut mieux **faire des phrases simples** plutôt que des phrases complexes.
- lorsque vous avez des moments d'hésitation, vous pouvez **gagner du temps** en utilisant des **gap-fillers** tels que : *Er...* ; *Well...* ; *So...* ; *What I mean is...* ; *Let me think...* ; *You know...* ; *You see...* ; *The thing is...* ; *The point is...* ; *I'd say that...* ; *I mean...* ; *I suppose...* ; *I guess...* ; *What I'm trying to say is that...* ; *In other words...*
- l'interaction orale aime l'imprévu ! Ne suivez pas aveuglément vos notes : réagissez à ce que vient de dire votre interlocuteur, posez-lui des questions, contrez ses arguments. Bref, **faites vivre la conversation** !
- le **contact visuel** avec vos interlocuteurs est fondamental. Essayez de ne pas les quitter des yeux ! Leurs gestes et l'expression de leur visage peuvent vous aider à comprendre ce qu'ils veulent dire.
- votre propre **gestuelle** et vos **mimiques** peuvent aussi faciliter la compréhension de vos camarades. N'hésitez pas à utiliser vos bras, vos mains, votre regard et le ton de votre voix pour faire passer votre message.
- votre discours aura plus d'impact si vous l'**illustrez avec des exemples**, qu'ils soient tirés de votre expérience personnelle, de l'actualité ou de vos connaissances culturelles.

» Quoi qu'il arrive, résistez à la tentation de repasser au français. Essayez de vous convaincre que votre camarade est anglais et ne parle pas d'autre langue. Si vous ne trouvez pas le mot que vous cherchez, expliquez, faites une périphrase, donnez un exemple ou mimez ! Plus vous jouerez le jeu, plus vous améliorerez votre fluidité.

Toolbox

Clarifying

- Do I make myself clear? /klɪəʳ/: *Est-ce que je me fais bien comprendre ?*
- Do you get my point? /pɔɪnt/: *Vous voyez ce que je veux dire ?*
- Do you understand? /ˌʌndə'stænd/

Giving your opinion

- I guess / reckon /'rekn/ / believe /bɪ'li:v/ that...
- I haven't got a clue. /klu/: *Je n'en ai pas la moindre idée.*
- In my opinion... /ə'pɪnjən/
- It seems to me that... /si:ms/: *Il me semble que...*
- On one hand... On the other hand... /hænd/: *D'une part... D'autre part...*

Reacting

- Do you really think so? /'rɪəlɪ/
- How awful! /'ɔ:fʊl/: *Quelle horreur !*
- I (dis)agree with you on that point. /ˌdɪsə'gri:/
- I see what you mean. /mi:n/
- I think you're right. /raɪt/
- I'm sorry but I can't answer that question. /'ɑ:nsəʳ ðæt 'kwestʃn/
- Let me finish please, I'd like to say that... /'fɪnɪʃ/
- Let me say something about that. /'sʌmθɪŋ/
- Let's move on to the next point. /mu:v ɒn/: *Passons au point suivant.*
- Of course, go ahead! /ə'hed/
- Seriously? /'sɪərɪəslɪ/: *Sérieusement ?*
- This is interesting but... /'ɪntrəstɪŋ/
- This is quite true. /kwaɪt tru:/
- Unbelievable! /ˌʌnbɪ'li:vəbl/
- Well, let me tell you something.
- Why not? /waɪ nɒt/

Participer à un débat

Le débat tel qu'il est pratiqué en classe est une sorte de jeu de rôle qui vise à vous entraîner à défendre un point de vue sur un sujet précis et à contrer les arguments de vos adversaires. Voici quelques conseils pour y participer dans les règles de l'art !

1. La préparation du débat

» Avant toute chose, lisez attentivement l'intitulé du débat pour savoir ce que l'on attend de vous :

- quel est le **thème** du débat (les avantages et inconvénients du multiculturalisme, l'influence du hip-hop sur les jeunes...) ?
- Vous impose-t-on une **opinion** (« pour » ou « contre ») ou pouvez-vous choisir votre camp ?

» Une fois l'intitulé élucidé, vous pouvez préparer vos interventions :

- en cherchant dans l'unité les **arguments** qui pourront servir à défendre votre position, et en y ajoutant vos propres idées. Si vous préparez le débat chez vous, cherchez sur Internet de quoi enrichir votre argumentation. Attention : n'écrivez **jamais de phrases complètes** et **banissez le français** !
- en trouvant des **exemples concrets**, tirés de l'unité, de votre expérience, de vos connaissances culturelles ou de l'actualité, pour illustrer chacun de vos arguments.
- en pensant aux **contre-arguments** que vos adversaires vont pouvoir avancer et en réfléchissant à la façon de les réfuter.

2. Le débat

» Le débat commence par une courte introduction de chaque équipe. Il s'agit de présenter le thème et d'indiquer brièvement la position adoptée.

» Lors des échanges qui suivent, c'est la qualité de l'interaction et de l'argumentation qui prime. Veillez donc à :

- **rester courtois** en toute circonstance : partagez la parole au sein de votre équipe et n'interrompez pas vos adversaires.
- **prendre en compte ce qui vient d'être dit**, en faisant éventuellement reformuler les paroles de votre interlocuteur ou en les répétant.
- **faire vivre le débat** en concédant certains points mais aussi en essayant de déstabiliser l'adversaire par des questions, des exclamations, des arguments supplémentaires, des exemples frappants, etc.
- prêter une attention particulière à votre **gestuelle**, vos **intonations**, votre **regard** et vos **mimiques** : votre message passera bien plus efficacement si vous avez l'air absolument convaincu et convaincant !

» À la fin du débat, vous aurez à formuler une conclusion en équipe. C'est le moment de réaffirmer votre position en reprenant brièvement vos idées principales. Attention à rester cohérent avec votre introduction : il ne s'agit pas de prendre soudain la position adverse !

Toolbox

Starting the debate
- First of all, I would like to say that...
- To begin with, I'd like to point out that... /bɪˈgɪn/
- By way of introduction, I will say that... /ˌɪntrəˈdʌkʃn/

Agreeing
- I couldn't agree more. /əˈgriː/
- You are absolutely right!
- How true! /haʊ truː/
- I'm with you there! /ðeə/

Disagreeing
- That's not how I see it.
- I disagree with her on this point. /ˌdɪsəˈgriː/
- I take a different view of the question. /ˈkwestʃn/
- I only agree up to a point.
- Yes, in a way, but...
- I understand you feel... yet...

Clarifying
- Sorry but I don't see what you mean. /miːn/
- Could you explain that in more detail? /ˈdiːteɪl/

Expressing cause/consequence
- as a result of /rɪˈzʌlt/
- because of /bɪˈkɒz/
- consequently /kɒnˈsɪkwentlɪ/
- due to /djuː/
- for this reason /ˈriːzn/
- since /ˈsɪns/
- therefore /ˈðeərfɔːʳ/

Giving an example
- for example /ɪgˈzɑːmpl/ / For instance... /ˈɪnstəns/
- Take the example of...

Making suggestions
- Don't you think...?
- Why not...?
- Perhaps we could... /pəˈhæps/

Repeating a statement
- You told us that...
- You mentioned that... /ˈmenʃənd/
- In other words you mean that... /miːn/

Concluding
- To conclude... /kənˈkluːd/
- To sum up... /sʌm ʌp/
- In short / In brief... /briːf/
- To reach a consensus... /kənˈsensəs/

Relire ses devoirs

Ça y est, vous venez décrire la dernière ligne de votre devoir d'anglais ! Vous avez fait le plus gros, certes, mais le travail n'est pas terminé ! Vous devez impérativement vous relire pour corriger ces erreurs qui hérissent le poil des correcteurs et vous font perdre des points bêtement. Voici ce à quoi vous devez faire attention.

1. Sujet, verbe, complément !

Une phrase en anglais, c'est comme en français : un sujet, un verbe et un complément. Attention à n'oublier aucun de ces trois éléments !

2. *He / she* ≠ *it*

He et ***she*** s'emploient pour des personnes alors que ***it*** fait référence à des choses. Pour parler d'une bande dessinée, de la malbouffe ou d'un stéréotype, on emploie ***it*** (et non ***she*** ou ***he***).

3. *-s*

Vous le savez... mais l'oubliez souvent ! À la 3e personne du singulier du présent simple, les verbes prennent un ***-s*** : *he eat**s**, she play**s**, it work**s**...*

4. *Be* + V-*ing*

Si vous employez un verbe en ***-ing***, vérifiez que vous avez bien conjugué (et pas oublié) ***be*** avant : ***I am*** *writing, she* ***is*** *wearing, they* ***are*** *talking...*

5. *Who* ≠ *which*

Who et ***which*** signifient « qui » ou « que » mais s'utilisent différemment. ***Who*** s'emploie pour une personne (*The man,* ***who*** *is singing in the street, is talented.*) et ***which*** pour un objet (*The book,* ***which*** *is on the table, is highly interesting*).

6. *There is / there are*

There is et ***there are*** signifient « il y a » mais l'un est suivi d'un mot au singulier (*There* ***is*** *a garden on the rooftop.*) tandis que l'autre est suivi d'un mot au pluriel (*There* ***are*** *tornadoes*). Soyez logique : si vous savez compter, vous savez conjuguer !

7. Modaux + base verbale

Retenez que tous les modaux s'utilisent de la même manière : ***can / must / should / will / may / might / could / would + BV*** (= verbe à l'infinitif sans *to* et sans *-ing*).

8. *To* + V

On ne met jamais ***for*** avant un verbe pour traduire « pour + verbe » ! On utilise **to + V**.

9. *Want TO* + V

« Vouloir faire quelque chose » se traduit par *to want* ***to*** *do something.* N'oubliez pas la préposition !

10. Verbes à préposition

Certains verbes se construisent avec une préposition. Attention : si vous l'oubliez, ils changent de sens ou n'en ont plus aucun ! Faites une liste des verbes prépositionnels les plus courants : ***to look at*** (regarder), ***to listen to*** (écouter), ***to deal with*** (parler de), ***to dream about / of*** (rêver de), ***to think about*** (penser à), ***to go to*** (aller à), ***to hear about*** (entendre parler de)...

11. Adjectifs

Les adjectifs se placent toujours **avant** les noms (même quand il y en a plusieurs) et sont **invariables**. Ils ne prennent donc jamais de ***-s*** : *Three* ***big black*** *wolves ate three* ***pink fat*** *pigs.*

12. Article Ø

En anglais, on n'emploie pas d'article quand on parle de quelque chose de général : **Ø** *Pollution is harmful for the environment.* ; **Ø** *British people like tea.* (il s'agit de la pollution en général et des Britanniques en général).

13. Article *a / an*

Rappelez-vous qu'on emploie l'article ***an*** et non ***a*** devant les mots qui commencent par une voyelle, pour en faciliter la prononciation : ***an*** *emotion,* ***an*** *arm...*

14. Majuscules

Pensez à mettre une majuscule à tous les noms de pays et à leurs dérivés (nationalités, habitants, langue, etc.) : *He's* ***S****cottish, but he also speaks* ***S****panish!*

15. Confusions fréquentes

Attention à ne pas confondre :

- ***you're*** et ***your***
  You are my friend. ≠ *Your pen is on the table.*
- ***they're***, ***their*** et ***there***
  They are happy. ≠ *Their life is fantastic.* ≠ *Put the book on the table over there.*
- ***it's*** et ***its***
  I love your house and its garden. It's a gorgeous place!

Index grammatical

A

Above, 166
Across, 166
Adjectif, 163-165
Adverbe, 164, 174-175
Ago, 171
A lot of, 162-163
And, 179
Any, 162
Article, 160
As soon as, 177
At, 166

B

Be / Be -ing, 167-170, 172
Be able to, 172-173
Be allowed to, 172
Be going to, 173
Behind, 166
Below, 166
Both, 163
But, 179

C

Can, 171-172
Capacité, 171-172
Cause, 166, 177-178
Certitude, 171-172
Collectif (nom), 159
Comparatif, 164-165
Concession, 166, 177-178
Condition, 173, 177
Conseil, 171-172

D

Dare, 172
Défini (article), 160
Démonstratif, 160
Dénombrable (nom), 159-160, 162
Devoir, 171-172
Discours rapporté, 176, 179
Distance, 160
Do, 167, 179
During, 170-171

E

Each other, 161-162
Either, 163
Enoncés emphatiques, 167, 173
Every, 162

F

Faire faire, 178-179
(A) few, 162
For, 170-171
Fréquence, 175
From, 166
Futur, 173, 177

G

(Double) génitif, 161, 165
Gérondif, 176

H

Have, 167-170, 172
Have -en, 168-170, 172
Have to, 172
Haut degré, 164
How, 173

I

Impératif, 173-174
In(to), 166
Incapacité, 172
Indéfini (article), 159-160
Indénombrable (nom), 159-160, 162
Infériorité, 164-165
Interdiction, 171-173, 176
In front of, 166

L

(A) little, 162
Lots of, 162

M

Many, 162
May, 171-172
Might, 171, 172
Modaux, 171-172
Most / the most, 163, 165
Much, 162
Must, 171-172

N

Nationalités, 164
Need, 172
Neither, 163, 174
No, 162
Nombres, 163
Noms, 159-160, 163, 164, 165
Noms composés, 160

O

Obligation, 171-173, 176
Of, 161
Off, 166
On(to), 166
Or, 179
Ought to, 172
Out of, 166
Over, 166

P

Particule (verbes à), 175
Passif, 174, 179
Past perfect, 169-170, 177, 179
Permission, 172
Périphrases, 172-173
Pluperfect, 170
Possession, 161, 167
Prépositions, 166, 175, 176, 178
Présent, 167-170, 173, 177, 179
Present perfect, 168-170, 179
Prétérit, 167-173, 177, 179
Probabilité, 171, 176
Pronoms, 161, 177
Proximité, 160

Q

Quantifieurs, 162-163
Questions, 168-169, 171, 173-174
Question tags, 174

R

Relatives, 160, 178

S

Shall, 171-173
Should, 171-173
Since, 170-171, 173, 177
So / so as to, 173-174, 177
Some, 162, 170
Subordonnées, 177-178
Such, 164, 173
Supériorité, 164-165
Superlatif, 165

T

Temps, 167-170
That, 176-178
The, 160
The two, 163
There is / there are, 175
This, 160
Through, 166
To, 176

U

Until, 177
Used to, 172, 175, 176

U

What, 173, 178
When, 177-178
Where, 178, 179
Whereas, 177
Which, 178
While, 161, 170, 173, 177
Who, 166, 168, 169, 173, 177, 178
Whom, 177, 178
Whose, 178
Why, 162, 178, 179
Will, 171-173
Would, 161, 171, 173, 174, 176, 177, 178, 179

Z

Zéro (article), 160

Autour du nom

Les noms (N)

1. Noms « dénombrables » et « indénombrables »

Les noms ne sont pas dénombrables ou indénombrables en eux-mêmes, c'est leur **fonctionnement** qui varie. Par exemple, le mot *hair* peut fonctionner de deux manières :

- indénombrable : *Her hair **is** beautiful.* (***Ses** cheveux **sont** magnifiques.*)
- dénombrable : *Waiter, there's **a hair** in my soup!* (*Garçon, il y a **un cheveu** dans ma soupe !*)

• Quand ils fonctionnent de manière **dénombrable**, les noms désignent des éléments qui peuvent être comptés : *a computer*, *two computers*, etc. Ils peuvent être employés avec l'article indéfini *a*, les numéraux cardinaux *one*, *two*, etc., et certains quantifieurs (voir **Les quantifieurs**, p. 162). Ils peuvent porter la marque du pluriel et les verbes s'accordent, avec eux, en nombre.

• Les terminaisons régulières du pluriel sont :
- ***-s*** pour la majorité des mots : *one guitar/two guitar**s**, a philanthropist/two philanthropist**s***
- ***-es*** pour les mots terminés par ***-s***, ***-o*** ou ***-y*** (qui devient ***i*** devant ***-es***) : *boss/boss**es**, domino/dominoes, baby/bab**ies**.*

• Certains noms ont un pluriel irrégulier :
- en ***-a*** : *medium/media*
- en ***-en*** : *child/children, man/men, woman/women*
- en ***-es*** : *crisis/crises, hypothesis/hypotheses*
- en ***-ice*** : *mouse/mice*
- en ***-ves*** : *knife/knives, leaf/leaves, life/lives, shelf/shelves, wife/wives*
- avec **une autre voyelle à l'intérieur du mot** : *foot/feet, tooth/teeth*

• Quand ils fonctionnent de manière **indénombrable**, les noms renvoient à une « masse » qui ne peut être comptée :
- concept (*life*, *death*)
- sentiment (*happiness*, *sadness*)
- phénomène de société (*unemployment*, *racism*)
- matière (*gold*)

• On ne peut les employer ni avec l'article indéfini *a* ni avec les numéraux cardinaux *one*, *two*, *three*, etc. Ils ne sont jamais au pluriel. Les verbes s'accordent toujours au singulier avec eux : *All the **money was** sent to charities.*

Les équivalents de certains noms « **indénombrables** » en anglais sont des « **dénombrables** » au pluriel en français : *This millionaire gave **sound advice** to the young investors.* (*Ce millionnaire a donné **de bons conseils** aux jeunes investisseurs.*)

Il en sera de même pour : *baggage/luggage* (*des bagages*), *furniture* (*des meubles*), *information* (*des renseignements*), *news** (*des nouvelles*), *progress* (*des progrès*). En revanche, pour désigner un seul élément, on utilise des **dénombreurs** suivis de ***of*** : *Mr Zuckerberg was shocked at that **piece of** news.* ; *Several **pieces of** furniture are named after English kings.*

*singulier

2. Fonctionnements particuliers

a. Collectif

People, *cattle* ou *police*, etc., désignent des éléments qui peuvent être comptés mais qui ne portent pas de marque visible du pluriel : ***Thousands of people** took part in the demonstration.* (***Des milliers de personnes** ont participé à la manifestation.*)

b. Collectif occasionnel

• *Committee*, *family* ou *government* désignent des éléments dénombrables : *My **family has** always been there for me.* ; *Several African American **families live** in the neighbourhood.* Mais en anglais britannique, ces mêmes noms peuvent aussi avoir un fonctionnement **collectif** : *My **family are** from London.* C'est pourquoi on parle de collectif « occasionnel ».

• Lorsqu'ils ont un fonctionnement collectif, ces noms doivent être considérés comme pluriels mais ils ne permettent pas, contrairement aux collectifs de type *people* ou *cattle*, le dénombrement au moyen de déterminants numéraux.

c. Indénombrable pluriel

Les indénombrables pluriels ne sont jamais au singulier : *morals*, *outskirts*, *clothes* (*des vêtements*), etc., et non ~~*one moral*~~, ~~*one outskirt*~~, ~~*one clothe*~~. Il en est de même pour les objets « doubles » : *binoculars*, *glasses*, *scissors* ainsi que les vêtements pour les jambes (*pants*, *pyjamas*, *trousers*). Ils sont alors dénombrés à l'aide de ***pair*** + ***of*** (*a **pair of trousers***, *two **pairs of trousers***).

d. Invariable

Plusieurs noms d'animaux que l'on chasse ou que l'on pêche (*fish*, *salmon*, *deer*) ainsi que le mot *sheep* sont invariables : ***A sheep** ate my muffin.* ; *I saw **ten sheep** in the barn.*

e. Nom singulier en *-s*

Certains noms de **disciplines** ou de **jeux** prennent toujours un *-s*, même au singulier (*linguistic**s**, mathematic**s**, physic**s**, billiard**s**, bowl**s***, etc.) : ***Billiards is** a game in which chance plays little part.*

Les noms de pays se terminant en ***-s*** sont singuliers en anglais mais pluriels en français : *The United States **is** a big country.* (*Les États-Unis **sont** un grand pays.*)

f. Nom en *-s* avec fonctionnement invariable

Certains noms se terminant en *-s* ont eux un fonctionnement invariable (*crossroads, means, series*, etc.) : *Natasha Walker gave **a/two series** of lectures.* Il en est de même pour certains noms de maladies (*the measles, the mumps*).

3. Noms composés

Dans les noms composés, c'est **le dernier mot** qui désigne la nature de l'ensemble : *a race **horse*** (*une course de **chevaux***), *a horse **race*** (*un cheval de **course***).

Les articles

1. Article zéro (Ø)

On emploie l'**article zéro** (Ø) pour désigner la **nature** des éléments désignés :

- **avec des noms dits « indénombrables »**, pour désigner des choses **de manière globale** (*Ø life, Ø unemployment, Ø bread*) ou quand on s'intéresse surtout à leur **nature** : *The detective saw Ø **blood** on the floor.*
- **avec des noms dits « dénombrables pluriels »**, pour désigner des personnes ou des choses **en général** (*Ø **Children** should lead healthier lives.*) ou quand on s'intéresse surtout à leur **nature** (*There were Ø **hamburgers** on the menu*).
- devant les **noms propres de personnes** (*Ø Rosa Parks*), **de pays** (*Ø England*), les **noms précédés d'un titre** (*Ø President Obama*) ou précisés par **un chiffre** ou **une lettre** (*Ø room 101, Ø staircase C*).

Les articles ne s'emploient pas de la même manière dans les deux langues : *That's Ø **life**.* (*C'est **la vie**.*) ; *Americans fear Ø **unemployment**.* (*Les Américains craignent **le chômage**.*) ; *Ø **Clouds** were floating over Dallas.* (***Des nuages** flottaient au-dessus de Dallas.*)

2. Article indéfini *a/an*

On écrit *a* devant un nom qui commence par un **son consonne** : ***a** book* ; ***a** painting* ; ***a** uniform* (/juː/) et *an* devant un mot qui commence par **un son voyelle** : ***an** apple* ; ***an** orange* ; ***an** hour* (/aʊə/).

- On utilise l'article indéfini devant des noms « dénombrables » pour désigner un **élément** parmi tous les autres quand celui-ci n'est **pas immédiatement identifiable par l'interlocuteur** : *I need **a** chair.* ; *There was **a** computer.*
- On peut aussi l'employer pour « classifier » les éléments désignés, c'est-à-dire pour désigner **n'importe lequel** des éléments concernés: ***A** philanthropist tries to promote human welfare.* ; ***A** platypus is a semi-aquatic mammal.*

Pour indiquer son métier, on emploie l'article indéfini : *I am **an** engineer.* (*Je suis **Ø** ingénieur.*)

3. Article défini *the*

- On emploie *the* pour désigner des personnes ou des choses particulières, censées être **immédiatement identifiables** par l'énonciateur : ***Athletes** need to be very careful about their diet.* (les athlètes en général) ; ***The athletes** were surprised by the announcement.* (des athlètes particuliers en une occasion connue de l'interlocuteur).
- Quelques emplois particuliers de *the* :
  - pour désigner des **groupes sociaux ou nationaux** : ***the** rich, **the** poor, **the** Americans.*
  - des **éléments uniques** que l'interlocuteur peut identifier immédiatement : ***the** sun.*
  - avant les noms de pays formés à partir de **noms communs** : ***the** United States, **the** United Kingdom.*
  - avant les groupes nominaux précisés par des **groupes prépositionnels** ou des **propositions relatives** : ***the** price **of the item**, **the** man **I met yesterday**.*

Les démonstratifs

On emploie ***this*** (pluriel ***these***) pour désigner ce qui est **à proximité** et ***that*** (pluriel ***those***) pour ce qui est **à distance**.

Démonstratif / Proximité ou distance	*this*	*that*
spatiale	***this** pupil* (cet élève-ci = à côté de celui qui parle)	***that** pupil* (cet élève-là = au fond de la salle)
temporelle	***this** year* (l'année en cours)	***that** year* (cette année-là = dans le passé ou l'avenir)
intellectuelle	***This** book is a masterpiece* (celui dont on est en train de parler)	***That** book was extraordinary.* (celui que l'on a fini de lire)
affective	*I like **this** little dog.*	***That** man is a monster.*

Les pronoms

1. Pronoms personnels

Les **pronoms personnels** ne désignent pas forcément des personnes : ***It's** raining.* Ils servent à marquer les trois types de personnes grammaticales (la 1re, la 2e et la 3e) et portent la marque du nombre. À la 3e personne du singulier, ils portent aussi la marque du genre :

- **pronoms personnels sujets** : ***I/you/he-she-it/we/you/they** gave Peter a lift.*
- **pronoms personnels compléments** : *Peter called **me/you/him-her-it/us/you/them** last night.* ; *Peter gave **me/you/him-her-it/us/you/them** a lift.*

2. Pronoms personnels possessifs

• Les **pronoms possessifs** permettent d'exprimer un **lien d'appartenance**. Ils s'accordent en nombre avec le **possesseur** (et non avec la chose possédée, contrairement à ce qui se passe en français) : *Janis Joplin had invited **her** friends.* (*Janis Joplin avait invité **ses** amis.*)

En anglais, on emploie les pronoms possessifs avec les parties du corps et parfois les vêtements. En français, on utilise l'article défini : *Don't forget to brush **your** teeth.* (*N'oublie pas de te laver **les** dents.*)

• À la 3e personne du singulier, les pronoms possessifs s'accordent aussi en genre : ***my/ your/ his-her-its/ our/ your/ their** computer.*

Pour désigner une même chose appartenant à plusieurs personnes, on emploie le pluriel en anglais : *The students raised **their hands**.* (*Les étudiants ont levé **la main**.*)

• On peut renforcer la possession en ajoutant ***own*** après le pronom : *The athlete beat **his own** record.* (*L'athlète a battu **son propre** record.*)

• Il existe aussi une deuxième série de pronoms personnels possessifs : ***mine/yours/his-hers-its/ours/yours/theirs*** (*le mien, le tien, etc.*) qui permettent d'omettre un nom tout en désignant l'identité du possesseur : *My meal was better than **yours**.* On évite ainsi de répéter le mot *meal*, en s'intéressant surtout au fait que c'est de *ton repas* que l'on parle.

3. *Of* + génitif ou « double génitif »

• Pour désigner un ou plusieurs éléments qui appartiennent à la sphère du « possesseur », il arrive que l'on ait besoin d'employer un **article** ou un **démonstratif** avant le groupe nominal qui contient le génitif. On emploie alors la structure **article** + GN + ***of*** + génitif : *Bob was **a** personal friend **of** John Steinbeck**'s**.* (*Bob était un ami personnel de John Steinbeck.*) ; *We got a call from **this** colleague of my father'**s**.* (*On a reçu un coup de fil d'un ami de mon père.*).

• Le mot qui porte le génitif peut être un pronom personnel. Dans ce cas, il faut employer les pronoms de la 2e série : *This friend of **mine/yours/his-hers/ours/yours/theirs** sang beautifully.*

4. Pronoms réfléchis et réciproques

• Les **pronoms réfléchis** permettent de désigner des actions dont le sujet est aussi l'objet : *Peter hurt **himself** while trying to repair his car.* (*Peter **s'est** blessé en essayant de réparer sa voiture.*) ; *He said to **himself** that he would have to eat healthier food.* (*Il **s'est** dit qu'il allait devoir manger plus sainement.*)

• Les pronoms réfléchis portent toujours la marque du nombre :

- *I hurt my**self**.*
- *You hurt your**self**.*
- *He/she/it hurts him/her/it**self**.*
- *We hurt our**selves**.*
- *You hurt your**selves**.*
- *They hurt them**selves**.*

They saw themselves in the mirror.

Certains verbes se construisent sans pronom même s'ils ont un équivalent réfléchi en français : *dress/get dressed* (*s'habiller*), *hide* (*se cacher*), *wash* (*se laver*), *get up* (*se lever*), *shave* (*se raser*).

• Les **pronoms réciproques** permettent de désigner des actions accomplies par plusieurs sujets qui les affectent mutuellement : *They smiled when they saw **each other**.* (*l'un l'autre*) et *The student athletes encouraged **one another**.* (*les uns les autres*).

They saw each other at the cinema.

They are talking to one another.

Les quantifieurs

1. *Many, much, a lot of, lots of, few, a few, little, a little*

• Les quantifieurs indéfinis permettent d'exprimer des quantités **importantes** ou **faibles**, **suffisantes** ou **insuffisantes**. Leur emploi varie :

		Fonctionnement dénombrable	Fonctionnement indénombrable
Quantité importante		***many*** *chairs*	***much*** *water*
		a lot of/lots of *chairs/water*	
Quantité faible	suffisante	***a few*** *chairs*	***a little*** *water*
	insuffisante	***few*** *chairs*	***little*** *water*

• ***Much*** et ***many*** ne sont pas toujours employés dans les énoncés affirmatifs, dans lesquels on leur préfère souvent ***a lot of*** ou ***lots of*** : *Mr Scrooge had **lots of** money* plutôt que *Mr Scrooge had **much** money*.

• ***A lot of***, ***lots of*** ou ***plenty of*** (quantité largement suffisante) peuvent être employés avec des fonctionnements dénombrables et indénombrables : ***a lot of*** *people*, ***a lot of*** *chairs*.

• Pour les **quantités suffisantes** et **insuffisantes**, comparer : *As soon as I have **a little** money, I will buy Jhumpa Lahiri's latest book.* et *I have **little** money and I cannot pay my bills.* Ou ***A few*** *people joined the charity.* (quelques personnes ont rejoint l'organisation caritative et même si leur nombre était faible, on présente la chose sous un angle positif) et ***Few*** *people joined the charity.* (on fait comprendre que trop peu de personnes l'ont fait pour que cela soit significatif.).

• On emploie ***a few*** dans le sens de *quelques* : *I've got **a few** questions to ask you.*

• ***Quite a few*** désigne une quantité importante (*pas mal de*) : ***Quite a few*** *philanthropists have supported our organisation*.

• D'autres quantifieurs indéfinis sont ***several*** + **dénombrable pluriel** (*plusieurs*), ***a small/great number of*** + **dénombrable pluriel** (*certains, un petit/grand nombre de*), ***a good/great deal of*** + **indénombrable** (*une bonne quantité de*).

> ⚠ ***A lot of*** et ***Ø lots of*** sont équivalents mais ~~***Ø lot of***~~ et ~~***a lots of***~~ sont agrammaticaux.

2. *Some* et *any*

Some et ***any*** permettent d'exprimer des quantités **indéfinies** sans préciser si elles sont faibles ou importantes :

- ***some*** + **dénombrable** ou **indénombrable** exprime **une certaine quantité** : *There is **some** tea left. Help yourself!* ; ***Some*** *millionaires want to pay more tax*.

> ⚠ ***Some*** diffère en ceci de l'**article Ø** qui exprime la **nature** des éléments et non leur quantité (voir **Article défini *the***, p. 160) : *There is Ø tea in this cake.* ; *Ø Millionaires are Ø ordinary people, after all*.

- ***any*** + **dénombrable** ou **indénombrable** désigne :

- une **quantité quelconque**, même la plus petite : ***Any*** *oil found in this area will be used to make fuel.*

- **n'importe lequel** des éléments désignés : ***Any*** *fool could do that!* ; ***Any*** *of these shirts will do.*

Not (...) any, not (...) a

Any n'a pas de valeur négative en soi. Après ***not*** ou dans des négations, on nie qu'il y ait une quelconque quantité ou un élément quelconque : *There is**n't any** reason why you should go.* (**pas la moindre**)

> ⚠ **On ne peut employer *not any* avec un « dénombrable » au singulier**. Il faut utiliser ***not a*** : *I have**n't** got **a** mobile phone.*

3. *No*

No + **dénombrable** ou **indénombrable** permet d'exprimer une **quantité nulle** : *There are **no** trees in this garden.* ; *There is **no** alternative.* ; *There was **no** money left.*

4. *Each, every* et *all*

Each, ***every*** et ***all*** permettent de désigner **tous les éléments d'un ensemble** en les **individualisant** plus ou moins :

- avec ***each*** + **dénombrable singulier uniquement**, on passe en revue chaque élément : *A customised training schedule was set up for **each** athlete.*
- avec ***every*** + **dénombrable singulier uniquement**, on passe tous les cas en revue de manière globale : ***Every*** *man has his shortcomings.*
- avec ***all*** + **dénombrable** ou **indénombrable**, la **totalité** est concernée : *They ate **all** the bagels and drank **all** the Coke.*

Whole n'est pas un quantifieur, mais un **adjectif** qui exprime l'**entièreté** : *He ate the **whole** cake.* (*Il a mangé le gâteau* ***tout entier***.)

5. *Most*

Most permet de désigner une **majorité d'éléments** ou la **plus grande partie** d'un tout :

- avec **dénombrable pluriel** (*la plupart*) : ***Most*** *eccentrics are harmless.* (***La plupart*** *des excentriques sont des gens inoffensifs.*)
- avec **indénombrable** (*la plus grande partie de*) : *He spent* ***most*** *of the money I had given him.*

⚠ ***Most of*** n'est employé que devant un groupe **défini** (avec l'article ***the*** ou un déterminant/pronom démonstratif ou possessif) : ***Most of*** *the boys I know like to play football.* ; ***Most***/~~***most of***~~ *boys like to play football.* De nombreux autres quantifieurs peuvent aussi être suivis de ***of*** avant un groupe défini : ***Many/ a lot of/few/all of*** *these students have been to Dallas.* ***Each of*** *them liked the place a lot.* ; ***Much of*** *this money was given to charities.*

6. *Both* et *the two*

Both et ***the two*** (+ **dénombrable pluriel**) permettent de **désigner deux éléments ensemble** :

- avec ***both***, les éléments forment un tout (***tous les deux, l'un comme l'autre***) : ***Both*** *men were Asian Americans.*
- avec ***the two***, ils sont distincts et entrent dans un rapport réciproque : ***The two*** *men greeted each other.*

7. *Either* et *neither*

Either et ***neither*** (+ **dénombrable singulier**) permettent de désigner **simultanément**, mais **individuellement**, les deux éléments d'une paire :

- ***either*** (*l'un(e) ou l'autre/l'un(e) et l'autre*) : ***Either*** *solution will do.* (***N'importe laquelle*** *de ces deux solutions fera l'affaire.*) ; *There were trees on* ***either*** *side of the street.* (*Il y avait des arbres de* ***chaque*** *côté de la rue.*)
- ***neither*** (*aucun(e) des deux*) : ***Neither*** *dress fitted Aretha.* (*Aucune des deux robes n'allait à Aretha.*)

En français, l'emploi de *aucun* appelle l'emploi du mot négatif *ne*. En anglais, ***no*** et ***neither*** contiennent déjà la négation et les énoncés construits avec ces quantificateurs ne comportent pas le mot ***not***.

Les nombres

- ***One***, ***two***, etc. sont des **numéraux cardinaux** qui servent à **compter** des éléments : ***one*** *car*, ***two*** *cars*, etc.
- Précédés de l'article défini, ***first***, ***second***, etc. sont des adjectifs **ordinaux** qui servent à **ordonner** les éléments : *the* ***first*** *day*, *the* ***second*** *car*, etc.

⚠ Pour lire une date ou désigner un monarque, on emploie des adjectifs **ordinaux** : *October 16 =* ***the*** *sixteen****th of*** *October*, *Henry VIII = Henry* ***the*** *eigh****th***.

- ***Dozen***, ***hundred***, ***thousand***, ***million***, ***billion*** sont **invariables** lorsqu'ils font partie de **nombres** et ne sont **jamais suivis de *of*** : *a hundr****ed*** *soldiers*, ***two*** *thousa****nd*** *people*. Ils sont alors précédés de l'article *a* ou de numéraux cardinaux, parfois de quantifieurs indéfinis.

En revanche, ce sont des **noms** lorsqu'ils désignent des quantités approximatives. Ils sont souvent précédés de l'article Ø, parfois de *the*, voire d'autres déterminants. Ils prennent la marque du pluriel et sont **toujours suivis de *of*** : *Ø hundred****s of*** *demonstrators* ; *Ø thousand****s of*** *soldiers* ; *the million****s of*** *stars in the sky*.

⚠ *Ø millions* ***of*** *stars* (***des*** *millions* ***d'****étoiles*) → **nom** ; ***two*** *million Ø people* (***deux*** *millions* ***de*** *gens*) → **nombre**.

Les adjectifs

⚠ Les adjectifs sont invariables en anglais. Ils ne prennent pas la marque du pluriel.

1. La place et l'ordre des adjectifs

- Les **adjectifs épithètes** se placent **avant** le nom même lorsqu'ils sont précédés d'un adverbe : *The British aristocrat owns a* ***big*** *house.* ; *These are* ***very convincing*** *arguments.*

⚠ Devant un nom, ne pas confondre adverbes et adjectifs : *a* ***particular***/~~***particularly***~~ *subject.*

- Les **adjectifs attributs** se placent après des verbes comme *be* ou *seem* : *This watch seems* ***broken***.
- Certains adjectifs ne peuvent être qu'attributs. C'est notamment le cas de *ill*, *content*, *cross*, *glad*, *well* et de bon nombre d'adjectifs commençant par *a-* : *afraid*, *alike*, *alone*, *asleep*, *alive*, *awake*...

Ces adjectifs expriment généralement un **état transitoire**.

Lorsque **plusieurs adjectifs se suivent**, ils respectent généralement l'ordre **TACOM** (**T**aille, **Â**ge, **C**ouleur, **O**rigine, **M**atière) : *an* ***old Chinese*** *woman*, *a* ***large brown leather*** *jacket*. Les adjectifs qui expriment un jugement subjectif se placent en début de la liste : *an* ***impressive*** *blue glass-fronted building*.

2. Les adjectifs verbaux

Les adjectifs verbaux sont **formés à partir de verbes** : *boring* (verbe *bore* + -***ing***), *broken* (verbe *break* + -***en***), *exciting* (verbe *excite* + -***ing***), *tired* (verbe *tire* + -***ed***).

> ⚠ Ne pas confondre la terminaison *-ing* (**sens actif**) : *This lecture was very interest**ing**.* (*Cette conférence était très intéress**ante**.*) et la terminaison *-ed* (**sens passif**) : *The audience was very interest**ed** in what the speaker said.* (*L'auditoire a été très intéress**é** par ce que l'intervenant a dit.*) et non ~~*The audience was very interest**ing** in what the speaker said*~~.

3. Adjectifs substantivés

• Pour désigner des catégories de gens, on peut employer des adjectifs précédés de l'article défini. Ils sont alors **invariables** : *the rich*, *the poor*, *the blind*, *the unemployed*.

• Plusieurs adjectifs de nationalité fonctionnent ainsi, notamment ceux qui se terminent par ***-sh***/***-ch*** (*the English*, *the Dutch*, etc.) ou ***-ese*** (*the Chinese*, *the Portuguese*, etc.).

> Les adjectifs de nationalité prennent une majuscule en anglais, contrairement à leurs équivalents en français : *an **A**merican movie* (*un film **a**méricain*) ; ***B**ritish actors* (*des acteurs **b**ritanniques*).

• En anglais, on emploie des noms pour désigner « les noirs » et « les blancs » : *the black**s***, *the white**s***.

> **Adjectifs de nationalité du tournoi de rugby « des six nations »**
>
> - **Emploi substantivé** : *the English* (*les Anglais*) ; *the French* (*les Français*) ; *the Welsh* (*les Gallois*) ; *the Irish* (*les Irlandais*) sauf *the Scots* (*les Écossais*) et *the Italians* (*les Italiens*).
> - **Emploi au pluriel**, comme pour la plupart des adjectifs en *-an* et en *-i* : *the Americans*, *the Indians*, *the Somalis*, etc.

• Dans les suites **nombre** + **N** + **adjectif**, le nom prend la marque du pluriel quand l'ensemble est attribut, mais reste invariable en position épithète. On met souvent des tirets entre les mots : *This boy is **ten years old**.* et *This is a **ten-year-old** boy.*

4. Haut degré

On peut rendre le sens d'un adjectif encore plus fort et montrer ainsi que ce qu'il exprime est vrai à un **haut degré** :

- avec un **adverbe** (*very*, *extremely*, etc.) : *Texans are said to be **very** friendly.*
- avec ***such*** placé avant l'ensemble du groupe nominal : *Aretha Franklin was **such a powerful singer**!* ; *I've never seen **such miserable weather** in my life.*
- ***so*** placé avant l'adjectif : *This book was **so wonderful**.*

Les comparatifs et les superlatifs

1. Comparatifs

On emploie le **comparatif** pour comparer **le degré d'une qualité** possédée par deux éléments.

a. Le comparatif de supériorité (adj. *-er* + *than* ou *more* + adj. + *than*)

• On ajoute généralement *-er* aux adjectifs d'une ou deux syllabes terminés par :

-er : *clever/clever**er***
-ow : *narrow/narrow**er***
-y (*y* devient *i* devant *-er*) : *friendly/friendl**ier***.

• On emploie ***more*** + adj. + ***than*** avec les autres adjectifs : *Texas is said to be **more conservative than** other American states.*

• Dans certains cas, on peut aussi employer ***more*** devant certains adjectifs d'une ou de deux syllabes terminés par ***-er***, ***-ow*** ou ***-y*** : *Lord Egerton tended to be **more close** to his dogs than to other people.*

b. Le comparatif d'égalité (*as* + adj. + *as*)

*Beyoncé is **as popular as** President Obama.*

c. Le comparatif d'infériorité (*less* + adj. + *than*)

*Being an athlete is **less dangerous than** being a firefighter.*

> On emploie plus rarement ***less*** + adj. + ***than*** en anglais que *moins + adj. + que* en français.

En anglais, on exprime fréquemment le comparatif d'infériorité **en niant l'égalité** (***not as*** *[parfois* ***so****]* + adj. + ***than***) : *Individual Rothschilds were* ***not as rich as*** *American tycoons. (Considérés individuellement, les Rothschild* ***n'égalaient pas en richesse*** *les grands hommes d'affaires américains.)*

Le comparatif de supériorité peut aussi être employé avec un adjectif de sens opposé : *Housing is* ***cheaper*** *in Texas* ***than*** *in California. (Le prix du logement est* ***moins élevé*** *au Texas* ***qu****'en Californie.)*

d. L'accroissement progressif

On peut exprimer un **accroissement progressif** en utilisant deux comparatifs de supériorité ou d'infériorité reliés par la conjonction de coordination ***and*** (voir **La coordination**, p. 179) : *Lance Armstrong rode* ***faster and faster****.* ; *The athlete is* ***less and less reliable****.*

2. Superlatifs

On emploie le **superlatif** pour comparer un élément à **tous les autres éléments de sa classe**.

a. Le superlatif de supériorité (***the*** + adj.-***est*** ou ***the most*** + adj.)

- Dans la plupart des cas, on emploie ***the... -est*** pour les adjectifs d'une syllabe : *Andrew Carnegie became* ***the richest*** *man of his age.*
- On tend à employer aussi ***the... -est*** pour les adjectifs de deux syllabes terminés :
  - par ***-er*** : *clever/****the*** *clever****est***
  - par ***-ow*** : *narrow/****the*** *narrow****est***
  - par ***-y*** *(****y*** devient ***i*** *devant -****er****)* : *funny/****the*** *funn****iest***

This is ***the friendliest Englishman*** *I've ever met.*

- On place généralement ***the most*** devant les autres adjectifs de plus d'une syllabe : *Muhammad Ali was* ***the most intimidating*** *boxer of all times.*

On emploie une forme particulière de superlatif (***the*** *adj.****-er****/****the more*** + *adj.*) pour dire qu'un élément est celui qui possède le plus ou le moins de propriétés dans un ensemble de deux éléments : *Ali and Liston were both very strong, but Ali proved* ***the*** *strong****er****.*

b. Le superlatif d'infériorité (***the least*** + adj.)

That location was ***the least romantic*** *place on earth.*

c. Les comparatifs et superlatifs irréguliers

Quelques adjectifs courts d'usage fréquent ont des formes irrégulières au comparatif et au superlatif :

Adjectif	Comparatif	Superlatif
good	better	the best
bad	worse	the worst
far	farther/further	the farthest/the furthest

La formation des comparatifs et des superlatifs reflète différentes influences exercées sur l'anglais au cours des siècles.

Les **formes régulières** et **irrégulières** des **adjectifs courts** sont germaniques alors que le **placement** de ***more*** et ***the most*** **devant les adjectifs** évoque l'influence du français, à laquelle l'anglais a été exposé après l'invasion de Guillaume le Conquérant.

Comparez l'anglais *more conservative* et *the most intimidating* avec le français *plus conservateur* et *le plus intimidant*.

Les constructions à plusieurs noms

Pour mettre **deux noms en relation** (le premier, N1, et le second, N2), il existe trois structures en anglais :

1. N1 of N2

Généralement employée lorsque **N2** désigne une chose ou une personne qui n'est **pas immédiatement identifiable** par l'interlocuteur ou qui n'est pas présente à son esprit :

The body of a man *was found in the woods.*

N1 N2

2. Génitif (N2's N1)

Généralement employée lorsque **N2** désigne une chose ou une personne **déjà présente à l'esprit** de l'interlocuteur ou **immédiatement identifiable** :

Churchill's elocution *was peculiar.*

N2 N1

- Quand N1 désigne des objets, des vêtements ou les parties du corps, on emploie souvent le **génitif**, car c'est la personne elle-même (N2) qui est immédiatement identifiable par l'interlocuteur : ***Muhammad Ali's legs*** *were long and nimble.* ; ***Charles Dickens's hat*** *was auctioned off last night.*

Pas d'article défini qui porte sur N1 dans une structure avec le génitif : *Mr. Zuckerberg's contribution* (*la contribution de M. Zuckerberg*) et non ~~*The Mr. Zuckerberg's contribution*~~.

- On peut pourtant avoir l'article défini s'il porte sur N2 : *la contribution du milliardaire* = ***the billionaire's*** *contribution (Mr. Buffett = the billionaire).*

- Quand une personne n'est pas identifiable par l'interlocuteur, on a souvent **N1 of N2** : *It was then that I first passed **the house of Neil Leifer**, a man who was to become a famous sports photographer.*
- Ce peut être vrai aussi quand elle est identifiable, mais non présente à son esprit : *This story reminds me of **the rise of Winston Churchill**.*
- Quand N1 désigne un objet, on emploie souvent **N1 of N2** car il est fréquent qu'un objet ne soit pas immédiatement identifiable ou présent à l'esprit de l'interlocuteur : *He looked down and saw **the broken leg of an armchair**.*
- Lorsque N1 désigne un objet immédiatement identifiable et présent à l'esprit de l'interlocuteur, on peut avoir **N2's N1**. Dans une publicité pour un fauteuil, c'est-à-dire un document dans lequel le fauteuil est le sujet principal (et donc présent à l'esprit de l'interlocuteur), on aura : ***The armchair's back** is designed to be comfortable.*

3. N2 N1

Avec **N2 N1**, on ne fait plus ressortir le fait qu'il existe une **relation** entre **deux éléments distincts** désignés par N1 et N2, mais on **restreint le type de l'élément désigné** à l'aide de N2.

Comparez : *the **World Cup's greatest moments*** (*les **meilleurs moments de la Coupe du monde***) et ***a World Cup match*** (un ***match de Coupe du monde***).
N2 (World Cup) N1 (match)

La première combinaison fait ressortir le fait qu'il y a eu la Coupe du monde et qu'il y a eu, pendant cette Coupe du monde, des moments particulièrement excellents. Avec la seconde combinaison, on montre que l'on ne parle pas de n'importe quel type de match, mais d'un match de Coupe du monde.

Les prépositions

Placées avant des groupes nominaux, les prépositions permettent de préciser les **lieux**, les **moments**, etc.

1. Repérer un élément dans l'espace

Pour choisir la bonne préposition, il faut se poser quatre questions :

- Est-ce que l'on repère par rapport à un **point**, une **surface** ou un **volume** ?
- L'élément que l'on veut repérer est-il **immobile** ou **en mouvement** ?
- Si l'élément est en mouvement, ce mouvement est-il **vers** ou **depuis** le repère ?
- Si le repère est une surface ou un volume, le mouvement **traverse-t-il** le repère ?

Repère / Élément	Point	Surface	Volume
Immobile	**at** *Wait for me **at** the bus stop.*	**on** *The scissors were **on** the table.*	**in** *The bacon is **in** the fridge.*
En mouvement vers le repère	**to** *I drove **to** Austin.*	**onto** *Angie flung the suitcase **onto** the desk.*	**into** *He walked **into** the room.*
En mouvement depuis le repère	**from** *Jessica is just back **from** Houston.*	**off** *I took the sheet **off** the bed.*	**out of** *The police brought the man **out of** the car.*
Mouvement qui traverse le repère		**across** *We sailed **across** the Channel.*	**through** *The visitors walked **through** the hall.*

Autres prépositions :

- ***over*** (ce qui recouvre quelque chose ou effectue un mouvement qui couvre quelque chose) : *One flew **over** a cuckoo's nest.*
- ***in front of*** (devant) : *A man was standing **in front of** the house.*
- ***behind*** (derrière) : *A figure was lurking **behind** the tree.*
- ***above*** (au-dessus d'un certain niveau) : *A 2-floor car park was built **above** ground.*
- ***below*** (en-dessous d'un certain niveau) : *New Orleans is located **below** sea level.*

2. Repérer un élément dans le temps

- **at** (heures ou points dans le temps) : ***at** 5pm*, ***at** Christmas*, ***at** that moment*
- **on** (jours de la semaine ou dates) : ***on** Monday*, ***on** the 6th of May*
- **in** (périodes étendues telles que siècles, années) : ***in** the 20th century*, ***in** the 70s (in the seventies)*, ***in** 2016*

⚠ ***in** the morning*, ***in** the afternoon*, ***in** the evening*, mais ***at** night*.

⚠ Après une préposition, on emploie la forme **V *-ing*** (et surtout pas ***to*** + **V**) : *Before going/~~to go~~ to the cinema,…* (voir **V *-ing*** (**le « gérondif »**), p. 176).

3. Usages divers des prépositions

D'autres prépositions permettent d'exprimer d'autres types de relations. Par exemple, la cause (***because of***, ***thanks to***), la destination (***for***), le moyen (***by***, ***with***), la concession (***in spite of***, ***despite***), le contraste (***contrary to***, ***unlike***), etc.

Be, have, do

Trois verbes jouent un rôle particulièrement important dans la formations des énoncés : ***be***, ***have*** et ***do***, qui sont tantôt verbes lexicaux et tantôt auxiliaires.

Au présent

- ***be*** conjugué a **trois formes distinctes** : *I* ***am****, you* ***are****, he/she/it* ***is****, we* ***are****, you* ***are****, they* ***are****.*
- ***have*** conjugué a **deux formes**, il devient ***has*** à la 3ᵉ personne du singulier : *I* ***have****, you* ***have****, he/she/it* ***has****, we* ***have****, you* ***have****, they* ***have****.*
- ***do*** conjugué a **deux formes**, il devient ***does*** à la 3ᵉ personne du singulier : *I* ***do****, you* ***do****, he/she/it* ***does****, we* ***do****, you* ***do****, they* ***do****.*

Au prétérit

- ***be*** conjugué a **deux formes** : *I* ***was****, you* ***were****, he/she/it* ***was****, we* ***were****, you* ***were****, they* ***were****.*
- ***have*** est irrégulier mais n'a qu'**une forme** : *I* ***had****, you* ***had****, he/she/it* ***had****, we* ***had****, you* ***had****, they* ***had****.*
- ***do*** est irrégulier mais n'a qu'**une forme** : *I* ***did****, you* ***did****, he/she/it* ***did****, we* ***did****, you* ***did****, they* ***did****.*

1. *Be*, *have* et *do* comme verbes lexicaux

• Quand ***be***, ***have*** et ***do*** sont **verbes lexicaux**, ils ont un sens :

- ***be*** exprime l'existence : *I think, therefore I* ***am****.*
- ***have*** exprime généralement la possession : *Mr Buffet* ***has*** *a Cadillac.*
- ***do*** a le sens de *faire* : *What did you* ***do*** *last night?*

• ***Be***, ***have*** et ***do*** peuvent aussi être employés comme **verbes-outils** dans les combinaisons temps grammaticaux / outils (voir **Les temps grammaticaux et leurs outils** ci-dessous) ou dans les énoncés négatifs, interrogatifs ou emphatiques (voir **Les énoncés interrogatifs, interro-négatifs, emphatiques et exclamatifs**, p. 173). On les désigne alors sous le nom d'**auxiliaires** plutôt que sous celui de verbes.

• Quand ***have*** et ***do*** sont **verbes lexicaux**, l'auxiliaire ***do*** intervient dans les énoncés :

- interrogatifs : ***Do you have*** *brothers and sisters?*
- négatifs : *"But I* ***didn't do*** *anything."*
- emphatiques : *"Oh yes, you* ***did do*** *something."*

2. *Be*, *have* et *do* comme auxiliaires

• Trois verbes jouent un rôle particulièrement important dans la formations des énoncés : *be*, *have* et *do*, qui sont tantôt verbes lexicaux et tantôt auxiliaires.

• Quand ***be***, ***have*** et ***do*** sont **auxiliaires**, ils portent eux-mêmes l'inversion, la négation et l'accent d'emphase. ***Do*** n'intervient pas dans les énoncés négatifs, interrogatifs ou emphatiques : *I* ***haven't*** *seen him for years.* (et non ~~*I didn't have seen him for years*~~.)

À l'oral

Au présent		Au prétérit
*am/are not → are**n't***	*is not → is**n't***	*was not → was**n't***
*have not → have**n't***	*has not → has**n't***	*had not → had**n't***
*do not → do**n't***	*does not → does**n't***	*did not → did**n't***

• Qu'il soit auxiliaire ou verbe lexical, ***be*** porte l'inversion, la négation et l'accent d'emphase.

L'énoncé

Énoncer consiste à affirmer, nier, demander, évaluer quelque chose qui concerne le monde réel ou agir sur celui-ci par la parole. Produire un énoncé nécessite de **mettre en relation** un **sujet** et un **ensemble verbe + compléments**. On dispose pour cela de **temps grammaticaux** et d'**outils**, comme ***be - ing***, ***have -en*** ou l'outil **Ø** ou encore les modaux (voir **Temps grammaticaux** ci-contre, **Outils grammaticaux**, p. 168 et **Les modaux**, p. 171).

Les temps grammaticaux et leurs outils

• Les **temps grammaticaux** ne doivent pas être confondus avec le temps « réel ». On peut, par exemple, se servir du temps appelé le présent pour se référer à un état ou une action qui s'est produite dans le passé ou se produira dans l'avenir (voir **Le présent**, p. 173).

• Un ou plusieurs outils grammaticaux peuvent par ailleurs **se combiner** aux temps (voir **Outils grammaticaux**, p. 168).

• **Ce n'est pas la nature des actions elle-même qui décide du choix des temps et des outils**. Celui qui parle choisit les temps et les outils en fonction de la manière dont il veut présenter tel état ou tel événement.

1. Temps grammaticaux

En anglais, il existe **deux temps grammaticaux** :

- **le présent** (*the present tense*) que l'on emploie pour présenter la mise en relation entre le sujet et l'ensemble verbe + compléments comme **conforme à la réalité dans la situation où l'on parle** : *Harry* ***loves*** *reggae.*
- **le prétérit** (*the preterite tense*) que l'on emploie pour présenter la mise en relation entre le sujet et l'ensemble verbe + compléments comme **en décalage avec la situation où l'on parle**. Ceci peut traduire :

- un **décalage temporel** lorsque l'état ou l'évènement a eu lieu à un **moment révolu** : *We* ***went*** *to Texas last year.*

- une **situation irréelle** lorsque l'état ou l'événement n'est pas **conforme à la réalité** : *Even if I* ***knew****, I wouldn't tell you.*

2. Outils grammaticaux

a. L'outil *be -ing*

• Pour construire des énoncés avec l'outil ***be -ing***, on conjugue l'auxiliaire ***be*** au temps requis – le présent ou le prétérit – et on ajoute ***-ing*** à la base verbale du verbe qui suit.

• Dans certaines combinaisons (voir **Le *present perfect be -ing*** et **Le *past perfect* ou *pluperfect be -ing***, p. 170), l'auxiliaire ***be*** porte lui-même la marque de l'outil ***have -en***.

• Avec l'outil ***be -ing***, celui qui parle **fait sentir sa présence** et présente des états ou des évènements comme **déjà perçus**, **envisagés** ou **réalisés**, parfois pour les **expliquer**, les **justifier** ou les **développer**. Il décrit toujours un **état**, un **état de fait**, une **situation** : *Every time you drive, **you are taking a risk***.

⚠ Contrairement à l'idée reçue, ***be*** + **V *-ing*** ne sert pas, en soi, à décrire une action en cours de déroulement. Il peut aussi, comme ici, permettre de revenir sur une action qui se répète ou sur une vérité générale.

b. L'outil *have -en*

• Pour construire des énoncés avec l'outil ***have -en***, on conjugue l'auxiliaire ***have*** au temps requis – le présent ou le prétérit – et l'on ajoute ***-en***, c'est-à-dire la marque du **participe passé**, à l'infinitif du verbe qui suit.

• Le participe passé est régulièrement marqué par la terminaison ***-ed*** : *cross/cross**ed**, jump/jump**ed**, remember/remember**ed***. Celle-ci prend la forme ***-d*** si le verbe se termine par un *e*.

• Les verbes dits « irréguliers » sont souvent des verbes d'origine germanique dont le participe passé a conservé sa forme d'origine ou une forme apparentée (*hear/heard*, *lie/lain*, *speak/spoken*).

• Avec l'outil ***have -en***, celui qui parle signale l'**existence d'un lien** entre **deux moments** dont l'un est **antérieur à l'autre** : *What **have** I **done** to deserve this?*

• Le **participe passé** renvoie, comme son nom l'indique, à un état ou un évènement **passé**. Souvent, sa forme n'est d'ailleurs pas sans rappeler celle du prétérit. L'outil ***have -en*** permet donc, en quelque sorte, d'attribuer au sujet la trace, parfois la conséquence ou le résultat, d'un état ou d'un événement passé : *I have done something* pourrait ainsi se comprendre comme *I did something*.

• Avec l'outil ***have -en***, celui qui parle signale l'**existence d'un lien** entre **deux moments** dont l'un est **antérieur à l'autre** : *What **have** I **done** to deserve this?*

moment présent (*have*) — évènement passé ayant une conséquence dans le moment présent (*done*)

c. L'outil Ø

Pour construire les énoncés avec l'outil **Ø**, on conjugue le verbe au temps requis ou on utilise l'auxiliaire ***do*** selon le type d'énoncé construit .

Avec l'outil **Ø**, celui qui parle **s'efface** et présente des états de fait ou des évènements comme « bruts », c'est-à-dire **non déjà perçus** ou **envisagés**. Il met l'accent sur la **nature de l'état** ou de l'**évènement** désignés par le verbe et ses compléments : *A philanthropist is someone who **takes** care of his fellow beings.*

d. Combinaisons des temps avec l'outil Ø

Le présent + l'outil Ø = le présent simple (V-/-*s*)

• Dans les énoncés affirmatifs, au **présent simple**, les verbes ont la même forme qu'à l'infinitif, sauf à la 3e personne du singulier, où ils prennent la **terminaison *-s*** : *give/gives*.

Celle-ci prend la forme :
-es après les sons /s/, /z/, /ʃ/, /tʃ/ et /dʒ/ : *catch/catch**es***
-ies pour les verbes terminés par *-y* : *carry/carr**ies***.

• Dans les questions, la négation et l'emphase, on emploie l'outil ***do*** ou ***does*** à la 3e personne du singulier (voir ***Be, have, do***, p. 167, **Les énoncés interrogatifs, interro-négatifs, emphatiques et exclamatifs**, p. 173) : *Delfín Carbonell Basset **does not** live in Spain. **Does** Delfín live in Spain? Delfín **does** live in Spain, contrary to what you think.* À l'oral, ***do(es) not*** se prononce ***d(oe)sn't*** : *Delfín Basset **doesn't** live in Spain.*

On peut employer le présent simple pour :

- nommer des états ou des actions en cours au moment où l'on parle : *Listen. I think Mr Armstrong **wants** to say something.* ; *I **pour** the milk and **add** the sugar.* (description de la réalisation d'une recette de cuisine à la télévision).
- accomplir des actes par la parole : *I **apologise**, I **promise** I won't do it again.*
- désigner des états ou des actions qui caractérisent le sujet : *Willie Nelson **plays** the guitar.* ; *"What **does** your father **do** for a living?" - "He **works** as an engineer in Amarillo."*
- relater des évènements passés dans le cadre d'un récit « animé » (présent de narration) : *I **turn** around, and what **do** I **see**? There**'s** this guy standing in front of me with a gun.*
- donner des précisions sur des états ou des évènements dont la réalisation doit se produire dans l'avenir : *My train **leaves** at 4pm.*

Le prétérit + l'outil Ø = le prétérit simple (V *-ed*)

• Dans les énoncés affirmatifs, **le prétérit** est régulièrement marqué par la **terminaison *-ed*** : *cross/cross**ed** ; jump/jump**ed** ; remember/remember**ed**.*

Celle-ci prend la forme **-*d*** si le verbe se termine par un *e* : *apologise/apologis**ed*** ; *cause/caus**ed*** ; *stare/star**ed***.

• Même remarque que pour les participes passés : les verbes dits « irréguliers » sont souvent des verbes d'origine germanique qui ont conservé au prétérit leur forme d'origine ou une forme apparentée : *lie → lay, stand → stood, wear → wore.*

• Dans les questions, la négation et l'emphase, l'auxiliaire ***do*** porte lui-même la marque du prétérit et devient ***did*** : *I **did not use** performance enhancing drugs.* (voir **Les énoncés interrogatifs, interro-négatifs, emphatiques et exclamatifs**, p. 173). À l'oral, ***did not*** se prononce ***didn't***.

On peut employer le prétérit pour :

- faire part d'évènements révolus ou en faire le récit : *Janis Joplin **died** in 1970.*
- désigner des états ou des actions caractéristiques du sujet : *Baron de Rotschild **drove** a carriage drawn by four zebras.*
- évoquer des situations irréelles : *She wishes her daughter **talked** to her more.*

e. Combinaisons des temps avec l'outil *be -ing*

Le présent + l'outil *be -ing* = le présent *be -ing* (*be* + V *-ing*)

• On peut employer le présent ***be -ing*** pour (voir le sens du **présent** et celui de l'**outil *be -ing***, p. 167-168) :

- expliquer ou réinterpréter un état ou un évènement déjà mentionné, expliciter ou faire expliciter le contenu d'un propos déjà tenu : *When a child whines and complains, **he is doing it** to get attention.* ; ***What are you trying** to tell me?*
- justifier / expliciter ou faire justifier / expliciter une situation déjà perçue par l'interlocuteur : *"**What are you doing**? We're all waiting for you." "Just a second! **I am finishing** an urgent piece of work."*
- justifier ou expliciter une situation en se référant à un événement à venir : *"Will you be there tonight?" - "I can't. I**'m having** dinner with Bill Gates."* (voir **Référence à l'avenir**, p. 173)
- établir un cadre pour les évènements d'un récit : *This song is about **a man who is digging** a hole in his garden. Suddenly his shovel hits something. He stops to see what it is...*

• La **présence de celui qui parle** peut parfois donner une **valeur affective** à l'énoncé : *Derek, **you're drinking** again!* (Celui qui parle n'informe pas ici son interlocuteur qu'il boit mais lui fait un reproche.). On peut aussi imaginer un client mécontent s'adressant à un vendeur : *This is too expensive. You**'re always wanting** too much.*

> ⚠ Contrairement à l'idée reçue, ***be*** + **V *-ing*** ne fonctionne pas qu'avec des verbes d'action. Il peut également être compatible avec des verbes d'état.

Le prétérit + l'outil *be -ing* = le prétérit *be* + V *-ing* (*be -ed* + V *-ing*)

On peut employer le prétérit ***be*** **+ V *-ing*** pour :

- décrire une situation, une scène : *People **were eating**, **drinking**, **dancing** and **having** a wonderful time.* Avec le prétérit, on nommerait seulement la nature des actions de façon neutre : *People **ate**, **drank**, **danced**. It **was** wonderful.*
- faire sentir la présence, « regard » d'un personnage dans un récit : *Lord Rokeby walked down to the shore. The sun **was shining** on the water.* Ici, la scène est décrite à travers le regard de Lord Rokeby alors qu'avec le prétérit, on n'aurait pas cet effet : *Lork Rokeby walked down to the shore. The sun **shone** on the water.*
- développer des évènements et en donner une explication en décalage avec la réalité : *The master looked at his slave **as if he was trying** to kill him with his stare.*

  Dans ce dernier cas, on peut employer l'auxiliaire ***be*** à l'indicatif : *as if he was...* (registre peu formel) mais aussi au **subjonctif** : *as if he were...* (registre plus formel).

f. Combinaisons des temps avec l'outil *have -en*

Le présent + l'outil *have -en* = le *present perfect* (*have* + V *-en*)

On emploie le *present perfect* pour montrer que la situation présente porte en elle la trace du passé : *Mr Smith is the man we need. He is an experienced salesman and **he has worked** in India.* (énoncé produit par un patron après un entretien d'embauche pour montrer que Mr Smith est le plus qualifié en raison de son expérience).

*Sheila will not be in class today. **She has broken her arm**.* (on fait comprendre qu'elle ne peut pas venir aujourd'hui en raison de ce qui s'est passé un peu auparavant).

> En anglais, quand on veut se référer à une situation présente qui dure depuis un certain temps, on emploie le *present perfect*, alors que le français emploie le présent : ***I have lived** in San Antonio for three years.* (*J'habite à San Antonio depuis trois ans.*)

⚠ Lorsqu'une action a « des conséquences dans le présent », on pense parfois qu'il faut employer le *present perfect*. Ce n'est pas toujours vrai : *Sheila* ***broke*** *her arm while getting off the bus yesterday.* Cet évènement a des conséquences dans le présent (Sheila souffre aujourd'hui). Le prétérit est utilisé pour présenter l'évènement comme en décalage avec la situation dans laquelle se trouve la personne qui parle.

Le passé composé français peut avoir la valeur du **prétérit** anglais (décalage par rapport au moment où l'on parle) : *It is in 1889 that Andrew Carnegie* ***wrote*** *his famous article.* (*C'est en 1889 qu'Andrew Carnegie* ***a écrit*** *son célèbre article.*) Ici, on n'emploie pas le *present perfect*, malgré sa ressemblance avec le passé composé.

Before that moment, it had rained.

At that moment, the grass was wet and slippery.

Le prétérit + l'outil *have -en* = le *pluperfect* ou *past perfect* (*had* + V *-en*)

On emploie le *past perfect* ou *pluperfect* pour :

- désigner un **évènement antérieur à un évènement passé** : *Last Monday, Terry used his car to go to The Alamo. The week before, he* ***had taken*** *the bus.*
- montrer qu'un **évènement passé portait la marque d'une situation antérieure** : *LeBron* ***had slept*** *like a log and felt better.* ; *He* ***had known*** *his sponsor for ages.*
- désigner une **situation irréelle qui porte la marque d'une situation passée** : *Chin wouldn't be in jail if he* ***had not tried*** *to fix the match.*

g. Combinaisons des temps avec les deux outils *be -ing* et *have -en*

Le présent + les outils *be -ing* et *have -en* = le *present perfect be -ing* (*have* + *been* + V *-ing*)

- On emploie ***have*** + ***been*** + **V *-ing*** pour **justifier l'état présent** du sujet. On met l'accent sur l'action qui est à l'origine de l'état présent : *"Your clothes are covered with paint. What* ***have you been doing****?" - "****I've been painting*** *my guitar."*
- Avec ***have + V -en***, on évoquerait ici le **produit des actions** accomplies par le sujet à un moment passé : *"What's new, Willie?" - "Well,* ***I've painted*** *my guitar in red."*

Le prétérit + les outils *be -ing* et *have -en* = le *past perfect* ou *pluperfect be -ing* (*had* + *been* + V *-ing*)

On emploie *had* + *been* + V *-ing* pour indiquer que la mise en relation sujet / verbe + compléments est **en décalage avec la situation où l'on parle** :

- **décalage temporel** : *Goretti was exhausted.* ***She had been working*** *like a Trojan.*
- **décalage** dû à une **situation irréelle** : *Ian Wright was speaking* ***as if he had been running****...*

Since, For, During, Ago

1. *Since* et *for*

Deux mots peuvent traduire *depuis* : ***since*** et ***for***.

- ***Since*** désigne un **point dans le temps**. Il est normalement suivi d'une **date** ou d'un **point de départ** marquant le début d'une période (*since last year, since he began to...*, etc). Si la période s'étend jusqu'au moment où l'on parle, on emploie le *present perfect* simple ou en *be -ing* : *Most Americans* ***have considered*** *Mary Wineberg a great athlete* ***since*** *2008.* ; *She* ***has been training since*** *she was very young.* Si la période est en rupture avec le moment où l'on parle, on emploie le *past perfect* simple ou en *be -ing* : *Americans* ***had considered*** *Armstrong a great cyclist* ***since*** *1990.* ; *He* ***had been cycling since*** *teenage years.*
- ***For*** exprime une **durée**. S'il est employé pour désigner une **période de temps** qui s'étend jusqu'au moment où l'on parle, on emploie *have* + V *-en* (+ V *-ing*) : *Beyoncé* ***has known*** *Jay-Z* ***for*** *years. They* ***have been performing*** *together* ***for*** *a while.* Si la période est en rupture avec le moment où l'on parle, on emploie le *past perfect* simple ou en *be -ing* : *Buddy Holly* ***had been*** *a great favourite* ***for*** *some time.* ; *Janis Joplin* ***had been singing for*** *years.*

2. *For* et *during*

Deux mots peuvent traduire *pendant* : ***for*** et ***during***.

- ***For*** exprime une **durée**. Normalement, cette période de temps est en décalage avec le moment où l'on parle. On emploie donc V *-ed* ou le *past perfect* : *Buddy Holly* ***played*** *rock and roll* ***for*** *a few years. Before his death, the public* ***had known*** *him for a relatively short period of time.*
- ***During*** permet de **situer une action** dans une période donnée : *I* ***met*** *Elton John* ***during*** *my stay in London.* Cette rencontre a eu lieu **pendant / durant mon séjour** à Londres, c'est-à-dire **à un moment donné** de ce séjour.

⚠ Malgré sa ressemblance avec le verbe du français *durer*, *during* **n'exprime pas la durée** : *I played **for** three hours.* (*J'ai joué durant trois heures.*) et non ~~*I played during three hours*~~.

On peut avoir l'impression que *during* exprime la durée dans *Hannah yawned **during** the whole meeting.* mais c'est ***whole*** qui produit cet effet.

3. *Ago*

Ago permet d'obtenir le sens de *il y a (+ durée)*. Il permet de **situer un évènement passé par rapport au moment où l'on parle**. Contrairement à *il y a*, ***ago*** se place **après** l'expression de la durée : *I visited Texas two years **ago***.

En français, l'expression ***il y a*** + ***durée*** a un sens temporel. C'est dans ce cas seulement que son sens correspond à celui de ***ago***. Lorsque ***il y a*** est employé pour affirmer l'existence ou la présence de quelque chose ou de quelqu'un (***Il y a** un ordinateur dans la pièce*), son sens est tout à fait différent et correspond à celui de la tournure *there is/there are* en anglais (voir **There is/there are**, p. 175).

Les modaux

1. Fonctionnement et sens

Les modaux sont des **outils** qui permettent à celui qui parle de **signaler sa présence** :

- pour **exprimer son degré de certitude** quant à la probabilité que la relation entre le sujet et l'ensemble verbe + compléments soit conforme à la réalité.
- pour **déclarer que le sujet doit ou peut agir** pour que cette relation devienne conforme à la réalité (valeurs d'**obligation**, d'**interdiction**, de **devoir**, de **conseil**, de **capacité**, etc.).

• Les modaux se placent **entre le sujet et le verbe et ses compléments** ou **entre le sujet et le 1er verbe-outil du groupe verbal** : *They **must** come at once.*

• Ils ne **prennent pas de -*s* à la 3e personne du singulier** : *Helen **may** be at home.*

• Ils ne peuvent être suivis que d'une **base verbale (V)** : *You **could work** harder.* ou d'une **base verbale + un outil** : *You **could have worked** harder.*

• Ils ne sont jamais suivis de ***to*** + **V**, d'une forme conjuguée ou d'un autre modal.

• Ils **portent directement la négation** : *Anthony **should not** have shouted so loud.*

• Ils **s'inversent avec le sujet** dans les questions : ***Can** you swim?*

• À l'oral, la plupart des suites de type ***modal + not*** sont **contractées** : *cannot* → *can't* ; *could not* → *couldn't* ; *must not* → *mustn't* ; *should not* → *shouldn't* ; *will not* → *won't* ; *would not* → *wouldn't*.

2. *Must*

Must exprime l'**obligation**. On l'emploie pour :

- **déclarer que le sujet doit ou peut agir** : *You **must** go.* (*Tu dois y aller.* C'est une **obligation**.)
- **exprimer un degré de certitude** : *They **must** be at home.* (*Ils doivent être à la maison.* C'est « **obligé** ».)

3. *Can* et *may*

Can et ***may*** expriment la **possibilité**. On les emploie pour :

- **déclarer que le sujet doit ou peut agir** : *You **can**/You **may** go now.* (*Tu peux y aller.* Cela t'est **possible** car je t'y autorise.) ; *I **can** swim.* (*Je sais nager.* J'en suis capable, cela m'est **possible**.)
- **exprimer un degré de certitude** : *They **may** be at home.* (*Il est **possible** qu'ils soient chez eux.*)

4. *Will* et *shall*

Will et parfois ***shall*** (registre soutenu) permettent de se référer à **l'avenir** (voir **Référence à l'avenir**, p. 173) avec diverses nuances.

• On emploie ***will*** pour :

- émettre un **pronostic**, une **prévision** : *Sally **will** come to the party.*
- accepter de **faire quelque chose**, faire une **promesse** : *OK. I **will** do it.*
- formuler une **demande** ou un **ordre** : *You **will** come with me, won't you?*
- décrire un **comportement caractéristique** : *My computer **will** crash if I run this programme.*

• On emploie ***shall*** pour :

- exprimer un **fort engagement** personnel : *I **shall** succeed.*
- donner un **commandement** (langue officielle, biblique ou très formelle) : *You **shall** not kill.* ; *Scotland **shall** be independent.* ; *The president **shall** hold office for five years.*

5. Modaux au prétérit

• ***Could***, ***might***, ***should*** et ***would*** sont respectivement les modaux ***can***, ***may***, ***shall*** et ***will*** au prétérit (***could*** = ***can*** + **-*ed***, etc.). Or, on sait que le prétérit est la marque d'un **décalage** (voir **Les temps grammaticaux et leurs outils**, p. 167).

• Avec les modaux ***could***, ***might***, ***should*** et ***would***, **-*ed*** peut :

- indiquer un décalage **temporel** : *When I was younger, I **could** run a marathon.*
- prendre une valeur d'**atténuation** : *You **shall** go!* (commandement péremptoire) / *You **should** go.* (conseil) ; *He **may** come.* (*Il se **peut** qu'il vienne.*) / *He **might** come.* (*Il se **pourrait** qu'il vienne*).

Pour parler d'un comportement qui caractérisait quelqu'un dans le passé, on utilise ***would*** : *When Jhumpa's mother screamed at her, she **would** scream back.*

> ⚠ Ne pas confondre cet usage avec ***used to*** + V qui permet d'insister sur le fait qu'une situation était vraie dans le passé, mais ne l'est plus au moment où l'on parle : *Getting a visa* ***used to be*** *easy, but the regulations have tightened up.*

6. Degrés de certitude

On emploie les modaux suivants, par ordre croissant de certitude exprimée :

The phone is ringing, it…	
… ***might/could*** *be Frances.*	(*Cela* ***pourrait*** *être elle.*)
… ***may***	(*Cela* ***peut*** *être elle.*)
… ***should***	(*Cela* ***devrait*** *être elle.*)
… ***must***	(*Cela* ***doit*** *être elle.*)
… ***will***	(*C'****est*** *elle, j'en suis sûr.*)

7. Énoncés négatifs avec des modaux

- Quand les modaux expriment un **degré de certitude**, la négation concerne la situation elle-même : *It* ***might/may*** *(etc.)* ***not*** *be Frances.* (*Cela pourrait / peut (etc.)* ***ne pas être elle.***)

> ⚠ Avec ***cannot/can't*** et ***could not/couldn't***, la négation porte sur le modal et non sur la situation elle-même : *It* ***can't*** *be Frances.* (*Cela* ***ne peut pas*** *être elle.*) ≠ *It* ***may not*** *be Frances.* (*Cela* ***peut ne pas*** *être elle*).

- Quand les modaux expriment un **degré de certitude**, la négation porte sur le modal :
  - interdiction : *You* ***mustn't*** *eat red meat.*
  - conseil de ne pas faire (parfois nuance de reproche) : *You* ***shouldn't*** *try to fix the match.*
  - commandement absolu de ne pas faire : *You* ***shall*** *not pass.*
  - permission refusée : *You* ***can't*** *walk on the lawn here.* ; *No, you* ***may not*** *smoke in my office.*
  - incapacité : *They* ***can't*** *beat Lebron James.*
  - promesse de ne pas faire, refus : *I* ***won't*** *do it again, I* ***won't*** *go with you.*

8. Effets particuliers

On a parfois des effets de sens quand l'énoncé est affirmatif ou interrogatif ou quand le sujet est à la 1re, la 2e ou la 3e personne. On peut :

- formuler **une requête**, une **invitation** dans un énoncé interrogatif (***will*** **+ sujet à la 2e personne**) : ***Will*** *you do this for me?* ; ***Will*** *you come with us?*
- proposer son **aide** dans un énoncé interrogatif (***shall*** **+ sujet à la 1re personne**) : ***Shall*** *I open the window?*
- proposer son **aide** dans des énoncés affirmatifs ou interrogatifs (***can*** **+ sujet à la 1re personne**) : ***Can*** *I help you?* ; *I* ***can*** *send you the link.*

9. *Need* et *dare*

Need (avoir besoin de) et ***dare*** (oser) fonctionnent parfois comme des modaux, parfois comme des verbes lexicaux : *You* ***don't need to*** *be/You* ***needn't*** *be from Texas to like ZZ Top.* ; *How* ***did he dare to*** *ask me if I was from Texas?/How* ***dared he*** *ask me if I was from Texas?*

10. Modaux avec V + *have -en*

On emploie un modal suivi d'une **base verbale +** ***have -en*** (l'infinitif parfait) pour intervenir sur un énoncé en décalage avec la situation où l'on parle et pour exprimer :

- un **jugement** / une **intervention** en rapport avec des **évènements révolus** : *I didn't see Alex. He* ***must have missed*** *his train.*
- un **jugement** / une **intervention** en rapport avec des **situations irréelles** : *If I had studied harder, I* ***might have passed*** *the exam.* (Celui qui parle a échoué.)

On peut aussi employer un modal dans un énoncé avec l'**outil** ***be -ing*** ou la **combinaison des outil** ***be -ing*** **et** ***have -en***. L'important est que le verbe qui suit le modal (ici, l'auxiliaire *have* ou *be*) soit toujours une **base verbale** : *Surely Lord Rokeby can't* ***be bathing*** *again!* ; *Could Lance Armstrong* ***have been taking*** *PEDs?*

11. Modaux et périphrases en *to*

- Il existe des périphrases en ***to*** dont le sens se rapproche de celui de certains modaux. Par exemple :

Modal	Périphrase en *to* correspondante	Sens
can	*be able to*	capacité
can/may	*be allowed to*	permission
must	*have to*	obligation, devoir
should	*ought to*	conseil

- Avec les modaux, celui qui parle se présente comme **directement à l'origine** de l'obligation, du devoir, du conseil, etc. Avec les périphrases en ***to***, ce n'est pas le cas. La source en est présentée comme extérieure ou objective. Comparez : *Now that's enough, Mr Armstrong. You* ***must*** *stop taking performance enhancing drugs.* et *Mr Armstrong* ***has to*** *stop taking performance enhancing drugs if he wants to be allowed to compete.*
- Il est impossible d'avoir deux modaux qui se suivent. Quand celui qui parle veut intervenir sur un énoncé qui exprime une possibilité, un devoir, une prédiction, etc., on peut utiliser des **périphrases** (c'est-à-dire une expression plus longue qu'un modal car constituée de plusieurs termes, dont le sens est plus ou moins équivalent à celui d'un modal) en ***to*** qui expriment des sens proches de ceux des modaux : *I will* ***have to*** *be more careful.* ; *They may* ***be***

***allowed to** go to the concert.* ; *Mary Wineberg should **be able to** run that marathon.*

Ne pas confondre ***do not have to*** (absence d'obligation : *You **don't have to** come. Tu **n'es pas obligé** de venir*) et ***must not*** (interdiction : *You **must not** go. Tu **ne dois pas** y aller.*)

12. Référence à l'avenir

a. *Will*

On peut se référer à l'avenir en employant ***will***. Cette référence peut être une simple prévision / prédiction ou peut se confondre avec l'expression de la volonté : *Wales **will** beat England.* ; *I **will not go** to university.* ***Shall*** est parfois employé à la 1re personne dans un style très formel (voir **Les modaux**, p. 171).

Will / would ne sont pas employés dans les subordonnées de temps introduites, par exemple, par ***when***, ***while***, ***as soon as***, ***as long as***, même si le futur y est employé en français : *As soon as **I get**/~~will get~~ **a job in Austin**, I will buy a flat near Zilker Park.* (*Dès que **j'aurai un emploi à Austin**, j'achèterai un appartement près de Zilker Park.*). Ils ne sont pas employés non plus dans les subordonnées de condition : *If you buy/~~will buy~~ this guitar, you will not be disappointed.*

b. *Be going to*

- On se réfère à l'avenir avec ***be going to*** lorsqu'on s'appuie sur des éléments présents pour annoncer ce qui va se passer dans l'avenir : *When I grow up, I**'m going to** be a billionnaire.* (la décision est déjà prise).
- ***Will*** exprime souvent une **conséquence** alors que ***be going to*** exprime un évènement **inévitable** dans les circonstances présentes : *Don't walk on that bridge. It **will** collapse.* (le pont va s'effondrer **si tu marches dessus**) et *Don't walk on that bridge. It**'s going to** collapse.* (on voit que ce pont va s'effondrer **de toute façon**).

c. Le présent

- On emploie le **présent simple** pour se référer de façon neutre à des évènements programmés dans l'avenir : *My train **leaves** at 6.* (voir **Le présent + l'outil Ø**, p. 168).
- On emploie le **présent *be -ing***, pour expliquer / justifier une situation présente par des dispositions prises pour l'avenir : *I **am** leaving tomorrow.* (voir **Le présent + l'outil *be -ing***, p. 169)

d. Les périphrases

Des périphrases en *to*, comme ***be to*** (quelque chose a été **organisé à l'avance**), ***be about to*** (être **sur le point de**), ***be bound to*** (quelque chose arrivera **forcément**) permettent également de se référer à l'avenir.

Au prétérit, ***be to*** est employé pour décrire un évènement après coup comme dicté par le destin : *Napoleon **was to** meet defeat on the plains of Waterloo.*

Les énoncés interrogatifs, interro-négatifs, emphatiques et exclamatifs

1. Énoncés interrogatifs

- Dans les ***Yes/No questions*** et les questions **ouvertes** (auxquelles la réponse est autre que oui ou non) où *who* ou *what* ne sont pas sujets, il y a une **inversion** entre le 1er auxiliaire du groupe verbal (voir ***Be, have, do***, p. 167) et le sujet : ***Did you** fix that match?* ; ***Have you** been feeling like that for a long time?* ; *Where **did hip-hop** come from?*
- Dans les **questions ouvertes** où ***who*** ou ***what*** sont **sujets**, il n'y a **pas d'inversion** : ***Who wrote** "A Christmas Carol"?* ; ***Who has** been eating my muffins?* ; ***What's** going on here?*

2. Énoncés interro-négatifs

Dans les **énoncés interro-négatifs**, on **combine** les marques de la négation et de l'interrogation : ***Don't you** like jazz?* ; ***Aren't you** leaving tomorrow?* (*Do you not like jazz?* et *Are you not leaving tomorrow?* sont très formels et s'emploient peu à l'oral).

3. Énoncés emphatiques

Les **énoncés emphatiques** servent à **affirmer** une chose qui a été ouvertement ou implicitement remise en question. L'auxiliaire (voir ***Be, have, do***, p. 167) est alors accentué : *"Since you don't like hamburgers, we'll have vegetables instead." – "But I **do** like hamburgers"* ; *"I'd like you to stay here and do your homework first." – "But I **have** done my homework."*

4. Énoncés exclamatifs

On peut former des énoncés exclamatifs :

- avec ***how*** **+ adj. en tête d'énoncé** (on omet alors parfois le sujet et le verbe, surtout si celui-ci est ***be***) : ***How** fantastic!* (Plus naturel que *How fantastic this concert was!*)
- avec ***what*** **(+ *a/an*) + adj. + nom** : ***What** a fool I've been!* ; *What a fantastic concert it was!* On omet parfois l'ensemble **sujet + verbe** : ***What** a fantastic concert!*
- avec ***so*** **+ adj.** : *This aristocrat is **so** eccentric!*
- avec ***such*** **(+ *a/an*) + adj. + nom** : *He is **such** an eccentric!* (voir aussi **Haut degré**, p. 164).

L'impératif

1. Formation des énoncés à l'impératif

- À la 2e personne du singulier et du pluriel, on forme l'impératif avec la base verbale : *Go!* ; *Wait a minute!*
- À la 1re et à la 3e personne du singulier et du pluriel, on fait précéder la base verbale personne de ***let*** + **pronom personnel** approprié : *Well, **let me** think!* (*Voyons ! Réfléchissons...*) ; *Let's go!* (*Allons-y !*) ; ***Let him** play!* (*Qu'il joue !*)

2. Formation des énoncés négatifs à l'impératif

- À la 2e personne du singulier et du pluriel, on a le schéma ***don't (do not)*** **+ V (+ complément(s))** : ***Don't*** *do that!*
- À la 1re et à la 3e personne, on a le schéma ***let's not (let us not)*** **+ V (+ complément(s))** : ***Let's not*** *panic!*

Le schéma ***don't (do not)*** **+ V (+ complément(s))** s'applique même quand ***be*** est le verbe principal. C'est le seul cas où l'auxiliaire ***do*** doit être employé avec le verbe ***be*** : ***Don't be*** *stupid!*

La voix passive (*be* + V *-en*)

On forme la voix passive en employant ***be*** suivi d'un participe passé (V *-en*) : *Lance Armstrong* ***was*** *ador****ed*** *by the public before he fell into disrepute.*

- On emploie la voix passive quand on veut parler de **la personne / la chose affectée par un événement** ou encore **l'objet d'une démarche** plutôt que des auteurs ou de la source de l'évènement / de la démarche : *Runaway slaves* ***were*** *punish****ed*** *by their masters.* ; *Lord Cornbury* ***was*** *hat****ed*** *by a great many people.*
- Le passif permet d'omettre ces auteurs ou cette source quand leur identité est évidente ou peu importante : *Zaha Hadid has often been criticised (~~**by her opponents**~~).* ; *The English are often considered as eccentrics (~~**by people of other nationalities**~~).*
- Certains verbes dont le sens s'apparente à *dire / demander* ou à *donner* (*advise, ask, give, lend, offer, promise, sell, send, show, tell*) permettent de former des énoncés à la voix passive à **deux objets** : ***The charity*** *was given* ***a new name.*** ; *I was told* ***to wait in the hall.***

En anglais, on utilise souvent la voix passive là où le français préfère le pronom indéfini ***on*** : ***I had been told*** *that the weather would be nice.* (***On m'avait dit*** *qu'il ferait beau.*)

- Certains verbes, dont le sens s'apparente à celui de *dire* ou de *croire* (*say, think, rumour, believe, report*), permettent de suggérer que quelque chose est vrai sans pour autant s'en porter garat. Ils sont employés au passif et suivis de ***to*** **+ infinitif *have*** **V *-en*** : *Francis Henry Egerton* ***is said/thought/believed/reported to have dined*** *with his dogs every day.* (*(À ce qu'on dit,) Francis Henry Egerton* ***aurait dîné*** *avec ses chiens tous les jours.*)

Reprises par des auxiliaires

1. Réponses dites « courtes »

À l'oral, pour éviter les répétitions, les auxiliaires peuvent reprendre un verbe qui vient d'être utilisé pour :

- **répondre à une question posée** : *"Do you like jazz?" - "Yes,* ***I do****." ; "Do you like rap?" - "I'm afraid* ***I don't****."*
- **contrer ce qui vient d'être affirmé** : *"You did not even try to call me." - "****I did****, but the line was busy." ; "You've been smoking again, Tony." - "****I haven't****."*
- **contraster deux sujets** : *Jay-Z never played the blues, but Bessie Smith* ***did****. ; "I enjoyed the concert very much.* ***Didn't*** *you?"* (l'élément contrasté est alors accentué).
- **maintenir le contact avec l'interlocuteur** : *"I really enjoyed the concert." - "****Did*** *you?" (Ah bon ? / Ça alors !) ; "I don't like hamburgers." - "****Don't*** *you?"* (*Ah bon ? / Vraiment pas ?*).

2. *So / Neither do I*, etc.

Les auxiliaires peuvent aussi permettre de reprendre des verbes lexicaux pour décrire des situations où le même état ou la même action est attribuée à des sujets différents (ils expriment alors le sens de *moi aussi, toi aussi, lui non plus*, etc.) :

- après un **énoncé affirmatif (*so* + auxiliaires / modal + sujet)** : *"I really enjoyed the concert." - "****So did*** *I"" ; "Mr Gates has been influenced by Andrew Carnegie and* ***so have*** *other American businessmen."*
- après un **énoncé négatif (*neither* + auxiliaires / modal + sujet)** : *"I did not enjoy the play." - "****Neither did*** *I." ; "John shouldn't eat so much junk food." - "****Neither should*** *you."*

Les *question tags*

On forme les *question tags* avec des auxiliaires dits de reprise. On les emploie en fin d'énoncé pour demander confirmation de ce que l'on vient de dire. Plus ou moins équivalents à *N'est-ce pas ?, C'est bien ça ?*, etc., ils sont très fréquents en anglais :

- après un **énoncé affirmatif**, le *question tag* est **interro-négatif** : *You're joking,* ***aren't you?*** (*Vous plaisantez,* ***n'est-ce pas ?***)
- après un **énoncé négatif**, le *question tag* est **interrogatif** : *You didn't really enjoy that show,* ***did you?*** (*Vous n'avez pas réellement apprécié ce spectacle,* ***si ?***)

Si l'on attend vraiment une réponse, l'intonation du *question tag* est **montante**. Si l'on désire seulement une confirmation, elle est **descendante**.

Les adverbes

Les adverbes qui portent sur la relation entre le sujet et le verbe peuvent se placer à différents endroits dans les énoncés, notamment certains adverbes de manière : ***Slowly****, he walked away.* ; *He* ***slowly*** *walked away.* ; *He walked* ***slowly*** *away.* ; *He walked away* ***slowly****.* Il existe cependant des tendances fortes.

1. Adverbes de fréquence indéfinie

• Les adverbes de fréquence indéfinie (*never*, *hardly ever*, *rarely*, *often*, *always*) se placent entre le sujet et le 1er élément du groupe verbal (le 1er verbe-outil ou le verbe) : *He **often** goes to Texas.* ; *He **never** listens to rock'n'roll.*

• ***Sometimes*** peut aussi être placé en début ou en fin d'énoncé : *Words can speak louder than actions **sometimes**.*

2. Adverbes de fréquence précise

Les adverbes de fréquence précise (*daily*, *weekly*, *monthly*, *yearly*) se placent en fin d'énoncé : *Magazines are often published **weekly**.* ; *Sometimes they are published **monthly**.* On leur préfère souvent des équivalents comme *every day*, *every week*, *every month*, etc.

⚠ Les adverbes ne se placent jamais entre un verbe et son complément d'objet : *He speaks Japanese very well.* et non ~~*He speaks very well Japanese*~~.

Les verbes à particule

Dans un registre peu formel, certains verbes peuvent être suivis de particules adverbiales qui ressemblent à des prépositions (*about*, *at*, *in*, *off*, *out*, *up*, *to*, etc.). L'ensemble forme **un tout** dont les constituants peuvent avoir un sens qui peut être plus ou moins différent de celui du verbe et de la particule seuls : *give up* (*abandonner*).

Certains verbes à particules ont plusieurs sens. Ainsi, *make up* peut signifier *se réconcilier*, *se maquiller*, *former* ou *composer*.

1. Points communs avec les verbes prépositionnels

• Comme les prépositions, les particules adverbiales peuvent désigner des mouvements dans l'espace : *He went **up** the hill.* (préposition) ; *The curtain went **up**.* (particule adverbiale).

• Les verbes à particules et les verbes prépositionnels peuvent avoir un sens différent de celui du verbe et de la particule seuls : *turn* (*tourner*) ; *turn on someone* (*s'en prendre à quelqu'un*, verbe prépositionnel) ; *take* (*prendre*) ; *take in* (*tromper*, verbe à particule).

2. Différences avec les verbes prépositionnels

• Les verbes prépositionnels sont toujours suivis d'un complément. Les verbes à particule, eux, peuvent ne pas en avoir :

- **verbe prépositionnel** : *The car went **off** the road.* (*La voiture a quitté la route.*)
- **verbe à particule adverbiale** : *The bomb **went off**.* (*La bombe a explosé.*)

Le complément des verbes prépositionnels suit toujours la préposition alors que le complément des verbes à particule peut être placé entre le verbe et la particule adverbiale :

- verbe prépositionnel : *Jhumpa's father **turned on** her mother.*
- verbe à particule adverbiale : *Lucy **turned** the TV **on**.*

• Quand le complément des verbes à particule est un pronom, il est toujours placé entre le verbe et la particule adverbiale mais il suit toujours les verbes prépositionnels :

- verbe prépositionnel : *Lucy **turned on** me.*
- verbe à particule : *Lucy walked to the TV and **turned** it **on**.*

Certains verbes à particule peuvent être suivis de prépositions :
Jhumpa wanted to **make up** (verbe à particule) **for** (préposition) *her behaviour.*
(*Après s'être mal conduite, Jhumpa voulait faire amende honorable.*)

There is/there are

• On emploie ***there is/there are*** pour **affirmer l'existence / la présence** d'une **chose** ou de **quelqu'un**.

En anglais, ***be*** s'accorde en nombre avec la chose dont on affirme l'existence / la présence : *There **are** many African Americans in show business.* En français, avec *il y a*, le verbe ne s'accorde pas avec la chose dont on affirme l'existence / ou la présence : *Il y a bon nombre d'Afro-Américains dans le monde du spectacle.*

• On peut parfois utiliser ***there exist(s)*** : ***There exist** charities which provide free health care.*

⚠ Ne pas confondre *there* avec *it*, même si en français, on dit *il y a* : ~~*It exist many species of fish*~~.

L'énoncé complexe

Un énoncé complexe est un énoncé comportant **plusieurs propositions**.

Les propositions subordonnées nominalisées

• Dans un énoncé, un **groupe nominal** peut typiquement remplir l'une des fonctions suivantes :

- sujet : ***Tobacco** can damage your health.*
- complément d'une préposition ou complément d'objet : *I'm used to **the cold**.* ; *Martin Luther King said **words that brought tears to my eyes**.*
- attribut : *Muhammad Ali was **the first man to win the heavyweight championship three times**.*

• Certains outils permettent à des propositions de remplir ces mêmes fonctions :

1. *That* + proposition avec sujet + verbe conjugué

• On emploie souvent ***that*** pour introduire une proposition de type **sujet + verbe conjugué (+ complément(s))** qui remplit les fonctions suivantes :

- **complément d'objet direct** : *He said **that he had never taken performance-enhancing drugs**.* (voir **Le discours rapporté**, p. 179).
- **attribut** : *His problem is **that he eats too much**.*

• On emploie souvent des propositions en ***that*** dans des schémas de type ***it is/was* + adj. + *that* + S / V conjugué (+ complément(s))** avec des adjectifs qui traduisent une probabilité, un jugement, une appréciation ou une obligation : *It is likely **that we will visit Dallas**.*

2. *To* + V (l'infinitif « complet »)

• Une proposition en ***to* + V** ne comporte pas toujours de sujet exprimé, mais un sujet est toujours sous-entendu. Les propositions en ***to* + V** remplissent souvent les fonctions suivantes :

- **complément d'objet direct** (après un verbe transitif) : *Henry wants **to go to Dallas**. Henry* est le sujet sous-entendu de *go*.
- **attribut** : *The best thing is **to tell the truth**. You* est le sujet sous-entendu de *tell*.

• Si l'on veut exprimer le sujet, on le fait précéder de ***for*** : *It's difficult **<u>for me</u> to believe this**.*

• On emploie souvent des propositions en ***to* + V** dans des schémas de type ***it is/was* + adj. + to + V (+ complément(s))** avec des adjectifs qui traduisent un jugement, une appréciation, une nécessité ou une obligation / interdiction : ***It's good** (for us) **to be in Texas**.* ; ***It is forbidden to smoke on the premises**.*

3. V-*ing* (le « gérondif »)

Une proposition en **V-*ing*** ne comporte pas toujours de sujet exprimé, mais un sujet est toujours sous-entendu. Les propositions en **V-*ing*** remplissent souvent les fonctions suivantes :

- **sujet** : ***Smoking** can damage your health. You* est le sujet sous-entendu de *smoke*. C'est vrai notamment pour les équivalents des infinitifs français en position de sujet (entre autres lorsqu'ils peuvent être précédés de « le fait de ») : *(Le fait de) Fumer peut nuire à votre santé*.
- **complément d'objet direct** : *This artist began **playing** the guitar at the age of 6.*
- **complément de préposition** : *Mandela succeeded in **freeing** his nation.*
- **attribut** : *This aristocrats's favourite pastime is **training** his dogs.*

Ne pas confondre la structure ***be used to* + V-*ing*** qui signifie *être habitué(e)* et ***used to* + V** qui permet d'insister sur le fait qu'une situation était vraie dans le passé, mais ne l'est plus au moment où l'on parle (voir **Les modaux** – ***would*** et ***used to***, p. 171-172).

⚠ Ne pas utiliser ***to*** + V après une préposition : *Before visiting London* et non ~~*Before to visit London*~~ (*Avant de visiter Londres*).

- **direct (après un verbe transitif)** : *I like **going to jazz concerts**. I* est le sujet sous-entendu de *go*.

4. Différence entre *to* + V et V -*ing*

• ***To* + V** permet de désigner des actions ou des états encore à venir alors que **V -*ing*** est employé pour se référer à des états ou des évènements déjà réalisés ou perçus. On dit : *Remember **to turn off** the lights when you leave the room.* (n'oublie pas de le faire quand tu sortiras) mais *I remember **turning off** the lights when leaving the room.* (je me souviens de l'avoir fait). Cette phrase est d'ailleurs équivalente à *I remember **having turned off** the lights when leaving the room.* (avec **L'outil *have -en*** p. 168-170).

• C'est pourquoi on emploie généralement **V-*ing*** après les verbes qui indiquent que les états ou les évènements qui suivent ont déjà été réalisés ou envisagés ou qu'ils ont déjà commencé (*stop*, *regret*, *remember*, *keep (on)*, *give up*, *quit*) : *Stop **smoking**.* (*Arrêter de fumer*) et non ~~*Stop to smoke.*~~

• C'est vrai aussi avec les verbes qui expriment l'appréciation (apprécier une activité suppose qu'on l'a déjà pratiquée) (*like*, *love*, *enjoy*, *appreciate*, *hate*, *can't stand*, etc.). On emploie aussi **V-*ing*** après les verbes suivants : *avoid*, *consider*, *deny*, *involve*, *mind*, *suggest*, etc.) : *Would you mind **judging** our speech competition?*

Avec ce type de verbes, on a parfois la possibilité d'employer les deux structures. Le sens peut alors être différent : *I like **to do the dishes as soon as dinner is finished**.* (*Je préfère faire la vaisselle aussitôt le repas terminé*) ; *I like **doing the dishes**.* (*J'apprécie en soi le fait de faire la vaisselle*).

• À l'inverse, on emploie généralement ***to* + V** après les verbes qui indiquent que les états ou les événements qui suivent sont encore à venir (*want*, *plan*, *intend*, *mean*, *promise*, *propose*, *offer*, etc.) : *Barack Obama **intends to give** a speech on environmental matters.*

5. Propositions de type nom + *to* + V / V-*ing* (+ complément)

• Parfois, les subordonnées nominalisées en ***to* + V** ou **V-*ing*** comportent un Groupe Nominal (GN) qui est à la fois complément du verbe de la principale et sujet du verbe de la subordonnée. C'est alors l'ensemble **GN + *to* + V / V-*ing* (+ complément)** qui remplit la fonction « nominale » : *Christina Lamb helped **Malala to write***

her autobiography. ; *They watched* ***William Wallace haranguing the warriors***.

• Dans ce type de structure, les verbes souvent employés avec ***to* + V** sont : *advise*, *allow*, *force*, *help*, *get* (voir **Faire faire**, p. 178), *persuade*, *push*, *want*, etc.

• Les verbes employés avec **V-*ing*** sont souvent des verbes de perception : *hear*, *see*, *watch*, etc., mais pas seulement.

• Dans ce type de structure, quand le GN sujet du verbe de la subordonnée est un pronom personnel, ce sont les pronoms compléments (***me/you/him-her-it/us/you/them***) qui sont utilisés (voir **Pronoms personnels**, p. 161) : *Christina Lamb helped* ***her*** *to write her autobiography.* ; *They watched* ***him*** *haranguing the warriors.*

• Dans les subordonnées nominales avec **V -*ing***, on a aussi parfois des pronoms personnels possessifs (voir **Pronoms personnels possessifs**, p. 161) : *I don't really mind him/****his*** *smoking in my office.*

Les propositions subordonnées « circonstancielles »

1. Subordonnées de condition

• Pour exprimer une **condition probable**, on utilise une subordonnée en ***If* + *sujet* + V au présent** suivie d'une proposition principale en ***will*** : ***If you work*** *hard, you* ***will*** *succeed.*

• Pour exprimer une **condition moins probable ou irréelle**, on utilise une subordonnée en ***If* + sujet + V au prétérit** suivie d'une proposition principale en ***would*** : ***If he got*** *the job, he* ***would*** *move to San Antonio.* ; ***If I had*** *more money, I* ***would*** *take a trip to Dallas.*

On exprime l'**irréel du passé** avec une subordonnée en ***If* + sujet + V au *past perfect*** suivie d'une proposition principale en ***would* + infinitif parfait** : ***If he had come*** *to the party, he* ***would have met*** *Mr Buffet.*

2. Subordonnées de temps

On peut construire des **subordonnées de temps** avec ***when*** (*quand*), ***as soon as*** (*dès que*), ***while*** (*pendant que*), ***as*** (*alors que*), ***before*** (*avant que*), ***after*** (*après que*), ***until*** (*jusqu'à ce que*), etc. : *William Wallace spoke* ***until*** *the sun began to set.*

Rappel : on n'emploie pas *will* (ou *will* + *-ed* = *would*) dans les subordonnées de condition ou de temps (voir **Les modaux,** p. 171), même si l'on y emploie le futur en français : *When* ***I see him****, I will tell him a piece of my mind.* (*Quand* ***je le verrai****, je lui dirai ma façon de penser.*)

3. Subordonnées de but

On peut construire des **subordonnées de but** avec ***in order to***, ***so as to*** ou simplement ***to*** (équivalents de *pour* en français) : *Mary walked faster* ***(in order) to*** *win the race.* (*Mary a accéléré le pas* ***pour*** *gagner la course.*)

Ne pas employer *for* (calque du français *pour*) dans les subordonnées de but : ~~*Mary will have to run faster for win/ winning the race.*~~

Attention à l'ordre des mots lorsque la négation précède un verbe à l'infinitif précédé de *to*. ***Not*** se place **avant *to*** : *She went on a diet (so as)* ***not to gain*** *more weight*. et non ~~*to not gain more weight*~~ ou ~~*to don't gain more weight*~~.

Penser à la question de Hamlet : *To be or* ***not to*** *be...?*

4. Subordonnées de cause

• On emploie ***because*** (*parce que*) pour présenter la raison comme inconnue de l'interlocuteur : *Jay-Z won't be singing tonight* ***because*** *he has a sore throat.*

• On emploie ***since*** (*puisque*) pour présenter la raison comme déjà connue de l'interlocuteur : *Mr Obama won't run for office again* ***since*** *no president can serve more than two successive terms.*

• ***As*** (*puisque*, *comme*, *car*) a parfois un sens proche de celui de *since* : *Mr Obama won't run for office again* ***as*** *no president can serve more than two successive terms.* On peut cependant présenter la raison comme non encore connue de l'interlocuteur : *Willie had to swap his guitar* ***as*** *a string had broken.*

• Avec ***for*** (*car*), on présente la raison comme non encore connue de l'interlocuteur : *We ate a lot* ***for*** *we were very hungry.* ***For*** ne peut pas être employé en début de phrase.

5. Subordonnées de contraste

• Pour exprimer le contraste dans une proposition subordonnée, on emploie ***whereas*** (*alors que*, *tandis que*) : *In the Unites States, they drink Coca Cola* ***whereas*** *in France, we drink wine.* On peut aussi employer ***while*** ou même ***when***, qui revêtent alors un autre sens que dans les subordonnées de temps

En français, *tandis que* peut aussi avoir un sens temporel ou un sens contrastif.

6. Subordonnées de concession

Pour exprimer la concession dans une proposition subordonnée, on emploie :

- ***although***, ***even though*** ou ***though*** (*bien que*, *même si*) en tête de proposition : ***Although*** *Karim's family is originally from India, he considers himself a born-and-bred Englishman.*

- deux propositions indépendantes et les adverbes ***however*** ou ***(and) yet*** (*cependant, toutefois, et pourtant*) au début de la seconde proposition : *Karim's family is originally from India. **However**, he considers himself a born-and-bred Englishman.*
- les prépositions ***despite*** et ***in spite of*** (*malgré*) suivis de **groupes nominaux** : ***Despite his family's Indian origins**, Karim considers himself a born-and-bred Englishman.*

Les subordonnées relatives

1. *That/which/Ø*

- ***Who*** et ***whom*** renvoient à un antécédent humain. On emploie :
  - ***who*** quand le relatif est sujet : *The students **who** took part in the speech competition did very well.*
  - ***whom*** quand le relatif est COD ou après une préposition : *The man to **whom** Dorothy had given her watch was standing on a rostrum.* (registre très formel)
- ***Which*** (relativement formel) renvoie à un antécédent non humain. Il peut être :
  - **sujet :** *Those competing in Original Oratory gave speeches **which** lasted 40 minutes.*
  - **COD :** *The arguments **which** they used were convincing.*
- Dans un registre moins formel, ***that*** ou **Ø** renvoient à un antécédent humain ou non humain : *The student **that/Ø** we heard had a stentorian voice.* ; *The arguments **that/Ø** he used were really original.*

Which et ***that*** peuvent être sujet, mais **Ø** ne le peut pas : *The students **that** spoke seemed to be afraid of the audience.* ; ~~*The students Ø spoke seemed to be…*~~.

2. *Which* relatif de « phrase » (ce qui, ce que)

Which, lorsqu'il est **relatif de phrase**, reprend **ce qui vient d'être dit**. Il est alors précédé d'une virgule : *He told me that he had got the job, **which** surprised me a lot.* (*Il m'a dit qu'il avait obtenu le poste, **ce qui** m'a beaucoup surprise.*) ; *This businessman decided to turn to crowdfunding, **which** I really appreciated.* (*Cet homme d'affaires a décidé de recourir au financement participatif, **ce que** j'ai réellement apprécié.*)

⚠ Quand ***ce qui / ce que*** reprennent ce qui vient d'être dit, ils ne doivent surtout pas être traduits par ***what*** : *He told me that he had got the job,* ~~***what** surprised me a lot*~~.

3. Relatives circonstancielles

Where, ***when*** et ***why*** introduisent des relatives dites **circonstancielles** et sont employés pour apporter des informations sur le lieu, le temps ou la cause. Leur sens est équivalent à celui d'un ensemble **préposition + *which*** :

- *The town **where** (= in which) we stayed was one of the smallest in Texas.*
- *The McGloughlin still remember the day **when** (= on which) they decided their home would become multigenerational.*
- *Do you know the reason **why** (= for which) they chose crowdfunding?*

- On emploie parfois **Ø** au lieu de ***when*** : *The day **when** they decided their home would become multigenerational, = The day **Ø** they decided their home would become multigenerational.*
- On emploie souvent ***why*** au lieu de ***the reason why*** : *Do you know **the reason why** they chose crowdfunding? = Do you know **why** they chose crowdfunding?*

4. *Whose*

Whose permet de reprendre un antécédent tout en lui associant un lien de relation ou d'appartenance semblable à celui qu'exprime un génitif ou ***of***. Il a un sens équivalent à celui du ***dont*** d'appartenance en français : *The start-up **whose** growth (= the growth **of** which) was so extraordinary was run by my friend.* (*La start-up **dont** la croissance était si impressionnante était dirigée par mon ami.*)

5. Relatives « nominales »

What peut aussi parfois être traduit par ***ce que / ce qui***. Il est alors équivalent à ***the thing that*** : ***What*** *(= The thing that) I would like to know is whether he got the job.* (***Ce que** j'aimerais savoir, c'est s'il a obtenu le poste.*)

Who, ***where***, ***when*** et ***why*** fonctionnent parfois de manière similaire. Les propositions qu'ils introduisent sont appelées relatives nominales car ces pronoms sont équivalents à ***the person*** (*who*), ***the place*** (*where*), ***the moment*** (*when*), ***the reason*** (*why*) :

- *You can choose **who (= the person who)** you like.* (*Tu peux choisir **qui** tu veux.*)
- *You can go **where (= the place where)** you like.* (*Tu peux aller **où** tu veux.*)
- *Tell me **when (= the moment when)** it started.* (*Dis-moi **quand** cela a commencé.*)
- ***Why (= the reason why)** he went was unclear to me.* (*J'ai eu du mal à comprendre **la raison pour laquelle** il y est allé.*)

Faire faire

- Avec ***make someone do something***, une **contrainte** est exercée sur le sujet : *Ali **made** Sonny Liston give up.* (Liston ne le souhaitait pas, mais Ali l'y a contraint.)
- Avec ***get someone to do something***, il n'y a pas d'idée de contrainte, on **parvient** à faire faire quelque chose à quelqu'un : *I **got** Lance **to** reconsider his decision.*

• ***Have someone do something*** est la formule la plus neutre. Il n'y a pas de contrainte ni d'idée de réussite explicite : *The doctor **had** me **go** to the lab for a blood test.*

• On utilise souvent ***cause someone / something to do something*** pour désigner des actions dont le résultat est quasi-automatique. Le sujet de *cause* est souvent non humain : *The wind **caused the ball to go** in the wrong direction.*

> Les schémas de type 2 (*get someone to do something*) et de type 3 (*have someone do something*) donnent lieu à des constructions à la voix passive : ***Have / Get something done***. On ne précise généralement pas l'agent : *Jim **had** his hair cut ~~(by the hairdresser)~~.* ; *I **got** my car repaired ~~(by a mechanic)~~.*

La coordination

• On peut coordonner deux énoncés indépendants au moyen de conjonctions de coordination :

- ***and*** (*et*) : *MLK was fond of anaphora **and** Mr Obama likes antitheses.*
- ***or*** (*ou*) : *You can use irony **or** you can opt for rhetorical questions.*
- ***but*** (*mais*) : *The Japanese like fish **but** I prefer red meat.*

> On omet parfois certains éléments dans le 2e énoncé coordonné pour éviter des répétitions : *MLK was fond of anaphora **and** Mr Obama **[Ø]** of antitheses.* ; *You can use irony **or [Ø]** opt for rhetorical questions.*

• Avec *and*, on a parfois aussi une suite **chronologique** : *Malala walked to the platform **and** delivered her speech.* Avec *and*, *or* et *but*, le 2e énoncé coordonné exprime parfois la **conséquence** du 1er : *Ali punched Liston **and** the champion fell down.* ; *Don't eat too much junk food **or** you'll become fat. He spoke up, **but** no one heard him.*

Le discours rapporté

• On peut rapporter des propos en utilisant :

- le **discours direct** : *Michelle Obama said, "Nearly one in three children in America are overweight."*
- le **discours indirect** (il n'y a plus de guillemets disparaissent alors et une **conjonction de subordination** suit le verbe introducteur de discours) :
  – **énoncés affirmatifs** (***that/Ø***) : *Michelle Obama said **that/Ø** nearly one in three children in America were overweight.*
  – **énoncés interrogatifs** (le point d'interrogation des questions directes devient un simple point) :
- **questions fermées** (***if/whether***) : *"Are you from Texas, Willie?", I asked.* ➞ *I asked Willie **if/whether** he was from Texas.*
- **questions ouvertes** (**mots en WH-**) : *"What's your job?", I asked Anthony.* ➞ *I asked Anthony **what** his job was..*

• Plusieurs **ajustements** sont nécessaires au discours rapporté :

1. Ajustements de personne

Au discours rapporté, la 1re personne du discours direct devient la 3e personne : ***I** am hungry., the boy said.* ➞ *The boy said **he** was hungry.* La 2e personne devient la 3e personne : *"Are **you** hungry?", I asked the boy.* ➞ *I asked him if **he** was hungry.* La 2e personne devient la 1re personne : *"Are **you** hungry?", he asked.* ➞ *He asked if **I** was hungry.*

2. Ajustements de temps

Dans un récit au prétérit, le présent du discours direct devient souvent le prétérit dans le discours rapporté : *"The only thing we **have** to fear **is** fear itself.", Mr Roosevelt said.* ➞ *Mr Roosevelt said that the only thing we **had** to fear **was** fear itself.* Ceci s'applique aussi aux auxiliaires : le prétérit ou le *present perfect* deviennent le *past perfect*, etc.

3. Ajustements d'outils et d'ordre des mots dans les énoncés interrogatifs

• Lorsqu'il y a inversion sujet / verbe (ou 1er auxiliaire du groupe verbal) dans le discours direct, il n'y a plus cette inversion dans l'énoncé équivalent au discours rapporté : *"**Why are you so excited about the class**?", I asked Frances.* ➞ *I asked her **why she was so excited about the class**.*

• L'auxiliaire ***do*** utilisé dans le discours direct disparaît au discours rapporté : *"**Where do you come from**?", I asked Willie.* ➞ *I asked Willie **where he came from**.*

> En français, on peut avoir une inversion dans certaines questions indirectes mais pas en anglais : *I wonder what these people were doing.* (*Je me demande <u>ce que faisaient ces gens</u>.*)

4. Ajustements de repères

Dans un récit au prétérit, les repères de **temps** et de **lieu** situent des évènements par rapport au **moment** et **à l'endroit où l'on parle**. Quand le récit passe au prétérit, ils sont remplacés par des repères qui situent ces événements par rapport à la **situation décrite dans la narration** : *"From **now** on, we will meet in **this very room** every day. You can expect to see me **tomorrow**", the president of the charity declared.* ➞ *The president of the charity declared that from **then** on, we would meet in **that very room** every day and that we could expect to see him **the following day**.*

> ⚠ Les ajustements ne sont pas automatiques, notamment lorsqu'ils concernent les temps ou les repères. Dans certains cas, le discours rapporté n'entraîne pas d'ajustements ou entraîne l'emploi de repères plus ou moins complexes.
>
> Au discours indirect, *"Leave the textbook **in this room**.", he said* pourra par exemple laisser place à *He told me to leave the textbook in **the room where we were**.*

Banque d'exercices

Noms « dénombrables » et « indénombrables »

1 Traduisez les énoncés suivants en anglais.

1. Ce professeur donne généralement d'excellents conseils.
2. La police a arrêté les cambrioleurs.
3. Les États-Unis ont réformé leur système de santé.
4. Les nouvelles sont bonnes.
5. J'ai pêché six saumons dans la Spey.
6. Zut ! Ce pyjama est trop grand.

2 Complétez les énoncés suivants avec les éléments appropriés (a, b, c ou d).

1. Drive to the ... and then turn right.
   a. crossroad **b.** crossed roads
   c. crosses road **d.** crossroads

2. I need .... Could you help me, please?
   a. information **b.** informations
   c. pieces of informations **d.** pieces of information

3. A lot of ... present when the accident happened.
   a. people were **b.** people was
   c. peoples were **d.** peoples was-

4. Some consider that ... the queen of sciences.
   a. linguistic is **b.** linguistic are
   c. linguistics is **d.** linguistics are

5. ... the only one that my parents have kept.
   a. This furniture is
   b. These furnitures are
   c. These pieces of furniture are
   d. This piece of furniture is

Les articles

3 Traduisez les énoncés suivants en anglais en prêtant une attention particulière à l'emploi des articles.

1. L'or est un métal précieux.
2. Son fils est pilote.
3. Les adolescents ont parfois des problèmes relationnels avec leurs parents.
4. Les organisateurs ont invité un artiste très connu.
5. Des bateaux étaient visibles à l'horizon.
6. Le Royaume-Uni comprend quatre pays, alors que la Grande-Bretagne n'en comprend que trois : l'Angleterre, le Pays de Galles et l'Écosse.

4 Complétez les énoncés avec Ø, *a*/*an* ou *the*.

1. ... man I saw in the lobby reminded me of my uncle.
2. Gwen is ... civil servant, and her sister is ... accountant.
3. ... polar bears are very dangerous animals.
4. ... cry of this bird is familiar to ... sailors.
5. ... European Union cannot compete with ... United States in terms of military power.
6. The film I saw yesterday was about ... freedom and ... happiness.

Les démonstratifs

5 Traduisez les éléments soulignés en anglais.

1. Cette année, nous partirons au Pays de Galles.
2. Cette année-là, Margaret Thatcher devint premier ministre.
3. Rien n'est bon marché ces jours-ci.
4. En ce temps-là, les pubs fermaient à 14 h 30 et à 23 h.
5. Faites entrer ce monsieur, je vous prie.
6. Cet individu me dégoûte !

Les pronoms

Pronoms personnels

6 Complétez les énoncés suivants avec la forme appropriée du pronom personnel entre parenthèses.

1. We went to Cornwall last year, and it reminded (we) of Normandy.
2. Mary gave (I) a present for (I) 14th birthday.
3. Meet Tim Timmerman and (he) wife. Tim's a colleague of (I).
4. "Ah! I've found (I) wallet." – "I'm afraid not". This is not (you). It's (I).
5. We saw (they) running down the stairs.*
6. Do you mind (I) opening the window?*

* voir aussi **Les propositions subordonnées nominalisées, Propositions de type nom + *to* + V / V-*ing* (+ complément)**, p. 176

7 Traduisez les énoncés suivants en anglais.

1. Cet ami de mon père travaille à Cardiff.
2. Le professeur a levé la tête.
3. Ma voiture est en panne, nous prendrons la leur.
4. La banque leur a prêté une grosse somme d'argent.
5. Tiens, tiens ! Tu t'es rasé la barbe ?

Pronoms réfléchis et réciproques

8 Complétez les énoncés suivants avec la forme appropriée d'un pronom réfléchi ou réciproque.

1. She recoiled when she saw ... in the mirror.
2. The crew members kept smiling at ... .

3. I would like to know how this village developed ... and became what it is today.
4. You should learn how to dress ... to look good.
5. As soon as they saw ... the two dogs jumped at ... 's throats.

Les quantifieurs

Many, much, a lot of, lots of, few, a few, little, a little

9 **Complétez les énoncés suivants avec les éléments appropriés (a, b, c ou d).**

1. The pub was packed and there was ... room at the bar, so the four of us drank our lemonade outside.
a. much **b.** a few **c.** a lot of **d.** little
2. "That concert's going to be a roaring success! There are ... people standing in the queue outside."
a. much **b.** a few **c.** few **d.** lots of
3. This candidate doesn't stand ... chance of being elected.
a. many **b.** much **c.** few **d.** little
4. Not ... people I know can speak Welsh.
a. many **b.** a few **c.** few **d.** much
5. Elderly people should drink ... water when it is very hot outside.
a. lot of **b.** a lots of **c.** a lot **d.** lots of

10 **Complétez les énoncés suivants avec *many, much, a lot of, few, a few, little* ou *a little*.**

1. I'm a bit out of pocket at the moment. Could you lend me ... pounds?
2. ... people have had the privilege of travelling to space.
3. There is ... cheese left in the fridge. There should be just enough for you and me.
4. This man eats ... fish. That's why he has such a good memory.
5. "I have ... money and can't even buy myself a mobile phone."
6. If I were a millionaire, I would buy ... clothes and a big house.

Some, any et no

11 **Complétez les énoncés suivants avec *some, any* ou *no*.**

1. Is it acceptable to eat chips with your fingers in a restaurant? I've seen ... people do it when I was in Paris.
2. Are there ... native English speakers round here?
3. "What if Robert asks me a question about my relationship with Lance Armstrong?" – "Don't worry, Robert never asks ... questions."
4. Is there ... wine left in the bottle? Otherwise I'll have ... water instead.
5. What! Are there ... athletes able to run a marathon in this district? This is really a pity.

Some, Ø, any, a

12 **Complétez les énoncés suivants avec *some*, Ø, *any* ou *a*.**

1. ... people like to eat their meat rare.
2. There is ... hydrogen in the earth's atmosphere.
3. There wasn't ... news of this in the papers this morning.
4. Do you know if this artist has ... girlfriend?
5. There's ... flour left in the cupboard. I'll use it for the cake.
6. ... politicians are usually very clever people.

Some, Ø, any, a, no

13 **Complétez les énoncés suivants avec les éléments appropriés (a, b, c ou d).**

1. There is ... beer left, I'm afraid. Would you like Coke instead?
a. some **b.** any **c.** Ø **d.** no
2. There's ... milk in the fridge. Help yourself!
a. no **b.** some **c.** a **d.** any
3. ... American president has ever delivered a speech like this.
a. any **b.** no **c.** a **d.** an
4. "Could you lend me your mobile phone, Terry?" – "Sorry, I haven't got ... mobile phone."
a. no **b.** Ø **c.** any **d.** a
5. What a shabby hotel! The room was stuffy and there were ... holes in the carpet.
a. Ø **b.** any **c.** no **d.** a
6. I was so excited that I couldn't get ... sleep.
a. no **b.** some **c.** any **d.** a

Either, both, the two, neither

14 **Complétez les énoncés suivants avec *either, both, the two* ou *neither*.**

1. ... men engaged in a fist-fight, trying to knock each other off.
2. Bystanders were assembled on ... sides of the street.
3. Guards were posted at ... end of the bridge.
4. Alistair asked Henry to accompany him, and then he asked Thomas, but as they shook their heads in shame, he quickly understood that ... would go with him.
5. ... children began to play together.

Each, every, all

15 Complétez les énoncés suivants avec *each*, *every* ou *all*.

1. ... men are created equal.
2. ... house had its own peculiar character.
3. ... child I saw seemed happy to be there.
4. This charity provides services to ... people with disabilities.
5. Not ... western movie has a happy ending, I'm afraid.

Les nombres

16 Traduisez les énoncés suivants en anglais en prêtant une attention particulière aux nombres.

1. On a dépensé dix millions de dollars dans ce projet.
2. Des centaines de personnes attendaient à l'extérieur.
3. Il y a des milliards d'étoiles dans notre galaxie.
4. Trois mille personnes ont assisté au concert.
5. Ce document comprend sept mille cent trente-six caractères.

Les adjectifs

17 Complétez les énoncés suivants avec les éléments appropriés (a, b, c ou d).

1. ... were listening to the speaker.
   a. very interesting pupils **b.** pupils very interesting
   c. pupils very interested **d.** very interested pupils
2. This scheme will be helpful for ... .
   a. the poor **b.** poor
   c. the poors **d.** poors
3. Tony was really scared, which is not surprising as he is a very ... little boy.
   a. afraid **b.** frightened
   c. fearful **d.** fearsome

18 Traduisez les énoncés suivants en anglais en prêtant une attention particulière à l'accord, la nature, la place et l'ordre des adjectifs.

1. Les Irlandais et les Écossais apprécient généralement les Français.
2. Les Anglais et les Gallois ont un tempérament très différent de celui des Italiens.
3. Il y avait un curieux petit chapeau de soie chinois sur la table.
4. Mon frère conduit une grosse voiture allemande bleue.
5. Nous avons vu des enfants endormis dans le jardin.

Le haut degré

19 Traduisez les énoncés suivants en anglais en prêtant une attention particulière aux éléments soulignés.

1. L'intrigue de ce roman est vraiment <u>très surprenante</u>.
2. Je n'ai jamais vu <u>un film si remarquable</u>. *(deux solutions)*
3. C'est dommage que nous ayons eu <u>un si mauvais temps</u>.
4. Cet homme d'affaires est <u>extrêmement intelligent</u>.
5. J'ai rarement entendu <u>des musiciens si doués</u>.

Comparatifs et superlatifs

20 Complétez les énoncés suivants avec les éléments appropriés (a, b, c ou d).

1. His girlfriend is ... him.
   a. cleverer that **b.** as clever than
   c. cleverer as **d.** more clever than
2. This pilot is probably one of ... in the world.
   a. the best **b.** the better
   c. the most good **d.** the goodest
3. Of these two athletes, William is the ... .
   a. faster **b.** most fast
   c. farther **d.** farthest
4. This film was not ... the one we saw yesterday.
   a. as interesting than **b.** more interesting as
   c. as interesting as **d.** as interesting to

21 Traduisez les énoncés ci-dessous.

1. George est plus rapide que Mark.
2. Mick est plus efficace que ses collègues.
3. Ce groupe est le meilleur que j'aie jamais entendu.
4. De tous les employés, Joan est la plus efficace.
5. L'homme le plus fort du monde est plus fort que le plus fort de ces deux personnages.
6. Cette émission de radio est plus amusante que le film, mais elle n'est pas aussi amusante que le livre original.

N1 *of* N2, N2's N1 et N2 N1

22 Traduisez les énoncés suivants en anglais en prêtant une attention particulière aux éléments soulignés.

1. <u>Les robes de Michelle Obama</u> ont souvent fait la une des magazines people.
2. Ce que vous voyez sur cette photo est <u>le visage de Benjamin Bathurst</u>. Monsieur Bathurst est un diplomate britannique qui a disparu mystérieusement lors d'une mission en Allemagne au XIXe siècle.

3. Tom me dévisagea longuement. Le regard de mon ami était à la fois grave et bienveillant.
4. Des gouttes de sueur perlaient sur son front.
5. Le design de la voiture est extrêmement intéressant.

Les prépositions

23 Complétez les énoncés suivants avec les éléments appropriés (a, b, c ou d).

1. Dylan will see his brother ... Christmas.
a. at **b.** on **c.** in **d.** to
2. The concert is scheduled ... 3 March.
a. out of **b.** at **c.** on **d.** from
3. A big black cloud as hovering ... our heads.
a. onto **b.** into **c.** from **d.** over
4. His IQ is well ... average.
a. beyond **b.** over **c.** up **d.** above
5. Wash your hands before coming ... the table.
a. to **b.** onto **c.** into **d.** at

24 Traduisez les énoncés suivants en anglais en prêtant une attention particulière à l'emploi des prépositions.

1. Le mariage a eu lieu l'après-midi.
2. Les cambrioleurs opèrent souvent la nuit.
3. Je propose que nous nous retrouvions à la gare.
4. Il pleuvait tellement que nous nous sommes réfugiés dans la gare.
5. Martin Luther King a prononcé son plus célèbre discours en 1963.

Les combinaisons temps/outils

25 Employez les combinaisons temps/outils appropriées pour les verbes entre parenthèses en tenant compte des éventuelles indications contextuelles.

1. Ten years ago Robert (make) a decision that changed his life.
2. I (never see) such a beautiful landscape in my life.
3. Yesterday Maggie cooked a cake for her sister. The day before, she (buy) a recipe book.
4. Six years ago the doctors (diagnose) Ann with a rare form of pneumonia.
5. *(Joan talking to her brother Ted who has been in the bathroom for next to 3/4h. A strange buzzing noise emanates from the inside of the bathroom).*
"What (you do), Ted? I (wait) at the door for more than half an hour, now."
"I (shave)."

26 Complétez les énoncés suivants avec les éléments appropriés (a, b, c ou d).

1. They ... breakfast when the telephone rang.
a. have had **b.** were having
c. have been having **d.** had
2. We ... in the waiting room for several minutes when the doctor came in.
a. have been sitting **b.** sat
c. had been sitting **d.** were sitting
3. "What's the matter, Lucy, you look exhausted!"
"Yes, I (write) letters all night."
a. have written **b.** was writing
c. had been writing **d.** have been writing
4. "Well, Sam, you look very satisfied with yourself."
"Indeed, I've been very efficient this morning. I (write) no less than seven letters."
a. have been writing **b.** had written
c. have written **d.** was writing
5. It smells of tobacco in here. You ... again!
a. have been smoking **b.** have smoked
c. had been smoking **d.** had smoked

27 Traduisez les verbes soulignés en employant les combinaisons temps/outils appropriées et en tenant compte des éventuelles indications contextuelles. Plusieurs solutions sont parfois possibles.

1. (*Commentaire sportif à la télévision.*) « Carrick court. Il tire. Oui ! Il marque ! C'est le but ! 2 à 0 pour Manchester United ! »
2. L'Europe traverse une crise aiguë depuis 2008.
3. « Que fais-tu, Sam ? » « Je m'entraîne pour le prochain marathon de New York. »
4. J'ai commis une grave erreur. Je jure que l'on ne m'y reprendra plus.
5. Cela faisait plus de deux heures que les élèves travaillaient lorsque l'alarme s'est déclenchée.

Since, for, during, ago

28 Complétez les énoncés suivants avec *since, for, during* ou *ago*.

1. I saw Bill Gates at a petrol station ... my holiday in Texas.
2. Georges has been playing for the national team ... 2009.
3. I worked for Walmart ... three years when I was living in the U.S.
4. I first Alice met many years ... when she was still an apprentice.
5. Lawrence had been ill ... the beginning of the year when her GP prescribed antibiotics.
6. Jane has worked as an accountant in Liverpool ... several years now.

Les modaux

29 Reformulez les énoncés suivants en exprimant le sens des termes soulignés avec un modal.

1. No doubt Susan is very angry after what you said.
2. Yes, I allow you to smoke in my office.
3. I advise you to do more exercise.
4. There seems to be some chance of his being at home.
5. Perhaps he missed his train.

30 Traduisez les énoncés suivants.

1. Jonathan a dû réussir son examen.
2. Il se peut que Mary n'ait pas reçu son colis.
3. Tu ne devrais pas écrire sur les tables.
4. Il se pourrait que Sam arrive en retard.
5. Je suis désolé. Je ne sais pas conduire.
6. Comment oses-tu me dire que je suis un menteur ?

Les périphrases en *to*

31 Reformulez les énoncés suivants en employant des périphrases en *to*.

1. You must go to bed, now.
2. No, you may not have any more chocolate.
3. You should tell me the truth, Jim.
4. This robot can perform amazing tasks.
5. You needn't worry so much.

La référence à l'avenir

32 Construisez des énoncés faisant référence à l'avenir à l'aide des verbes entre parenthèses.

1. I assure you that I (not lie) anymore.
2. Be careful. I can see that this tree (fall).
3. I can't come to Larry's party because I (go) the dentist's.
4. "What time is your plane scheduled?" "It (leave) at 6.30."
5. As soon as I (get) back home, I'll run myself a hot bath.*
6. The Republican candidate (probably be elected). All the polls give him a lead.

* voir aussi **Les propositions subordonnées « circonstancielles » de temps**, p. 177

Les énoncés interrogatifs, interro-négatifs, emphatiques et exclamatifs

Énoncés interrogatifs

33 Formulez des *yes/no questions* à partir des énoncés suivants.
Exemple : *Cats eat mice.* → *Do cats eat mice?*

1. GW Bush was elected President of The United States twice.
2. Napoleon was planning to invade the United Kingdom with about two thousand ships.
3. William Wallace defended Scotland against the English.
4. He has been to Japan several times in the past six months.
5. They have not seen their uncle last year.
6. They were not having lunch when it started raining.

34 Formez les énoncés interrogatifs qui permettront d'obtenir des réponses contenant les éléments soulignés.
Exemple : *Barack Obama became the first black American president in 2008.* → *When did Mr Obama become the first black American president?*

1. Barack Obama became the first black American president in 2008.
2. I met David Cameron during my stay in London last summer.
3. Natasha spent her holiday in Majorca.
4. A noise behind him caused Peter to turn around.
5. Some people are fat because they eat too much.

Énoncés interro-négatifs et emphatiques

35 Traduisez les énoncés suivants.

1. « N'as-tu pas laissé ton portefeuille dans la cuisine ? »
2. « Vous vous êtes perdus parce que vous n'avez pas regardé la carte avant de partir. Mais nous, nous avons regardé la carte ! »
3. « Vous n'avez pas le droit de vous garer ici. Vous ne savez pas lire ? »
4. « Comment pouvez-vous vous attendre à ce que la chambre soit prête alors que vous n'avez pas appelé pour la réserver ?
   – Mais nous avons appelé. Mon mari a réservé hier. »

Énoncés exclamatifs

36 Traduisez les énoncés suivants. Plusieurs solutions sont parfois possibles.

1. Quel athlète que cet homme !
2. Quel dommage ! Un si beau blouson !
3. Comme ces gens sont égoïstes !

4. La mer est si bleue ici lorsqu'il fait beau !
5. Ce cycliste a nié avoir pris des produits dopants ? Tiens, comme c'est étrange !
6. Quelle patience il vous a fallu pour ne pas vous mettre en colère !

L'impératif

37 Traduisez les énoncés suivants.

1. Courez ! Sautez ! Levez les bras !
2. Qu'ils fassent plus attention la prochaine fois.
3. Aidons-les. Ils en ont besoin.
4. Ne sois pas ridicule. Donne-moi ce téléphone portable tout de suite !
5. Allons-y, maintenant ! Ne perdons pas de temps.

La voix passive

38 Reformulez les énoncés suivants en employant la voix passive.

1. According to a rumour, this millionaire has sold his property in Texas for 100,000 dollars.
2. Some believe that Samantha has been invited to the White House.
3. People think that this match was rigged.
4. Many people say that this man has swum across the Channel several times.

Les reprises par des auxiliaires

Réponses dites « courtes »

39 Traduisez les énoncés suivants.

1. « On m'a dit que les impôts allaient baisser, mais moi je crois que non. »
2. « J'ai terminé mes devoirs. Et toi ? »
3. « – Tiens ! Ce boucher gallois vend des hamburgers d'agneau.
   – Ah bon ? »
4. « – Le directeur n'a pas encore appelé ?
   – Je ne pense pas. »
5. « – Regarde ! Ce piéton danse en plein milieu de la rue !
   – Mais oui ! Tu as raison. »

So/Neither do I, etc.

40 Traduisez les énoncés suivants.

1. Burt n'aime pas la pizza, et moi non plus.
2. Je suis allé au Pays de Galles l'année dernière, et ma sœur aussi.
3. Je n'ai jamais vu une si grosse voiture, et mes parents non plus.
4. Je ne peux pas soulever un sac si lourd, et toi non plus.
5. Il se pourrait qu'il soit à la maison, et sa sœur aussi.

Les *questions tags*

41 Complétez les énoncés suivants avec le *question tag* approprié.

1. This boy is eight years old, ... ?
2. You haven't seen that film yet, ... ?
3. You don't mind if I stay in your office, ... ?
4. Harold will call a taxi, ... ?
5. These people have been standing in the hall for almost half an hour, ... ?
6. The police arrested the burglar, ... ?

Les adverbes

42 Formulez des énoncés comportant les adverbes entre parenthèses en prêtant une attention particulière à leur place. Plusieurs solutions sont parfois possibles.

1. He goes to the gym with his sister. (never)
2. This programme is broadcast. (daily)
3. This newspaper is circulated. (weekly)
4. Some people say that only black people can sing the blues. (very well)
5. I feel like giving it all up. (sometimes)
6. This man seems to have disappeared. (mysteriously)

Les verbes à particule

43 Déterminez si les termes soulignés sont des verbes à particule ou des verbes prépositionnels. Aidez-vous d'un dictionnaire si besoin est.

1. Simon took the book off the shelf.
2. The plane took off at 6pm as scheduled.
3. The letters you put on my desk are not addressed to me.
4. Your wallet is in the jacket you put on last night.
5. We ran down the stairs and jumped into the car.
6. A motorist ran down a pedestrian not far from where I live.
7. The car broke down and we had to call a mechanic.

There is/there are

44 Traduisez les énoncés ci-dessous.

1. Il y a un grand jardin devant sa maison.
2. Est-ce qu'il y a des ours dans ce zoo ?
3. Il y avait de l'eau dans la bouteille.
4. Y avait-il beaucoup de monde à ce concert ?
5. Il y avait beaucoup de meubles dans la pièce.

L'énoncé complexe

Subordonnées nominales

45 Complétez les énoncés suivants avec la forme appropriée des verbes entre parenthèses (*to* + V ou V *-ing*).

1. Don't forget (tell) Terry that the appointment has been cancelled.
2. The suspect denied (commit) the murder.
3. The supervisor reminded me (fill in) the form.
4. The manager asked his employees (be) there on time.
5. Always take your time before (answer) the interviewer's questions.
6. He managed to open the door by (use) a duplicate key.
7. Laura hesitated (accept) my offer. She told me she was afraid (sign) the contract.
8. I love (be) alone in my room.
9. I'd really love (discover) Scotland. I am actually thinking of (book) a trip to the Highlands next summer.

46 Reliez les éléments de la colonne de gauche avec ceux de la colonne de droite (plusieurs solutions sont souvent possibles).

1. He said	a. that the cat was hungry.
2. We were told	b. to keep quiet.
3. She believes	c. his being there at the party.
4. I remember	d. talking about that painful experience.
5. Eileen was advised	
6. We carefully avoided	

Subordonnées de condition

47 Complétez les énoncés suivants avec les verbes entre parenthèses en employant les structures appropriées.

1. If you work hard, you (succeed).
2. If Alex (work) harder, he would sail through that exam.
3. If Elinor (live) in North Wales, she would probably have been fluent in Welsh.
4. If I (be) an astronaut, I (fly) to the moon every month.
5. If Laura (learn) Spanish when she was young, she (be able to) talk to these people.

Subordonnées de temps

48 Complétez les énoncés suivants avec *when*, *as soon as*, *while*, *as*, *before*, *after*, *until*. Tous ces mots ne seront pas utilisés et plusieurs solutions sont parfois possibles.

1. Stay here and wait for me ... I get back.
2. I'll buy myself something nice ... I go to the shops.
3. ... she saw Freddy, she ran towards him and flung herself into his arms.
4. We were getting more and more excited ... the wedding drew nearer.
5. ... David worked in his office, Sally was talking on the phone.
6. You are to return to sports only ... the manager has given you the go-ahead.

Subordonnées de but

49 Complétez les énoncés ci-dessous avec les éléments appropriés.

1. He opened the box ... what was inside.
   a. for see — b. for seeing
   c. to see — d. to seeing
2. The foreman raised his voice ... heard above the noise.
   a. so as to be — b. to being
   c. for to be — d. for being
3. The boy hid in the cupboard ... seen by the warden.
   a. for not be — b. to not be
   c. for not being — d. not to be
4. They ran faster ... late at their appointment.
   a. in order to not be — b. in order not to be
   c. in order to don't be — d. for not being

Subordonnées relatives

50 Complétez les énoncés ci-dessous avec le relatif approprié.

1. The woman ... I saw at the station was wearing a beautiful dress.
   a. which — b. who — c. Ø
2. The person ... wrote that speech happens to be a professional playwright.
   a. that — b. which — c. Ø
3. The socks ... you were wearing yesterday used to belong to my grandfather.
   a. whom — b. that — c. where

4. I was surprised to discover the email ... you sent me the other day.
   a. which b. who c. when

5. The moment ... I saw him, I knew he was going to become my best friend.
   a. whom b. where c. Ø

6. I remember that day ... we went to the beach with Samantha and Joan.
   a. where b. when c. why

51 Traduisez les énoncés ci-dessous. Plusieurs solutions sont parfois possibles.

1. La personne que vous essayez de contacter ne pourra pas vous répondre aujourd'hui.
2. La raison pour laquelle cette entreprise a fait faillite reste mystérieuse.
3. Il faudra que je lise les livres que tu m'as prêtés.
4. L'étudiant dont le père est footballeur professionnel s'appelle Patrick.
5. L'endroit où vous nous avez emmenés nous a beaucoup plu.
6. Je lui rendrai sa montre le jour où je le verrai.*

* voir aussi **Les propositions subordonnées « circonstancielles », Subordonnées de condition**, p. 177

« Ce qui, ce que » : *which* relatif « de phrase » et *what* dans les surbordonnées nominales

52 *Which* ou *what* ? Quel est l'équivalent des éléments soulignés ?

1. Le dessert était de couleur bleue, ce qui m'a paru étrange.
2. Ce que je voudrais qu'il me dise, c'est l'endroit où il habite.
3. Vivre à la campagne, c'est ce que j'aime par-dessus tout.
4. J'ai insisté pour qu'il sorte de la pièce, ce qui lui a déplu.
5. Il n'est pas responsable de l'accident. Du moins, c'est ce qu'il affirme.
6. Il a été très honnête, ce que j'ai beaucoup apprécié.

La coordination

53 Reliez les énoncés ci-dessous en employant *and*, *or* ou *but*. Modifiez la ponctuation et supprimez les éléments devenus inutiles.

1. I turned the ignit on key. The engine started immediately.
2. Lucie wants to take me to the gym. I don't like exercising in front of other people.
3. You can come at 2pm. You can come at 3pm. It doesn't matter to me as I'll be there all afternoon.
4. Paul was praised for his honesty. Suzan was praised for her exemplary behavior.
5. I promised that I would play the guitar at Sam's birthday party. I will do it.
6. Please put out your cigarette. I will leave the room.

Le discours rapporté

54 Formulez des énoncés au discours indirect à partir des énoncés suivants.

1. "Where are you going?" Rupert asked me.
2. "Does he really have time to read all these books?" Alice wondered.
3. The teacher said, "You are all going to discover something that you have never seen before". We were very excited.
4. "I'm sorry, but I can't swim", she told me.
5. "Give me this letter. I'll leave it here and put it in the post tomorrow," he said.*

* voir aussi **Les subordonnées nominalisées, Propositions de type nom + *to* + V / V-*ing* (+ complément)**, p. 176

Verbes irréguliers

Base verbale	Prétérit	Participe passé	Traduction
Trois formes identiques			
bet /e/	bet /e/	bet /e/	*parier*
bid /ɪ/	bid /ɪ/	bid /ɪ/	*offrir*
broadcast /a:/	broadcast /a:/	broadcast /a:/	*diffuser / émettre*
burst /ə:/	burst /ə:/	burst /ə:/	*éclater*
cast /a:/	cast /a:/	cast /a:/	*lancer*
cost /ɒ/	cost /ɒ/	cost /ɒ/	*coûter*
cut /ʌ/	cut /ʌ/	cut /ʌ/	*couper*
forecast /a:/	forecast /a:/	forecast /a:/	*prévoir*
hit /ɪ/	hit /ɪ/	hit /ɪ/	*taper*
hurt /ə:/	hurt /ə:/	hurt /ə:/	*blesser*
let /e/	let /e/	let /e/	*laisser / louer*
put /ʊ/	put /ʊ/	put /ʊ/	*mettre / poser*
quit /ɪ/	quit /ɪ/	quit /ɪ/	*abandonner / arrêter*
read /i:/	read /e/	read /e/	*lire*
rent /e/	rent /e/	rent /e/	*louer*
set /e/	set /e/	set /e/	*fixer*
split /ɪ/	split /ɪ/	split /ɪ/	*fendre*
shut /ʌ/	shut /ʌ/	shut /ʌ/	*fermer*
spread /e/	spread /e/	spread /e/	*répandre*
sweat /e/	sweat /e/	sweat /e/	*suer*
Prétérit et participe passé identiques			
bend /e/	bent /e/	bent /e/	*plier / (se) courber*
bleed /i:/	bled /e/	bled /e/	*saigner*
breed /i:/	bred /e/	bred /e/	*élever*
bring /ɪ/	brought /ɔ:/	brought /ɔ:/	*apporter*
build /ɪ/	built /ɪ/	built /ɪ/	*construire*
burn /ə:/	burnt /ə:/	burnt /ə:/	*brûler*
buy /aɪ/	bought /ɔ:/	bought /ɔ:/	*acheter*
catch /æ/	caught /ɔ:/	caught /ɔ:/	*attraper*
deal /i:/	dealt /e/	dealt /e/	*distribuer*
dream /i:/	dreamt /e/	dreamt /e/	*rêver*
dwell /e/	dwelt /e/	dwelt /e/	*habiter*
feed /i:/	fed /e/	fed /e/	*nourrir*
feel /i:/	felt /e/	felt /e/	*(se) sentir / éprouver*
fight /aɪ/	fought /ɔ:/	fought /ɔ:/	*(se) battre*
find /aɪ/	found /aʊ/	found /aʊ/	*trouver*
get /e/	got /ɒ/	got /ɒ/	*obtenir*
hang /æ/	hung /ʌ/	hung /ʌ/	*accrocher / pendre*
have /æ/	had /æ/	had /æ/	*avoir*
hear /ɪə/	heard /ə:/	heard /ə:/	*entendre*
hold /əʊ/	held /e/	held /e/	*tenir*
keep /i:/	kept /e/	kept /e/	*garder*
lead /i:/	led /e/	led /e/	*mener / guider*
leap /i:/	leapt /e/	leapt /e/	*sauter / bondir*
learn /ə/	learnt /ə/	learnt /ə/	*apprendre*
leave /i:/	left /e/	left /e/	*laisser / partir*
lend /e/	lent /e/	lent /e/	*prêter*
light /aɪ/	lit /ɪ/	lit /ɪ/	*allumer*
lose /u:/	lost /ɒ/	lost /ɒ/	*perdre*
make /eɪ/	made /eɪ/	made /eɪ/	*faire / fabriquer*
mean /i:/	meant /e/	meant /e/	*signifier*
meet /i:/	met /e/	met /e/	*(se) rencontrer*
pay /eɪ/	paid /eɪ/	paid /eɪ/	*payer*
say /eɪ/	said /e/	said /e/	*dire*
seek /i:/	sought /ɔ:/	sought /ɔ:/	*chercher*
sell /e/	sold /əʊ/	sold /əʊ/	*vendre*
send /e/	sent /e/	sent /e/	*envoyer*
shine /aɪ/	shone /ɒ/	shone /ɒ/	*briller*
shoot /u:/	shot /ɒ/	shot /ɒ/	*tirer / filmer*
sit /ɪ/	sat /æ/	sat /æ/	*s'asseoir*
sleep /i:/	slept /e/	slept /e/	*dormir*
slide /aɪ/	slid /ɪ/	slid /ɪ/	*glisser*
spell /e/	spelt /e	spelt /e/	*épeler*
spend /e/	spent /e/	spent /e/	*dépenser / passer du temps*
spill /ɪ/	spilt /ɪ/	spilt /ɪ/	*renverser*
spit /ɪ/	spat /a/	spat /a/	*cracher*
spoil /ɔɪ/	spoilt /ɔɪ/	spoilt /ɔɪ/	*gâcher / gâter*
stand /æ/	stood /ʊ/	stood /ʊ/	*être debout / être posé*

stick /ɪ/	stuck /ʌ/	stuck /ʌ/	*coller*
sweep /iː/	swept /e/	swept /e/	*balayer*
swing /ɪ/	swung /ʌ/	swung /ʌ/	*(se) balancer*
teach /iː/	taught /ɔː/	taught /ɔː/	*enseigner*
tell /e/	told /əʊ/	told /əʊ/	*dire / raconter*
think /ɪ/	thought /ɔː/	thought /ɔː/	*penser*
understand /æ/	understood /ʊ/	understood /ʊ/	*comprendre*
weep /iː/	wept /e/	wept /e/	*pleurer*
win /ɪ/	won /ʌ/	won /ʌ/	*gagner*
wind /ɪ/	wound /uː/	wound /uː/	*enrouler*

Deux formes identiques

beat /iː/	beat /iː/	beaten /iː/	*battre*
become /ʌ/	became /eɪ/	become /ʌ/	*devenir*
come /ʌ/	came /eɪ/	come /ʌ/	*venir*
overcome /ʌ/	overcame / eɪ/	overcome /ʌ/	*surmonter*
run /ʌ/	ran /æ/	run /ʌ/	*courir*

Trois formes différentes

awake /eɪ/	awoke /əʊ/	awoken /əʊ/	*(se) réveiller*
be /iː/	was /ɒ/ were /ə/	been /iː/	*être*
bear /ɛə/	bore /ɔː/	borne /ɔː/	*porter / supporter*
begin /ɪ/	began /æ/	begun /ʌ/	*commencer*
bite /aɪ/	bit /ɪ/	bitten /ɪ/	*mordre*
blow /əʊ/	blew /uː/	blown /əuː/	*souffler*
break /eɪ/	broke /əʊ/	broken /əʊ/	*casser*
choose /uː/	chose /əʊ/	chosen /əʊ/	*choisir*
do /uː/	did /ɪ/	done /ʌ/	*faire*
draw /ɔː/	drew /uː/	drawn /ɔː/	*dessiner*
drink /ɪ/	drank /æ/	drunk /ʌ/	*boire*
drive /aɪ/	drove /əʊ/	driven /ɪ/	*conduire*
eat /iː/	ate /eɪ/	eaten /iː/	*manger*
fall /ɔː/	fell /e/	fallen /ɔː/	*tomber*
fly /aɪ/	flew /uː/	flown /əʊ/	*voler*
forbid /ɪ/	forbade /eɪ/	forbidden /ɪ/	*interdire*
forget /e/	forgot /ɒ/	forgotten /ɒ/	*oublier*
forgive /ɪ/	forgave /eɪ/	forgiven /ɪ/	*pardonner*
freeze /iː/	froze /əʊ/	frozen /əʊ/	*geler*
give /ɪ/	gave /eɪ/	given /ɪ/	*donner*
go /əʊ/	went /e/	gone /ɒ/	*aller*
grow / əʊ/	grew /uː/	grown /əʊ/	*grandir / pousser*
hide /aɪ/	hid /ɪ/	hidden /ɪ/	*cacher*
know /əʊ/	knew /uː/	known /əʊ/	*connaître / savoir*
lay /eɪ/	laid /eɪ/	lain /eɪ/	*poser*
lie /aɪ/	lay /eɪ/	lain /eɪ/	*s'allonger*
ride /aɪ/	rode /əʊ/	ridden /ɪ/	*monter / chevaucher*
ring /ɪ/	rang /æ/	rung /ʌ/	*sonner / téléphoner*
rise /aɪ/	rose /əʊ/	risen /ɪ/	*(se) lever*
see /iː/	saw /ɔː/	seen /iː/	*voir*
shake /eɪ/	shook /ʊ/	shaken /eɪ/	*secouer*
show /əʊ/	showed /əʊ/	shone /əʊ/	*montrer*
sing /ɪ/	sang /æ/	sung /ʌ/	*chanter*
sink /ɪ/	sank /æ/	sunk /ʌ/	*couler*
smell /e/	smelt /e/	smelt /e/	*sentir*
speak /iː/	spoke /əʊ/	spoken /əʊ/	*parler*
steal /iː/	stole /əʊ/	stolen /əʊ/	*dérober*
stink /ɪ/	stank /æ/	stunk /ʌ/	*puer*
strike /aɪ/	struck /ʌ/	stricken /ɪ/	*frapper*
swear /ɛə/	swore /ɔː/	sworn /ɔː/	*jurer*
swell /e/	swelled /e/	swollen /əʊ/	*gonfler / enfler*
swim /ɪ/	swam /æ/	swum /ʌ/	*nager*
take /eɪ/	took /ʊ/	taken /eɪ/	*prendre*
tear /eə/	tore /ɔː/	torn /ɔː/	*déchirer*
throw /əʊ/	threw /uː/	thrown /əʊ/	*jeter*
undergo /əʊ/	underwent /e/	undergone /ɔ/	*subir*
wake /eɪ/	woke /əʊ/	woken /əʊ/	*réveiller*
wear /eə/	wore /ɔː/	worn /ɔː/	*porter*
withdraw /ɔː/	withdrew /uː/	withdrawn /ɔː/	*(se) retirer*
write /aɪ/	wrote /əʊ/	written /ɪ/	*écrire*

Verbes irréguliers

Sport

meet /i:/	met /e/	met /e/	*(se) rencontrer*
beat /i:/	beat /i:/	beaten /i:/	*battre*
hurt /ə:/	hurt /ə:/	hurt /ə:/	*blesser*
quit /ɪ/	quit /ɪ/	quit /ɪ/	*abandonner /arrêter*
strike /aɪ/	struck /ʌ/	struck /ʌ/	*frapper*
hit /ɪ/	hit /ɪ/	hit /ɪ/	*taper*
shoot /u:/	shot /ɒ/	shot /ɒ/	*tirer/filmer*
fall /ɔ:/	fell /e/	fallen /ɔ:/	*tomber*
lead /i:/	led /e/	led /e/	*mener/guider*
overcome /ʌ/	overcame /eɪ/	overcome /ʌ/	*surmonter*
slide /aɪ/	slid /ɪ/	slid /ɪ/	*glisser*
throw /əʊ/	threw /u:/	thrown /əʊ/	*jeter*
bleed /i:/	bled /e/	bled /e/	*saigner*
bet /e/	bet /e/	bet /e/	*parier*
fight /aɪ/	fought /ɔ:/	fought /ɔ:/	*se battre*
win /ɪ/	won /ʌ/	won /ʌ/	*gagner*
swear /eə/	swore /ɔ:/	sworn /ɔ:/	*jurer*
swim /ɪ/	swam /æ/	swum /ʌ/	*nager*
swing /ɪ/	swung /ʌ/	swung /ʌ/	*(se) balancer*
run /ʌ/	ran /æ/	run /ʌ/	*courir*
catch /æ/	caught /ɔ:/	caught /ɔ:/	*attraper*
lose /u:/	lost /ɒ/	lost /ɒ/	*perdre*

Daily Routine / At Home

sleep /i:/	slept /e/	slept /e/	*dormir*
shut /ʌ/	shut /ʌ/	shut /ʌ/	*fermer*
hold /əʊ/	held /e/	held /e/	*tenir*
find /aɪ/	found /aʊ/	found /aʊ/	*trouver*
rise /aɪ/	rose /əʊ/	risen /ɪ/	*(se) lever*
lay /eɪ/	laid /eɪ/	lain /eɪ/	*poser/ étendre*
wake /eɪ/	woke /əʊ/	woken /əʊ/	*réveiller*
lie /aɪ/	lay /eɪ/	lain /eɪ/	*(s')allonger*
sit /ɪ/	sat /æ/	sat /æ/	*s'asseoir*
dream /i:/	dreamt /e/	dreamt /e/	*rêver*
light /aɪ/	lit /ɪ/	lit /ɪ/	*allumer*
set /e/	set /e/	set /e/	*fixer*

Movement

be /i:/	was /ɒ/, were /ə/	been /i:/	*être*
leave /i:/	left /e/	left /e/	*laisser/quitter/ partir*
seek /i:/	sought /ɔ:/	sought /ɔ:/	*chercher*
ride /aɪ/	rode /əʊ/	ridden /ɪ/	*monter/ chevaucher*
go /əʊ/	went /e/	gone /ɒ/	*aller*
hide /aɪ/	hid /ɪ/	hidden /ɪ/	*cacher*
bring /ɪ/	brought /ɔ:/	brought /ɔ:/	*apporter*
fly /aɪ/	flew /u:/	flown /əʊ/	*voler*
drive /aɪ/	drove /əʊ/	driven /ɪ:/	*conduire*
come /ʌ/	came /eɪ/	come /ʌ/	*venir*
send /e/	sent /e/	sent /e/	*envoyer*
bend /e/	bent /e/	bent /e/	*plier/(se) courber*

Conversation

withdraw /ɔ:/	withdrew /u:/	withdrawn /ɔ:/	*(se) retirer*
begin /ɪ/	began /æ/	begun /ʌ/	*commencer*
do /u:/	did /ɪ/	done /ʌ/	*faire*
deal /i:/	dealt /e/	dealt /e/	*distribuer*
feel /i:/	felt /e/	felt /e/	*(se) sentir/ éprouver*
forget /e/	forgot /ɒ/	forgotten /ɒ/	*oublier*
mean /i:/	meant /e/	meant /e/	*signifier*
hear /ɪə/	heard /ə/	heard /ə/	*entendre*
forbid /ɪ/	forbade /eɪ/	forbidden /ɪ/	*interdire*
bear /eə/	bore /ɔ:/	borne /ɔ:	*porter/ supporter*
forgive /ɪ/	forgave /əɪ/	forgiven /ɪ/	*pardonner*
weep /i:/	wept /e/	wept /e/	*pleurer*
say /eɪ/	said /e/	said /e/	*dire*

Food

feed /iː/ – fed /e/ – fed /e/ – *nourrir*

split /ɪ/ – split /ɪ/ – split /ɪ/ – *fendre*

make /eɪ/ – made /eɪ/ – made /eɪ/ – *faire/fabriquer*

bite /aɪ/ – bit /ɪ/ – bitten /ɪ/ – *mordre*

burn /ɜː/ – burnt /ɜː/ – burnt /ɜː/ – *brûler*

smell /e/ – smelt /e/ – smelt /e/ – *sentir*

spread /e/ – spread /e/ – spread /e/ – *répandre*

eat /iː/ – ate /eɪ/ – eaten /iː/ – *manger*

drink /ɪ/ – drank /æ/ – drunk /ʌ/ – *boire*

shake /eɪ/ – shook /ʊ/ – shaken /eɪ/ – *secouer*

spoil /ɔɪ/ – spoilt /ɔɪ/ – spoilt /ɔɪ/ – *gâcher/gâter*

sink /ɪ/ – sank /æ/ – sunk /ʌ/ – *couler*

grow /əʊ/ – grew /uː/ – grown /əʊ/ – *grandir/pousser*

Weather

shine /aɪ/ – shone /ɒ/ – shone /ɒ/ – *briller*

forecast /aː/ – forecast /aː/ – forecast /aː/ – *prévoir*

freeze /iː/ – froze /əʊ/ – frozen /əʊ/ – *geler*

broadcast /aː/ – broadcast /aː/ – broadcast /aː/ – *diffuser/émettre*

Shopping

take /eɪ/ – took /ʊ/ – taken /eɪ/ – *prendre*

choose /uː/ – chose /əʊ/ – chosen /əʊ/ – *choisir*

buy /aɪ/ – bought /ɔː/ – bought /ɔː/ – *acheter*

hang /æ/ – hung /ʌ/ – hung /ʌ/ – *accrocher/pendre*

get /e/ – got /ɒ/ – got /ɒ/ – *obtenir*

tear /eə/ – tore /ɔː/ – torn /ɔː/ – *déchirer*

pay /eɪ/ – paid /eɪ/ – paid /eɪ/ – *payer*

have /æ/ – had /æ/ – had /æ/ – *avoir*

sell /e/ – sold /əʊ/ – sold /əʊ/ – *vendre*

cut /ʌ/ – cut /ʌ/ – cut /ʌ/ – *couper*

lend /e/ – lent /e/ – lent /e/ – *prêter*

break /eɪ/ – broke /əʊ/ – broken /əʊ/ – *casser*

steal /iː/ – stole /əʊ/ – stolen /əʊ/ – *dérober*

keep /iː/ – kept /e/ – kept /e/ – *garder*

give /ɪ/ – gave /eɪ/ – given /ɪ/ – *donner*

put /ʊ/ – put /ʊ/ – put /ʊ/ – *mettre/poser*

wear /eə/ – wore /ɔː/ – worn /ɔː/ – *porter*

spend /e/ – spent /e/ – spent /e/ – *dépenser/passer du temps*

cost /ɒ/ – cost /ɒ/ – cost /ɒ/ – *coûter*

School

teach /iː/ – taught /ɔː/ – taught /ɔː/ – *enseigner*

stick /ɪ/ – stuck /ʌ/ – stuck /ʌ/ – *coller*

read /iː/ – read /e/ – read /e/ – *lire*

draw /ɔː/ – drew /uː/ – drawn /ɔː/ – *dessiner*

understand /æ/ – understood /ʊ/ – understood /ʊ/ – *comprendre*

see /iː/ – saw /ɔː/ – seen /iː/ – *voir*

let /e/ – let /e/ – let /e/ – *permettre / louer*

build /ɪ/ – built /ɪ/ – built /ɪ/ – *construire*

ring /ɪ/ – rang /æ/ – rung /ʌ/ – *sonner/téléphoner*

tell /e/ – told /əʊ/ – told /əʊ/ – *dire/raconter*

speak /iː/ – spoke /əʊ/ – spoken /əʊ/ – *parler*

sing /ɪ/ – sang /æ/ – sung /ʌ/ – *chanter*

learn /ɜː/ – learnt /ɜː/ – learnt /ɜː/ – *apprendre*

know /əʊ/ – knew /uː/ – known /əʊ/ – *connaître/savoir*

think /ɪ/ – thought /ɔː/ – thought /ɔː/ – *penser*

stand /æ/ – stood /ʊ/ – stood /ʊ/ – *être debout/être posé*

become /ʌ/ – became /eɪ/ – become /ʌ/ – *devenir*

write /aɪ/ – wrote /əʊ/ – written /ɪ/ – *écrire*

Crédits photos/illustrations

Page 8: Media24/Gallo Images/Contributor; **Page 9:** © Hongqi Zhang (aka Michael Zhang); The Venus Project designed by Jacque Fresco; Robert R. McElroy/contributor; © LLDC - Queen Elizabeth Park, Stratford (Aquatics Centre); Neil Leifer/Contributor; **Page 11:** "Coffee And Donut", © copyright 2015, Ralph Goings, all rights reserved.; © A1977; Ebet Roberts/Contributor; **Page 13:** © Juan Moyan; © Bettmann/CORBIS; **Page 14:** (b) Ryan Pierse/Staff; (h) Kevin Winter/Staff; **Page 15:** (h) © David Paul Morris/San Francisco Chronicle/San Francisco Chronicle/Corbis; (b) Media24/Gallo Images/Contributor; **Page 16:** © TCU Marketing and Communication; **Page 17:** © Morgan Levy; **Page 18:** (h) From Public speaking How-To by Ian Patterson / Courtesy of Thrive Foundation for Youth/Ian Patterson; (b) Bloomberg / Contributor; **Page 19:** From *I Am Malala : The Girl Who Stood Up for Education and Was Shot by the Taliban* by Malala Yousafzai with Christina Lamb © Little, Brown and Company; **Page 20:** © Memegenerator.net; **Page 21:** © Hongqi Zhang (aka Michael Zhang); **Pages 22-23:** (h) © Danny Ghitis; (b) Buero Monaco; **Page 23:** Mike Harrington; **Page 24:** (h) aarp.org (American Association of Retired Persons); (b) © Chromorange; (b) http://nwc.co/; **Page 25:** © Enplug; **Page 26:** © Zipcar; **Page 27:** (h) © Reproduced by kind permission of *Private Eye Magazine* / Graeme Keyes; (b) From Peers: Growing the sharing economy movement, © Peers; **Page 28:** (h) From Within Reach - Journey to Find Sustainable Community by Within, © Within Reach; Brian «Ziggy» Liloia at The Year of Mud; **Page 29:** *Pocket Neighborhoods* by Ross Chapin (The Taunton Press, 2011); **Page 30:** (h) © Cover from *Divergent* by Veronica Roth. Copyright © 2012 Reprinted by permission of HarperCollins Publishers.; (b) © Jaguarps; **Page 31:** The Venus Project designed by Jacque Fresco; **Page 32:** © Claudiad; **Page 33:** © alvarez; **Page 34:** © Mar Guixé; **Page 35:** (g) © 2010 Clothing Swap, Inc. All Rights Reserved; (d) Jonathan Kim; **Pages 36-37:** © Mar Guixé; **Page 38:** (g) © Frazervg; (d) http://galleryhip.com/; **Page 39:** © Renee Mazurek; **Page 40:** (h) From The Alamo - San Antonio, Texas by Travel Thru History © Series created by Joe Dorsey, John DeMaio, Cassie Yde. Narration by Jillian Young. Music by SJ; (b) © Davel5957; **Page 41:** © Matt Doeden, Charles Barnett, Phill Miller; **Page 42:** (h) © MikeyLPT; (m) © Skvoor; (b) From Discover Houston © Greater Houston Partnership; **Page 43:** (h) Jose Lozano @ Magic Spoon Productions - magicspoonproductions.com; (b) From Discover Unforgettable San Antonio - With permission of the San Antonio Convention & Visitors Bureau for educational use.; **Page 44:** (h) From *Travels with Charley: In Search of America* by John Steinbeck, © (c) 1961, 1962 by The Curtis Publishing Co.; copyright (c) 1962 by John Steinbeck; copyright renewed (c) 1989, 1990 by Elaine Steinbeck, Thom Steinbeck, and John Steinbeck IV. Used by permission of Viking Penguin, a division of Penguin Group (USA) LLC.; (b) © Charlie Powell; **Page 45:** (h-g) Robert R. McElroy/contributor; (h-d) John Rodgers/Contributor; (m) © Contender1; (b) Peter Pakvis/Contributor; **Page 49:** (g) Copyright 2014 by James J. Griffin, Cover design by Livia Reasoner, Texas Ranger badge image courtesy of the Texas Ranger Hall of Fame and Museum, Waco; (d) © Jerry Coli; **Page 50:** (h) © Plmrue; (m) © Tinarayna; (b) © Willeecole; **Page 51:** (h-g) © Scanrail; (h-d) © Bahadir Yeniceri; (m) © Christopher Elwell; (b) © Palo_ok and © Al; **Page 52:** (h) © Alex Ameye (Art Director), Thomas François (Photographer), Chez Eddy in Paris (3D artist), Eurostar (Client); (b) © Hugleikur Dagsson - www.dagsson.com; **Page 53:** © Karsten Schley (cartoonist); **Page 54:** Cover from *Ready, Steady, Go!* by Shawn Levy © 2002 by Shawn Levy. Used by permission of Doubleday, an imprint of the Knopf Doubleday Publishing Group, a division of Penguin Random House LLC. All rights reserved.; **Page 55:** (h) © Visit Britain - www.gov.uk/britainisgreat/http://www.visitbritain.org; (m) From Music is great (video) © Visit Britain; (b) From Fashion is great (video) © Visit Britain; **Page 56:** RyanJLane; **Page 57:** (h) caters/sipa; (b) Anadolu Agency/Contributor; **Page 58:** (h) Artwork © Published by arrangement with The Random House Group Limited.; (b) © Julian James; **Page 59:** (h) © Visit Britain - www.gov.uk/britainisgreat/http://www.visitbritain.org; (b) © LLDC - Queen Elizabeth Park, Stratford (Aquatics Centre); **Page 60:** © Photosanda; **Page 62:** © From *Hullabaloo in the Guava Orchard*, Faber & Faber, UK, Commissioned by Donna Payne, Art Director, Design & Illustration by Mecob; **Page 63:** (g) Published by Bradt travel guides; (d) From Awfully thorough guide to Being British © Me:Mo Interactive Ltd. - www.memointeractive.com; **Page 64:** (h) © The Atlantic/Alex Ostroy (artist); (b) © Icon magazine February 2012 - Zim & Zou/Media 10 Images - www.iconeye.com; **Page 65:** (h) © Fairfax Syndication; (b) © Edible Brooklyn, Photo: Truck Farm by Ian Cheney; **Page 66:** © KATE E WEYBRIET – KATE EMMA PHOTOGRAPHY & DESIGN; **Page 67:** Courtesy of no meat for a week; **Page 68:** (h) From Jamie Oliver's Food revolution, © FremantleMedia Ltd/ Fresh One Productions ltd; (b) ©2015 King Features Syndicate, Inc. ™ Hearst Holdings, Inc.; **Page 69:** AFP/Stringer; **Page 70:** © Thomas Weil and Quentin Weisbuch/www.studiofurious.com; **Page 71:** (h) © Ento; (b-g) caters/sipa; (b-d) AFP/Stringer; **Page 72:** (h) © *The Wind from the Sun* by Arthur C. Clarke, The Orion Publishing Group, London; (b) Robert Nickelsberg/Contributor; **Page 73:** (h) "American Favorites", © copyright 2015, Ralph Goings, all rights reserved.; (b) "Coffee And Donut", © 2015, Ralph Goings, All rights reserved.; **Page 74:** © Gabriel Blaj; **Page 76:** (g) © Mark Vorobev; (m) © Paco Riera; (m) © Piotr Marcinski; (d) © Godfer; **Page 77:** (g) Andrew Burton/Staff; (d) © pixitive; **Page 78:** Ithaca College Asian American Alliance (AAA), jacksonli93 (photographer), Chenteng (model); **Page 79:** (h) © Canadian Race Relations Foundation | Fondation canadienne des relations raciales; (b) © 2104 - I Too Am Harvard; **Page 80:** (h) From *American Born Chinese* © 2006 by Gene Luen Yang. Reprinted by permission of First Second, an imprint of Roaring Brook Press, a division of Holtzbrinck Publishing Holdings Limited Partnership All Rights Reserved.; (b) From How has integration changed Britain? by Nick Robinson, BBC, © BBC Worldwide Learning; **Page 81:** Vittorio Zunino Celotto/Staff; **Page 82:** (h) © Etsy; (b) Ithaca College Asian American Alliance (AAA)/jacksonli93 (photographer), Mchu (model); **Page 84:** (g) © Nigel Spiers; (d) © Mike Clegg; **Page 85:** (h) © Bobby Smith & Margaret Oshindele-Smith/Troubador Publishing Ltd; (b) John Parra/contributor; **Page 86:** (h) © From *The Buddha of Suburbia* by Hanif Kureishi (1990), Faber & Faber, UK; (b) Ulf Andersen/Contributor; **Page 87:** (h) © A1977; (b) Chalkie Davies/Contributor; **Page 88:** (h-g) © Pongphan Ruengchai; (h-d) © Dimitrieong; (b) © Nitr; **Page 90:** (b-m) © Michał Rojek; (b-g) © RapidEye; (b-d) Pitti; **Page 91:** (g) © Brick Lane by Monica Ali, Transworld Publishers Ltd; (d) © Mike Tauber; **Page 92:** Mark Venema/Contributor; **Page 93:** (h) GAB Archive/Colaborador; (b) catwalker; **Page 94:** (h) © Josh Coen and Blues Comix, Excerpt from the comic book; (b) From *My Bondage and My Freedom* by Frederick Douglass © Penguin Group (USA) LLC; **Page 95:** © Richard Knight (author)/Trailblazer guides; **Page 96:** (h) © ARTEFACT MEDIA; (b) From *Soundtrack for a Revolution* / Dylan Nelson; **Page 98:** Sugar Hill Records; **Page 99:** © Sbukley; **Page 100:** (h) © From Going to meet the man, Penguin Random House LLC; (b) Jenkins/Stringer **Page 101:** (h) *From the Platform: Subway Graffiti* by Paul Cavalieri; image courtesy of the publisher, Schiffer Publishing Ltd; (b) Ebet Roberts/Contributor; **Page 102:** (h-g) © Carrienelson1; (h-d) © Sbukley; (b) Jack Robinson/Contributor; **Page 103:** (1) © Anna Krasnopeeva; (2) © Le-thuy Do; (3) © Flavijus; (4) Horiyan; (5) © Uatp1; (6) © Martijn Mulder; (7) © Kenneth Vaughn; (8) © Thomas Dutour; (9) © Rui Matos; **Page 104:** (b-g) © Neustockimages; (h-g) catwalker; (h-m) © WN2015; (h-d) © Sbukley; (b-g) © Delta Blues Museum; (b-m) Robert Johnson Studio Portrait Hooks Bros., Memphis, circa 1935 ©1989 Delta Haze Corporation; (b-d) Nikola Spasenoski; **Page 105:** (g) From *I Know Why the Caged Bird Sings* by Maya Angelou, Publisher Penguin Random House LLC; (d) Jamie McCarthy/Staff; **Page 106:** © Canadian Paralympic Committee | Comité paralympique canadien; **Page 107:** (h) @ UK Anti-Doping 2015; (b) Show your colours; **Page 108:** Copyright 2015 Miracle League National Association. All Rights Reserved. www.MiracleLeague.com; **Page 109:** (h) Aaron Davidson/Stringer; (b) © Mary Wineberg; **Page 110:** Vincent Kompany; **Page 111:** Doug Pensinger/Staff; **Page 112:** © Mark Knight; **Page 113:** (h-g) Popperfoto/Contributor; (h-m) Paul Gilham/staff; (h-d) / Staff; From 1968 Summer Olympics, *Black Power Salute* by I love Ancestry, Produced and distributed by the Media Education Foundation, www.notjustagamemovie.org; **Page 114:** (h) From *The Art of Fielding* by Chad Harbach © 2011 by Chad Harbach. Used by permission of Little, Brown and Company. All rights reserved.; (b) © Chad Harbach; **Page 115:** (h) © Neil Leifer; (b) Neil Leifer/Contributor; **Page 118:** © radarreklama; **Page 119:** (g) Getty images/From *No limits: The Will to Succeed*, Free Press (2008); From *Inside the Numbers: Athletes as Role Models*, CNN; **Page 120:** 'The image on page 120 'Oxfam Loves a Sceptic', 2012 is reproduced with the permission of Oxfam GB, Oxfam House, John Smith Drive, Cowley, Oxford OX4 2JY, UK www.oxfam.org.uk. Oxfam GB does not necessarily endorse any text or activities that accompany the materials.'; **Page 121:** (h) Reproduced with permission from the Singapore Red Cross.; (b) © Jimmy Swindells - www.jimmyswindells.co.uk/British Heart Foundation; **Page 122:** 'The image on page 122, from Lift Lives for Good, 2013 is reproduced with the permission of Oxfam GB, Oxfam house, John Smith Drive, Cowley, Oxford OX4 2JY, UK www.oxfam.org.uk. Oxfam GB does not necessarily endorse any text or activities that accompany the materials.'; **Page 123:** (h) From Angels Among Us – Café by Jennifer Roscoe, WCIA 3 news - WCIA 3 News/Nexstar Broadcasting; (b) © Yanlev; **Page 124:** From The Giving Pledge: Warren Buffet, © ABC NEWS; **Page 125:** (h) Paul Morigi/Stringer; (b) Bloomberg/Contributor; **Page 126:** From Microcredit and the Future of Poverty by byutv, Used with permission of BYU Broadcasting; **Page 127:** © United colors of Benetton/James Mollison; **Page 128:** (h) Scott McKowen (illustrator) - Sterling Classics Series; (b) © Georgios Kollidas; **Page 129:** (h) © F11photo; (m) © Juan Moyan; (b) Tony Vaccaro/Contributor; **Page 133:** (g) From The Third Wave by Alison Thompson, Publisher: Scribe Publications Pty Ltd (2011); (d) © Charity: water; **Page 134:** (h) Education Images/contributor; (b) © Peace Arch Entertainment/Showtime; **Page 135:** (h) © Albert Knapp/Alamy; (b) Spencer Platt/staff; **Page 136:** (h) Pool/pool; (m) From 9/11 Memorial museum by CBC News, CBC licensing; (b) From Top Billing explore Kolmansko ghost in Namibia by SABC, Visual material owned and supplied by SABC Ltd.; **Page 137:** ©English heritage - www.english-heritage.org.uk; **Page 138:** Sebastian Granata/stringer; **Page 139:** (g) VIDEO VISION ENTERTAINMENT/DISTANT HORIZON/PATHE/THE KOBAL COLLECTION; (m) PARAMOUNT PICTURES/THE KOBAL COLLECTION; (d) GK FILMS/THE KOBAL COLLECTION; **Page 140:** (h) © Stateside - www.stateside.com.au; (b) © Verizon Wireless/Photographer : Jon Darren; **Page 141:** (h) © lovemax; (b) © Bikeworldtravel; **Page 142:** (h) From Code Talker: A Novel About the Navajo Marines of World War Two Paperback by Joseph Bruchac - Speak; Reprint edition (July 6, 2006); (b) © Eric Jenks; **Page 143:** (h) © Bettmann/CORBIS; (b) The Art Archive; **Page 144:** (h) © JuSun; (b) © coverdale84; **Page 145:** PARAMOUNT/PATHE/HARPO FILMS/THE KOBAL COLLECTION; **Page 146:** © no_limit_pictures; **Page 147:** © ABC - Rob Herric; **Page 152:** © Flynt | Dreamstime.com; **Page 154:** © Lesia_G; Barbara Chotard.

Crédits textes

Page 16: *Bitter Melon* by Cara Chow © 2010 by Cara Chow. All rights reserved; **Page 17:** © Morgan Levy; **Page 18:** (1) Words matter, Democratic Party of Wisconsin Founders Day Gala, Barack Obama; (2) Excerpt from *Braveheart* © 1995 Courtesy of Twentieth Century Fox. Written by Randall Wallace. All rights reserved.; **Page 19:** © Malala Yousafzai, July 2013; **Page 24:** Robyn Griggs Lawrence, Contributor, NextAvenue.org, Reprinted with permission from NextAvenue.org. All rights reserved; **Page 25:** Kyle Russell, businessinsider.com/Wright's Media; **Page 26:** © VentureBeat - http://venturebeat.com; **Page 27:** © Telegraph Media Group Limited 2014; **Page 28:** Brian "Ziggy" Liloia at The Year of Mud; **Page 30:** © *Divergent* by Veronica Roth, 2012. Reprinted by permission of HarperCollins Publishers.; **Page 38:** © Leah Walker - www.LeahTravels.com; **Page 39:** © Renee Mazurek; **Page 41:** www.biographyself.com; **Page 42:** © Nikki and Dusty Green, USA Today, 05/01/2014.; **Page 43:** Michael Esposito, Texas Report; **Page 44:** *Travels with Charley: In Search of America* by John Steinbeck © 1961, 1962 by The Curtis Publishing Co.; © 1962 by John Steinbeck; copyright renewed © 1989, 1990 by Elaine Steinbeck, Thom Steinbeck, and John Steinbeck IV. Used by permission of Viking Penguin, a division of Penguin Group (USA) LLC.; **Page 53:** © Telegraph Media Group Limited 2014 ; **Page 54:** Excerpt from *Ready, Steady, Go!* by Shawn Levy, © 2002 by Shawn Levy. Used by permission of Doubleday, an imprint of the Knopf Doubleday Publishing Group, a division of Penguin Random House LLC. All rights reserved.; **Page 56:** © Jessica Tooze/First appeared on www.britain-magazine.com (BRITAIN magazine website); **Page 57:** http://www.historic-uk.com/Ben Johnson; **Page 58:** from *Notes from a Small Island* by Bill Bryson, Published by Doubleday, Reprinted by permission of The Random House Group Limited.; **Page 66:** Let's move!; **Page 69:** © Ron Rosenbaum/First appeared in Smithsonian Magazine, July 2014, http://www.smithsonianmag.com/arts-culture/anthony-bourdains-theory-foodie-revolution-180951848/#vZ6y041Wp26BsKOq.99; **Page 70:** Excerpts from pp. 1-3 [218 words] from *The Taste of Tomorrow* by Josh Schonwald © 2012 by Josh Schonwald. Reprinted by permission of HarperCollins Publishers.; **Page 72:** © Arthur C. Clarke, «The Wind from the Sun», *The Food of the Gods*, 1972 / Corgi Childrens (publisher); **Page 81:** © Jhumpa Lahiri, 2008, *Unaccustomed Earth*, Bloomsbury Publishing Plc; **Page 82:** Excerpt(s) from HALF AND HALF: WRITERS ON GROWING UP BIRACIAL AND BICULTURAL by Claudine C. O'Hearn © 1998 by Claudine Chiawei O'Hearn. Used by permission of Pantheon Books, an imprint of the Knopf Doubleday Publishing Group, a division of Penguin Random House LLC. All rights reserved.; **Page 83:** © Delfín Carbonell; **Page 84:** © Ben Norum, *Pea Soup Magazine*; **Page 85:** © Bobby Smith & Margaret Oshindele-Smith/Troubador Publishing Ltd; **Page 86:** © *The Buddha of Suburbia* by Hanif Kureishi (1990), Faber & Faber, UK; **Page 95:** © Richard Knight (author)/Trailblazer guides; **Page 97:** Abkco/Sony ATV/EMI; **Page 98:** (1) From *Can't Stop Won't Stop: a History of the Hip-Hop Nation* © 2005 by Jeff Chang and D. J. Kool Herc. Reprinted by permission of St. Martin's Press. All rights reserved.; (2) © Urban Dictionary; **Page 100:** Excerpted from "Sonny's Blues" © 1957 by James Baldwin. Copyright renewed. Collected in *Going to Meet the Man*, published by Vintage and Penguin Books. Reprinted by arrangement with James Baldwin Estate.; **Page 108:** Hannah Woodworth, MIAA Student Sportsmanship Essay; **Page 109:** © Christian Marin, Pros Give Back; **Page 110:** *The Fix: Soccer and Organized Crime* by Declan Hill - Non Basic Stock Line; Reprint edition (13 April 2010); **Page 112:** © Nigel Towson, The British at Play; **Page 114:** From *The Art of Fielding* by Chad Harbach. Copyright © 2011 by Chad Harbach. Used by permission of Little, Brown and Company. All rights reserved.; **Page 123:** Joel Harper/www.volunteernow.co.uk; **Page 124:** Tom Butler-Bowdon, 50 Prosperity Classics: Attract It, Create It, Manage It, Share It, 2008 - Nicholas Brealey Publishing.; **Page 125:** (1) Giving Pledge - Sara Blakely; (2) Giving Pledge - Leon Cooperman; **Page 126:** CARE; **Page 127:** Benetton.com; **Page 128:** From *A Christmas Carol* by Charles Dickens; **Page 137:** From *Reaching Boys, Teaching Boys: Strategies that Work and Why* by Michael Reichert and Richard Hawley/Wiley Publication; **Page 138:** (1) The Corries (Music) Ltd; (2) CNN; **Page 141:** © Nicole Breedlove; **Page 142:** From *Code Talker: A Novel About the Navajo Marines of World War Two* Paperback by Joseph Bruchac - Speak; Reprint edition (July 6, 2006).

éditions maison des langues
www.emdl.fr